Applied Communication Skills for the Construction Trades

Steven A. Rigolosi

Upper Saddle River, New Jersey
Columbus, Ohio

Library of Congress Cataloging in Publication Data

Rigolosi, Steven A.
    Applied communication skills for the construction trades / Steven A. Rigolosi.
       p. cm.
    Includes bibliographical references and index.
    ISBN 0-13-093355-4
    1. Communication in the building trades. 2. Building trades—Employees—Life skills
guides. 3. Building—Vocational guidance. I. Title.

TH215.R54 2002
624'.068'3—dc21   2001036901

Editor in Chief: Stephen Helba
Product Manager: Jamie Van Voorhis
Managing Editor: Lori Cowen
Production Editor: Stephen C. Robb
Design Coordinator: Diane Y. Ernsberger
Cover Designer: Ali Mohrman
Production Manager: Pat Tonneman
Production Supervision: Lisa Hessel, Carlisle Publishers Services

Pearson Education Ltd., *London*
Pearson Education of Australia Pty. Limited, *Sydney*
Pearson Education Singapore Pte. Ltd.
Pearson Education North Asia Ltd., *Hong Kong*
Pearson Education Canada Ltd., *Toronto*
Pearson Educación de Mexico, S.A. de C.V.
Pearson Education—Japan, *Tokyo*
Pearson Education Malaysia Pte. Ltd.
Pearson Education, *Upper Saddle River, New Jersey*

ISBN 0-13-093355-4

Foreword

Construction is the largest single industry in the United States, and it is the only one where each product must be designed and created specifically for the customer. Imagine what the auto industry would be like if every car was completely different, based on the needs of each individual customer. Also think about the soft drink industry. What would happen if each can or bottle of soda was designed specifically for each customer? It just could not be done. The building industry, however, does exactly that. Each product, no matter how big or small, is designed specifically for each individual customer.

Construction is an industry that requires dozens and sometimes hundreds of unrelated companies to work together to create someone's dream. Each of these companies has a unique service that it can offer in the process. A large project can provide work for thousands of skilled workers, most of whom never even meet. How does it all work? Communication is the key. Every building starts as an idea, a dream, or a solution to a problem. There is only one way that the dream becomes reality, and that is through the process of communication.

You may be saying to yourself, "I have been communicating since I was a kid. Why do I need to learn this stuff?" The answer is very simple: Mistakes can be costly, and in this industry, mistakes can kill. Misreading a blueprint or a specification can mean project delays or cost overruns. Cutting a hole in the wrong place for a switch or an outlet can be an embarrassing experience, and it takes valuable time to make things right. Communication on all levels is absolutely the key to success.

The four types of communication that this book addresses are reading, writing, speaking, and listening. Individually, these skills are very important. But together, they are the basis of an extremely successful construction career. A person who is skilled in all four forms of communication has an excellent chance of advancing in the construction industry. This book will allow you to develop your communication skills. Working well with others, getting your thoughts across, understanding what others need, reading for content, using e-mail efficiently, and writing so that others understand are all skills that you will hone as you proceed through the various exercises in this book.

The difference between this book and others is that it is written specifically for the construction industry. The author has used real-life examples that are found on construction sites every day. Construction professionals throughout the country have reviewed this material and have been impressed. I am sure that you will be also. Approach the material in this book with an open mind and a willingness to improve. You will be surprised at the results.

Wayne Belanger
Director of Education
Associated Builders & Contractors of Wisconsin
Apprenticeship & Training Trust

Preface

Construction professionals have long been valued for their technical expertise. Employers and clients expect that electricians will know electricity, plumbers will know piping, masons will know brick, and carpenters will know wood.

To this end, most construction training programs have long focused on teaching the technical aspects of the job. After elementary courses in mathematics and an overview of tools and safety regulations, workers-in-training follow a very specific path designed to make them expert in the tools, techniques, and terms of their chosen trade.

But the construction industry has begun to change to meet the demands of the twenty-first century, and instructors and trainers have now identified another set of skills in which construction professionals must be trained: communication skills. *Applied Communication Skills for the Construction Trades* is the first text to offer comprehensive instruction to construction trainees (and even experienced workers) in the four key areas of on-the-job communication:

- Listening
- Speaking
- Reading
- Writing

Unlike other communication texts, which are often written for the general public or for people who will work in an office atmosphere, this book has been prepared specifically to meet the needs of the construction industry. All the examples in the text are drawn from construction-related documents (such as OSHA regulations, training manuals, materials lists, job specs, and blueprints) and construction-related settings and situations. To ensure that the book meets the needs of today's construction industry, it has been extensively reviewed by construction personnel.

CONTENTS AND ORGANIZATION

Applied Communication Skills for the Construction Trades is designed for maximum flexibility. For this reason, the text is composed of "modules" rather than "chapters." Trainers and instructors can teach topics in any order they choose. They need not start at Module 1 and continue in a linear fashion through Module 8. In short, the text's flexibility allows instructors to customize the text to meet the needs of their students, which may vary from class to class or from program to program.

Each of the four communication skills is taught in two back-to-back modules. The first module provides the basics of that skill. The second module treats advanced topics in that skill. The advanced modules are particularly well suited to training programs for experienced workers, who may have already mastered the basics. The focus throughout the text is on improving skills that students already have to a certain extent. Thus, while the text offers tips on how to read more effectively and improve comprehension and retention, it is not intended as a basic literacy text.

An overview of the topics found in each module follows.

Modules 1 and 2: Listening Skills

- The communication process
- Listening actively

- Nonverbal communication
- Body language
- Barriers to effective listening
- Taking notes
- Following instructions
- Handling criticism
- Using telephones and cell phones
- Participating in meetings

Modules 3 and 4: Speaking Skills

- Talking with co-workers, supervisors, and clients
- Jargon and slang versus formal English
- Speaking clearly, concisely, and effectively
- Group dynamics
- Communicating ethically
- Public speaking
- Leading meetings
- Courtesy and etiquette
- Delivering bad news
- Workplace diversity
- Conflict management

Modules 5 and 6: Reading Skills

- Tips for reading effectively
- Reading to find information
- Improving comprehension skills
- Reading construction-related business correspondence
- Following directions
- Understanding visual aids (including tables, charts, maps, and Web pages)
- Reading blueprints, isometrics, orthographics, and schematics
- Managing your information load
- Reading critically

Modules 7 and 8: Writing Skills

- Understanding your audience
- The hallmarks of good writing (objectivity, economy, clarity, simplicity, legibility)
- Writing to convey information
- Writing for a variety of purposes (persuasion, direction, summary, synthesis, analysis, evaluation)
- Filling out forms
- Formatting business documents properly
- Writing field and progress reports
- Proofreading
- Tips on spelling, grammar, and punctuation

FEATURES

Applied Communication Skills for the Construction Trades is designed as an interactive text. Students are encouraged to work directly in the text, to think about what they've learned, to practice their new skills, and to collaborate with team members or classmates.

Each module offers the following features:

SKILLS INSTRUCTION.   Each module offers five to eight "mini-modules," numbered for easy reference. For example, instruction on "Reading Visual Materials" appears in Section 6.1, which is the first section in Module 6. Instruction on the role of listening in on-the-job safety is found in Section 1.4, which is the fourth section in Module 1. Because each section is designed to stand on its own, instructors can choose to skip individual sections without worrying about issues of transition or "flow." Cross-references to other parts of the book are clearly noted when necessary.

Instructors and trainers can get very creative with the tips and suggestions included with the skills instruction. You might want to offer additional suggestions of your own or ask students to provide examples from their own experience.

ACTIVITIES.   *Applied Communication Skills for the Construction Trades* includes more than 100 activities. Designed to provide practice in the skills being learned, these activities come in a variety of formats: self-assessment exercises, action plans, questionnaires, and quizzes in multiple formats (multiple choice, fill-in-the-blank, true/false, short answer). Several exercises (indicated with an asterisk in the table of contents) are specifically designated *collaborative exercises* because they require more than one person to complete.

The activities can be used in many ways. They may be assigned as homework, completed in class, or used as quizzes. Even those activities not specifically designated as "collaborative" can become so with only minor adjustments.

Answers to all activities are provided at the end of the text.

In addition, the text offers several additional resources that may be valuable to trainees:

- **Appendix A, "Working with Technology,"** provides tips on integrating technology into every facet of one's construction career, offering tips on working with computers, personal digital assistants (PDAs), and fax machines.
- **Appendix B, "Managing Your Construction Career,"** is an all-in-one career starter kit. It takes the novice through the basics of preparing a résumé, writing a cover letter, and sitting for an interview.
- **Appendix C** contains a **glossary of construction terms.**

We'd Like Your Thoughts and Contributions

We are very interested in your experiences with this text. Have you found it useful in your classes? Have students responded positively? Would you like to see additional topics included in future editions of the text? Do you use any special activities in your class that you'd like to contribute?

Please feel free to share your thoughts with us. We can be reached via the Construction Craft Training Program at Prentice Hall. Please write to us in care of the managing editor: Lori Cowen, Room 5E-92, Career, Health, Education, and Technology Division, Pearson Education, Inc., One Lake Street, Upper Saddle River, NJ 07458. Her e-mail address is Lori_Cowen@prenhall.com.

We hope that you and your students enjoy using *Applied Communication Skills for the Construction Trades*.

Acknowledgments

The expertise and experience of many seasoned construction professionals have made this a much better book. First and foremost, I would like to thank all of the reviewers who took the time to comment extensively on the manuscript and to provide "real-world" materials for the text. They include: John Yencho, vocational instructor, Trenton High School, Trenton, FL; Dick Johnson, quality manager, Triple Crown Construction, Harrisburg, PA; and Bill Yeager, Yeager Plumbing, Heating, and Air Conditioning, Newton, IA.

Special thanks go to Wayne Belanger, director of education at the ABC Wisconsin Apprenticeship & Training Trust. Wayne has been incredibly supportive of this project, and his suggestions have made every page of the text better.

At Prentice Hall, there is no substitute for Lori Cowen, whose official title is "managing editor" but whose true title should be "editor extraordinaire." Our many brainstorming sessions helped to shape this book at every stage of development. I am truly fortunate to have Lori as my editor and friend.

Finally, some thanks to other friends and colleagues: Thank you to Ellen Greenberg, as always, for just being there. Thanks to Marc Lieberman for excellent advice, and to Greg Karpijian for help on just about everything.

Steven Rigolosi

Contents

---

*Indicates a collaborative activity.

Listening Skills I
The Basics

66 God gave us two ears and one mouth. Must mean we should listen twice as much as we talk. 99

—Proverb

Human communication takes place in two ways: through the *spoken* word and through the *written* word. While construction professionals are expected to be experts in technical skills, the best workers not only know their trades but also know how to communicate effectively with co-workers, supervisors, clients, and suppliers.

In this module, and in the three that follow, we examine the *spoken* word. There is good reason to improve the skills associated with the spoken word—specifically, listening and speaking skills. Did you know that 45% of our communication time is spent listening, and 30% is spent speaking?[1]

If you doubt the importance of good listening and speaking skills, just think how difficult your job would be if you couldn't talk with your co-workers, or if you had to learn your trade solely from books. The written word standardizes and records; but teaching, training, and learning are accomplished through speaking, demonstrating, and listening.

This module teaches the basics of active listening, including an overview of the communication process and the barriers to effective listening. Module 2 offers instruction in advanced listening skills, such as note taking, following spoken instructions, and communicating on the telephone.

1.1 THE COMMUNICATION PROCESS: HOW SPOKEN COMMUNICATION WORKS

Before we discuss how to become a more effective listener, it is helpful to understand how spoken communication works. Figure 1.1 outlines the communication process.

Sender and Receiver

Spoken communication begins with a *sender* who has a message to send to a *receiver*. The sender must *encode* the message and then use a *communication channel* to deliver it to the receiver. In spoken communication, the messages are usually encoded with words, numbers, gestures, tone of voice, and body language. The communication channel may be a conversation, a speech, a meeting, or any other channel that allows two people to communicate.

Noise

Spoken communication is effective only if the receiver can *decode* the message. In other words, the receiver must be able to understand what the sender is saying. Anything that interferes with decoding the message is called *noise*.

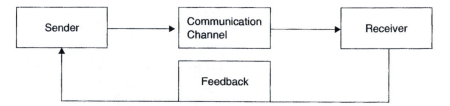

Figure 1.1: The Communication Process

---

[1]Paul Rankin, Proceedings of the Ohio State Educational Conference's Ninth Annual Session, 1929.

Noise can arise from many factors. It can occur when the sender uses words the receiver doesn't understand, or when the sender's body language is hard to interpret. It can also arise when the listener is tired or isn't paying attention, or when there is real background noise that makes it hard to listen or concentrate. Construction sites are filled with many types of noise, which can sometimes make it hard to listen effectively.

One-Way and Two-Way Communication

In some cases, communication goes in one direction only—from the sender to the receiver. This is called *one-way communication*. One-way communication often gives rise to misunderstandings. For this reason, the best communications allow for *feedback*. That is, they allow the receiver to communicate back with the sender, to make sure that everything is understood. This type of communication, called *two-way communication,* is common in construction. Whether you are speaking or listening, two-way communication ensures that everybody is working with the same expectations and striving toward the same goal.

Application of the Communication Process

Let's move the communication process, and Figure 1.1, out of the realm of theory and into practice on the construction site. Consider the following scenario:

> Jeanne Jones is a supervisor at Cartwright Construction. She has called a meeting of her three senior people—Mike Callahan, Rich Hughes, and Wendy Frasier. She wants to ask their advice about a difficult drainage situation that the company is having trouble solving. She holds the meeting at lunchtime in a quiet area. Mike is distracted because he's very hungry. After Jeanne has presented the problem, she asks Mike, Rich, and Wendy for their suggestions on how the drainage problem can be solved.[2]

In this scenario:

- Jeanne Jones is the *sender.*
- Mike Callahan, Rich Hughes, and Wendy Frasier are the *receivers.*
- The *communication channel* is a meeting.
- Even though the meeting takes place in a quiet area, *noise* is present in the form of Mike's hunger pangs.
- This is a situation in which *two-way communication* is called for. Jeanne asks the advice of her three senior people.

As you continue through this module and those that follow, keep the components of the communication process in mind. They will help you communicate more effectively. Remember:

- When you are the *sender* (speaker), you need to select the appropriate communication channel.
- When you are the *receiver* (listener), you need to ensure that you're decoding the message properly. Do you understand all the words being used? (If not, ask for clarification.) Are you sensitive to tone of voice and what it means in the conversation? Are you interpreting body language and other forms of nonverbal communication (see Section 1.3) correctly?

---

[2]Steven A. Rigolosi, *Tools for Success: Soft Skills for the Construction Industry* (Upper Saddle River, NJ/Columbus, OH: Prentice Hall, 2000), p. 75.

- If *noise* is present, you could seriously misunderstand the message being conveyed. Are you aware of your surroundings and the effects they have on your listening abilities? Can distractions and other types of noise be eliminated? Should the communication be postponed or moved to another location?
- Whether you are the speaker or the listener, you need to establish two-way communication to maximize *feedback*. Are you responding to the questions you've been asked? Are you actively engaged in the conversation? If you haven't listened carefully, you won't be able to respond appropriately.

Activity 1.1: Understanding the Communication Process

The diagram below summarizes the communication process. Look at the diagram and answer the questions that follow.

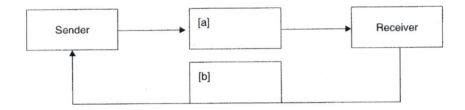

1. What should the block marked [a] be labeled? _____

2. What should the block marked [b] be labeled? _____

3. Because the block marked [b] is present, what type of communication is represented in the diagram? _____

4. Suppose that something interferes with the message being sent to the receiver from the sender. What term is used to describe this interference? _____

5. Suppose the block marked [b] is not present in the diagram. What type of communication would the diagram represent? _____

Activity 1.2: Applying the Communication Process

The goal of this activity is to understand and apply the components of the communication process. For each mini-case, complete the grid that follows.

▓ *Mini-Case #1*

Mark Singer works for a small family-owned business. At the start of each day, the foreman, Billy Hutchins, calls a meeting of Mark and his five teammates to discuss status, procedures, and other relevant matters. Today, Billy has chosen a quiet location, away from the site, because he wants to demonstrate a new procedure. After explaining the procedure, he asks Mark and his team if they have any questions about it.

Sender(s)	Receiver(s)	Communication Channel(s)	Is Noise Present? If So, What Is It?	Is This One-Way or Two-Way Communication?

■ *Mini-Case #2*

Rachel Bennington receives a memo from her boss, Carol Mayfield. The memo directs Rachel to place a phone call to Curtis Johnson at 3 P.M. on Friday afternoon. Steve Franklin and Gregg Kastell also receive copies of the memo. The purpose of the call Rachel has to make is simple: to get a schedule for a specific project. Rachel reads the memo very quickly because she has so much other paperwork on her desk. She misses the fact that she is supposed to wait until Friday to call, so she calls today.

Sender(s)	Receiver(s)	Communication Channel(s)	Is Noise Present? If So, What Is It?	Is This One-Way or Two-Way Communication?

■ *Mini-Case #3*

Melanie Harkness, the director of personnel, calls Julie Gold into her office for a meeting. It's time to fill out the paperwork for benefits, and Melanie is meeting with each employee individually to make sure that the paperwork is filled out correctly. An important part of Melanie's job is to answer any questions that employees might have about their benefits. Julie finds Melanie very helpful, but she wishes that Melanie's phone wouldn't ring so much, and that Melanie would stop answering the phone every time it rings. The meeting should have taken only 15 minutes, but because of the ringing phone, it ended up taking half an hour.

Sender(s)	Receiver(s)	Communication Channel(s)	Is Noise Present? If So, What Is It?	Is This One-Way or Two-Way Communication?

1.2 ACTIVE LISTENING

Why is it so important to be a good listener? First and foremost, we learn by listening, not by speaking. You learn your trade by watching and listening to experienced people.

Many people think that listening is something that just happens—some people talk and other people hear it. But listening is an *active* process. Successful understanding comes from active listening.

The good news is: You can train yourself to be an active listener by keeping the following suggestions in mind.

UNDERSTAND THE POSSIBLE CONSEQUENCES OF NOT LISTENING. Poor listening skills can cause costly mistakes in both time and money. Be aware of what can happen if you don't listen. A message not fully understood can have serious consequences. For example, a worker who doesn't listen to safety rules endangers not only himself but also co-workers. A worker who doesn't listen attentively to the boss can make mistakes that cost thousands of dollars to fix.

CONSIDER THE BENEFITS OF EFFECTIVE LISTENING. Good listening skills lead to higher efficiency, greater productivity, and better on-the-job relationships. Think about it this way: Aren't you more likely to enjoy the company of someone who listens to every word you say? When you're listening, you should grant the speaker your full attention. Listen to others in the same way you'd like them to listen to you.

STAY FOCUSED. Because people are busy and everyone has so much to do, it's easy to let your mind wander. Fight that temptation and stay focused. For example, when you're listening to the foreman give instructions, don't think about the football game you watched last night or the road trip scheduled for this weekend.

One way to stay focused is to make eye contact with the person who's speaking. It's harder for your thoughts to wander when you're looking directly at someone else.

DON'T JUMP AHEAD. If you think that the speaker is going to say something you already know, you may not listen closely. Your mind may jump ahead, thinking that it already knows what's coming. Resist this urge, and allow your mind to move at the same pace as the speaker. You may learn some new things or hear some unexpected information.

KEEP AN OPEN MIND. It's easy to shut our minds—and our ears—when we hear something we disagree with or when a person we don't like is doing the talking. On construction sites, though, all communications are important, especially those with supervisors. Don't tune people out. Remember that even people you don't like can have good things to say.

BE AWARE OF YOUR BODY LANGUAGE. You listen not just with your ears but with your whole body. Nodding your head shows that you're listening. Other types of body language show that you're impatient or *not* listening. Whenever you find yourself rolling your eyes, drumming your fingers, sighing, or yawning, you aren't listening actively.

SHOW THAT YOU'RE LISTENING. The person who's speaking needs to know that you're listening. To show that you are, nod your head or express your interest in some other way. For example, you might simply say "OK" every few minutes. Or you might occasionally restate the speaker's message in other words to demonstrate your understanding.

ASK QUESTIONS IF YOU DON'T UNDERSTAND. Sometimes you may not understand a particular word, term, or instruction. If this happens, ask for clarification before the speaker goes too much further.

Don't be embarrassed if you can't follow a conversation. It's always better to ask questions than to assume the wrong information and make a costly error. Also, senior people fully expect apprentices and journeymen to ask questions—it's an important part of their training. On a job site, there is no such thing as a "stupid question."

TIP: Don't interrupt without good cause. You can't listen when you're speaking! Consider whether you should interrupt the speaker, or whether your question can wait until he's done speaking.

PAY ATTENTION TO THE DETAILS.   In your construction job, you'll be asked to perform very specific tasks. Just understanding the general gist of what's being said will not be enough. For example, an order from your foreman to "Have the fuse box installed by tomorrow" is very different from an order to "Have the fuse box installed by 10 A.M. tomorrow." So pay attention to the details of what you're hearing. Remember that most projects are time sensitive, so always ask about the time frame involved.

TAKE NOTES.   If the speaker is presenting a lot of information, it often helps to take notes on a small pocket notepad. Later on, if any confusion arises or if you forget anything, you can refer to your notes.

Supervisors love it when their workers take notes. It shows that they're paying attention and care about the details. Notes also prevent you from having to bother your supervisor later if you have questions. (Section 2.1 offers detailed instructions on taking notes effectively.)

DON'T GUESS ABOUT IMPORTANT PARTS OF INSTRUCTIONS YOU'RE RECEIVING. If a word or an instruction can be interpreted in different ways, find out exactly what the speaker means. Suppose your supervisor tells you to change the tolerance on a machine part. Does "change the tolerance" mean you should *increase* the tolerance or *decrease* it? To what *exact setting* should the tolerance be adjusted? Don't assume that your supervisor means one or the other. Ask her which one she wants.

SUMMARIZE AT THE END OF A CONVERSATION.   The best way to make sure you understand what's been said is to repeat everything you've heard at the end of the conversation. This way, you will find out immediately if you've misunderstood anything.

Suppose the foreman tells you to secure the site and return all protective equipment to a storage trailer between 5 and 6 P.M. You should listen to what he says, then say something like, "OK—between 5 and 6 o'clock tonight, I'll secure the site and bring back all the protective equipment to the trailer." When the foreman nods, you'll know that you've understood everything correctly.

REMEMBER: You can't listen when you're talking. Don't interrupt people when they're talking. Let them finish what they have to say before you respond.

Activity 1.3: Active Listening Quiz

Choose the best answer for each of the following questions.

_____   1. All of the following are the results of active listening, except
   a. improved on-the-job relations
   b. greater productivity
   c. higher costs
   d. higher efficiency

_____   2. One effective way to show the speaker that you're listening would be to
   a. nod your head
   b. look over her shoulder
   c. tap your fingers
   d. read while she is speaking

_____   3. Suppose your boss tells you to meet him in the home office later that day. What would be your best response?
   a. "OK, will do."
   b. "Great . . . should I bring anything with me?"
   c. "All right, but I might be a little late."
   d. "I'll be there. What time?"

_____   4. What is one nonverbal indicator that someone is not listening actively?
   a. rolling one's eyes
   b. making eye contact with the speaker
   c. summarizing at the end of a conversation
   d. asking questions for clarification

_____   5. You're in a meeting with one of the senior members of the team— a man you don't like very much. You find yourself thinking about other things while he speaks. What advice would you give yourself in this situation?
   a. "You really don't need to listen closely, because you know this stuff already."
   b. "You may not like this guy, but he is experienced and may have good things to say. So you'd better listen up."
   c. "It's no big deal if you don't listen now. Later on, if you have any questions, you can always ask someone else who attended the meeting for clarification."
   d. "You're right not to listen to this guy—he doesn't know what he's talking about."

Activity 1.4: Listening Actively (Collaborative Activity)

For this activity, you need a partner.

Step One: Decide whether you will be Participant A or Participant B.

Step Two: If you are Participant A, stop reading here.

Step Three: Participant B will read the following questions out loud to Participant A. Person A needs to listen actively and answer the questions accurately.

SET 1:

A plumber with brown hair is in charge of completely gutting and rebuilding the plumbing in Mrs. Johnson's house. The plumber's name is Jack Friday. To help him with the job, the plumber has asked an old friend of his, Peter Jones, to meet him at the house at 8 A.M. on Tuesday. When the plumber arrives at the arranged time, he sees that his friend is already there. The two friends drink a cup of coffee together, then knock on the homeowner's door.

QUESTIONS:

1. What color is the plumber's hair? _____

2. Who owns the house? _____

3. On what day are the plumber and his friend meeting at the house?
   _____

SET 2:

Freddy MacIntyre is a mason who lives in Pennsylvania. He does about 60% of his work in his home state, 30% of his work in New Jersey, and an occasional job in Delaware. Today's job is to pick up the brick for a new staircase he will be building on a small house in Roosevelt, New Jersey. When he goes to the brickyard, he is told that the color of brick he wants has been discontinued, but he has three options instead: terra cotta, burnt red, or Arizona cactus color.

QUESTIONS:

1. What percentage of Freddy's work is not done in either Pennsylvania or New Jersey? _____

2. In what town will Freddy be working today? _____

3. Does Freddy ever work in Arizona? _____

4. Name two of the three brick color options Freddy has for the job he will be starting today._____

SET 3:

To get to my house, take Interstate 94 to Exit 95. At the end of the ramp, make a left onto Morrison Road, and stay on that street for three miles. You'll come to a traffic light. Make a right at that light onto Michaels Road. Continue past a supermarket on the right, and then take the third left after the supermarket. That's Alps Road. I'm at number 59 Alps Road, fourth house on the left.

QUESTIONS:

1. What is the name of the street you'll be driving on as soon as you get off Interstate 94? _____

2. What exit number off the highway should you take? _____

3. On what street is the supermarket located? _____

4. What number is the house? _____

1.3 NONVERBAL COMMUNICATION AND BODY LANGUAGE

Remember the old saying, "A picture is worth a thousand words"? It's equally true that one gesture, or one small movement, can convey a huge amount of information. In fact, research has shown that more than 90% of all communication is nonverbal. That is, we communicate not only through words but also through many unspoken methods. Though we may be unaware of it, our bodies and our facial expressions sometimes communicate a message—approval, agreement, enthusiasm, confusion, anger, distaste—that conflicts with the words we're saying.

For example, picture the following two conversations:

Foreman: Marty, call JK Plumbing and find out when they're gonna get here. They're two hours late already!

Marty (nodding his head): Will do, Al.

Foreman: Marty, call JK Plumbing and find out when they're gonna get here. They're two hours late already!

Marty (rolling his eyes and sighing): Will do, Al.

The words are the same in both situations. But in the first one, Marty's nonverbal signals are positive. In the second situation, Marty's nonverbal signals are negative, and the foreman is sure to pick up on them.

As part of your active listening strategy, be aware of the following aspects of nonverbal communication and body language, and adjust your behavior accordingly.

POSTURE. When you're listening to someone, don't slump down. Slouching usually makes you look tired, bored, or uninterested. Try to keep your arms and legs loose. (Generally, people fold their arms or cross their legs when they're listening to or talking with people they don't like. Other people pick up on these signals easily.)

EYE CONTACT. Look directly at the person who's talking to you. Don't stare at that person, of course; it's OK to look away occasionally. Don't roll your eyes or look at the ceiling. These gestures make you look doubtful, arrogant, or dismissive.

VOICE QUALITY. Just about everyone on earth is sensitive to a raised voice, which conveys anger or frustration. In conversation, *never* yell or curse in response to something you disagree with.

Table 1.1 summarizes some types of body language and the way they are usually interpreted. Be aware of your own body language as you listen, and change that body language if it's conveying the wrong message.

TABLE 1.1   Nonverbal Behavior and Body Language

Nonverbal Behavior	Interpretation
Standing with hands on hips	Readiness, aggression
Arms crossed on chest	Defensiveness
Rubbing hands	Anticipation
Tapping or drumming fingers or a pen/pencil	Impatience
Patting or fondling hair	Lack of self-confidence; insecurity
Tilted head, leaning forward	Interest

Nonverbal Behavior	Interpretation
Stroking chin	Trying to make a decision
Biting nails	Insecurity, nervousness
Rubbing the eyes	Doubt, disbelief
Sitting with hands clasped behind head, legs crossed	Confidence, superiority
Brisk, erect walk	Self-confidence
Turning one's back on another person	Dismissal
Foot tapping	Impatience
Looking out of the corner of the eyes	Disdain, scorn

Source: Adapted from V. A. Seitz, "Your Executive Image." [Online]
http://www.careercity.com/edge/getjob/prep/dress/dress4.htm (Adams Media Corporation, 1996).

Activity 1.5: Understanding Body Language

For each of the nonverbal signals listed below, choose the most likely interpretation.

_____ 1. Crossed arms
    a. high interest level in the conversation
    b. dislike of the speaker
    c. boredom
    d. sexual attraction

_____ 2. Raised voice
    a. calmness, tranquility
    b. frustration, anger
    c. lack of self-confidence, insecurity
    d. intense curiosity

_____ 3. Nail biting
    a. nervousness
    b. excitement
    c. happiness
    d. creativity

_____ 4. Rolled eyes
    a. self-confidence
    b. anticipation
    c. scorn
    d. rivalry

_____ 5. Playing with one's hair
    a. sexual attraction
    b. interest
    c. aggressiveness
    d. insecurity

_____   6. Standing with hands on hips
           a. aggressiveness, readiness
           b. snobbery
           c. impatience
           d. ridicule

Activity 1.6: Interpreting Body Language (Collaborative Activity)

This activity requires five people (one foreman and four workers). Only the people playing the roles should read the dialogue that follows. After the role play, answer these questions.

1. Do you think the crew will be able to do the job correctly?

2. How do you think the foreman felt about the behavior of Bob, Sally, and Charlie?

3. Two weeks from now, when the foreman is promoted and is asked to recommend one of the crew to replace him as foreman, whom will the foreman recommend?

4. Which member of the crew is the best worker? The most intelligent?

Dialogue

Foreman: Bob, you and Sally take these two fittings—this one and this one—and go up to the compressor deck. Pete, you and Charlie get a come-along and bring it up there. I'll meet you on the compressor deck with the permit.

Bob: (Take out your pocketknife and begin to clean your fingernails as soon as the foreman begins giving instructions.)

Pete: (Look directly at the foreman or whatever he points to the entire time he is giving instructions. Nod occasionally; say "OK" once in a while. When the foreman finishes, say "Got it!")

Sally: (As soon as the foreman starts talking, bend down and pick up something from the ground. Look at it for a second. Then look off to the side as if you're watching someone leave. Point and say under your breath to Charlie, "Who's that leaving? You know whose truck that is?" Keep looking off to the side.)

Charlie: (Look uninterested, with your eyes down at the floor. When Sally speaks to you, look interested in the truck she points to. Reply in a low voice, "I'm not sure. Looks like Mike Cook.")

1.4 LISTENING AND ON-THE-JOB SAFETY

Throughout this module, we've been emphasizing two important aspects of active listening: (1) the "human relations" aspect, and (2) the safety aspect. When you listen carefully, you are more likely to build good relationships with your supervisors and co-workers. (Of course, the same is true in your nonwork life as well. You benefit greatly from listening closely to your friends and family.) And, perhaps more importantly, when you listen actively you are much more likely to remain safe and unharmed on the job.

The importance of safety on any construction site requires you to ensure that you've *listened to* and *heard* every instruction you've been given. Suppose, for example, that you wear glasses and you are just learning how to weld. Your supervisor is explaining basic welding safety to you, and he says the following:

"Never wear contact lenses when welding."

Now suppose that some heavy equipment is being moved in the background while your supervisor is speaking. Because so much noise is present, you might hear:

". . . wear contact lenses when welding."

By not hearing one simple word ("never"), you could think that your boss is telling you to wear contact lenses instead of glasses, and you could make the serious mistake of wearing contact lenses when you weld.[3]

The tips listed in Section 1.2 for active listening all apply to situations in which job safety is concerned. Here are some additional safety-related tips to keep you safe on the job.

ELIMINATE NOISE. In Section 1.1 we showed how noise can interfere with a message. Always try to eliminate distractions. Ask to move to a quieter location if necessary. If doing so is impractical, move closer to the person speaking.

READ AND FOLLOW UP. Many procedures on the job site are written down in manuals or summarized in memos. It's always a good idea to read those materials as a follow-up to verbal instructions. If you notice any discrepancies between what you read and what you hear, talk to your supervisor.

PROTECT YOUR HEARING, AND GET IT CHECKED PERIODICALLY. Always wear the required protective hearing equipment. Your hearing is precious, and you should do everything in your power to protect it. Have your hearing checked annually. Many people with hearing loss don't notice the problem; some even refuse to accept it.

REMEMBER: If you can't hear properly, you endanger other people, not just yourself.

---

[3]The reason you shouldn't wear contact lenses while welding is as follows: The ultraviolet rays may dry out the moisture beneath the contact lens, causing it to stick to your eye. When you try to remove the lens, you might damage the eye.

UNDERSTAND WHICH NOISE YOU SHOULD *NOT* IGNORE.   In a world full of distractions, we've become masters of ignoring the noise around us. People who live near airports say they don't even hear the planes taking off! But, on a construction site, tuning out noise can be dangerous. Whistles usually mean something important. So do those "beep-beep-beep" sounds that indicate heavy machinery backing up. Understand the noises you should ignore, and those you should not.

Activity 1.7: Differentiating Noise

An important part of listening actively and working safely is knowing which noises you can safely ignore and to which noises you should pay attention. In the list that follows, mark those workplace noises that you should ignore with an "I." Mark those workplace noises you should pay attention to with a "P."

_____   1. Airplanes flying overhead

_____   2. Loud whistles

_____   3. Music on the radio

_____   4. Fire alarms

_____   5. Beeps to indicate machinery backing up

_____   6. Communications over two-way radio from the foreman

_____   7. Noise from local rivers and streams

_____   8. Traffic from the local interstate highway

_____   9. Loudspeaker announcements

_____ 10. Gossipy conversations of co-workers who are talking in the area where you're working

1.5 BARRIERS TO EFFECTIVE LISTENING

To be an effective listener, it's helpful to be aware of the factors that can interfere with effective listening. Barriers fall into two general categories: (1) external barriers, and (2) internal barriers.

External Barriers

An *external barrier* is one that is beyond the listener's control. External barriers include some types of noise, soft-spoken speakers, differing expertise or experience levels, and language barriers.

NOISE.   As we've seen, noise can come from a variety of sources, from a radio that's playing too loud, to traffic on a nearby road, to the sounds made by construction equipment. Noise is an unfortunate fact of life. It can't be completely avoided.

The best approach to noise is to be aware of it. Understand the environment in which you must work, and determine how best to listen when noise is present. Use the tips presented in this chapter and determine the system that works best for you. For example, on one construction site, workers leave their cars in a parking lot a mile away from the job site. Each morning, the foreman holds a 15-minute meeting in the parking lot, where there is almost no construction noise.

INEFFECTIVE SPEAKERS.   Sometimes listening can be negatively affected by an ineffective speaker. The person speaking may speak too softly for you to hear, too rapidly for you to take notes, or too slowly to hold your interest.

In such situations, your best bet is to take charge! Respectfully ask the speaker to speak up, to slow down, or to speed up. Always feel free to ask questions if you need clarification. Speakers are often unaware of their effect on listeners, and they usually appreciate knowing how they can improve.

Modules 3 and 4 offer an extended discussion of effective speaking skills.

DIFFERENT EXPERTISE/EXPERIENCE LEVELS.   Imagine that you were to attend a conference of nuclear physicists, all of whom were presenting the results of their research. Would you be able to understand one word of what they were saying? Most likely, you wouldn't!

Good speakers use the appropriate level of terminology for their audience. With experienced co-workers, they use the terms of the trade and can safely assume that these terms will be understood by the listeners. With clients or inexperienced people, they explain more and speak more slowly. However, not all speakers are audience-centered. They might use terms they don't explain or assume knowledge that their audience doesn't have.

In such situations, your best bet is to follow as best you can. Try not to tune out. Listen as closely and carefully as possible. You might learn something valuable. But you'll definitely need to follow up with questions and/or further reading materials.

LANGUAGE BARRIERS.   In our multicultural world, different accents (whether national or regional) can get in the way of effective listening. People who do their best to speak effective English may still not be understood by native speakers of English. In fact, people from different parts of the United States sometimes don't understand one another! People from the South, the Northeast, and the Midwest all have distinct speech patterns that people from other regions might not understand.

Deal with language barriers as sensitively and tactfully as possible. (People who learn English as adults are likely to have accents for the rest of their lives.) If you don't understand something, ask the speaker to repeat what she's said. Ask nicely; don't get impatient. Try to sympathize with the speaker, who is most likely doing the best she can.

You can also make the effort to learn something about the speaker's language, particularly if you'll be working with many people who speak the same native language. For example, native speakers of Spanish often add an "e" to the beginning of words that start with the letter "s." So, instead of saying "space," they may say "e-space." (This happens because the word for space in Spanish, *espacio,* starts with "e" instead of "s.") Knowing a little something about the speaker's native language can be very helpful.

Internal Barriers

Internal barriers to listening emanate from the listener himself. These are barriers influenced by personality, perspective, or attitude. They include an unwillingness to listen, inattentiveness, impatience, and ego and other personality factors. Fortunately, all these barriers can be overcome.

UNWILLINGNESS TO LISTEN.   Some people want to talk much more than they want to listen. Their main goal is to offer their own thoughts, rather than to hear what other people have to say. This is frustrating to both parties—both of whom want to be heard simultaneously. In effect, each becomes "noise" to the other.

If you're aware of this tendency in yourself, you can ask others to point it out to you. Being reminded when you're interrupting can help you become a better listener.

INATTENTIVENESS.   With all the distractions in the world, it's easy to "tune out" of a conversation, especially when you're not interested in the topic or when you think you know what's going to be said.

Monitor yourself. Don't let your mind wander. Force yourself to pay attention. Think about your job and what needs to get done. Focus on the benefits of listening—maybe this conversation will someday save your life, save you time, or get you promoted!

> **TIP:** Don't bring problems at home to the job. Being preoccupied with nonwork worries can impair your ability to listen and concentrate. If you do have personal problems that affect your ability to do your job, talk to your supervisor.

IMPATIENCE.   Because people are so busy and rushed, they sometimes feel they don't have the time to sit down and listen closely. So they might try to hurry the speaker along, either by interrupting or finishing the speaker's sentences. They might also express their impatience nonverbally, perhaps by looking at their watch or looking around.

If you are an impatient listener, try using an *empathetic* approach. That is, put yourself in the speaker's place and imagine how you'd feel if someone were as impatient with you as you are being with the speaker. If you truly don't have time to listen, ask the speaker if the discussion can be postponed until later. (This usually is not an approach to take with your supervisor, however.)

EGO AND OTHER PERSONALITY FACTORS.   A host of other personality factors can also get in the way of effective listening. People sometimes stop listening when:

- They disagree with what's being said
- They don't like the person speaking
- They consider themselves more intelligent than the speaker
- They are attracted to the speaker
- The speaker reminds them of someone they don't like
- Something about the speaker makes a bad impression—such as clothing or hairstyle

None of these are valid reasons to stop listening. Remember not to judge a book by its cover, and to remain open-minded.

Table 1.2 lists some ineffective listening styles. If you exhibit any of these styles, consider their effects on the speaker and work to improve your listening skills.

TABLE 1.2   Ineffective Listening Styles

Listener Type	Listening (Responding Behavior)	(Mis)interpreting Thoughts
Static listener	Gives no feedback, remains relatively motionless, reveals no expression	Why isn't she reacting? Am I not producing sound?
Monotonous feedback giver	Seems responsive but the responses never vary; regardless of what you say, the response is the same	Am I making sense? Why is he still smiling? I'm dead serious.
Overly expressive listener	Reacts to just about everything with extreme responses	Why is she so expressive? I didn't say anything that provocative.
Reader/writer	Reads or writes while "listening" and only occasionally glances up	Am I that boring?
Eye avoider	Looks all around and at others but never at you	Why isn't he looking at me? Do I have spinach in my teeth?
Preoccupied listener	Listens to other things at the same time, often with headphones so loud that it interferes with your own thinking	When is she going to shut that music off and really listen? Am I so boring that background music is needed?
Waiting listener	Listens for a cue to take over the speaking turn	Is he listening to me or rehearsing his next interruption?
Thought-completing listener	Listens a little and then finishes your thought	Am I that predictable? Why do I bother saying anything? He already knows what I'm going to say.

Source: Adapted from Joseph A. DeVito, *The Interpersonal Communication Book,* 9th ed. (New York, NY: Addison Wesley Longman, 2001), p. 119.

Activity 1.8: Self-Assessment: Identifying Bad Listening Habits

The following are some signs of poor listeners. Check any boxes that you think apply to you. Be *honest* in your self-assessment! Once you're aware of these bad habits, you can work on improving them.

- ☐ Making jokes when the other person is trying to be serious
- ☐ Arguing with everything the other person says
- ☐ Interrupting the other person constantly
- ☐ Doubting what the other person says, and showing it on your face
- ☐ Thinking about other things while having a conversation
- ☐ Acting fidgety or playing with things (pencils, etc.) when someone else is talking
- ☐ Disagreeing constantly with the other person's suggestions
- ☐ Finishing sentences for the other person

☐ Changing the subject to something you're more interested in

☐ Saying things like "Cool" or "No doubt" instead of taking an active part in the conversation

☐ Looking at your watch while somebody is talking to you

☐ Jumping to conclusions before the other person is finished

☐ Tuning out because you don't like someone's appearance

☐ Being distracted by noise

☐ Becoming frustrated by someone's accent

☐ _____

☐ _____

My action plan for improving my listening skills:

1. _____

2. _____

3. _____

4. _____

5. _____

6. _____

Activity 1.9: Eliminating Barriers to Effective Listening

In this activity, your job is to assess the situation and offer advice to the person featured in each mini-case.

▦ Mini-Case #1

Dave McManus has been working for Northgate Construction for over ten years. He is well liked by just about everyone, particularly by the apprentices and journeymen, because he is so good at his job and so good at explaining techniques and procedures to less experienced workers. One day, a few of the younger workers come to Dave and tell him how frustrated they are with their foreman, Gary Stangis. They complain that Gary talks much too quickly and that they don't understand the terms he uses. In addition, Gary was born in Germany, and his accent distracts them. So, rather than listen closely to Gary, they just tune out of the conversation. If they have questions later on, they come to Dave, who they know will explain everything to them carefully.

QUESTION:
If you were Dave McManus, what advice would you give the younger workers about improving their listening skills?

▦ Mini-Case #2

Darlene Nichols has been assigned to work on a two-person project with Fran Romani. The two women are both very qualified carpenters (both have been doing their jobs for more than ten years), but they have different styles of communication. Darlene likes to do everything by the book. She has one way of doing things, and she doesn't like to move off that path. She's not much of a talker;

she just works. In contrast, Fran is creative and is always looking for new, more productive ways to get the job done. She likes to laugh and chat while she works.

The problem is: The two women do not seem to communicate very effectively. Darlene complains that Fran talks too much and distracts Darlene while she's working. She doesn't think she can learn much from Fran, because they've been in the business for the same amount of time. On her side, Fran thinks that Darlene is uncommunicative, and that they could get the job done much more quickly if they'd just put their heads together.

QUESTION:
What advice would you give Darlene about improving her listening skills? What advice would you give Fran?

Listening Skills II:
Advanced Topics

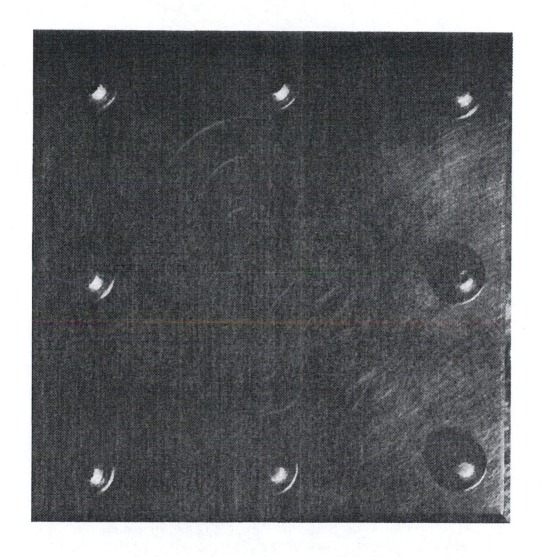

> " In seeking wisdom, the first step is silence, the second listening,
> the third remembering, the fourth practicing,
> the fifth—teaching others. "
>
> —Ibn Gabirol, poet and philosopher (c. 1022–1058)

Module 1 explained the basics of the communication process, active listening, and nonverbal communication. With those basics mastered, this module explores some additional listening-related topics: how to take notes, how to listen to instructions, how to handle criticism and bad news, and how to listen effectively on office phones, on cellular phones, and in meetings.

2.1 Taking Notes

Books, memos, and manuals all exist for one reason: All human beings have limited memory capacity. Even people with excellent memories forget what they've heard or learned after a while. Nobody is able to remember *everything* he or she sees, hears, or does.

It's not surprising, then, that most working adults have taken to carrying a small notepad around with them. Business executives rarely attend a meeting without paper and pen. Contractors and subcontractors don't give an estimate without taking notes. Could you imagine how challenging it would be to write up an estimate based on memory alone?

Taking notes while you listen has many benefits:

- When you take notes, your listeners know that you're paying close attention to them.
- Taking notes helps ensure accurate information. If you try to memorize a phone number, you might get it wrong later. But if it's written down, you'll never have to worry about calling the wrong number.
- Employees who take notes get noticed by their supervisors. Foremen and other managers like their workers to take notes. It's a sign of dedication to the job.
- Taking notes increases your productivity. When you have the information you need in front of you, you won't waste time searching for answers or asking co-workers for help.

Good notes must accomplish two things:

- They must serve as an accurate summary of what you've heard.
- They must include enough details so that they make sense when you reread them later.

Later in this module we give an example of a presentation and the notes taken during that presentation. First, however, it is helpful to outline some effective note-taking techniques.

LISTEN FOR CUES.   While talking, the speaker may use words or phrases that signal important ideas or concepts. She might say something like, "Always remember that," "Keep in mind," or "It's really important that. . . ." Listen carefully when you hear such phrases. It's probably worth jotting down a note that summarizes the points introduced by these phrases.

DON'T WRITE EVERYTHING DOWN.   Note taking requires a careful balance between listening and writing. If you write down everything, you're likely to miss some of what is being said. Don't become so involved in note taking that you stop listening. Write down only the most important things.

BE CAREFUL WITH NUMBERS.   Quite often, you will be writing quickly when you take notes. Slow down when you write numbers, because on a construction site accuracy in numbers is *essential.*

USE ABBREVIATIONS. Because human beings write more slowly than they speak, good note taking requires quite a lot of abbreviating. You'll waste valuable time if you try to write out complete words, so come up with a series of abbreviations that you'll be able to understand. For example, instead of writing "electrical," you can write "elec." Instead of "air conditioning," you can write "AC."

CARRY A NOTEBOOK AND PENCIL WITH YOU. You never know when you'll need to take notes, so keep a pencil and notebook handy whenever possible. Put a date on your notes so that you know when you took them.

KEEP A LIST OF QUESTIONS. Sometimes it isn't practical to interrupt a speaker with your questions. Yet, if you don't ask the question when it occurs to you, there's a chance that you might forget it. So feel free to write down questions so that you can ask them later on.

USE A FORMAT THAT WORKS FOR YOU. Some people like to take notes in a list format (1, 2, 3, etc.). Others prefer a more free-flowing style. Use whichever format works best for you. Just be sure that your format allows you to go back and access the information you need easily.

DRAW DIAGRAMS. A picture can be worth a thousand words. Simple sketches or drawings can be quite helpful for future reference.

With these tips in mind, let's imagine that you are an HVAC specialist, and you're attending a local conference on piping. You're sitting in an audience of 40 people, and the speaker gets up and starts talking, as follows:

Many types of piping are used in HVAC work. Copper pipe is used to transport refrigerant in residential and smaller commercial air conditioning systems. In large commercial and industrial systems, welded steel piping is more common. Steel is also used with special refrigerants, such as ammonia. Steel and plastic piping are used to transport water in HVAC systems that use water as a heat exchange mechanism. Black iron pipe is used to transport natural gas for heating systems.

It's really important that HVAC technicians take six precautions when working with pipe. First, protect all piping from exposure to dirt and other contaminants. Don't leave open ends of piping stocks exposed. Even tiny amounts of contaminants can damage an HVAC system. Second, remove the charge from a pressurized system before opening any solder joints. It's dangerous to work on piping when the system is under pressure, and it's illegal to release refrigerant into the atmosphere. Third, use only ACR copper piping and fittings in refrigeration work. Type M and DWV copper piping and fittings, which are used in plumbing, aren't suitable for refrigeration work. Fourth, use as few fittings as possible. Fewer fittings mean a smaller chance of leaks and pressure drops. Fifth, use extreme caution in making every solder connection. Use correct solder and techniques. Don't cut corners. Finally, pitch horizontal lines in the direction of refrigerant flow. Otherwise, oil may cling to the inner walls of the tubing. Tubing pitch will allow oil to flow in the right direction. It also avoids backward flow during shutdown. Use half an inch of pitch per 10 feet of run.

You can get a copy of these HVAC technician guidelines free by calling Laura Pearson at 201-555-7783. If you have any questions, you can call me, Wayne Cowen, at 904-555-9898.[1]

---

[1]Adapted from National Center for Construction Education and Research, *Heating, Ventilating, and Air Conditioning Trainee Guide* (Upper Saddle River, NJ/Columbus, OH: Prentice Hall, 1999), Task Module 03104, p. 5.

Since you're new to the HVAC field, you may want to jot down some notes.

As you prepare to take notes, notice that the speaker, Wayne Cowen, is talking about two topics: (1) types of piping, and (2) HVAC precautions. Wayne signals the important part of his presentation by saying "It's really important that...." He concludes by giving a couple of phone numbers that you can call for more information. Your notes based on this presentation might look like this:

Piping
1-copper—res & sm. comm a/c
2-welded steel—lg comm/indus
3-steel—ammonia
4-steel & plastic—water
5-blk iron—nat. gas

Cautions
1-No dirt on pipe, no open ends
2-Depress. b4 opening solder jts
3-Use only ACR pip/fit, no M/DWV
4-Use few ftgs
5-Careful w/solder connex.
6-Pitch horiz lines toward ref. flow — 1/2"/10 ft.

Laura Pearson 201-555-7783
Wayne Cowen 904-555-9898

REMEMBER AS YOU TAKE NOTES:
- Focus on the most important points and details.
- Write efficiently. Use abbreviations and shortened forms whenever possible.
- Tune out distractions. Imagine that the world is composed of just two people: you and the speaker.

Activity 2.1: Taking Notes (Collaborative Activity)

The goal of this activity is to practice your note-taking skills. Two people are required for this activity. Proceed as follows:

- The first person will read the first lecture out loud to the second person. Be sure to read at a normal pace.
- The second person will take notes as the first person speaks.
- For the second lecture, the second person reads out loud while the first person takes notes.

Lecture #1: The History of the Plumbing Trade[2]

The distribution of water occurs constantly in nature. Sunlight causes water to evaporate and form clouds. These clouds are moved by wind currents.

---

[2]Adapted from National Center for Construction Education and Research, *Plumbing Trainee Guide* (Upper Saddle River, NJ/Columbus, OH: Prentice Hall, 1992), Task Module 02101, pp. 1–8.

When they encounter cold air, the moisture condenses and falls as precipitation, either in the form of rain or snow. Some of this precipitation penetrates into the earth while much of it flows into lakes, streams, or rivers. Eventually, the water flows to one of the major bodies of water, such as the Pacific Ocean. By tapping this cycle, by drilling wells and creating drainage and sewage systems, man is able to improve his quality of life. Water is made continuously and conveniently available for domestic and industrial use. Sanitation is greatly increased because water is used to dispose of waste.

The work of constructing water supply and sewer systems is divided into two major categories. The piping systems, which are buried below ground, are generally installed by workers who specialize in pipeline construction. The installation of piping and the fixtures and controls within buildings is done by skilled tradesmen called plumbers.

The English word "plumber" comes from the Latin word "plumbum," which means lead. Because most early plumbing was made from lead, the workers who specialized in this field were called "plumbarius," meaning one who works with lead. The existence of plumbing as an identifiable craft can be traced back to the ancient Roman empire, even though the Palace of Knossos in Crete had vented "toilets" about 4,000 years ago. By 400 B.C. the first public bath house had been erected in Greece, and by 312 B.C. the Romans began building 11 aqueducts to move huge volumes of water to Rome. In 100 A.D., the average resident of Rome was supplied with 300 gallons of water per day! Despite their sophisticated water supply mechanisms, though, the Romans had no means of treating water. The typical practice was to obtain water upstream from a city and discharge sewage back into the river downstream from the city.

During the fifth century and through the Dark Ages (400–1400 A.D.), the Goths invaded Rome, and little was done to maintain the aqueducts. They gradually deteriorated, and by the 11th century, they were completely inoperable. In the period 1347–1351, almost a quarter of Europe's population was wiped out by the bubonic plague, which probably could have been prevented through sanitary water and waste disposal systems.

As the Dark Ages were ending, London, England laid its first water supply pipe. By 1721, the London Water Company began pumping water through wooden pipes to supply the city. In 1775, Alexander Cummings patented the first valve toilet. In the 1870s Thomas Twyford produced the first washout toilet made from a single piece of glazed earthenware. This development was followed by rapid expansion of the use of indoor plumbing facilities.

The rapid advancement of plumbing since the mid-1800s may be better appreciated by the following example. In most American cities, people were still dumping sewage and garbage in the streets for pigs to scavenge. By 1855, Chicago was a city of 75,000 people. Bathing was a once-a-week experience which utilized a washtub filled with water which had been carried from a well and heated on a stove. All members of the family took turns using the same tub of water!

In 1937, Al Moen introduced the double valve faucet with a cam to control the two valves, and the 1950s saw the introduction of stainless steel to the plumbing fixture industry. In 1958, centrifugal pipe casting machines were developed. In 1961, compression gaskets were introduced, followed in 1964 by hubless couplings. In recent years, given the booming population and huge amount of waste, much time and money have been spent on antipollution measures.

Lecture #2: Treating Your Customers with Respect[3]

In the painting trade, treating customers with respect is always important, but in residential work, it is even more critical. Admitting you into their home or business is a gesture of faith by customers—faith that you will do no harm, and that you will treat the premises and occupants with respect.

So, it's important to always ask yourself these questions: Do you refrain from smoking? Do you remember to protect the work area? Do you carry rags and clean up after yourself? Do you have dropcloths to protect hardwood floors and carpets? Do you respect the customers' home by not tracking in dirt? Do you remember to return the home to its original condition, wiping off dirty fingerprints, cleaning up dropcloths, and replacing covers?

As the number of homes with more than one income has increased, the need to arrive on time has become more critical than ever, since in these cases someone has to take off from work to wait for the craftsperson. Be on time. Call if you are going to be late. Show the customers that you realize that their time is valuable.

Customers notice if you arrive with a full set of tools, neatly packed. Using a wrong tool not only leaves behind poor results, it tells your customer that you are unprofessional. They notice your attitude, and whether it shows a good work ethic. They can see if you neatly repack your tools when you finish the job, too. It's part of how they judge you and your company. It's also a large contributor to whether they call your company back for more work.

Also ask yourself these questions: Do you tackle the job promptly? Do you arrive fully informed and ready to do the job? Do you politely avoid general conversations while working? The answer to all these questions should be "Yes"!

Finally, remember that your customers always appreciate a positive attitude. For example, it's best to be professional and avoid "bad mouthing" different products and/or competitors. Likewise, for example, if you are late—but it is not your fault—focus on the positive, getting the job done, rather than blaming someone else. Say something like: "I understand how you feel. I'm sorry. Please know that I will do my best to have your room professionally painted as soon as I can."

2.2 LISTENING TO (AND FOLLOWING) INSTRUCTIONS

Spoken instructions are extremely common on any construction site, and to do your job well you must know how to follow instructions to the letter.

How should you proceed? First and foremost, when listening to directions, apply the rules of active listening outlined in Section 1.2. Stay focused, pay attention to the details, take notes, and show that you're listening. In addition, do the following:

CAREFULLY WATCH DEMONSTRATIONS THAT ACCOMPANY THE INSTRUCTIONS. Sometimes the people giving instructions will also be demonstrating the process at the same time. For example, a foreman might talk about how to operate a piece of machinery while demonstrating on the actual machinery. So, in addition to listening closely to the directions, pay close attention to the step-by-step demonstrations.

---

[3]Adapted from National Center for Construction Education and Research, *Painting Trainee Guide* (Upper Saddle River, NJ/Columbus, OH: Prentice Hall, 1997), Trainee Module 07101, pp. 17–18.

IF A DEMONSTRATION IS NOT PROVIDED, VISUALIZE.   When listening to a set of instructions, picture yourself actually doing each step as you hear it. Visualizing can help you remember the directions. It also increases the chances that you'll accomplish the task correctly the first time you try.

ASK QUESTIONS.   Active questioning is always an essential part of active listening, but it's particularly important when you're listening to instructions. While you should make every effort not to interrupt the speaker, remember that instructions are cumulative. That is, you might not be able to continue with Steps 4, 5, and 6 if you haven't understood Steps 1, 2, and 3. In such a case, it's acceptable to ask the speaker to clarify Step 3 at the time he's discussing it.

> **TIP:** When you have questions, be sure to ask the speaker, rather than the co-workers or people around you. The speaker is the expert, after all. Also, by whispering while the speaker is talking, you distract other people in the audience.

Activity 2.2: Following Spoken Directions (Collaborative Activity)

The goal of this activity is to practice your listening skills. Two people are required for this activity. Proceed as follows:

- The first person will read the first set of directions out loud to the second person. Be sure to read at a normal pace.
- The second person will do as instructed.
- For the second set of instructions, the second person reads out loud and the first person follows the directions.

SET #1

1. Take out a piece of paper.
2. At the top of the paper, write the words "construction trades." Leave space between each of the letters, but keep the two words on one line.
3. Cross out all A's, I's, and O's.
4. Cross out all T's.
5. On the next line, rewrite what is left.
6. Where you see "U" and "C" together, cross them out and write in "P" and "E" instead.
7. After the "C," add an "A."
8. Change the "D" to a "T."
9. Cross out the second "R."
10. Between the last letter and the next-to-last letter, add an "R."
11. Cross out the third and fourth letters from the left.
12. What word do you now have?

Set #2

1. Stand up.

2. Pick up a writing implement and place it in your left hand.

3. Take six steps forward, but only after you have taken two steps backward.

4. Move the writing implement to your other hand, but first take a step to the left.

5. Hand the writing implement to me. On second thought, keep it.

6. Check your watch. What time is it?

7. Take two steps backwards while clasping your hands together. Keep the writing implement between your hands.

8. If 10×5 equals 40, move two steps to the right. If $10 \times 5 = 50$, move two steps to the left.

9. What is your name—last name first?

10. If half an inch is more than a quarter of an inch, return to your seat. If half an inch is less than a quarter of an inch, give me the writing implement.

11. Is it now the same time it was when I asked you the time a little while ago?

2.3 Listening to (and Accepting) Criticism

All human beings make mistakes. Nobody is perfect, and there's no human being without flaws. In our daily lives, we can overlook mistakes, but on a job site a foreman's job is to correct any mistakes she sees. This means that when you do something wrong, someone will probably tell you about it. In addition, each year, you will receive an evaluation in which your supervisor summarizes your job performance for the year. In most companies, the supervisor will not only congratulate you on what you did well, but also point out areas that can be improved.

It's easy to take criticism personally, to get upset by it or angry because of it. But criticism need not be something that causes hurt feelings. There are two types of criticism:

- *Destructive criticism* aims to hurt or insult people. It strips them of their self-esteem and makes them feel worthless. It also creates hostility and bad feelings. Destructive criticism doesn't offer support or suggestions for improvement. Rather, it closes down the lines of communication.

  Has anyone ever said to you: "What did you do that for? Man, that was stupid." Or "What's wrong with you? Didn't you listen to what I was saying? Or are you just deaf?" These are examples of destructive criticism.

- *Constructive criticism* is the opposite of destructive criticism. Its goal is to correct mistakes tactfully, offering support and advice to help workers correct their mistakes. The results of constructive criticism are better on-the-job relations and increased productivity.

  Some examples of constructive criticism are: "I see why you made a mistake here . . . let me show you a better way to handle this situation, one that will be less work for you," or "So, you made a mistake. No big deal. It'll only take a few minutes to fix it. While we're fixing it, I can show you how to use the correct tool so that this doesn't happen again."

To benefit from constructive criticism, it's important to keep an open mind and to listen to the criticism as carefully as you would any other communication on the job. When we're being criticized, it's tempting to shut out the speaker. Doing so allows us to protect ourselves. But learning from our mistakes is a valuable way to improve our skills. If you look on criticism as a learning opportunity, it will be much easier to stay open minded.

Some suggestions for listening (and responding) to criticism follow.

ANTICIPATE CRITICISM.   It's easier to deal with criticism if you expect it to happen sooner or later. Remember: Every criticism offers the potential for growth.

DON'T TAKE CRITICISM OF YOUR JOB PERFORMANCE PERSONALLY.   Remember that your foreman's comments about the difficulties you've had wiring a house are *not* comments about you as a person. Your foreman may like you very much, but it's his job to make sure the job is done right. He needs to make sure you meet the company's standards.

LOOK AT YOURSELF FROM YOUR SUPERVISOR'S—OR THE CRITICIZER'S—POINT OF VIEW.   Imagine that you're outside your body, evaluating the work you've just done. Deep down inside, you know when you haven't done a good job. Try to see your work as other people do, and you'll realize that you can benefit from the constructive criticism you receive.

DON'T GET DEFENSIVE. MAINTAIN CONTROL OVER YOUR EMOTIONS.   When somebody criticizes you, your first reaction may be to defend yourself or fight back. Resist that temptation. Be willing to listen. The worst thing you can do is return criticism with a comment like, "Yeah, and you think you're so perfect? You make more mistakes than I do."

DON'T MAKE EXCUSES.   You may sometimes want to explain your mistake or shift the blame. But it's much better to take responsibility for your errors. Don't bring other people into the criticism. For example, don't say something like, "I could have done this a lot better if only Wally had helped me more."

ASK FOR CLARIFICATION AND SPECIFICS.   When you receive criticism, you have an excellent opportunity to demonstrate a positive attitude and a strong sense of teamwork. Rather than become angry, ask how you can fix the situation. It also doesn't hurt to express regret for what you've done wrong and to reassure your foreman that it won't happen again.

If you don't understand the criticism, don't be afraid to ask for details. Sometimes criticism can be vague, and you may not fully know what your boss means. Respectfully ask for examples or explanations. For instance, you might respectfully say, "I want to do a better job, but I don't have a handle on what exactly I'm doing wrong. Can you give me some specific suggestions?"

MAKE AND STATE A PLAN TO IMPROVE YOUR PERFORMANCE.   There's no better way to impress your boss than to take her criticism seriously. So, after she's pointed out your mistake, let her know what you'll do to correct the situation. For example, if she criticizes you for being late, you might say something like, "I am going to buy a new alarm clock so that I don't oversleep ever again."

UNDERSTAND YOUR RIGHT TO DISAGREE WHEN THE CRITICISM IS NOT WARRANTED.   Sometimes, after carefully evaluating the criticism you receive, you may feel that it's not justified. Sometimes you *are* right, and the other person is wrong. In that case, offer your side of the story respectfully and clearly. Give examples to support your point of view. Don't begin by saying, "You're totally wrong about that—get lost." Instead, say "I see things differently. Let me explain what happened."

Activity 2.3: Responding to Criticism

When someone criticizes you, it's important that you respond in some way. If you say or do nothing, you may come across as hostile, angry, or defensive.

To complete this activity, respond to the following criticisms appropriately. Some of the criticism you'll be responding to is constructive, while other criticism is destructive. Think about the best way to respond before you write your answer. Give the most professional response, which may not necessarily be the same as what you might *want* to say.

1. **Criticism**—Your boss says to you: "You're not a team player."

   Your response: _____

   _____

   _____

2. **Criticism**—The foreman says to you, "I think you've lost interest in doing a good job."

   Your response: _____

   _____

   _____

3. **Criticism**—A co-worker says to you, "You talk way too much while we're working . . . could you please just shut up?"

   Your response: _____

   _____

   _____

4. **Criticism**—A teammate says to you, "I'm sick and tired of the sloppy way you work."

   Your response: _____

   _____

   _____

5. **Criticism**—A co-worker says to you, "You're really slowing me down. You're too young and you don't know what you're doing yet. I need to work with someone who has more experience than you do."

   Your response: _____

   _____

   _____

6. **Criticism**—Your supervisor says to you, "I know you are trying really hard, but you don't seem to be getting this right. Do you need some additional training?"

   Your response: _____

   _____

   _____

7. **Criticism**—Your foreman says to you, "How many times do I have to teach you the same thing? We keep going over this. Are you dense or something?"

   Your response: _____

   _____

   _____

8. **Criticism**—Your supervisor says to you, "This is the third day in a row that you've been late. I'm not going to put up with it. You're lazy and unreliable."

   Your response: _____

   _____

   _____

9. **Criticism**—The owner of the company says to you, "I hear that you have come up with some innovative ideas and have saved us a lot of money. I wanted to personally thank you for your contributions. Next time, please tell me about them directly."

   Your response: _____

   _____

   _____

10. **Criticism**—At lunch, a friend says to you, "Ugh! You talk with your mouth full, like a pig!"

    Your response: _____

    _____

    _____

Activity 2.4: Converting Destructive Criticism into Constructive Criticism

The best criticism is constructive, not destructive. Constructive criticism seeks to correct mistakes gently, and it takes other people's feelings into account. Destructive criticism seeks only to harm or belittle.

   To prevent yourself from offering destructive criticism, think before you speak. The following table lists several situations, along with destructive criticism. Your goal is to make the criticism constructive rather than destructive. The first one has been completed as an example.

Situation	Destructive Criticism	Constructive Criticism
1. You're teaching somebody to pitch a curve ball. Your student can't seem to do it right. He needs to spread his fingers over the seam of the ball, but he's not doing that. He keeps his fingers too close together, and he doesn't snap his wrist when he releases the ball.	"You're never going to get this if you don't pay attention to what I'm saying."	"Not a bad try. But your fingers are too close together. Spread them a little. When you release the ball, snap it even more. Right now, you're just giving a small snap—give it even more snap!"

Situation	Destructive Criticism	Constructive Criticism
2. You're working on a team of four people. Three of you are reliable and on time. The fourth person calls in sick a lot, takes long lunches, and likes to sneak home early.	"You're not a good team player. The three of us are better off without you."	
3. You've asked someone to cut a 2 × 4 at a 45-degree angle. It's your last 2 × 4, and the person cuts it at the wrong angle. Now you can't finish the job today, and your foreman is going to be upset.	"Hey! I said cut that at a 45-degree angle! Were you sleeping? You know, you really messed me up. Thanks a lot."	
4. You're the foreman. One of your workers is constantly trying to put things over on you. He lies, covers up his mistakes, and blames other people for things he's done wrong. He thinks he's fooling you, but he isn't.	"I guess you think I was born yesterday, huh? Well, guess what— I'm onto you, and I know what you're all about. So does everyone else, and that's why nobody likes you."	
5. You're working side by side with someone who keeps losing things. First, he misplaced an important tool. Now he's lost the nails and screws you need to get the job done.	"I think you'd lose your head if it wasn't attached. Don't forget, someone who loses things is a *loser*."	

2.4 HANDLING BAD NEWS

In life, things don't always go according to plan. The ups and downs of life mean that on some days you'll receive good news, and on some days you'll receive bad news. Good news is easy to handle. It's cause for laughter, smiles, and celebration. In contrast, bad news can affect your job performance quite negatively if you don't manage it properly.

What types of bad news might you receive? In your personal life, your "significant other" might break up with you, or your rent might go up. At work, you may find that someone else has been promoted into a job you wanted, or your boss might announce that everyone needs to work overtime on a weekend you'd planned to take a mini-vacation. At a more extreme level, the company might announce cutbacks in benefits or even layoffs.

For your personal well-being, as well as continued effectiveness on the job, it's essential that you learn how to cope with bad news. Here are some tips for doing so.

AS HARD AS IT IS TO LISTEN, STAY FOCUSED.   Bad news is hard to hear, and it's tempting to shut it out. But instead of closing your ears, listen carefully. It may turn out that the bad news isn't as bad as you thought it was. Or the bad news may be accompanied by some important information. For example, if the company is announcing layoffs, it might also be announcing severance packages at the same time. Knowing that you'll receive eight weeks' severance pay could soften the blow somewhat.

CONTROL YOUR EMOTIONS.   You may be tempted to respond to bad news in many ways: by yelling, by crying, or even by punching someone or something. All these things are counterproductive and might even make the situation worse.

Try to remain calm, and then express your emotion in an acceptable way. For example, you might decide to go to the gym to work off some excess tension.

MAINTAIN YOUR PERSPECTIVE.   It's easy to let bad news overwhelm you. A piece of negative information can sometimes make you lose perspective. You might think, "Why me?" or "Why do bad things keep happening?" Stop yourself from thinking these negative thoughts. Try to keep things in perspective. As hard as it may be, try to see the positive side. For example, you might say to yourself, "Okay, I have to work much more overtime than I wanted to, but I can sure use the money."

Another hint: Remind yourself of the good things in your life. Let those things make up for the bad news. Think: "All right, Joe got the job that I wanted, but that job would have taken a lot of my time. This way, I get to spend more time with my wife and kids, and I'll have another chance next year to get promoted."

> **TIP: Take the ten-year test.** When you get bad news, ask yourself, "Will this matter ten years from now?" Most likely, the answer will be "No." Knowing that this bad news doesn't matter in the big scheme of things will help you keep it in perspective.

DON'T TAKE IT PERSONALLY.   Section 2.3 emphasized that you shouldn't take work-related criticism personally. The criticism is directed against something you've done, not against you as a person. The same guideline holds true for bad news. Don't take it personally. Most of the time, bad news is the result of a situation beyond your control.

TALK IT OUT.   In the 1600s, the Englishman John Donne wrote, "No man is an island, entire of itself." By this, he meant that human beings are social creatures who rely on one another for companionship and perspective. It's much easier to cope with bad news when you can talk about it with other people. Sometimes your spouse is the right person. Other times, you might want to talk about the news with your co-workers. If something truly tragic has happened (such as the death of a loved one), you might consider talking to a professional, licensed counselor or clergy member.

MAKE A PLAN OF ACTION.   People are happiest when they feel the most in control of their surroundings. You may not be able to control what has happened, but you can control what happens afterward, at least with regard to your personal well-being. So take charge of the situation emotionally. If you find out that you're losing your job, immediately begin looking for another one. Talk to friends, co-workers, and relatives to find out about possible job openings. Look in the paper and/or surf the Internet. By taking active steps to improve your situation, you become much more in control and much less a victim of circumstances.

Activity 2.5: Self-Assessment: Handling Bad News

The following list summarizes some behaviors or reactions that people have when they receive bad news.

Step One: Check those boxes that apply to you. As with all self-assessments, honesty is essential.

Step Two: Once you've determined your weak areas, make an action plan for improvement.

When I receive bad news, I tend to:

- ☐ Get extremely upset
- ☐ Lose perspective
- ☐ Become extremely angry
- ☐ Lose my ability to concentrate
- ☐ Blame myself
- ☐ Keep the bad news to myself
- ☐ Take it personally
- ☐ Lash out at others
- ☐ Become defensive
- ☐ Scream or yell at the person who delivered the bad news
- ☐ Shut down emotionally and become unable to take action
- ☐ Cry
- ☐ Drink too much alcohol
- ☐ Use legal or illegal drugs
- ☐ Get depressed
- ☐ Stop listening to what is being said
- ☐ Feel bad about myself
- ☐ _____
- ☐ _____
- ☐ _____

Action Plan for Improvement:

EXAMPLE:

Problem: Drinking too much beer after getting bad news

Action Plan: 1. Go see a good funny movie instead to lighten my mood
2. Play softball or go to the health club to relieve some frustration
3. Have some friends over for a barbecue

Problem: _____

Action Plan: _____

_____

_____

_____

Problem: _____

Action Plan: _____

_____

_____

_____

Problem: _____

Action Plan: _____

_____

_____

_____

Problem: _____

Action Plan: _____

_____

_____

_____

2.5 TIPS FOR CONCENTRATING DURING DIFFERENT COMMUNICATION MODES

Throughout Modules 1 and 2, the listening skills we've focused on have assumed face-to-face communication—in other words, one or more people speaking to an audience of one or more people. Yet, in the real world, much communication takes place when people cannot see one another, particularly via telephone or cell phone.

Modules 1 and 2 have also assumed fairly informal communications—that is, communications that aren't very structured. But, in the real world, many communications take place in the form of structured business meetings, where workers are expected to listen and contribute.

For all these reasons, we close this module with tips on how to communicate effectively via telephone and cell phone, and how to participate effectively in business meetings.

2.5.1 Telephones and Cell Phones

Telephones used to be anchored in trailers and offices. Making a phone call required you to stop what you were doing, go to a different location, and place the call. Today, with cellular telephones, you can make a phone call from just about anywhere on a construction site.

When you're speaking with people face to face, you can see them and their reactions to your words. This is not the case when you're talking on the telephone. Because proper telephone behavior is such an important part of good business practice, here are some guidelines for using the phone on the job.

When Placing a Call

IDENTIFY YOURSELF AND DETERMINE TO WHOM YOU ARE SPEAKING. Begin your conversation by saying who you are: "This is Ernesto Morales. I'm a mason with JKL Company. Who am I speaking to?"

SPEAK DIRECTLY INTO THE RECEIVER, AND FOCUS ON THE PHONE CALL.   Make sure that you speak directly into the phone's receiver so that the person on the other end can hear you. And, when speaking on the phone, focus all your attention on the call. That is, refrain from doing other activities (such as answering e-mail, cleaning up, or having a side conversation) when you're on the phone.

STATE YOUR PURPOSE.   Don't simply ask to speak to someone. Rather, explain your purpose for calling. Instead of saying, "Is Pete there?" say, "I'm calling to set up an appointment with Pete. I'm supposed to pick up some supplies from him tomorrow."

SPEAK CLEARLY, AND SLOW DOWN WHEN APPROPRIATE.   Talking on the phone requires both parties to speak and listen more carefully than they would in person, because they cannot see the other person. Use simple, nontechnical language whenever possible. Also, speak more slowly when going over technical or tricky information. Repeat key information, especially numbers. For example, you might say, "We are going to use part number 46115. That's 4 . . . 6 . . . 1 . . . 1 . . . 5."

> **TIP:** Be yourself on the telephone. Speak pleasantly, crisply, and clearly. Try to visualize the person to whom you're talking. The person will seem much more "real" in your mind if you do so.

TAKE NOTES.   Much important information is communicated over the phone. Using the tips in Section 2.1, take notes to help you remember what's been said and the decisions that have been reached.

NEVER DIAL OR TALK ON THE PHONE WHILE DRIVING OR OPERATING HEAVY EQUIPMENT.   This is an extremely dangerous practice, and it is illegal in many states.

IF YOU'RE LEAVING A VOICE MAIL MESSAGE, KEEP IT BRIEF.   Voice mail is common, so assume that you will get an answering machine and prepare your message before you pick up the phone to call. When you leave the voice mail, state your name and purpose, as well as the date and time. Then leave a number at which you can be reached, as well as the best time to reach you. (Say your phone number twice, slowly.) Leave all the necessary information, but keep the message as short as possible.

> **TIP:** If you're going away on vacation, or will not be on the job for a few days, change your voice mail message to alert callers to your absence. When appropriate, leave the name and phone number of a qualified contact person. Return all calls within 24 hours, or sooner if the situation demands it.

BE AWARE OF PRIVACY CONCERNS.   Cell phone frequencies can sometimes be picked up by other sources. This means that others may be able to eavesdrop on your conversation without your knowledge. For this reason, do not communicate any confidential or sensitive information on a cell phone.

When Receiving a Call

IDENTIFY YOURSELF AS SOON AS YOU PICK UP THE PHONE.   Don't simply say "Hello." Instead, say "Cedric Jefferson—Plumbing."

DON'T KEEP PEOPLE ON HOLD.   Everyone is busy these days, and people resent being put on hold. If you don't have the time to talk, say so. Then arrange for a better time to talk.

USE COURTESY WHEN TRANSFERRING CALLS.   If you need to transfer a call, briefly explain the situation to the person who will take the call. This prevents the caller from having to explain himself or his situation all over again.

KEEP IT SHORT!   Cell phone time is expensive, and you're charged not only for outgoing calls but also incoming calls. Use the cell phone for business calls only, and keep your calls brief. (You may find it helpful to plan what you're going to say before you pick up the phone. This way, you keep your calls short and productive.)

If You Get Disconnected

Cell phones are subject to unexpected service interruptions. If you get disconnected, wait a few seconds for the line to clear. If you placed the call to begin with, call the person back. If the other person called you, keep your line clear and assume that he or she will call you back.

> **TIP:** Don't talk on the phone while co-workers, supervisors, or customers are waiting. This is considered rude.

Taking Messages

You may sometimes need to take a message for a co-worker. When you do, be sure to write down all the relevant information, including:

- Who the call was intended for
- Date/time
- Caller's name, properly spelled (ask the caller to spell his or her name)
- Caller's telephone number
- Your name or initials
- The specific message or information

Be sure to leave the message in a conspicuous place.

2.5.2 Meetings

While most craftspeople spend much of their day working with their hands, they are sometimes called into meetings. The higher you go in an organization, the more time you will spend in meetings.

What exactly is a meeting? Simply stated, a *meeting* is a gathering of three or more people sharing common objectives, where communication (verbal and/or written) serves as the primary means of achieving those objectives.[4]

---

[4]Marion E. Haynes, *Effective Meeting Skills* (Los Altos, CA: Crisp Publications, 1988), p. 2.

As a participant in the meeting, your close attention and feedback are expected. For example, your foreman may call a meeting with several workers to discuss a drainage problem on the job site and how it can be resolved. The foreman expects everyone to come to the meeting prepared with his or her ideas.

How can you listen carefully and get the most out of meetings? Here are some suggestions.

PREPARE.   Generally, the topic of the meeting will be announced in advance. So take some time to familiarize yourself with the subject to be discussed at the meeting. This is an excellent way to make a good impression.

FOCUS ON THE AGENDA. TAKE NOTES AS APPROPRIATE.   In formal meetings, an agenda is usually circulated. The *agenda* is a sheet of paper outlining the attendees, the topics to be considered and discussed, and the time to be spent on each topic. The agenda usually touches on the most important aspects of the meeting, so it makes an excellent "summary sheet" for future reference.

> **TIP:** It's sad but true that some meetings are long-winded and boring. During such meetings, work your hardest to pay attention and focus on the important aspects. Don't show your boredom! Don't sigh, or tap your fingers, or look at your watch. Doing so is disrespectful to the speaker.

PAY ATTENTION TO THE MEETING LEADER.   Usually, the person who has called the meeting is the one who leads it. Use active listening techniques to concentrate on what the speaker is saying. Jot down any questions you might have, and ask them at the appropriate time.

OFFER YOUR OPINION OR SUGGESTIONS.   Meetings are effective only when the attendees actively participate. So, when asked, offer your ideas. Present them simply and clearly. Your contributions will be valued!

> **TIP:** Time your suggestions well. It's not a good idea to interrupt someone who is speaking, particularly a boss or supervisor. Wait your turn. Write down your questions so that you don't forget them.

STICK TO THE TOPIC.   When you're surrounded by co-workers—or other people with whom you have a lot in common—it's easy to let the conversation wander off the topic. The more digressions you allow, the longer the meeting will go, and the more frustrated people will get. So, stick as closely to the agenda (or specified topic) as possible. If need be, schedule a separate meeting to discuss other issues that arise.

DON'T ENGAGE IN PRIVATE CONVERSATIONS.   Anything you say in a meeting should be intended for everyone at the meeting. Reserve side chat about other topics for personal conversations. Side conversations distract other people from listening to the main topic of conversation.

FOLLOW UP.   Usually, meetings call for some sort of post-meeting follow-up. If you're assigned tasks at the meeting, complete these tasks on time. In some cases, you may be asked to prepare a report or summary of what you've done.

A new type of meeting, called a *video conference,* uses video cameras, satellites, and/or the Internet to let you see and interact with people far away. Video conference technology is still in its infancy, and it is quite expensive. However, this emerging technology is likely to become more common in the future. If you find yourself in a video conference, be especially careful to speak concisely, pay attention, and stay focused.

Activity 2.6: Speaking on the Telephone

Here is your situation: Your name is Frank Torres, and you are an electrician with Valerian Brothers Plumbing. You need to place a phone call to one of your suppliers, New England Electric, to order six units of Part Number 7833. You need the parts delivered by tomorrow at 4 P.M. to your home office, which is located at 9894 Paddington, New Orleans, Louisiana. Your office phone number is 504-555-7494.

The phone is now ringing at New England Electric. Complete the following dialogue. Take your cues from the other person's responses.

Note: This activity can also be done as a collaborative activity. One person plays the role of Frank Torres. The other person plays the role of the people at New England Electric.

Dialogue #1

Operator: Hello, New England Electric.

You: _____

_____

Operator: You need the order department. I'll put you through. Hold on, please.

[ring, ring]

Voice: This is Joe in Electrical Supply.

You: _____

_____

Joe: OK, let me see if we have those in stock. . . . Yup, looks like we do. When do you need 'em by?

You: _____

_____

Joe: That should be no problem. Address?

You: _____

_____

Joe: OK, the total comes to $325.50. Anything else I can help you with today?

You: _____

_____

Dialogue #2

In this situation, you are a general contractor named Fred Washington, and you own a company called Total Remodeling, Inc. You receive a phone call from a homeowner, Janice Wiggins. She is interested in having her kitchen and bathroom completely remodeled. She calls you because she has heard good things about your company and would like an estimate.

Background information: The person who does your estimates is named Perry Knight, and he usually goes out on estimates between 8 A.M. and 4 P.M., Monday through Friday. He is also available for estimates on Wednesday evenings between 6 and 9 P.M. You recently remodeled a home in Ms. Wiggins's neighborhood. The owners of that house are Jack and Mindy Garcia, and their phone number is 801-555-0851. They were very pleased with your work. They've told you that you can give their phone number to potential customers who are looking to double check your reputation.

Complete the following dialogue. You are sitting at your desk in your office when the phone rings.

[ring, ring]

You: _____

_____

Ms. Wiggins: Hello, my name is Janice Wiggins. I live over on Elm Street, and I've been thinking about redoing my kitchen and bathroom. I heard good things about your company from my friend, Mary Ellen Grabonski.

You: _____

_____

Ms. Wiggins: Well, basically, both the kitchen and the bathroom are really, really old. The house was built in 1940, and it still has the original kitchen and bathroom. I want all new cabinets in the kitchen, plus a big new sink. The bathroom has a really old bathtub and fixtures, and I'd like all those replaced. The tile is falling apart, so I'd like all new tile in there as well.

You: _____

_____

_____

Ms. Wiggins: I would really love to see some samples of your work. You did a great job for Mary Ellen, but you only did her kitchen. Have you done any bathrooms in the area?

You: _____

_____

_____

Ms. Wiggins: Great, thanks. When would you be able to come by and give me the estimate?

You: _____

_____

_____

Ms. Wiggins: Well, I work during the week, and it's really hard for me to get away during the day.

You: _____

_____

_____

Ms. Wiggins: Sure, this Wednesday would be fine. Can you make it around 7 P.M.?

You: _____

_____

_____

Ms. Wiggins: Yes, it's 2123 Elm Street—that's 2—1—2—3 Elm, near the corner of Prospect.

You: _____

_____

_____

Ms. Wiggins: Sure, my work number is 801-555-7766, and my home number is 801-555-4297.

You: _____

_____

_____

Ms. Wiggins: Thanks, I'll see your guy on Wednesday!

Activity 2.7: Taking Phone Messages (Collaborative Activity)

This activity requires two people. Proceed as follows. Pretend that this is a phone call or a voice mail message. The first person reads Phone Message #1. The second person fills out a phone message form. For Phone Message #2, the second person reads the message and the first person completes the phone message form.

Phone Message #1 [Call taken by you at 10:15 A.M., Monday, December 3]

"Hi, this is Marty Fredericks over at 1-2-3 Plumbing. I'm looking for Joe . . . Joe Nahanic. Oh, he's not around? OK, can you let him know I gave him a call? I'm supposed to pick him up tomorrow around 6:30 A.M. to go over to that new mall they're building along Interstate 10 . . . yeah, I think I'm going to be about 15 minutes late getting to his house because there's all kinds of construction on Main Street . . . yeah, it stinks . . . I know . . . been taking me twice as long to get home from work! Yeah, and now they closed down a few of the side streets so I can't cut through. . . . OK, great, man, thanks a lot. Bye."

```
┌──────────────────────────────────────────────────────────────┐
│                      PHONE MESSAGE                             │
│  To: _____│
│  Caller: _____  Date: _____  Time: _____│
│  Phone: _____│
│  Message: _____│
│           _____│
│           _____│
│           _____ Initials: ___│
│  ☐ Urgent          ☐ Please Call Back      ☐ Wants to Meet     │
│  ☐ Sent a Fax      ☐ Check Your E-Mail     ☐ No Need for Return Call│
└──────────────────────────────────────────────────────────────┘
```

Phone Message #2 [left on answering machine on Friday, April 18 at 1:00 P.M.]

"Hey Marcy! It's me, Jackie. Sorry you're not there . . . I wonder where you are? If I know you, you're probably out there swinging that hammer around. . . . I saw Jake and the kids the other day, I can't believe how big Callie is getting, what is she—like three or four years old now? Unbelievable how time flies. Anyway, the reason I'm calling is, I just got this awful news—my company is going out of business. Can you believe it—after all these years? Art is just shutting everything down and retiring to Florida. So I'm out of a job. You know I'm a great secretary—I know all the computer programs and I'm great with the customers. Is your place looking for help? Can you get me in with the owner? I know you said he is a good guy. I'm going to send you an e-mail with my resume attached—can you pass it on? Anyway, give me a call—555-6166 is work, or at home 555-8432. Thanks, I owe ya one!"

```
┌──────────────────────────────────────────────────────────────┐
│                      PHONE MESSAGE                             │
│  To: _____│
│  Caller: _____  Date: _____  Time: _____│
│  Phone: _____│
│  Message: _____│
│           _____│
│           _____│
│           _____ Initials: ___│
│  ☐ Urgent          ☐ Please Call Back      ☐ Wants to Meet     │
│  ☐ Sent a Fax      ☐ Check Your E-Mail     ☐ No Need for Return Call│
└──────────────────────────────────────────────────────────────┘
```

Activity 2.8: Practicing Meeting Etiquette

How much do you know about attending and participating in meetings? Take this brief quiz. For each question, choose the best answer.

_____ 1. How many people must be present for a meeting to take place?

    a. two

    b. at least three

    c. at least four

    d. no more than three

_____ 2. Which of the following is not considered acceptable behavior at a meeting?
   a. taking notes
   b. asking questions
   c. sticking to the agenda
   d. whispering to the person sitting next to you

_____ 3. Suppose you're at a very boring meeting. What is your best course of action?
   a. Work hard to pay attention and stay focused.
   b. Doodle on your notepad to make the time go faster.
   c. Think about your work schedule for the next day.
   d. Excuse yourself to go to the bathroom, and don't come back.

_____ 4. When is the best time to ask questions?
   a. when the speaker has finished speaking, or at a natural break
   b. as soon as they occur to you
   c. when the meeting is over and everyone else has left
   d. It isn't acceptable to ask questions at a meeting.

_____ 5. Which of the following is not included on an agenda?
   a. topics to be discussed
   b. time allotments for each topic
   c. rules of the meeting
   d. names of the attendees

_____ 6. Suppose a meeting has been called to discuss the company's new safety guidelines. Two days before the meeting, your supervisor gives you a copy of the new guidelines. What should you do?
   a. File the guidelines away. There's no need to read them, because you'll be hearing about them in a few days, anyway.
   b. Read the safety guidelines and skip the meeting.
   c. Read the safety guidelines before the meeting, so that you can ask any questions you might have at the meeting.
   d. Ask someone else to read the safety guidelines and give you a summary of them.

_____ 7. Suppose the topic of a meeting is "hand tools." Which of the following would not be an appropriate item on the agenda?
   a. backhoes
   b. hammers
   c. wrenches
   d. screwdrivers

_____ 8. Who is expected to speak during a meeting?
   a. owners only
   b. owners and supervisors
   c. only those with more than ten years' seniority
   d. all attendees

_____   9. Who usually runs a meeting and sets the agenda?
            a. There is no leader. A meeting is just a forum for the exchange
               of ideas.
            b. the person who has called the meeting
            c. the attendees
            d. all high-level employees

_____   10. You're in a meeting about fire safety. What would not be an
             appropriate question to ask?
            a. Where are the fire extinguishers located in the building?
            b. Can you summarize the differences between the different
               types of fire extinguishers?
            c. How many days of vacation will the company be giving us this
               year?
            d. Would it be a good idea to appoint a "fire safety inspector"
               from one of the crewmen?

Speaking Skills I
The Basics

66 If you know, tell me in words so I can understand.
If you don't know, tell me so I can find someone who does. 99

—Art Holtz, Line Judge (Retired), National Football League

As we'll see in the second half of this book, reading and writing are two sides of the same coin. The two activities form an endless loop. People write something, and other people read what's been written. Those other people then respond to what they've read, perhaps by writing a response. The response is part of the all-important feedback process that is essential to effective two-way communication (see Figure 1.1 on page 2).

In the same way, *listening* and *speaking* are two sides of the same coin. Person A speaks, and Person B listens. B then responds to A, who in turn responds back to B—and so on. Like reading and writing, speaking and listening form a loop that allows for two-way communication.

Modules 1 and 2 presented techniques for becoming an effective listener. This module and the next continue our analysis of spoken communication, but now from the speaker's perspective. This module focuses on the basics of speaking effectively, from understanding your audience to communicating ethically. Module 4 discusses advanced topics in spoken communication.

3.1 UNDERSTANDING YOUR AUDIENCE

An extremely important part of speaking effectively involves tailoring your words to your *audience*. Before you speak, you must first consider the person or persons to whom you're speaking, then choose your words accordingly. For example, a discussion with a co-worker can be informal and conversational, while a conversation with your foreman should be formal and carefully worded.

We discuss techniques for speaking clearly and effectively in Section 3.4. Here we examine how your presentation will differ from audience to audience.

3.1.1 Talking to Co-Workers

Because all construction jobs rely on a team of highly skilled workers—yourself among them—there is one element that should form the basis of all communications between you and your co-workers. That element is *respect*.

To show respect while speaking with co-workers, keep the following tips in mind.

- Allow other people to speak their ideas as freely as you express your own. Don't interrupt others while they are talking.
- If you work with people from a different ethnic group or gender, do not make comments that draw attention to their gender or ethnic background.
- When you disagree with something a co-worker has said or done, disagree or criticize gently and respectfully. Never call attention to a person's mistakes or problems in public.
- Never use the phrase "It's not my job." The construction professional's job is to be an actively contributing member of the team.
- When appropriate, praise your co-workers. Everyone loves a compliment. So, when you're impressed by somebody's work, tell her about it. A compliment costs nothing, and it is an effective way to build team spirit.
- Share the credit. When a job is well done, there's plenty of credit to go around, so be sure to share any recognition you receive with your co-workers. Similarly, be willing to acknowledge your mistakes. Don't ask or expect your co-workers to cover for you.

Many times, when speaking with co-workers, you can feel confident that they'll speak the same "construction language" as you. Thus, you won't need to worry about explaining terms or speaking more slowly so that they can follow you. However, there may be times when you're talking to a group of people with different experience levels. In this situation, you have two options:

- Speak more slowly and explain the terms and procedures as you go along (see Section 3.1.3).

- Break your audience into several groups, organized by experience or ability level. In your talk with the more experienced people, assume higher levels of existing knowledge. With the less experienced people, take more time, perhaps demonstrating as you speak.

TIP: Laughing and jokes are completely acceptable—even desirable—when talking with co-workers. Humor lightens the mood and builds team spirit. Just be sure that humor doesn't overtake the conversation or overshadow the purpose of the conversation. And, of course, make sure your humor is appropriate.

3.1.2 Talking to Supervisors

Many people are fortunate to have foremen and supervisors whom they like a great deal. Nonetheless, a certain formality is usually expected between bosses and workers. For supervisors to offer constructive criticism, there needs to be some distance between them and their workers.

The good news is: Both bosses and workers usually prefer it this way. It's important that you maintain a friendly and good relationship with your boss, but you should not treat your boss as "one of the guys." Friendly conversation with the boss is highly recommended, but most of your talks with the boss should focus on business. Of course, as with co-workers, *respect* should lie at the foundation of every conversation you have with your boss.

Here are some suggestions for communicating effectively with your supervisor.

- *Remember that the boss is not the enemy.* Some people mistakenly assume that the boss is the enemy, a sort of evil creature who exists to make life a living hell. This could not be farther from the truth. Supervisors greatly trust and appreciate reliable workers. In fact, because supervisors have been in the business a while, they tend to have a lot of sympathy for the challenges faced by the crew. Because supervisors have so much experience, they understand the demands of your job.

- *Don't argue, and don't complain.* When the boss tells you to do something, do it immediately and without complaining. Of course, you should feel comfortable asking questions for clarification. But don't question your boss's authority or right to give you orders.

- *Disagree respectfully.* If you truly believe that your boss is wrong about something, talk with her about the situation in a mature and respectful way. Don't be confrontational. Don't ever raise your voice.

- *Remember that your boss has a boss, too.* Just as you must account for your actions to your supervisor, your boss must do the same to his supervisor. The difference is: Your boss's boss is at an even higher level in the company than your boss is! Your boss's higher-ups hold him responsible for any problems that arise. If you ever get frustrated with your boss, remember that he may only be following orders from *his* boss.

- *Admit your mistakes.* If you have made a mistake, don't try to cover it up. The boss will find out about it eventually. The best approach is to admit your mistakes and take responsibility for them. While your boss may react negatively in the short run, she'll also respect your honesty and your willingness to make things right. If you cover things up, you look sneaky and dishonest.

From time to time, you may need to have difficult conversations with your boss. For example, you may feel that you've been treated unfairly, or you may need to bring a problem to your boss's attention. When you need to have such nonroutine conversations, keep the following in mind:

- *Choose the appropriate time and place to talk.* Foremen and other supervisors are busy. They're willing to answer questions, provide guidance, and help to solve problems, but you should time your questions and requests properly. If the boss is having a bad day, wait a few days to ask for vacation time or a raise. If the owner will be visiting the site the next day, your boss may be a little nervous or uptight. Don't bother him with unimportant details that aren't urgent.
- *Communicate in private, depending on the situation.* If a problem that requires immediate attention comes up while your supervisor is talking to other people (owner, architect, engineer), ask your supervisor to step away from the group so that you can discuss the problem in private. Don't say anything that might alarm the guests or embarrass your supervisor in front of the group.

TIP: If you're having troubles on the job, don't go directly to your supervisor's boss. Doing so makes your boss look incompetent. The best way to solve problems is to go to your supervisor directly. As a general rule, go over the boss's head only as a last resort, after you've exhausted all other options. If you have to go to your boss's boss to get a problem solved, be sure to tell your boss that you're doing so.

Perhaps the most critical thing to keep in mind when talking with your boss is the importance of *empathy*—of putting yourself in your boss's shoes and understanding his or her point of view. Sometimes your boss may frustrate you. Instead of getting upset, try to see the situation from your boss's perspective.

For example, suppose that your supervisor, Jim, has been coming down hard on your friend, Bob. Jim has been on Bob's case every day because Bob comes in late and talks more than he works. You like Bob, and you feel that Jim is being too hard on him. But try to see things from Jim's perspective. Everybody else has to be at work on time, so why doesn't Bob? Everybody else has to put in a solid day's work, so why shouldn't Bob?

TIP: Never bad-mouth your boss to co-workers. While it's tempting to complain about the boss during a softball game or over lunch, it's also hard to prevent people from repeating what you've said. A good rule of thumb: Never say anything about anyone unless you'd be willing to say the exact same thing directly to that person.

3.1.3 Talking to Laypeople and Clients

When talking with co-workers and supervisors, you can assume a strong working knowledge of construction terms and practices. This is not the case, however, when talking to *laypeople* (that is, people who are not construction professionals) and clients. For example, suppose you've been hired to renovate the kitchen in an old house. While the homeowner may know a little something about plumbing, electrical, and heating and air conditioning systems, it's unlikely that he'll have a strong background in any of these areas.

Just as *respect* is the watchword in conversations with colleagues, it should be the basis of any conversation with a layperson or client. To demonstrate this respect, make use of the following suggestions.

- *Take the time to explain.* When talking with a layperson, *slow down.* Explain terms, procedures, and materials in as much detail as necessary.
- *Be patient.* Your client may ask you many questions whose answers seem obvious to you as a construction professional. Be patient with these questions, which can seem annoying. Remember, most people have little or no construction background.
- *Recognize the client's emotional investment.* Let's return to the example we used above: the kitchen renovation job. As a contractor, you may renovate kitchens every day, so a typical renovation is no big deal to you. But for the homeowner, the renovation is an extremely costly project that will likely disrupt the household for weeks or even months. Understanding the homeowner's concerns and emotional investment in any project is a critical component of the construction professional's job.
- *Communicate ethically.* The opportunities to take advantage of people with no construction background are numerous. For example, unethical workers will drastically overcharge someone to correct a very minor problem, claiming that the problem was "life threatening." The person being overcharged doesn't have the knowledge base to know that he's being taken advantage of. It goes without saying that such practices are immoral and disgraceful.

Activity 3.1: Talking with Different Audiences

Test your understanding of how to speak with different audiences. Choose the best answer for each of the following questions.

_____ 1. What should form the basis of all spoken communications with co-workers, supervisors, and laypeople?
   a. technical understanding of construction
   b. respect
   c. rapid understanding
   d. friendliness

_____ 2. Joe has a small company that installs and replaces gutters on houses. He receives a call from an elderly lady who says she thinks she needs new gutters because when it rains, the gutters drip horribly. Joe visits the house and sees that the gutters are jammed with mud and leaves, and that the problem could be solved by simply cleaning the gutters. Instead of telling the client this, he replaces the gutters for a cost of $750. The cost of cleaning the gutters would have been $125.

How would you assess the ethics of Joe's actions?

a. Joe just did what the client asked, so there is no problem here.

b. Joe cheated the client.

c. Before replacing the gutters, Joe should have told the client that the problem could be solved more cheaply by simply cleaning the gutters.

d. Joe should have referred the client to someone else who could do the job better.

_____ 3. In the last week, your boss has become extremely strict about safety regulations. In the past, she was fairly easygoing about such regulations, but all of a sudden, for no apparent reason, she has gotten tough. She has started sending workers home for violating safety rules.

Use the empathy rule. Why might your boss have started behaving this way?

a. Because someone from headquarters has gotten on her case and has told her that she needs to start being stricter about safety matters.

b. Because she has been fighting with her husband and wants to take her problems out on the people who work for her.

c. Because she has it in for certain workers, and is looking for an excuse to fire them.

d. Because she has suddenly become a jerk for no apparent reason.

_____ 4. Suppose you are about to address a room full of people. Your goal is to demonstrate how a new piece of machinery works. In the room are men, women, African-Americans, and Latinos of all ages, from construction companies across the country. Which of the following would be an appropriate greeting?

a. "Hello, ladies and gentlemen of all colors and ages."

b. "Good afternoon. My name is Jack Spencer and I'm going to show you how to operate the new Excalibur 2200i."

c. "Guys, girls, Blacks, and Hispanics . . . welcome."

d. "Wow, this room makes it clear that construction isn't just a white man's job anymore! Welcome, everybody! I'm happy you're all here."

_____ 5. When speaking with someone who knows little about construction, you should do all of the following except:

a. speak more slowly

b. explain the meanings of unfamiliar words

c. be patient if the other person doesn't catch on right away

d. speak more rapidly

_____ 6. Suppose you're in a meeting with your boss and your teammates. Your boss says, "I'd like to congratulate this team on finishing up the project two days early. Great work, everyone." But the boss has made a mistake—the team has actually finished two *weeks* early. How should you point out this error to your boss?

a. Correct him in front of everyone in the room.

b. Wait until the meeting is over and everyone has left. Then mention the error respectfully.

    c. Wait until he's done speaking, then, with everyone present, let him know that he has his dates mixed up.

    d. Rather than telling the supervisor himself, call up *his* boss and give him the correct information.

_____ 7. Suppose you need to call a meeting of your team to discuss new OSHA regulations. Basically, there are two types of people present: people who've been working in construction for a long time and are very familiar with OSHA regulations, and brand-new apprentices who just started last week. What would be your best method of conveying the new information?

    a. Gather everyone together and present the information, assuming that if the apprentices have any questions, they will ask.

    b. Gather everyone together, but speak very slowly and explain much of the background information, so that the new apprentices are fully informed.

    c. Meet with only the apprentices, and send a memo to the experienced workers.

    d. Have two separate meetings, one for the apprentices and one for the experienced workers.

_____ 8. On your current job, you have been putting in much more overtime than anyone else. You feel that your life is being affected by all this overtime, and you can't figure out why you're the only one putting in all these hours. You feel you need to talk to someone about this problem. What should you do?

    a. Choose a quiet time and place to convey your concerns directly to your supervisor.

    b. Go to the director of personnel to talk about your issues.

    c. Go to your boss's supervisor to let her know that you think your boss is not treating you fairly.

    d. Just call in sick on a day that you are scheduled to work overtime.

_____ 9. Suppose your boss has asked you to do a task that isn't part of your everyday job. Which of the following would be the ONLY appropriate response you could make?

    a. "Sorry, it's not my job."

    b. "Can't you ask someone else to do it?"

    c. "I'll be glad to, but I don't know how. Can you get someone to show me?"

    d. "I'll do it, but I really don't think I should have to."

_____ 10. You made a mistake. Instead of ordering 100 2 × 4s, you ordered 400 2 × 4s. Now you have a surplus of expensive wood on the job site, and your boss is bound to be angry. What is the best way to proceed?

    a. Have the lumber hauled off to another place and hope that the boss doesn't find out.

    b. Ask your co-workers if they'll cover up for you.

    c. Go to your boss, admit your mistake, and ask how you can improve the situation.

    d. Try to find another use for the lumber.

3.2 JARGON, SLANG, AND FORMAL ENGLISH

In Section 3.1, we pointed out that it's generally acceptable to use construction *jargon*—that is, construction terminology—when talking with co-workers or supervisors. However, in speaking with supervisors, your speech should be more formal. With co-workers, it's more likely to be informal.

What exactly do we mean by *jargon* and *formal English?*

Jargon

Jargon is common in the construction and technical trades. *Jargon* is a widely inclusive term that means, basically, "the language of the trade." Computer specialists talk about interfacing and protocols; bankers talk about calls and puts; and handwriting analysts talk about slant and pressure. All disciplines have their own special terms to describe common objects, occurrences, processes, and theories. Construction is no different. Table 3.1 summarizes some common construction jargon, along with their "English translations." Undoubtedly, you will be able to add to this list.

In on-the-job communications—whether written or spoken—jargon is completely acceptable. Just keep the following precautions in mind:

- *Avoid using jargon with laypeople.* If you must use jargon in conversations with laypeople and clients, be sure to explain every term you use.
- *Watch for regional differences in jargon.* A term or phrase may mean different things in different parts of the country or even at different companies. Or different areas of the country may use different words to define the same concept. For example, the terms "spigot," "tap," and "faucet" all mean the same thing, but each is used in a different part of the country. Check with experienced people to make sure you're using the correct term for the meaning you want to convey.
- *Don't over-jargon your speech.* Use as many terms of the trade as you need to, but remember that too much jargon may be confusing. Consider the following example from a discussion of preventive maintenance:

Jargon Version

Let's look at how Jack could have benefited from a little PM. He burned a lot more number two than he needed to before he got around to running the rack on his Slam-bang. A maintenance schedule would have pointed out any problems long before the engine started smoking. Same thing with the front SQ drop-in. He wouldn't have cooked it if he periodically checked and renewed the oil.[1]

TABLE 3.1   Construction Jargon Translated

Jargon	Translation
Specs	Specifications—descriptions of materials and workmanship required in a structure
Work the dog	Work the late shift
Ugly book	Electrician's Technical Handbook
Take-off	Laying out work from a blueprint
Take-out	In pipefitting, the measurement for allowance of a fitting

[1]Jo Sprague and Douglas Stuart, *The Speaker's Handbook,* 5th Ed. (Fort Worth, TX: Harcourt Brace, 2000), p. 216.

Isn't the following rewrite, phrased in common English, easier to follow?

Plain English Version

Let's look at how Jack could have benefited from a little preventive maintenance. He burned a lot more diesel fuel than he needed before he got around to adjusting the fuel injection system on his dump truck. A maintenance schedule would have pointed out any problems long before the engine started smoking. Same thing with the drive axle gears. They wouldn't have overheated and failed if Jack periodically checked and renewed the oil.[2]

Slang and Formal English

Formal English is the English that is considered widely acceptable for conversations between workers and managers, or between two companies. *Informal English,* in contrast, is usually marked by the presence of *slang,* a series of colorful words that are quite expressive but not considered appropriate for formal English. In addition, informal English makes use of contractions (*it's* for *it is*; *couldn't* for *could not; won't* for *will not,* and so on). In formal English, contractions are sparse or not used at all.

The best way to understand the differences between informal and formal English is by way of example.

Informal (with slang)	I was really *bummed out* when the foreman told me I had to put in overtime. That really *sucked.*
Formal	I was disappointed when the foreman told me I had to work overtime. It could not have come at a worse time.
Informal (with slang)	Jim didn't show up for work yesterday because he was *whacked out* on Nyquil.
Formal	Jim didn't show up for work yesterday because he took too much Nyquil, which affected him badly.
Informal (with slang)	*Say what, man?*
Formal	Excuse me, I couldn't hear you. Would you repeat that, please?

Slang and informal English make the language fun to speak and hear. In fact, the best conversationalists are usually the people who speak the most colorfully. Just keep in mind a few guidelines for using slang and formal English:

- *When speaking with clients, supervisors, or anyone outside the company, avoid slang and use formal English.* Formal English is particularly important when talking with people outside the company. Your speech reflects on the reputation of your company.

- *Be careful not to use slang that is racist, sexist, or prejudiced in any way.* Some slang is considered offensive, and shouldn't be used in business. For example, most women do not like to be called "chicks." Elderly people don't like to be called "old farts." African-Americans do not like to hear the phrase "to call a spade, a spade." When using slang, be aware of the possible negative associations and avoid using terms that give offense.

- *In your quest for formal English, don't overburden your speech.* When speaking formally, avoid using overly long words, phrases, or sentences

---

[2]Ibid.

in an effort to appear formal. The best speech is simple and clear, and not burdened with excess verbiage. "Yo! Dudes! Slam on the hard hats!" is too informal, but "Ladies and gentlemen, you are hereby requested to don your protective headgear—to wit, your hard hats" is too far in the other direction. Simply saying "Please put on your hard hats" is both formal and effective.

Activity 3.2: Changing Slang to Formal English

Each of the following sentences makes use of some sort of slang or other element of informal English. Some sentences even include slang that is considered offensive. Rewrite each sentence in formal English.

1. My boss nearly had a cow when he found out that half the crew was illing with the flu.

   _____

   _____

2. Joe spent the night puking his brains out.

   _____

   _____

3. I was used to seeing mostly white dudes on construction sites. But lately there have been lots of babes, too.

   _____

   _____

4. I told the supplier there was no way in hell I was going to pay his jacked-up prices.

   _____

   _____

5. That old broad was really bent out of shape when her new roof blew off in the thunderstorm.

   _____

   _____

6. Matt and Casey spent Saturday night behaving like drunken Irishmen and going ape.

   _____

   _____

7. We had a job to do in the colored section of town. Lots of Hispanics live there, too.

   _____

   _____

8. I got the best price because I was the first person in line in the morning. One of my buds showed up late. I told him, "You snooze, you lose."

   _____

9. Even though the speed limit was 55, Janet was barreling down the highway like a bat out of hell.

_____

_____

10. People from the South like to mosey along, but Yankees are always in a rush.

_____

_____

3.3 PREPARING YOUR MESSAGE

Spoken communications fall into two categories: formal and informal. In the informal category are conversations with friends about the news, chats with co-workers about sports or other topics of interest, and discussions in which information is traded freely among all the people present. Informal conversations have only a few "rules":

- Listen before you speak.
- Do not interrupt others while they're speaking.
- Do not complete someone else's thoughts.
- Be respectful in your choice of words.
- Speak clearly.

When you participate in an informal conversation, you're not expected to present information in any specific or organized manner. Rather, you ask or answer questions as the discussion dictates, and you include humor as the mood strikes you.

However, there are times when you will participate in formal discussions. Perhaps the best known and most common formal discussion is the job interview.[3] At the job interview, you will be asked a series of questions. It will then be your turn to ask questions.

Once you get the job, you may find yourself calling meetings or engaging in formal discussions with contractors and subcontractors for bids. The key to an effective formal discussion is _preparation_. In friendly conversations, you just take it as it comes. But in a formal discussion, you need to have goals in mind and a message to present. In the job interview, for example, one of your goals will be to determine whether you want to work for the company or not.

What can you do to prepare for a formal discussion? The following suggestions can help.

CONSIDER AND DEFINE YOUR GOALS. What do you hope to get out of the discussion? What should be the outcome? Go into your conversation with a determination to make the most of it. Don't be too ambitious. Rather, set realistic goals that you can achieve.

THINK ABOUT YOUR AUDIENCE AND HOW IT WILL REACT. Before you speak, consider the effects that your words are likely to have, and tailor your message to the audience. For example, suppose you're a supervisor and you want to bring up employee lateness problems at a monthly meeting. Will the people who are always on time be offended? If so, might there be a better time or place to discuss the issue?

Another example: Suppose you wish to make a suggestion to the owner about a process improvement. What will be more persuasive to the owner—the

---

[3]We discuss how to ace a job interview in Appendix B, Section B.3.

fact that the improvement will save money, or the fact that the improvement is being used by other companies? Owners are responsive to the bottom line, so you may be more persuasive if you focus on money.

TIMING IS EVERYTHING.   Choose a time and place to speak when others will be best able to listen. Ask yourself: What other activities are on my listeners' minds? When will they be the least distracted? When will I have their undivided attention? Is this the best place to speak, or should we move to a place that is quieter or subject to fewer interruptions?

For example, suppose you need to give co-workers some detailed instructions. Would it be better to talk to them first thing in the morning or just before lunch? In the morning, everyone is likely to be fresh and focused. But just before lunch, people will be tired and anxious to eat. When they're tired, they're less likely to listen closely.

REMEMBER THAT SHORTER IS BETTER.   Because people are so busy, everyone likes a conversation that is short, sweet, and to the point. When planning, ask yourself: How can I make the biggest impression in the least amount of time? How much do I really need to say? Which details can be excluded?

CONDUCT RESEARCH TO SUPPORT YOUR MESSAGE.   If you're planning to make a request or a suggestion, use facts and examples to back up your claims. Demonstrating that you've done your homework makes a positive impression on your audience, which makes them more likely to see matters from your perspective.

CONSIDER THE BEST ORDER FOR YOUR MAIN POINTS.   Do you want to provide background information, then end with your request? Or do you want to state right at the beginning what you're looking to do? There is no single best way to order your points. Think about which order will be most likely to appeal to your audience.

DELIVER BAD NEWS TACTFULLY AND SENSITIVELY.   If the purpose of your discussion is to deliver bad news, think long and hard about how the listeners will feel. Never lie, but spare the feelings of your audience as much as possible. We discuss additional techniques for delivering bad news in Section 4.5. Once you've thought about and planned your spoken message, follow the advice presented in the next section (3.4) to deliver it crisply and clearly.

Activity 3.3: Preparing Your Message

Read the following scenario, then complete the grid that follows.

Your plumbing supply company is thinking about opening another store in a city about one hour from your current location in Columbia, South Carolina. As the director of personnel, you are interested in seeing if any of your current employees would be willing to work at the new office. You know that your current staff is excellent, and you think they could get the new store up and running very quickly and effectively. But the long drive is going to be a problem for many of them, especially those with children at home. Thus, to motivate employees to work in the new location, you are going to offer them additional vacation time, as well as a raise of $2 per hour.

You want to call a meeting to announce the opening of the new store and to outline the package the company is offering to people willing to work in the new location. At the meeting, you will provide information in writing. You'll also ask those who are interested to come to talk to you by the end of the month. Finally, you will make sure everyone knows that working in the new store is completely voluntary. No one will be required to relocate, and nobody's job is in jeopardy.

What is your goal for the meeting?	
How is your audience likely to react?	
When would be a good time to have the meeting?	
What will be your main points? In what order will you present them?	
What specific information will you provide to entice workers to sign on as staff members of the new store?	
How much time do you think you will need for this meeting?	

3.4 Speaking Clearly, Concisely, and Effectively

Whether you're speaking to a friend, a co-worker, or a seated audience, you can take several steps to deliver your message in the most effective manner possible.

CHOOSE YOUR WORDS CAREFULLY.   Make sure you're using the right words for your audience. Always avoid sexist, racist, and other offensive language.

ADJUST YOUR VOLUME.   Make sure that you are speaking loud enough for everyone in your audience to hear. Similarly, be sure that you're not speaking *too* loud. You don't want to come across as overbearing.

WATCH YOUR PACE.   Customize your speaking pace to the individual situation. When chatting lightly or telling amusing stories, it's fine to speak somewhat rapidly. But, when conveying important information, it's better to use short sentences or long pauses when going over the most important points. Slow down when giving numbers, and repeat them if necessary.

ENUNCIATE.   People will understand you much better if you enunciate your words carefully. Don't chew gum or tobacco while speaking. Doing so interferes with your ability to pronounce words accurately.

In addition, watch for words that are often mispronounced. Some common mispronunciations appear in Table 3.2.

VARY YOUR TONE.   A person who speaks at the same level all the time (called a *monotone*) quickly puts his listeners to sleep. The most effective speakers vary their tone and pitch to keep the audience on its toes.

AVOID PHYSICAL DISTRACTERS.   When you speak, you want your audience to listen. However, your audience can be distracted by things like your clothing and jewelry. Whenever possible, avoid distracting your audience with physical

TABLE 3.2 Commonly Mispronounced Words

Word	Proper Pronunciation	Improper Pronunciation
across	a cross	a crost
ask	ask	ax
comparable	*com* per a bull	com *pair* a bull
drowned	drown'd	drown ded
escape	es cape	ex cape
et cetera (etc.)	et cet era	ex cet era
get	get	git
government	govern ment	gover ment
just	just	jist
library	library	lie berry
mischievous	miss che vus	miss chee vee us
nuclear	nuke lee ur	noo cyou lur
strict	strict	strick

items like hairstyles and garments. (We discuss some other barriers to communication in Section 3.7.) Also avoid distracting mannerisms, such as running your hand through your hair frequently or cracking your knuckles.

AVOID VOCAL DISTRACTERS.   Certain verbal tics or habits can prevent you from delivering your message effectively. For example, audiences lose their train of thought when a speaker uses phrases like "well," "um," "er," or "you know" too often. Try to keep your speech streamlined and free of distracters.

TRY TO ENGAGE THE AUDIENCE'S INTEREST.   Some topics are inherently more interesting than others. Effective speakers try particularly hard to make boring material interesting. You can do this by telling stories, making appropriate and tasteful jokes, and even admitting openly how dull the topic is. An audience always appreciates honesty!

You can also keep your audience's interest by walking around as you speak, mingling with the crowd. Walking around makes you seem like a "regular person," as opposed to one who is speaking from a distance.

MAINTAIN EYE CONTACT.   Look at your audience as you speak to them. It's important to establish one-on-one contact between speaker and listener.

PROJECT A POSITIVE ATTITUDE.   An audience is much more receptive to speakers who convey an upbeat and positive outlook. Of course, there are times when a more somber tone is required—as when presenting bad news. But, for the most part, speak in a way that draws your listeners to you, rather than pushes them away.

BE CONCISE.   Don't take more of your listeners' time than absolutely necessary. Make your point, summarize, and be done!

USE EXAMPLES AND NONVERBAL SIGNIFIERS.   When giving instructions or information, begin with a quick overview. Then give directions in the order they should be followed. Use hand gestures, or (better yet) demonstrate the procedure. Emphasize the most important steps. Repeat or reword any directions that are especially complicated. Use facial expressions to support your words, and vary those expressions as appropriate. Don't be stone-faced!

EXPLAIN THE BACKGROUND AND BENEFITS. If you're asking for help or looking for a solution, explain the background of the problem you're facing. Your listeners are more likely to help if you explain the situation in detail. If you're asking for a favor, explain the benefits others will receive from helping you.

GIVE YOUR LISTENERS TIME TO ASK QUESTIONS. At various points in your conversation or presentation (not just at the end), ask the listeners if they understood you. Encourage them to ask questions or offer suggestions. By asking for suggestions, you create a two-way dialogue and an atmosphere of respect. Also encourage your listeners to take notes. If questions come up, answer them clearly and patiently. Question-and-answer sessions can be an extremely effective method of building a relationship between the speaker and the audience.

LEAVE NO DOUBT ABOUT YOUR MEANING. Speaking well means getting your point across forcefully and directly. Spoken communication is useless if the listener comes away not knowing what is expected of him or her. So, make sure you spell out *exactly* what you mean and what your expectations are. In one-on-one situations, it can also be helpful to ask your listener to repeat what you said to ensure that she heard you correctly.

Activity 3.4: Speaking Clearly

Using the tips provided in this section, recite the follow sentences out loud. Keep in mind that the entire class should be able to hear you, so speak at the appropriate volume.

1. My Social Security number is 969-55-1449.

2. The mischievous child almost drowned when trying to get across the river.

3. Nuclear physicists are experimenting with methods to harness nuclear power in a safe, effective, and inexpensive way.

4. She sells sea shells by the sea shore.

5. Rubber baby buggy bumpers.

6. The librarian narrowly escaped an accident when the scaffolding collapsed around her.

7. I'm not sure how to do this. I should ask several people's opinions.

8. Some say the government is comparable to a backhoe: slow, loud, and inefficient.

9. My supervisor requires strict adherence to safety regulations.

10. I want to get an Internet hookup in my apartment. It will be useful for finding information, ordering books, etc.

Activity 3.5: Choosing Words Carefully

In each of the following sentences, choose the word or phrase that best completes the sentence. Choose words that are not likely to give offense.

1. Jesse Jackson is a major spokesperson for the (negro, black, African-American) community.

2. My boss (works us very hard, is a real slave driver).

3. Three (women, ladies, broads) work as file clerks in our home office.

4. We don't have enough (manpower, workers) to finish this job on time.

5. The homeowner asked us to use (cheap, inexpensive) paint in the basement.

6. I went to visit my grandfather at the (old folks', senior citizens') home.

7. John is an extremely (nit-picky, fastidious, anal-retentive) carpenter.

8. Many (Asian-Americans, Orientals) live in the San Francisco area.

9. Mary's father is an African-American, while her mother is white. For this reason, Mary is (biracial, a mulatto).

10. The owner of my company is extremely (profit-oriented, cheap, tight-fisted).

Activity 3.6: Avoiding Distracters While Speaking

The following is a list of behaviors that speakers sometimes engage in. Check those behaviors that tend to distract audience members, thereby decreasing their attentiveness and comprehension. (In other words, check the behaviors that should be avoided while speaking.)

- ☐ Asking questions
- ☐ Moving around the room
- ☐ Running your hand through your hair
- ☐ Summarizing key points at the end of the discussion
- ☐ Speaking very softly
- ☐ Wearing bracelets that make jingle/jangle sounds
- ☐ Using hand gestures to emphasize key points
- ☐ Telling tasteful jokes
- ☐ Speaking in the same tone throughout the discussion
- ☐ Using nonwords like "um" or "uh" to pace the discussion
- ☐ Providing background information
- ☐ Chewing tobacco or gum while speaking
- ☐ Ending with a question-and-answer period
- ☐ Speaking at great length
- ☐ Making eye contact
- ☐ Projecting a positive, supportive attitude
- ☐ Cracking your knuckles
- ☐ Wearing a holographic tie that shines light directly into your listeners' faces

3.5 Fact versus Opinion

When speaking (and when writing), it's important that your audience understand the difference between the facts you're presenting and your personal opinions. A *fact* is a statement that can be proven true or false. In contrast, an *opinion* cannot be proven true or false. It is based on someone's personal point of view or interpretation of facts. Different people can have different opinions about the same fact.

For example, it is a *fact* that the death penalty is in effect in several states. However, some people hold the *opinion* that the death penalty is cruel and inhumane, and should be illegal. Others hold the *opinion* that the death penalty is the best way to punish criminals and prevent crime.

As the speaker, it's your job to clearly indicate the presence of facts or opinions so that no misunderstandings take place. Your audience needs to know when you're presenting information that has strong basis in fact, and when you're making recommendations (giving your opinions) based on those facts.

It's quite easy to signal the presence of facts and opinions by using specific phrases or "verbal markers." To indicate a *fact*, you can begin by saying:

- "Research shows that . . ."
- "It has long been accepted that . . ."
- "It is not disputed that . . ."
- "There is no question that . . ."
- "A general consensus exists that . . ."
- "Everyone agrees that . . ."
- "A rule of our industry states that . . ."
- "Government regulations require that . . ."

To indicate an opinion or recommendation, you can begin by saying:

- "I think that . . ."
- "It is my opinion that . . ."
- "I would recommend that . . ."
- "There are different schools of thought. My belief is that . . ."
- "I suggest that we do the following . . ."
- "Based on my experience, my strong feeling is that . . ."
- "Some may disagree, but my sense is that . . ."

Of course, feel free to mix and match these phrases as they suit your purpose in speaking. Ultimately, your goal is to have your audience share your point of view. The more facts, evidence, and support you provide for your opinions, the more likely you are to convince your audience. Clearly signaling the presence of an opinion shows your audience members that you respect their intelligence, and that you're not trying to "put one over" on them.

Activity 3.7: Distinguishing Fact from Opinion

Reading the following passage, which repeats the words your boss said at a recent meeting, then answer the questions that follow. Be careful; some of the questions are tricky!

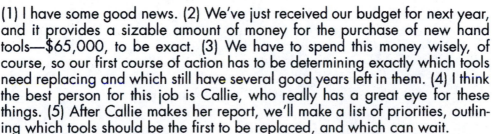

(1) I have some good news. (2) We've just received our budget for next year, and it provides a sizable amount of money for the purchase of new hand tools—$65,000, to be exact. (3) We have to spend this money wisely, of course, so our first course of action has to be determining exactly which tools need replacing and which still have several good years left in them. (4) I think the best person for this job is Callie, who really has a great eye for these things. (5) After Callie makes her report, we'll make a list of priorities, outlining which tools should be the first to be replaced, and which can wait.

(6) Our next step will be determining the prices of the tools we need. (7) Our research has shown that, of the three major brands, Acme Tools are the most expensive, while Rutgers Tools are the least expensive. (8) However, I am going to recommend that we spend the extra money on Acme Tools. (9) I've always found them to be durable and reliable. (10) I don't think anyone makes a more reliable tool. (11) I checked about ten Web sites for recommendations, and eight out of those Web sites recommend Acme Tools above all others. (12) Two recommend Rutgers Tools.

1. Is Sentence (1) a fact or an opinion? _____

2. Is Sentence (2) a fact or an opinion? _____

3. Is Sentence (4) a fact or an opinion? _____ Which word or words in that sentence give you the clue? _____

4. Is Sentence (7) a fact or an opinion? _____ Which word or words in that sentence give you the clue? _____

5. Is Sentence (10) a fact or an opinion? _____ Which word or words in that sentence give you the clue? _____

6. Is Sentence (11) a fact or an opinion? _____

7. Is Sentence (12) a fact or an opinion? _____

8. Suppose you are the person to whom this passage has been spoken. Do you think the person speaking has presented his case fairly? Would you agree with his conclusion? Explain your answer._____

_____

_____

3.6 PERSONALITY FACTORS AND GROUP DYNAMICS

Throughout this module, we've emphasized the importance of audience awareness, of taking account of the whole atmosphere surrounding spoken communications. An important factor that we haven't yet discussed is the role of individual personalities and how these can affect spoken communications.

In a sense, the speaker must be as much of a psychologist as any trained therapist. To prevent your message from being misunderstood or resented, you may need to take into account personality factors. What makes this tricky is the fact that people are so different from one another. For example, one foreman may prefer to be called "Mr. Smith" rather than "Fred," while another insists that you call him "Mike" instead of "Mr. Stiles." Sometimes these personality factors are easily detected. Other times, you need to spend time around someone before you can have a true sense of his needs, weaknesses, and soft spots.

Realistically, it may not be possible to get to know everyone on the job personally. But there are steps that you can take to ensure that your spoken communications remain respectful of almost all personality types.

- *When you're younger, show respect for older, more experienced employees.* If you're the "new kid" on a job and you have to talk to experienced people, it's best to demonstrate a high level of respect for their experience. This usually means being serious and not joking around much. You may be able to joke more with people your own age, and with more experienced people after you've earned their respect.

- *Pay attention to your audience's reactions.* Selected members of your audience may indicate to you that you've misspoken. Verbally, they might heckle you. Nonverbally, they might roll their eyes, get up and walk away, or sit with their arms folded over their chest. If you think you've misspoken, try to clear the air as quickly as possible. Depending on the sensitivity of the issue, you can either address the group directly or talk with the offended individual privately, later on.

- *Be aware of group dynamics.* When speaking to a group of people, remember to speak to everyone in the group. Avoid one-on-one conversations in a group, because these conversations tend to make other people feel excluded. If necessary, group people according to their experience levels and address each group separately.

Activity 3.8: Understanding Group Dynamics

Read the mini-case, then answer the questions that follow.

▪ *Mini-Case: The New Team*

You've been assigned to work on a six-person team. The team is composed of the following people:

- **Jim Mason,** team leader. He has worked for the company for ten years and is widely respected. However, he is not known for being very friendly, and he prefers newer people on the job to listen more than they speak.

- **Karen Aldridge.** She has just joined the company, but she and Jim have been friends for a long time. They grew up together and are the same age. Jim recommended that the company hire Karen because he respects her abilities greatly and thinks she is a very hard worker. Karen is an extremely friendly person who enjoys chatting. She is also known for keeping up with the latest changes and trends in construction technology.

- **Mike Morgan.** He is an apprentice who has just been assigned to the team. He is enthusiastic, but has very little experience or technical knowledge. He tends to ask a lot of questions. Mike calls the team leader "Mr. Mason."

- **Rich Benton.** He has been with the company for nearly 20 years, and he is starting to slow down. He can't do the heavy work like he used to. He is a good worker, but he is old-fashioned, and he isn't very open minded to new ways of doing things. He thinks construction is a "man's business" and doesn't like having to work with Karen Aldridge. However, he is a friend of your father, and he has told you to feel free to ask him for advice.

- **Zach Sullivan.** He has been with the company for six months, and has worked for Jim Mason before. While the two men are not friends, they seem to share a good working relationship, and Jim trusts Zach to get the job done. Zach's one quirk is that he gets impatient very easily. For this reason, he prefers to work with experienced people.

- **You.** You are a brand-new apprentice. You are excited to work with this team, because you have heard great things about Jim, Karen, and Zach. Plus, you have known Rich a long time, so you already have a friend on the team. You know that you're talented at what you do, but you also realize that you have a lot to learn.

1. It's your first day on the job, and you need to ask Jim Mason an important question. Should you call him "Jim" or "Mr. Mason"? Why?

   _____

   _____

2. Suppose you have a question about a very simple technique that is used widely on this particular job. To whom would you address your question? Why?

   _____

   _____

3. Now suppose you have a technical question that is very complex. It requires a knowledge of modern techniques and recent advances in construction technology. To whom would you address this question? Why?

4. Jim Mason has some important information to convey. Rather than talking to everyone on his team at once, he has decided to hold two separate meetings with two groups of people from the team. Suppose you are Jim. Which team members would you include in the first group? The second group? Why?

5. Of the people on this team, with whom do you think you would develop the most friendly relationship? With whom would you probably maintain more of a business-oriented, professional relationship? Explain your answers.

3.7 BARRIERS TO EFFECTIVE COMMUNICATION

The same factors that can prevent you from listening carefully can also stand in the way of clear, effective speaking.

Language Barriers and Accents

If English is not your first language, you may have difficulty pronouncing certain English words. Or, if the English word is particularly specialized, it may not have a corresponding word in your native language. Similarly, if you have a regional accent, members of your audience may not always be able to follow you. For example, people from the South and from New England sometimes speak quite differently than Midwesterners and New Yorkers.

It's understandable if you feel sensitive about your language barrier or accent, and it may be tempting to simply brush it under the table. But this is the easy way out. Your speech can be effective only when your audience understands you.

So, be upfront and honest with yourself and with your audience. Admit to yourself that it might be difficult to understand you. To your audience, you might say, "I know I speak with a Spanish accent. I will try to pronounce every word correctly, but I may make a few mistakes. Please stop me if you can't understand me. My feelings will not be hurt." By working harder to make your speech understandable by all, you will become a more effective speaker.

Also, if you are not a native speaker of English, you can follow these two simple tips to make your spoken English more understandable:

1. Prolong your vowel sounds. Unlike many other languages, spoken American English carries more meaning in vowels (a, e, i, o, u) than in consonants. It may sounds odd to you, but make each vowel last a long time. "Maaaake eeeeeeach voooooweeeel laaaaaaaast aaa looooooong tiiiiime."

2. Try to blend the end of one word into the beginning of the next word, for this is the natural rhythm of spoken English. In contrast, languages like Spanish pronounce each word distinctly. When English words are pronounced very distinctly in sentences, the sentences sound choppy and highly accented.

Levels of Expertisex

Understanding the various levels of expertise in your audience is a critical part of audience awareness. Are the people you're speaking to experts in their field? Are they novices? Is there a mixture of people, some with high levels of expertise, some with no knowledge base whatsoever?

As you speak, be sure to watch your audience for nonverbal signs that signal their comprehension level. If they're nodding their heads up and down, that's a good sign that they are following you. If their eyes are narrowed and they look confused, they probably *are* confused.

If your audience is less informed than you expected, take the following steps:

- Stop and ask, "Is everyone following me? Any questions? Am I going too fast?"
- To get the audience up to speed, use more examples and provide more background information.
- Use fewer technical terms, if you can do so without changing the important parts of your message.

If your audience is more informed or prepared than you expected, you can:

- Talk less about the basics and more about advanced topics.
- Cut your talk short and open up the discussion so that it becomes a brainstorming session or a question-and-answer session.

Race, Gender, and Cultural Factors

An important tenet of effective communication is *inclusiveness*. The principle of inclusiveness means that good speakers always try to involve every member of the audience. That is, they try to be aware of their audience's background, and they choose their words so that nobody feels excluded or offended. To be inclusive, speakers must be aware of the racial, ethnic, gender, and cultural makeup of their audience.

RACE AND ETHNICITY. In 21st-century America, racial and ethnic diversity is common in just about all jobs. On a construction site, you will often be working with Latinos, African-Americans, and Asian-Americans, as well as people of European descent. Let respect be your watchword. Don't say anything that belittles a race or ethnic group. Rather, focus on the common ground that we all share as Americans.

Also, don't call attention to the presence of various ethnic or minority groups in a particular room or setting. It may seem friendly to say, "I'm happy to see all my Latino colleagues here today," but a statement like this would set Latinos apart from the rest of the audience, making them feel as if they're not as much a part of the team as their Anglo co-workers.

GENDER. While construction jobs are still filled mostly by men, more and more women are working in all areas of construction. Always be respectful of your female co-workers. As with members of different racial and ethnic groups, don't call attention to the fact that women are present. In other words, don't say, "I see that we have the lovely ladies from carpentry with us today. . . ."

Much research has focused on the different communication styles of men versus women. In general, men tend to be more direct in their speech, and they favor an emphasis on problem solving. In contrast, women tend to speak less directly, and they see conversation as an opportunity for building relationships. Keep these differences in mind, and adjust your speaking style (if necessary) when talking with members of the opposite sex.

CULTURAL FACTORS.   It is impossible to know the cultural characteristics of every culture on the earth. But, with experience, you will come to learn certain cultural traits that will influence you when you speak. For example, people from Asian cultures are often unwilling to share details of their personal lives in a group setting. So, if you were to ask a Korean co-worker to tell you about his family in the middle of a meeting, he might very well feel embarrassed or awkward. Your best bet, when working, is to keep the conversation focused on the job and job-related issues. If you do so, you are unlikely to say the wrong thing.

Undesirable Speaking Styles

Speaking well is a skill that takes time to learn. But, because we have all been speaking since we were young children, we may not take the time to stop and examine our own speaking styles to see how effective they are. How can we improve? What can we do better?

The best way to improve your effectiveness as a speaker is to ask people you know and trust for their opinions. Do you do anything that interferes with your message? Do you have any habits that would be annoying to your listeners? For example, do you tap a pencil while you talk, or do you say "um" or "you know" a lot?

Here is a list of some undesirable speaking styles:

- Excessive negativity—Are you too much of an pessimist or "downer"?
- Excessive positivity–Are you too upbeat, so much so that you seem like a dreamer?
- Monotony—Does your voice remain at one pitch no matter what you say?
- Egotism—Are you too focused on yourself? Do you keep saying "Me, me, me"?
- Detours—Do you jump from topic to topic before you can finish a complete thought?
- Complaints—Do you complain or whine too much?
- Excess verbiage—Do you use many more words than necessary to get your point across?
- Interruptions—Do you cut people off or interrupt them while they're speaking?
- Inappropriate words—Do you use profanity or other offensive language?

Do any of these traits apply to your style of speaking? If so, think of ways to eliminate them. Ask a friend or co-worker to tell you when you're exhibiting these negative behaviors so that you can correct them.

REMEMBER: If your audience is annoyed or distracted, it will not be fully listening to you.

Activity 3.9: Examining Differences in Speaking Styles Between Men and Women

As noted in this section, research has shown that men and women tend to communicate quite differently. Because women and men are working together more often in construction jobs, it pays to be aware of these differences.

The following table lists some of the differences in communication styles between men and women.[4] For each style, mark "M" if you think this style is more typical of men, "W" if you think it is more typical of women. (Answers appear below.) In the third column, offer some tips for how the opposite sex can better work with each communication style. The first entry has been completed as an example.

M or W?	Communication Style	Tips for the Opposite Sex
M	1. These people communicate mostly for information. They're not usually into talking about their feelings or their emotional needs.	Women should not take it personally if men don't want to discuss their feelings, or if men want to discuss only "business" on the job site.
	2. These people often like to base their relationships on the sharing of their personal experiences and feelings.	
	3. These people like to talk quite a bit—for them, it's the "glue" that holds relationships together.	
	4. These people tend to base their friendships and relationships around activities, such as going places together or playing sports.	
	5. These people are more often "loners," and have fewer close friendships.	
	6. These people prefer to avoid confrontation. They would rather build consensus or give in, rather than fight or argue.	
	7. These people can be very aggressive and often enjoy confrontation or competition. They can even become friendly with the people they feel most competitive with.	
	8. These people tend to make more direct eye contact, and to sit closer to other people.	
	9. When these people talk about a problem they're having, they are more interested in having somebody listen to their problems, as opposed to offering solutions to those problems.	
	10. When these people talk about problems, their main goal is to find a solution to the problem. They're not really looking for emotional or moral support.	

ANSWERS: 1(M); 2(W); 3(W); 4(M); 5(M); 6(W); 7(M); 8(W); 9(W); 10(M).

(continued)

---

[4]Based on the work of Deborah Tannen. For more information, read her books *You Just Don't Understand* (New York: Ballantine, 1990) and *Talking from 9 to 5* (New York: Morrow, 1994).

Activity 3.10: Self-Assessment: Do You Speak Effectively?

The following is a list of behaviors or habits that interfere with clear speaking. Check each box that applies to you, then make an action plan for improvement. As with all self-assessments, honesty is essential.

POOR SPEAKING HABITS

- ☐ I am a downer—I always talk about the negative side of things
- ☐ I talk too much and don't let others get a word in edgewise
- ☐ I speak too softly; people are always asking me to repeat what I said
- ☐ I am so upbeat that others find me annoying
- ☐ I tend to get sidetracked when I speak, and I lose my train of thought
- ☐ I complain a lot when I'm talking to other people
- ☐ I focus a lot on myself—I'm constantly saying "I, I, I" or "me, me, me"
- ☐ I use the same steady tone whenever I'm speaking
- ☐ I chew gum or tobacco, which makes me garble my words
- ☐ I don't pay attention to how the people around me are reacting when I talk
- ☐ I talk a lot—once I get started, I keep going
- ☐ I don't make eye contact with others when I'm speaking to them
- ☐ I make intense eye contact with others while I'm speaking, and never look away
- ☐ I interrupt others when they are talking
- ☐ I finish other people's thoughts or sentences for them
- ☐ I speak slowly or hesitatingly
- ☐ I say "um," "like," "uh," or "you know" a lot
- ☐ I have nervous habits like biting my fingernails while I talk
- ☐ I mumble or cover my mouth when I talk
- ☐ I can't sit still; I have to be moving around when I talk
- ☐ Other: _____
- ☐ Other: _____
- ☐ Other: _____

ACTION PLAN FOR IMPROVEMENT:

Problem: _____

Solution: _____

_____

_____

Problem: _____

Solution: _____

_____

_____

Problem: _____

Solution: _____

_____

_____

Problem: _____

Solution: _____

_____

_____

3.8 COMMUNICATING ETHICALLY

Throughout this module, we've assumed that spoken communication takes place for shared good. We've assumed that the exchange of information and ideas is the primary reason for spoken communication. To that end, we have focused on ways to speak clearly and dynamically so that all parties are actively involved in two-way communication.

However, there are cases where spoken communication is meant to deceive, mislead, or spread negative information. All of these results turn the positive aspects of communication on their head. Because communication can be used negatively as well as positively, we close this module with a few words on rumors, gossip, and lies.

3.8.1 Rumors and Gossip

Rumors are bits of unverified information. For example, you may hear a rumor that your company is going out of business, or a rumor that a co-worker has a drinking problem. Rumors are usually spread in the form of *gossip,* informal and casual conversations in which two people talk about a third person.

Gossip is a universal part of life. It would be unrealistic to suggest that it be eliminated completely. However, you should try to gossip about the personal lives of co-workers as little as possible. It is particularly unethical to gossip when you:

- Repeat information that has been entrusted to you as a secret.
- Repeat information or rumors that violate another person's right to privacy, especially with regard to personal matters.
- Repeat rumors that you know to be untrue.

Throughout this module we've emphasized the need for *respect* as an underlying principle of effective communication. Spreading rumors and gossip usually displays a lack of respect. Before you engage in gossip about Person X, ask yourself, "How would X feel if she knew I was saying this about her?" If X would feel upset or hurt, that's good enough reason not to gossip about her.

3.8.2 Lies

A *lie* is a deliberate attempt to provide incorrect or misleading information. When information is purposely withheld, this withholding may be considered a "lie by omission." Even though no untruth has been spoken, a lie has been committed because the underlying purpose is to mislead.

Lies vary in degree from harmless, "little white lies" (for example, "I love your new haircut" or "Of course you don't look like you've put on weight") to lies that are very serious indeed. Most people agree that to save a person's feelings, a little white lie is acceptable. But, in general, and as the old saying goes, "Honesty is the best policy."

A few things to keep in mind about the truth and lies:

- *Getting caught in a lie will forever jeopardize your credibility.* Once you've been caught in a lie, people are likely never to trust you again.
- *Taking responsibility is preferable to lying.* If you lie to cover up something you've done wrong, expect to be found out eventually. It's much better to take responsibility for your actions, and your mistakes, right from the beginning.
- *Lying to your boss can result in immediate dismissal.* Many companies have a zero-tolerance policy for lying.

Activity 3.11: Identifying Gossip and Lies

Do you know gossip when you hear it? Read each statement below. Next to it, indicate whether information is being communicated ethically (E), whether gossip is involved (G), or whether a lie is being told (L).

_____ 1. I just got the news—Bill and Patti had a baby girl! Eight pounds, five ounces. Her name is Maria.

_____ 2. Did you hear? Frank saw Jill and Walt having a huge fight in the middle of the park on Saturday.

_____ 3. Sally asked me not to tell anyone, but get this: She is thinking of moving to Texas!

_____ 4. The boss told me that we're due for an OSHA inspection on Monday, so we need to spend the next few days making sure everything is up to code.

_____ 5. Miami Contractor's Supply is going out of business because the IRS is closing them down for tax evasion. Now we have to find another supplier that will give us good prices.

_____ 6. I told my boss I was home sick, but I was actually at the Yankee game.

_____ 7. I know a nurse who works for Dr. Reynolds, and she told me that Barbara is having really serious kidney problems. I don't think Barbara wants anyone to know, though.

_____ 8. Bill and Hank are out sick today, so we need a couple of volunteers for overtime.

_____ 9. I took home a few boxes of nails, but didn't say so when the boss asked where the nails had gone. I figured what he doesn't know won't hurt him.

_____ 10. I overheard Andy tell his brother that he is thinking of leaving his wife!

Speaking Skills II
Advanced Topics

66 I am convinced that the ability to speak clearly and comfortably in front of a group of people is critical for supervisors and managers in the construction industry. More and more, our field supervisors are expected to present information to owners, lead project meetings, and conduct training sessions. 99

—David Muehlbauer, Director of Training,
The Sundt Companies, Inc., Phoenix, AZ

Module 3 introduced the basics of effective spoken communication. We focused on understanding the audience, speaking clearly, and communicating ethically. In this module, we discuss advanced topics in speaking. We begin with some suggestions on making effective presentations, then move on to discussions of meeting etiquette, sensitivity in speaking, and conflict management.

4.1 MAKING PRESENTATIONS (PUBLIC SPEAKING)

At various times in your construction career, you may be asked to give a formal presentation to a group of people. Perhaps, as a foreman, you'll need to brief the owner on the progress made to date. Or, as the representative of a large contracting firm, you may need to present your estimates on a project to a group of decision makers.

Such occasions call for preparation. While all the suggestions for effective speaking, as outlined in Module 3, hold true in a formal presentation, there are several additional points to keep in mind.

REMAIN CALM. PRACTICE BEFOREHAND.   A certain amount of nervousness is expected in public speaking situations. You can make sure you deliver the best presentation possible by practicing beforehand. Try to remain calm at all times. Take a deep breath to calm yourself down, if necessary.

DRESS APPROPRIATELY WHEN DELIVERING YOUR SPEECH.   During a formal speech, the audience expects the speaker to be dressed well. Being dressed neatly lends much credibility to your presentation. Often, presentations are made to people higher up in the company or to parties outside the company. Consider on the presentation as your chance to impress, and begin with your attire.

SPEAK, DON'T READ.   It may be tempting to write out your entire presentation, and then go in front of your audience and simply read it from index cards. While this method may help you deliver all the right information, audiences are bored to tears by speakers who read their presentations. Practice talking *to* the audience instead of *at* them. Make eye contact with your listeners. Imagine yourself as having a conversation with a room full of friendly people, all of whom like you. This will put you at ease and make your speech sound more friendly and interesting.

MAKE SURE EVERYONE CAN HEAR YOU.   A presentation usually requires you to speak louder than you normally do. Speak from the stomach rather than the throat. This will help your voice carry better.

WHEN POSSIBLE, USE VISUAL AIDS.   Visual aids can help your audience understand key points, so plan to include summary charts or visual highlights—such as diagrams, tables, or maps—whenever you can. Copy the visuals and distribute them to the audience. If you'll be projecting the visuals onto a screen, be sure that they are readable from a distance. (In other words, don't jam-pack too much onto one slide. Keep the words large and easy to read.)

Some easy-to-use computer software programs make creating visual aids a snap. For example, Microsoft's PowerPoint program allows you to create electronic "transparencies" that can be projected onto a screen.

Note that not all visual aids need to be presented on paper. For example, if you're a sales representative for a tool manufacturer, you'll certainly want to bring samples of the tools for everyone in the audience to touch and feel. If you're demonstrating a technique, you'll want to bring all the materials and supplies you need to get the job done effectively.

> **TIP:** When creating visuals, have each visual represent one main idea only. Cramming too much information onto one slide or one chart defeats the purpose of visual aids, which is to clarify and simplify.

CLOSE ON A HIGH NOTE.   Make the end of your presentation something to remember. Tell a story, make a strong recommendation, summarize the data—anything that will keep your audience involved.

And, as always, keep your speech tight and focused. Try not to digress. Say what you need to say, answer any questions that come up, thank the audience, and then sit down!

Activity 4.1: Making a Presentation

Make a five-minute presentation to your instructor and classmates on the topic of your choice. Pretend this is "the real thing," so be sure to dress appropriately and speak at the proper volume so that everyone can hear you. If at all possible, use visual aids to help make your points.

If you can't think of a topic to speak on, ask yourself, "What is something I do well?" and speak on that subject. Choose a topic that will be interesting to your audience. Here are some suggested topics of general interest:

- Getting your finances in order/getting out of debt
- The car of the future
- Using the Internet to get good deals, great information, or free products
- Organizing your time so that you can get everything done
- Inexpensive ways to have fun in your city, town, or neighborhood
- Interesting historical facts about a particular sports figure or sports team
- A brief history of your city or town

4.2 LEADING MEETINGS

In Section 2.5.2, we examined some ways to listen closely while attending a meeting. Here we look at the other side of the coin: How can you *lead* a meeting successfully when you are in charge?

You can take several steps to ensure that any meeting you call will be effective.

BEFORE YOU BEGIN: IS A MEETING REALLY NECESSARY?   Don't call meetings unless they truly are necessary. Would a phone call, an e-mail, or a one-on-one discussion serve your purpose just as well? If so, these are all preferred options. Meetings should be called only when the immediate input and feedback of a group of experts is required.

Step 1: Plan your agenda. The *agenda* spells out which topics will be discussed, as well as the amount of time to be devoted to each topic. Keep your agenda focused. Don't try to cover too many bases in one meeting. The best meetings last no longer than one hour. Longer meetings should include planned break times.

Step 2: Invite the necessary participants. It's tempting to invite just about everybody to a meeting. There are problems with doing so, however. First, too many participants can turn a meeting into a free-for-all. Second, the people who are sitting in a meeting are *not* out doing their jobs! All meetings take time away from other activities, so be sure to invite only those people who are absolutely necessary.

Figure 4.1 reproduces a meeting planning form. You can use this form to estimate the cost of any meeting, to determine the necessary participants and materials, and to plan your agenda.

Date Scheduled _____ Time _____

Title _____
Purpose _____
Results Desired _____
Location _____

SCHEDULED			ACTUAL			MEETING COST		
Start	Stop	Total Hours	Start	Stop	Total Hours			

Persons Attending	✔	Value Per Hour	Total
1			
2			
3			
4			
5			
6			
7			
8			
9			
10			

Items To Be Discussed	(Sequence) →	✔
1		
2		
3		
4		
5		
6		
7		
8		
9		
10		

Materials Needed (Number Each Item)	Person Responsible
1	

Figure 4.1:   Meeting Planning Form

Source: Jack Smith, "The Nuts and Bolts of Effective Meetings" (Overland Park, KS: Encompass Electrical Technologies), p. 11.

TABLE 4.1   Meeting Management Techniques

Problem	Solution
More than one person is speaking.	"Excuse me, but we really should listen to one person at a time."
The discussion strays from the topic.	"I believe we have strayed from our agenda. We really should be discussing. . . ."
The group has divided into two or more factions on an issue.	"Maybe we should turn to something else today and each of us think about. . . ."
The discussion on an issue seems to have run its course.	"Have we finished on this? Should we go on to the next item on our agenda?"
A few meeting participants do most of the talking.	"Are we listening to everyone's point of view?"
There seems to be confusion.	"Why don't we write these ideas on a flip chart so that everyone can follow?"
The meeting is running behind schedule.	"We're running low on time for this subject. Should we discuss it five more minutes, and then move on?"

Source: Adapted from Jack Smith, "The Nuts and Bolts of Effective Meetings" (Overland Park, KS: Encompass Electrical Technologies), p. 9.

Step 3: Manage the meeting. The meeting leader is in charge of ensuring that the agenda is followed. Because people in meetings can be very chatty or digressive, the leader may need to interrupt or cut off speakers in the interest of keeping to the agenda.

Generally, interrupting others is considered rude. However, meeting participants expect the leader to keep the conversation focused, so it isn't considered inappropriate for the leader to interrupt. Still, the leader should be as polite and respectful as possible without being dictatorial.

Table 4.1 summarizes some respectful ways of interrupting others and other techniques to keep the meeting moving.

Step 4: Summarize and follow up. The meeting leader's final task is to summarize, as much as possible, what went on in the meeting. He or she should also thank the participants and make a follow-up plan for implementing the suggestions or decisions that resulted from the meeting. Figure 4.2 on page 76 reproduces a simple form that can be used to plan follow-up activities.

> **REMEMBER:** Follow-up is very important. Participants feel frustrated when they don't see meeting results being implemented.

Activity 4.2: Planning Meetings

The most important step in planning a meeting is determining whether or not a meeting should be called in the first place.

Four scenarios follow. For each, determine whether a meeting of at least three people is needed or whether some other form of communication would be more effective, less expensive, or less time consuming.

Scenario #1

The company, Vander Hoven Contracting, has long worked exclusively on residential building and renovation projects. The company's owners have now

Follow-Up Action Plan

	Who?	Is Going To Do What?	By When?	Completed
1.	_____	_____	_____	_____
2.	_____	_____	_____	_____
3.	_____	_____	_____	_____
4.	_____	_____	_____	_____
5.	_____	_____	_____	_____
6.	_____	_____	_____	_____
7.	_____	_____	_____	_____
8.	_____	_____	_____	_____
9.	_____	_____	_____	_____
10.	_____	_____	_____	_____
11.	_____	_____	_____	_____
12.	_____	_____	_____	_____

Figure 4.2: Follow-Up Action Plan

Source: Jack Smith, "The Nuts and Bolts of Effective Meetings" (Overland Park, KS: Encompass Electrical Technologies), p. 12.

decided to move into commercial work, which will require many employees to receive additional training in their specialties. In addition, Vander Hoven Contracting will need to hire about 15 additional people. Vander Hoven's owners, Hans and Fritz, are excited about all the additional business they expect to receive, and they know the employees will be happy to hear about the advancement opportunities that this change will bring. Hans and Fritz Vander Hoven want to find a way to announce the company's plans to the company's current employees.

Scenario #2

Michelle Williams is the foreperson on the construction of a new, freestanding commercial building in the downtown area. The structure will be three stories tall. She is responsible for the work of 25 people. Of these 25 employees, 23 are always on time and rarely, if ever, call in sick. However, there are two employees—Roger Newman and Mark Hartwell—who are routinely late for work and have a long history of calling in sick unnecessarily. Michelle needs to re-iterate the company's policy on lateness and sick leave.

Scenario #3

Martinson Heating and Cooling Co. is on an automated payroll system. The company's office manager, Carol Harliss, has just heard from the payroll processing company. Apparently, all of Martinson's 300 workers are going to have a minor error in this week's paycheck. For some reason, the computer rounded each worker's final payment up or down to the nearest dollar. So, for example, if the paycheck was to have been for $291.36, the computer mistakenly issued a check for $291.00. If the check was to have been for $185.76, the computer mistakenly issued a check for $186.00. All of these problems will be corrected in the next pay period. Carol needs to let the company employees know about this small error.

Scenario #4

New Jersey Excavating, a large excavating company, has just won a bid to do the excavation on a large new shopping mall project. The company had not expected to win the bid, and was pleasantly surprised when it received a phone call with the good news. But now the owner and general manager, Ross Hernandez, feels unprepared. Much work needs to be done in the next two months to plan the project. He needs all of his top people—the personnel director, the soil analysis director, the three foremen, and a few others—to begin working together to get everything prepared. In essence, he needs his people to come up with a plan of action for getting everything ready to begin the job in two months.

Activity 4.3: Reading an Agenda

A meeting agenda is reproduced below. Read it, then answer the questions that follow.

AGENDA: NEWTON TOWNHOUSES PROJECT
August 3, 2002

8:30–9:00	Breakfast
9:00–10:00	Concrete and Masonry
10:00–11:00	Doors and Windows
11:00–11:30	Break
11:30–12:30	Thermal and Moisture Protection
12:30–1:30	Lunch
1:30–3:00	Electrical
3:00–3:15	Break
3:15–4:00	Permit Planning
4:00–4:15	Wrap-Up

Attending: Will Owens, Steve Moravian, Tom Wintriss, Carmen Nunez, Jan Schmidt, Oliver Washington, Tyrone Jenkins, Miguel de la Hoya

1. What project will be discussed at this meeting? _____

2. On what day will the meeting take place? _____

3. Jan Schmidt has been asked to attend the meeting only for the discussion of thermal and moisture protection matters. At what time should she arrive? _____

4. How many breaks are scheduled (in addition to breakfast and lunch)?
   _____

5. Which topic is scheduled to take the greatest amount of time?
   _____

6. Of the following people, who will not be attending this meeting: Tom Wintriss, Phyllis Minichetti, Miguel de la Hoya, Will Owens, or Oliver Washington? _____

7. At what time will the meeting end? _____

8. Which of the scheduled discussions is expected to take only 45 minutes?
   _____

4.3 ASSERTIVENESS

When asked for your opinion, do you state it openly and respectfully, with no reservations? When you're not happy about something, do you say so?

If you answered "Yes" to either of these questions, it's likely that you are *assertive*. An assertive person stands up for his rights and isn't likely to be taken advantage of. In contrast, a nonassertive person won't stick up for himself and may end up in negative situations because of it.

In modern America, it's sometimes a challenge to be assertive without being aggressive. An assertive person clearly states his or her needs, but does so in a way that is respectful of others. In contrast, an *aggressive* person takes a "me, me, me" approach, placing his or her needs above those of others.

How can you be assertive and stand up for your rights while not offending others? Here are a few suggestions.

USE "I-TALK" RATHER THAN "YOU-TALK."   Aggressive people tend to attack others verbally. They say, "You did this, you did that." The listener is automatically put on the defensive. In contrast, an assertive person uses "I" or "We." For example, suppose someone next to you is chewing gum very loudly, and it's distracting you. An aggressive person would say "The way you chew gum is really annoying me." An assertive person would take more of an I-approach and say, "I find it very hard to concentrate when I hear someone chewing gum."

TREAT OTHER PEOPLE AS EQUALS.   An aggressive person sends signals of his own superiority. His messages tend to be insulting, condescending, or snide. In contrast, an assertive person treats others as equals. Where the aggressive person would say, "Enough already! Do you think you could stop chewing gum like a cow?", the assertive person would ask, "Could I ask you not to chew your gum so loudly? It's very distracting to me as I work."

WATCH YOUR TONE.   Aggressive people let anger or impatience show in their voices. Assertive people keep their tones modulated. They never raise their voices, yell, or shout at co-workers.

AVOID VAST GENERALIZATIONS.   Two words that can get a speaker into a lot of trouble are "always" and "never." Examples: "You are always late." "Why are you never here on time?" Such questions put people on the defensive, and defense mechanisms often lead to arguments. When talking with people, modulate your words. Speak the truth, but don't exaggerate for effect. Such exaggerations can shut down the lines of communication.

Consider when it is appropriate to be assertive and when it is not. Not all situations call for assertiveness. For example, if a little old lady accidentally cuts in front of you in line at a bank, do you really gain anything by being assertive?

Activity 4.4: Practicing Assertiveness, Avoiding Aggressiveness

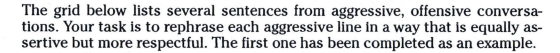

The grid below lists several sentences from aggressive, offensive conversations. Your task is to rephrase each aggressive line in a way that is equally assertive but more respectful. The first one has been completed as an example.

Aggressive	Assertive
Hey! Either show up on time, or I'm reporting you to the foreman. I'm sick of waiting around for you to start my job.	I'd appreciate it if we could get to work at the same time. This is a two-man job, and it doesn't make sense for me to stand around waiting to begin the day's work.
What were you thinking? I asked you to deliver those parts here by Tuesday, not Friday! It's already Thursday and you're two days late. I want to talk to your manager about this.	
The only car you should ever buy is one made in America. If you buy any foreign car, you're not a good American, and I want nothing to do with you.	
Why are you always interrupting me when I speak? For God's sake, just shut up for a minute.	
Waiter, take this hamburger back right now. I asked for it well done, and it's only medium. Are you deaf, or is the cook just stupid? And don't think I'm paying for it unless I get it cooked *exactly* the way I want it cooked.	

4.4 COURTESY AND ETIQUETTE

Some may argue that chivalry is dead, but the fact remains that common courtesy makes life much more pleasant for all concerned. A pleasant smile and a kind word make a difficult day easier for everyone. In fact, the rules of courtesy exist for a reason: They act as a social lubricant, making communication easier between people of all ages, genders, races, ethnicities, and walks of life.

The basis of all courtesy and etiquette is *respect*. Throughout this text, we've focused on respect as a necessary component of all face-to-face communications. Here we offer some tips on common courtesy when speaking with someone you cannot see.

4.4.1 Telephone Etiquette

Some businesspeople spend more time on the phone than anywhere else. Follow these suggestions for communicating effectively via telephone.

- *When speaking on a telephone, remember that the person you're speaking to cannot see you.* Therefore, she can't pick up on any facial expressions or other nonverbal signals you may be sending. So, speak very clearly. When giving numbers or important information, slow down so that the other person can take notes.
- *Answer the phone pleasantly and identify yourself.* A simple "Hello, Mike Rogers here" or "Good morning, this is Alice Langan" is a nice way to begin a phone call. Don't bark into the phone.
- *Before you begin a long conversation, ask the other person if she has time to talk.* You may not realize it, but you may be interrupting something important with your phone call.
- *Close on a positive note.* Most people expect a pleasant "Good-bye" as a way to end a phone call. Don't just hang up the phone. Say "Good-bye," "Adios," or "See you soon."

4.4.2 Voice Mail Etiquette

When you place a call, you're just as likely to get an answering machine as a real person. In fact, some people spend all day going back and forth between phone calls and their voice mail messages. For this reason, it's important to keep your voice mail messages short and to the point. Some other tips:

- *On business voice mails, keep messages focused on business.* Avoid gossip or unnecessary chat on voice mail. Save that for personal conversations.
- *Consider whether to leave a message at all.* Generally, you shouldn't just hang up when you get an answering machine. However, if you have a lot to say, it's unlikely that you'll fit it all in a three-minute message. In such cases, you might simply say, "Hi Lori, it's Steve. I need to talk to you about the Delta Freight project. Give me a call. Thanks."
- *When leaving your phone number, say it twice.* This way, if the receiver misses it the first time, he won't have to listen to your entire message again.
- *Don't trust voice mail.* Like most electronic systems, voice mail systems hit occasional glitches. If somebody hasn't called you back, there's a chance that your message was not delivered properly.
- *Don't deliver bad news via voice mail.* Voice mail should be used only for quick, neutral messages or questions. Serious issues should be discussed, and bad news should be delivered, in person or in a one-to-one phone conversation.

4.4.3 Cell Phone and Beeper Etiquette

The "wireless explosion" has truly revolutionized communication. People can now talk just about anywhere, at any time, via cellular technology. People can also reach one another instantly via beepers.

Like all modes of communication, a system of courtesy has developed surrounding the use of cell phones and beepers. Specifically:

- *Be keenly aware of the time spent on cell phone calls.* Cell phone subscribers are charged not only for outgoing calls but also for incoming calls. Thus, when you call someone, that person incurs a charge. Keep cell phone conversations as short as possible. Use a cell phone only when a land line isn't available.

- *Know when to beep, and when not to beep.* Beeps always convey a sense of urgency—in general, a beep is a request for you to return someone's call immediately. So, before you beep someone, ask yourself: Must I really speak to this person now? Or can I leave a message on her voice mail, and we'll talk later?

- *When speaking on a cell phone, find a quiet, solitary place to talk.* Imagine this scenario: You're having lunch with four friends. A cell phone rings. One of your friends answers the phone, then spends 15 minutes chatting with the caller. How do the rest of you feel? Excluded? Impatient? Annoyed?

    Or suppose that you're talking with a building owner (the customer) on the job site. Your cell phone rings; the caller is another customer. How would the first customer (who is paying you by the hour) feel about you stopping your conversation with him to talk to someone else?

    It's quite rude to talk on a cell phone around other people who aren't involved in the conversation. If you get a call when you're not alone, your two most courteous options are: (1) don't answer the phone, or (2) answer the phone, say you're busy, and call the person back later on. A third option is to excuse yourself to take the call in private.

- *Turn beepers and cell phones off during performances.* Turn cell phones off, and set beepers to vibrate, during movies, plays, concerts, and other events where their noises would disturb others.

- *Don't walk and talk, or talk and drive.* When driving, your full concentration should be on the road—not on the phone. When walking down a busy street, you lose awareness of hazards when you're talking on the phone. When talking on a cell phone, you should be sitting in a safe, quiet place.

4.4.4 Two-Way Radio Etiquette

On many job sites, and in jobs with public utilities, two-way radios are common means of communication. When talking on a two-way radio, keep the following pointers in mind.

- *Listen carefully and speak especially clearly.* Two-way radios are prone to static and other types of interference. So be sure to speak slowly and carefully, and repeat key information.

- *Never use profanity or inappropriate language.* Two-way radios are often on public frequencies, which means that unintended parties may hear pieces of your conversation. Keep your conversation free of offensive words or topics.

- *Don't interrupt others.* A two-way radio makes it impossible for two people to speak at the same time and hear each other. If you interrupt someone, you may miss important information because you won't hear what he is saying. Be sure someone is done talking before you respond.

Activity 4.5: Practicing Etiquette

Take this brief quiz to test your knowledge of telephone, voice mail, and beeper etiquette. Mark "T" if the statement is true, "F" if it is false.

_____ 1. In general, you should speed up when you're leaving a voice mail message and you have to give your phone number.

_____ 2. It is OK to convey bad news over voice mail, as long as you end up speaking to the other person face to face later on.

_____ 3. In a business situation, it's acceptable to just hang up the phone without saying "good-bye" or something similar.

_____ 4. Beepers and cell phones should be set to "vibrate" mode, or turned off, during meetings.

_____ 5. Voice mail systems can always be counted on to get your message to the right person.

_____ 6. If you need to have a long phone conversation with someone, it's a good idea to ask her if she has the time to talk before you begin.

_____ 7. If you have to leave a very complex message on someone's voice mail, it might be better to simply leave a message asking for a call back.

_____ 8. Talking on a cell phone while driving is a perfectly safe activity.

_____ 9. Today's "wireless explosion" has made it acceptable to talk on cell phones pretty much anywhere and at any time.

_____ 10. Generally, you should place a call to someone's beeper only for urgent matters.

4.5 DELIVERING BAD NEWS

By utilizing the advice in both this module and Module 3, you will have little difficulty in conveying information to your audience. All the suggestions made so far apply to all instances of spoken communication.

There is, however, a special case of spoken communication that needs to be considered. What approach should you take when you need to deliver bad news? Clearly, this situation requires much more sympathy and delicacy than the average conversation or discussion.

Unfortunately, we all occasionally need to convey bad news. When faced with such a situation, consider the following suggestions.

- *Whenever possible, convey bad news in a one-to-one conversation.* Suppose you're a foreman. Your company has decided to lay off 15% of its workforce, and you've been told that you'll need to lay off three members of your crew. Although an announcement of the layoff will soon be coming from headquarters, you should meet with the three crew members individually and talk with them one at a time.

- *Choose the proper time and place.* It's best to deliver bad news at the end of a day or at the beginning of the week. If you give someone bad news early in the day, he or she is likely to think about it, and be distracted by it, all day long. If you tell that person on Friday, he or she is likely to think about it all weekend.

- *Deliver your message concisely; don't beat around the bush.* When giving bad news, get it over with quickly. After a brief introduction, get right to business. Delaying the message only increases everyone's tension and anxiety. For example, the best way to give someone news of a layoff might be, "Nick, you're a valuable employee. But headquarters has told me that I have to lay off three crewmen. You are the junior man here, and seniority is the main factor we're using to determine layoffs. I am very sorry about this, but we need to lay you off effective April 15th."

- *Do your best to reassure the other person.* Suppose that, as a foreman, you've decided to promote John into a higher level job, instead of Bob. It's your opinion that Bob is a good worker but simply isn't ready for the promotion. When you give Bob the bad news, follow up immediately by emphasizing the positive. For example, you might say, "Bob, don't take this too hard. You're still young, and you're a hard worker. You just aren't quite ready yet, and John is. There will be other promotion opportunities in the coming months, and I hope you will apply for them."

- *Let the other person speak or express emotion.* People react to bad news in different ways. Some people clam up. Others cry, others scream and yell. Your job is to remain calm and cool—the voice of reason. Let the other person vent, and be willing to listen. Answer any questions calmly and clearly.

- *Above all, be as understanding and as sympathetic as possible.*

Activity 4.6: Conveying Bad News with Sensitivity

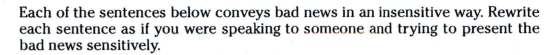

Each of the sentences below conveys bad news in an insensitive way. Rewrite each sentence as if you were speaking to someone and trying to present the bad news sensitively.

EXAMPLE:

Insensitive: Guess what? We're cutting you from the bowling team. Your scores are too low, and we don't want you messing us up in the state championship.

Sensitive: I'm really sorry about this, but the state championship is coming up, and the bowling team can only send the players with the highest scores. Several other people have much higher scores than you, so they are the ones who will be going to the championship. I'm sure you understand that this is our best strategy for winning.

1. "Brad, your grandmother kicked the bucket last night." _____

   _____

   _____

2. "We're way behind on this job. You guys are going to have to put in a boatload of overtime in the next few weeks, whether you want to or not."

   _____

   _____

   _____

3. "I'm giving Jack the promotion instead of you. He's just a really hard worker, and I know he's the right choice. Better luck next time."

   _____

   _____

4. "I just got a call from your father. Your mother was in a terrible car accident, and she's lying half dead at the hospital."

_____

_____

5. "Dave, I can't see you any more. I need to date a generous guy, and you're cheap. We can be friends, though, but try not to call me too much."

_____

_____

4.6 DIVERSITY IN THE WORKPLACE

The United States is very different today than it was 20 years ago. Before 1980, the workforce was composed of mostly white men working to support a family. Relatively few women worked outside the home.

Today, this is no longer true. About two-thirds of all single mothers today are in the labor force. So are about 45% of all mothers with children under three years old. People of every age, race, color, gender, and ethnic background now work together in all parts of the country. In fact, by the year 2020, minorities and women in the workplace will outnumber white men.

What does all of this mean? Many of the workers in the construction industry are still white men, but this situation is changing slowly but surely. Not just women, but also men from minority (nonwhite) groups, are discovering that they have the talents needed to be successful construction professionals. Many are attracted to the pay and fringe benefits that construction provides. Earning more money helps them better provide for themselves and their families.

Appreciating the benefits of a diverse workforce is an important part of being a good team member. A working knowledge of diversity is also important in helping you develop your spoken communication skills. Specifically, diversity requires that you be sensitive to the diverse characteristics of your audience, and adjust your language to be as inclusive and nonoffensive as possible.

4.6.1 What Is Diversity?

The word "diversity" is used often these days. But what exactly does it mean? Basically, _diversity_ refers to the many different ("diverse") kinds of people on a job site. People can be different in many ways. They can differ by:

Gender	Male, female
Race or ethnic group	Black, white, Latino, Native American
Nationality	Italian, Irish, Russian, Swedish, Chinese
Religion	Catholic, Baptist, Hindu, Jewish, Buddhist
Age	Young, middle-aged, retired, elderly
Education	Grammar school, high school, college
Physical disabilities	Deaf, blind, unable to walk
Mental disabilities	Dyslexia, attention deficit disorder
Marital status	Single, married, divorced, widowed

Weight	Thin, average, heavy, obese
Hair	Short hair, long hair, bald, curly hair
Tobacco status	Smoker, nonsmoker, tobacco chewer
Area of specialization	Plumber, electrician, mason, carpenter, engineer
Personality traits	Outgoing, shy, quiet, boisterous

Diversity enriches our lives, bringing a wealth of perspectives and experiences to our friendships and the workplace.

Because many minority groups have long suffered discrimination, it's very important to speak in a manner that is sensitive to their histories and needs. For example, you may have heard the term "African-American," and you may have said to yourself, "Why do I need to use this term? Isn't 'black' a good enough term?" To answer this question, put yourself in the shoes of an African-American. Unlike most other Americans, who have a strong sense of where their families emigrated from—Italy, Spain, Mexico, Vietnam, and so on—black people often do not know their origins. By calling themselves African-Americans, they are seeking a nationality, a sense of place, that was denied to them. From this perspective, isn't it easy to see why the term "African-American" is preferable to "black"?

4.6.2 Communicating with Diverse Groups

Throughout Modules 3 and 4, we've talked about the importance of showing respect for your co-workers during spoken communications. This means respecting *everyone,* not just those who share your background. Let respect be your cardinal rule, and you're not likely to ever run into trouble with anyone, regardless of age, gender, or color.

That said, here are some further tips for communicating in a diverse world.

BE AWARE OF CULTURAL DIFFERENCES, AND MAKE ALLOWANCES FOR THEM. Different cultural groups celebrate different holidays. They may also have different ways of approaching the same problem. For instance, Asian cultures tend to encourage a lot of group problem solving, while Americans believe in the "rugged individual." Don't take these cultural differences personally. Instead, be willing to learn from them. Keep in mind that there usually is no single "best" way to solve a problem. Remain open-minded and willing to listen to other ideas, even if they're different from yours.

NEVER MAKE FUN OF THOSE WHO ARE DIFFERENT FROM YOU. This is a simple rule of life. Remember the empathy rule: Think how you would feel if someone insulted you, your family, your religion, or your way of speaking.

FIND COMMON GROUND. On the job, you'll undoubtedly work with some people who don't share your background, beliefs, or culture. However, you do have one important thing in common: You are all working on the same job, and you all have the same goals: to do quality work, to finish the job on time, and to earn a living for yourselves and your families. Focus on what you have in common, and it will be much easier to accept differences.

THINK BEFORE YOU SPEAK, AND THINK BEFORE YOU ACT. If you are a young white man, it may be hard for you to understand how, say, an older African-American man or a young Asian woman might think. Here are some guidelines to consider when communicating with different kinds of people:

- **Women**—Women want to be taken seriously as co-workers and team members. They want their talents recognized. They don't want to be spoken to as if they're idiots who know nothing about construction. They don't want to be called "baby," "sister," or "hon," or to be touched in inappropriate places. Finally, they don't want to be whistled at or made to feel uncomfortable on the job. In general, the rule is simple: Assume that women are as competent as men are, and show them the same level of respect you'd demonstrate for male co-workers.

- **Older people**—Older people want to be respected for their life experiences. They don't want to be called "Gramps." They don't want young people acting superior, and they certainly don't want people assuming that they can't do things just because they're getting on in years.

    Some older people experience hearing loss. If you suspect that you're speaking with someone who can't quite hear you, raise your voice and look directly at the listener while you speak. Be prepared to repeat yourself a few times, and do so patiently.

- **People of color and people from different ethnic backgrounds**—African-Americans, Latinos, and Asian-Americans all want the same thing: to be valued as individuals, not seen as representatives of their ethnic group. Most of all, they want to be accepted members of the team. If you're talking to a group of people who speak English with a foreign accent, don't assume that they are less intelligent than you because their native language isn't English. While it may be helpful for you to speak more slowly and clearly with non-native speakers of English, it rarely helps to speak in a raised voice.

- **People with disabilities**—Disabled people want others to feel comfortable around them. They don't want to be pitied. They sometimes need to have special concessions made for them, but in general they don't want to put people out. When talking with a disabled person, it's acceptable to refer to the disability when doing so is relevant to the work at hand, but the disability itself should not be a primary topic of conversation.

    Sometimes a person with a disability will make specific requests to help the two of you communicate better. For example, a deaf person may ask you to look directly at her while you speak so that she can read your lips. Do whatever you can to accommodate these needs.

- **Shy people**—Shy people are often at a disadvantage in life and at work. Others often mistakenly assume that shy people are standoffish or conceited. In fact, most shy people welcome the opportunity to talk or build relationships. It just takes someone else to get the ball rolling. So don't be afraid to strike up a conversation with someone who seems shy. He or she is likely to be very happy you did.

REMEMBER: Above all else, approach people as individuals, not as members of a "group." Don't lump all members of a minority group into one category—doing so is *stereotyping,* which leads to vast (and incorrect) generalizations about that group. People are more than just members of their ethnic or social groups. They are living, breathing human beings with feelings and passions. Don't let any idea you have about a group affect your perception of an individual.

Activity 4.7: Increasing Your Awareness of Diversity

Almost anyone you meet can tell a story about misunderstandings that have arisen due to cultural differences. To expand your cultural awareness, see how many of the following questions you can answer correctly. Don't look for the answers in this module—they're not there! This quiz is designed to help you increase your multicultural knowledge, so don't feel upset if you get a low score. (Answers are at the end of the activity.) As with new knowledge you receive on the job, look on this activity as a learning experience.

1. Several years ago, the Chevrolet Motor Company had an extremely successful car named the Nova. Chevy decided to start exporting the car to South America, expecting it to be equally successful there. To the company's surprise, the car bombed, because Chevy failed to realize something important about its product. What do you think the problem was?
   a. Chevy didn't realize that there was not much demand for cars in South America.
   b. Chevy didn't understand that it goes against South Americans' religious beliefs to drive cars.
   c. Chevy didn't know that the car's name, Nova, means "doesn't go" in Spanish.

2. You are working on a large job site for a client who comes from Japan. One day, the Japanese owner comes to visit the site, and the foreman brings him around to meet some of the workers. When you go to shake his hand, he makes it clear he doesn't want to shake. Why do you think this happened?
   a. Because Japanese people consider it offensive to shake hands in public.
   b. Because Japanese businessmen believe that they are better than the people who work for them.
   c. Because, in general, the Japanese do not like Americans.

3. In the year 2000, approximately what percentage of the U.S. work force was composed of women and minorities?
   a. 30%
   b. 50%
   c. 85%

4. A recent phenomenon in the United States is called the "graying of America." This means that people are living longer, and that older people are making up a larger percentage of the population than ever before. In 1970, the median age in the United States was 27 years old.[1] What do you think the median age in the United States was in the year 2000?
   a. 39
   b. 35
   c. 30

5. It is a well-known fact that, unfortunately, women are often paid less than men for doing the same job. For every $1 earned by a man, a woman in a similar job earns:
   a. 95 cents
   b. 88 cents
   c. 73 cents

---

[1]A "median age" of 27 means that half the population of the country is younger than 27, and half the population is older than 27.

6. Which is the largest minority group in the United States?
   a. Asian-Americans
   b. African-Americans
   c. Latinos

7. When the Coca-Cola company first began selling its product in China, it hired a translator to translate the words "Coca-Cola" into Chinese. Unfortunately, the translation in Chinese sounded a lot like "Bite the wax tadpole." The product sold very poorly, and is it any wonder? When Coke realized its mistake, it changed its packaging so that the Chinese translation spells out a much more pleasant phrase. What do you think this phrase is?
   a. For a quick pick-up!
   b. Happiness in the mouth
   c. It's the real thing

8. When disabled people are asked to name the problem they face most often at work, what do you think their most common response is?
   a. Being asked too often about their disability
   b. Being resented by others, who think that disabled people receive "special treatment"
   c. Being asked to perform tasks that are beyond their abilities

9. After English, what is the most commonly spoken language in the United States?
   a. French
   b. Spanish
   c. Japanese

10. Numerous studies have compared male versus female attitudes toward work. Which of the following best describes the results of these studies?
    a. Women work for money, while men work because they're expected to.
    b. Men are more interested in advancing on the job, while women prefer to stay in one job for a long time.
    c. Both men and women want the same things from their work: a good salary, personal satisfaction, and the chance to prove themselves.

ANSWERS: 1(c); 2(a); 3(c); 4(a); 5(c); 6(b); 7(b); 8(a); 9(b); 10(c).

Activity 4.8: Understanding Diversity in Yourself and Others (Collaborative Activity)

This activity asks you to take a closer look at yourself and to share some of your background with others. The goal is to help you see diversity in yourself and others.

Working with a teammate, complete the following Diversity Questionnaire. The first part of the questionnaire asks you for information about yourself. For the second part of the questionnaire, you'll need to interview your teammate.

DIVERSITY QUESTIONNAIRE

Part I: Your Personal Diversity

Answer these questions about yourself. You do not have to answer any questions you do not feel comfortable answering.

1. What is your name? _____

2. What are your ethnic backgrounds?_____
   List any languages you speak in addition to English._____

3. Do you think people hold stereotypes of people from your background? If so, what are they? Do you think these stereotypes are true? _____
   _____
   _____

4. What is your religious background?_____

5. Name something that people might be surprised to know about you. _____
   _____
   _____

6. List one or two misconceptions that other people hold about you. _____
   _____
   _____

7. Give three words that describe yourself very accurately: _____
   _____

8. Complete the following sentences:
   a. If I could visit any place on earth, the place I'd go would be _____ .
   b. If I could do anything I wanted for a career, I would be a _____ .
   c. The quality I value most in another person is _____ .
   d. The person who has influenced me the most is _____ .
   e. Something that makes me really mad is _____ .
   f. If I could excel in any one sport, the one I'd choose would be _____ .
   g. I'm better than most people at _____ .
   h. I think my co-workers would describe me as _____ .

9. Have you ever encountered prejudice from other people? If so, describe the situation. How did you react? _____
   _____
   _____

10. Do you think you ever have the tendency to be prejudiced? If so, against whom? Why do you hold this prejudice? What steps can you take to eliminate it?_____
    _____
    _____

Part II: Your Teammate's Diversity

Interview your teammate, and write down his or her answers to these questions. The interviewee can choose to skip any questions that he or she is not comfortable discussing.

1. What is your name? _____

2. What are your ethnic backgrounds? _____
   List any languages you speak in addition to English._____

3. Do you think people hold stereotypes of people from your background? If so, what are they? Do you think these stereotypes are true? _____

   _____

   _____

4. What is your religious background? _____

5. Name something that people might be surprised to know about you._____

   _____

   _____

6. List one or two misconceptions that other people hold about you. _____

   _____

   _____

7. Give three words that describe yourself very accurately: _____

   _____

8. Complete the following sentences:
   a. If I could visit any place on earth, the place I'd go would be _____ .
   b. If I could do anything I wanted for a career, I would be a _____ .
   c. The quality I value most in another person is _____ .
   d. The person who has influenced me the most is _____ .
   e. Something that makes me really mad is _____ .
   f. If I could excel in any one sport, the one I'd choose would be _____ .
   g. I'm better than most people at _____ .
   h. I think my co-workers would describe me as _____ .

9. Have you ever encountered prejudice from other people? If so, describe the situation. How did you react? _____

   _____

   _____

10. Do you think you ever have the tendency to be prejudiced? If so, against whom? Why do you hold this prejudice? What steps can you take to eliminate it? _____

    _____

    _____

Did any of your teammate's answers surprise you? What have you learned from this activity? Has this activity changed the way you think about your teammate?

4.7 CONFLICT MANAGEMENT

Throughout this book we've emphasized the importance of building positive relationships with your supervisor and co-workers. Sometimes, though, arguments arise and relationships become strained.

To prevent disagreements from getting out of control, you must manage and resolve conflicts as they arise. The best way to end a conflict is to gather the parties involved and talk the issue through.

4.7.1 The Causes of Conflict

We've all experienced conflict in our lives. But what exactly causes conflict?

The answer is simple. *Conflict arises when people disagree.* Disagreements can arise from just about anything, from differences in opinion to differences in personality to differences in age.

As the first step to managing conflict on the job, you must be aware of the sources of conflict. When you know the sources, you can take steps to prevent the conflict from escalating.

Conflict Between Co-Workers

Conflict can exist among co-workers for many reasons. Some of the most common causes of this type of conflict follow.

DIFFERENT WORK HABITS.   People have very different ways of working. Some are neat; others seem sloppy and unorganized. The "Oscar Madisons" and "Felix Ungers" of the world rarely get along. Some people work quickly, while others are slow and methodical. Both types of people get annoyed by the other type. The faster workers think the slower workers are dragging their heels. The slower workers think the fast workers don't take the time to do things right.

To prevent conflict: Understand that different people can use different methods to get the same job done. Your preferred style of working is not necessarily the best. Be flexible. Hold your tongue.

DIFFERENT ATTITUDES TOWARD THE COMPANY OR JOB.   In every company, in every industry, people take widely different approaches to their jobs. Some take great pride in working. Others hate to get out of bed in the morning. Some work just to pay the rent, while others are workaholics. People who like their jobs may get accused of being brown-nosers, while people who don't like their jobs may be considered lazy or incompetent.

To prevent conflict: Maintain a positive attitude toward your job. Associate only with co-workers who share your positive attitude. Don't let others bring you down. If negative people say or do things to annoy you, don't take the bait. Walk away instead.

DIFFERENCES IN PERSONALITY AND APPEARANCE.   People have vastly different ways of expressing themselves. Some are reserved in nature and in the way they express themselves. Others pepper their conversation with jokes or controversial comments. Reserved people may be perceived as snobbish, while outgoing people may be perceived as rude. In addition, workers can have very strong reactions to their co-workers' physical appearance—disapproving of those who have long hair or are overweight, for example.

To prevent conflict: Remember that the world is big enough to hold all kinds of people. Does the fact that someone is fairly quiet make her a bad person?

Does it prevent her from being a good carpenter? Probably not—maybe she's just shy. Does the fact that someone has long hair prevent him from being a good electrician? Of course not.

DIFFERENCES IN AGE.   People born in different eras often have different sets of values. For example, "Baby Boomers" (who were born between 1946 and 1959) often feel a loyalty to the company they work for, and often care deeply about what other people think. They like to work with others and may not feel comfortable with technology. In contrast, "Baby Busters" and "Generation X" (those born after 1965) tend to be much less loyal to their company, and they feel that they work best alone. Also, younger people tend to be more comfortable with technology.[2]

To prevent conflict: Respect the values of others. Younger people can and should try to learn from people who are more experienced. Older people should be willing to learn from those who are younger.

PROBLEMS OUTSIDE THE JOB.   Sometimes, factors outside the job—such as family issues, legal issues, or money issues—can create high levels of stress. When people feel a lot of stress, they may be uncooperative or inattentive, or pick fights with co-workers. If you're not careful, these kinds of conflicts can escalate and affect team spirit.

To prevent conflict: Don't bring your personal problems to work. If you're dealing with a particularly difficult issue, discuss it with your supervisor and your team members. If one of your team members is experiencing a problem, show sympathy and understanding.

Conflict Between Workers and Supervisors

Most workers experience conflict with their supervisor at one time or another. Most of this conflict is caused by one of the following factors.

WORKLOAD.   The supervisor's job is to keep workers as productive as possible. But workers can become resentful if they feel they're being pushed too hard.

To prevent conflict: Use the empathy rule: Think how you'd feel if you were in your boss's position. Your boss's supervisor is making sure that your boss gets the most productivity, and the highest-quality work, out of the crew. You are a member of that crew.

ABSENTEEISM AND LATENESS.   Construction supervisors point to absenteeism and lateness as their two biggest problems on the job. Both problems can cause serious delays and conflict. When workers arrive late, leave early, or don't show up, their co-workers usually have to work harder. And if the job doesn't get done on time, everybody suffers.

To prevent conflict: Arrive at your job on time. Don't call in sick unless you really are sick. Don't use the excuse, "I couldn't get a ride to work." Instead, find a way to get there. Always call your supervisor if you're sick and can't make it to work. Don't make your supervisor guess your whereabouts. Remember: You may be an outstanding worker who is very knowledgeable about your job. But none of that matters if you're not at work. Also keep in mind that showing up on time, and not calling in sick, will reflect well on you at raise time.

---

[2]From Associated Builders and Contractors, Inc., *Training for Apprenticeship Mentors* (Madison, WI: 1997), pp. 15–18.

CRITICISM.   It's the manager's job to point out workers' mistakes. It's also her job to help workers be as efficient as possible. Sometimes workers take it personally when their performance is criticized or corrected (see Section 2.3). The result can be a strained relationship between worker and foreman.

To prevent conflict: Constructive criticism can be a valuable learning tool for you. Say to yourself: "I don't know everything. I can always learn more. I need to keep an open mind." If you truly believe that you're doing things the right way, discuss the situation with your supervisor calmly and clearly.

4.7.2 Simple Ways to Prevent Conflict

Most experienced supervisors try to build teams of people who can work well together. But, despite the best intentions, conflict sometimes does arise.

Many times, you can avoid conflict by derailing it before it flares up. Here are some suggestions:

THINK. THEN WALK AWAY. CHOOSE NOT TO GET ANNOYED.   In any situation with the potential for conflict, your best choice is to *think* before you react. Before you get into an argument, ask yourself: "Is this worth fighting about? Will any of this matter ten years from now?" Nine times out of ten, it won't. When you've realized that what you're about to argue about isn't important, it's much easier to walk away.

DON'T TAKE IT PERSONALLY.   You may sometimes think that other people's habits or personalities are specifically geared toward annoying you. This simply isn't true. Other people developed their habits and personalities long before they met you. Very rarely do people purposely *try* to annoy others. So, try to cut people some slack. Remember, "Don't sweat the small stuff."

AVOID GETTING INVOLVED IN OTHER PEOPLE'S ARGUMENTS.   Sometimes you may feel that you can offer advice to help other people resolve their conflicts. Thus it may be tempting to get drawn into other people's arguments. However, this is generally not a good idea. To prevent yourself from becoming involved in the conflict, mind your own business. If you do find yourself in the middle of an argument, don't take sides.

4.7.3 Resolving Conflicts Quickly and Effectively

The methods discussed in Sections 4.7.1 and 4.7.2 are useful for preventing minor conflict. However, it's unrealistic to expect that *all* conflict on the job can be avoided.

When conflict cannot be prevented, it's best to deal with it as quickly as possible. Conflict affects everyone negatively, and for the good of the project—as well as for everyone's mental health—serious conflicts should be addressed immediately. Let's discuss how to resolve conflict among co-workers, then how to resolve conflict that might arise between you and your boss.

Resolving Conflicts with Co-Workers

To neutralize a conflict, all the people involved must actively want the conflict to end. Thus, it's important that everyone have a say in how the issue will be resolved.

Resolving conflicts requires all co-workers to approach the problem rationally and with an open mind. Proceed as follows:

Step 1: Bring the conflict into the open. The first step in resolving conflict is admitting that the conflict exists. All parties must openly acknowledge the conflict. Nothing will be accomplished if someone won't admit that a problem exists.

Suppose, for example, that you've been assigned to work with Larry on a two-man job. You've been working together for three months, and you feel that Larry isn't pulling his share of the weight. He's been working for the company longer than you have, and you think he has a superior attitude. At the same time, you feel that his attitude towards you is hostile—he thinks you are a young punk. In addition to this personality conflict, you feel that Larry doesn't pay much attention on the job and that your safety is in jeopardy.

To get the conflict out into the open, look for an opportunity to have a private discussion with Larry. You might say, "Larry, we've been working together for three months, and it seems like it's not a good match. Do you agree, or am I imagining it?" If Larry agrees with you, that's the first step to opening up the dialogue.

Step 2: Analyze and discuss the problem. Once you've brought the conflict into the open, your next step is to find the cause(s) of the problem. To begin analyzing and discussing the problem, you might ask these questions:

- How did the conflict arise? What keeps it going?
- Is the conflict based on personality issues, or did a specific event trigger it?
- Has this conflict been building up for a while, or did it start suddenly?
- Has the conflict arisen because of differing expectations?
- Could the conflict have been prevented?
- Do all parties have the same perception of what's going on?

To continue our example, Larry may feel that the problem began when he overheard you complaining about having to work with him. You may feel that you sensed hostility coming from Larry the very first day you met him.

One thing to keep in mind when discussing the conflict: **Do everything you can to keep emotion out of the discussion.** Conflict can be emotionally upsetting, but when discussing the problem you need to be as rational as possible. If you get angry, you'll just prolong the conflict. If you sense too much anger developing, postpone the discussion until you can approach it more calmly.

Step 3: Develop possible solutions. After you've decided on the causes of the conflict, you need to address the underlying issues. You can use two techniques to develop possible solutions:

- **Collaboration.** When people *collaborate,* they put their heads together to determine a solution that will work for everyone. Collaboration allows the people involved to work together and find a solution agreeable to all.

  To be a good collaborator, you must remain open minded. You must also take responsibility for the role you played in the conflict. For example, you and Larry may collaborate and decide that you've misunderstood each other and that you'll both make a new beginning the next day.

- **Compromise.** When a solution is achieved through *compromise,* both parties give in a little bit. Giving in is a good way to show others that you're willing to work toward a resolution. When you compromise, you don't get everything you wanted, but you get enough to make you happy. The same holds true for everyone else involved in the conflict.

  For example, you and Larry may decide that you're just too different to ever get along. But you must work together effectively. You and Larry will never be friends, but you can make the rest of your time together as painless as possible. So you both compromise. You promise not to wear the T-shirt with the saying that annoys Larry, and he agrees not to make sarcastic remarks.

In both these techniques, it's important that you *listen* as much as you *talk*. When looking for solutions, you should:

- Search for common ground and work towards that.
- Be willing to admit when you're wrong and to apologize for your mistakes.
- Accept that other people think differently and have different needs than you do.
- Focus on the issues at hand rather than the people involved in them.
- Deal with only one issue at a time.
- Avoid name-calling and threatening behavior. Also avoid words that will produce a negative reaction. For example, don't use words like "never" and "always."
- If you decide to compromise, be sure to keep your end of the bargain.

Step 4: Choose and implement a solution. After you've analyzed the alternatives, it's time to choose and implement the best solution. All people involved in the conflict must agree to the solution. They must then make a commitment to implementing that solution. So, once you and Larry have decided on the best way to resolve your conflict, you must both dedicate yourselves to making that solution work.

Step 5: Evaluate the solution. When the solution has been in place a while, revisit the conflict to make sure no issues remain unresolved. Is the solution working for all parties? Have the results been uniformly positive, or are some adjustments necessary? Following up in this manner prevents the same issues from cropping up again later. It may be difficult for you to bring up the conflict with Larry after you think it's solved, but as the saying goes, "An ounce of prevention is worth a pound of cure."

Resolving Conflicts with Supervisors

When you set out to resolve a conflict with a co-worker, you usually approach him or her as an equal—as someone who's in the same position as you, more or less. However, if you're experiencing conflict with your foreman, you need to take a different approach. Most importantly, you must remember that the foreman is your boss. You can't stomp off if you don't like what he has to say.

Here are some tips for resolving conflict with your supervisor.

GATHER YOUR THOUGHTS.   Before you approach your supervisor, take a moment to gather your thoughts. Think deeply about the conflict and what has caused it. Some people find it helpful to write out their thoughts on a piece of paper; the act of writing helps to put things in perspective. After thinking or writing about the conflict, you may decide that there really is no conflict at all, or you may come up with a simple solution on your own. You may even decide that the best solution is already in place.

APPROACH YOUR BOSS WITH RESPECT.   Supervisors are busy people. So don't just march up to your boss and launch into your problem. Rather, study your supervisor's routine to figure out when would be the best time to approach him. The best time, of course, is when he's less busy and less stressed out. Sometimes it may be better to write the boss a note asking him for an appointment at his convenience.

When you do approach the boss, you might begin by saying, "I have something I'd like to discuss with you. When would be a good time to talk?" Then let him set the time for the discussion. If the only time he can talk is at the end of the day, be willing to stay after hours. When you do meet, do so in private so that you won't be interrupted.

SPEAK CALMLY.   In all conflicts, emotions can get the upper hand if you're not careful. If you feel you're not being treated fairly, for example, you may be tempted to get argumentative or sarcastic. A negative attitude will only escalate the conflict. Remain calm and rational throughout the discussion. Speak slowly and focus on the facts. Don't say anything you can't prove. And remember that your body language conveys as much about your emotions as your words do, so don't let your body convey a threatening or angry stance. (For more on body language, see Section 1.3.)

MAKE YOUR CASE CLEARLY.   Don't begin by throwing accusations at your boss. As much as you can, keep other people out of your conflict—don't mention any names unless you have to. If there is a situation you need fixed, make your case clearly, outlining the reasons behind the conflict. If you are suggesting any changes, explain your reasons and how they will benefit everyone concerned. If you bring up problems that need to be addressed, offer possible solutions that will benefit everyone on the team.

Suppose you feel that your boss makes you work much harder than the other two people on your crew. There is a right way and a wrong way to approach this issue.

> *Wrong way:* You know, Al, I'm not some kind of workhorse. Everyone else gets to sit around drinking coffee while I'm hauling 2×4s all over the lot. What do I look like, a jackass?

> *Right way:* Al, lately I feel I've been pulling more than my share of the weight. I'm happy to go the extra mile, but I feel like I'm the only one who does that. Do you remember yesterday when we got that load of 2×4s? I had to unload the truck all by myself, while the other guys were just putting away tools and sweeping up. I think the job would have gone a lot faster if someone had helped me.

RESPECT YOUR SUPERVISOR'S DECISIONS.   Once your boss makes a decision, it's final. Respect the boss's decision, understanding that she has the authority to make that decision. Sometimes supervisors feel backed into a corner when their employees confront them, and they may react hastily. Very often, they will sleep on the issue, then try to make amends the next day. So give your supervisor the benefit of the doubt. She wants to do the right thing as much as you do.

Activity 4.9: Recognizing the Potential for Conflict (Collaborative Activity)

Sometimes the best way to prevent conflict is to recognize the *potential* for conflict. When you're aware of situations that can result in conflict, you can take steps to improve the situation before conflict arises. Read the following case study. Then, in groups of four, answer the questions that follow.

KATE'S TEAM

Kate Davis is a 26-year-old African-American woman. She attended a state college for two years and took courses in surveying and soil analysis. She then went to work for a construction company, where she worked for four years. She is the new foreperson at McManus Construction, and her crew is made up of the following five people:

- **Martin** is an African-American man, age 45. He has 20 years experience in construction, and has worked for McManus Construction for the last 15 years. He is a high school graduate and was an exceptional football player much admired by all the cheerleaders. He is an excellent worker, and he expected to be promoted when the last foreman left. He was surprised when he found out that Kate Davis would be the new foreperson.

- **Sam** is a white man, age 30. He worked at several sales jobs after graduating from high school, then came to work for McManus Construction. He has been with the company for seven years. When he was a teenager, his mother took a trip to Mexico, where she got mugged.

- **Mary** is a white woman, age 28. After one year of college, she got married and subsequently had three children. For eight years she was a homemaker, hoping to someday complete her education. But a divorce forced her to go to work. She has worked for McManus Construction for two years.

- **Raul** is a Mexican-American, age 40, with 20 years' construction experience. For several years he owned his own company, but times have been tough and he had to shut the business down.

- **Trevor** is African-American, 19 years old. His job at McManus is his first construction job. He has a bossy older sister.

TEAM MEMBERS:

1. _____   2. _____
3. _____   4. _____

Identify at least five possible sources of conflict on Kate's team.

1. _____
2. _____
3. _____
4. _____
5. _____

For each possible source of conflict, suggest two ways to prevent that conflict.

1. (a) _____

   (b) _____

2. (a) _____

   (b) _____

3. (a) _____

   (b) _____

4. (a) _____

   (b) _____

5. (a) _____

   (b) _____

Activity 4.10: Resolving Conflict

Your goal in this activity is to work through the conflict resolution process. After you've read and thought about the situation, complete the grid that follows.

THE SITUATION

Three construction crews have been assigned to a new project in the Miami area. You are on one of the crews.

To keep the job moving, the three crews take three staggered lunch shifts. Each day, both the drink and the snack machines are completely empty by the time the second lunch shift begins. As a result, about half the workers end up without something to eat or drink during lunch. Workers in the second and third lunch shifts have been very upset about this.

You realize that this situation is causing bad feelings on the job, and you want to do something about it.

Conflict Resolution Grid	
1. What exactly is the conflict?	
2. What has caused the conflict?	
3. People grumble about this situation, but no one is doing anything about it. How can you bring this conflict into the open?	
4. You can't resolve this conflict on your own. You need the cooperation of others. How will you get their cooperation?	
5. What are some possible solutions? Is collaboration or compromise possible? What is the common ground? That is, what outcome will benefit everybody?	
6. Once you've resolved the problem, how will you go about making sure that the conflict doesn't arise again?	

Activity 4.11: Self-Assessment: How Well Do You Handle Conflict?

Can you quickly resolve disagreements with co-workers, or are you more likely to let conflicts linger? Take this quiz to find out. Answer each question *truthfully*, then add up your score.

	Often, Usually	Sometimes, Occasionally	Rarely, Never
1. I feel the need to prove to other people that my opinions are right.	☐	☐	☐
2. I have a tough time working with people whose work habits are different from mine.	☐	☐	☐
3. I get impatient easily.	☐	☐	☐
4. When discussing problems, I lose my temper.	☐	☐	☐
5. When somebody makes a mistake, I get annoyed and point out the mistake angrily.	☐	☐	☐
6. Rather than walk away from someone who's shouting at me, I shout back.	☐	☐	☐
7. I tend to get involved in other people's squabbles, and I take sides with the person I think is right.	☐	☐	☐
8. I think there are a lot of annoying people in the world, and I think that they're purposely trying to get on my nerves.	☐	☐	☐
9. Rather than openly confront a problem, I tend to keep quiet about it and hope it goes away.	☐	☐	☐
10. When I'm trying to resolve an argument, I feel that the most important thing is to get my way.	☐	☐	☐
11. I find it hard to admit when I'm wrong.	☐	☐	☐
12. It's tough for me to apologize when I've done something wrong.	☐	☐	☐
13. I don't think I do anything to annoy my co-workers.	☐	☐	☐
14. When somebody is annoying me, I'm pretty blunt about telling them so.	☐	☐	☐
15. I think that "giving in" means "losing."	☐	☐	☐

SCORING: Give yourself 1 point for each "Often/Usually" you checked, 2 points for each "Sometimes/Occasionally," and 3 points for each "Rarely/Never."

Number of "Often/Usually"   _____ × 1 = _____
Number of "Sometimes"   _____ × 2 = _____
Number of "Rarely/Never"   _____ × 3 = _____
Total   _____

ASSESSMENT AND SUGGESTIONS:
- 40–45 points: You are adept at handling and resolving conflict, and you know how to act as a "peacemaker."
- 30–39 points: You are swayed by different moods. Sometimes you actively try to resolve differences with other people, but other times you may not deal with conflict effectively. Keep in mind that both collaboration and compromise can help to resolve conflict.

- 29 points or lower: You may have the tendency to contribute to conflict rather than resolve it. Try to achieve greater flexibility in your thinking and behavior. Try to see both sides of the issues you confront, and work on keeping your emotions separate from your job.

Activity 4.12: Resolving Conflicts: A Quick Quiz

Choose the best answer for each of the following questions.

_____ 1. It's summertime, and you have a lot of roofing work to do. You've shaved your head so that the heat doesn't get to you. Mike is one of your co-workers, and he has a big nose. Mike sees you in the morning and says, "Hey, baldie! You look like Mr. Clean!" What's your best response?

    a. You say, "Yeah, and you have a nose bigger than the Grand Canyon!"

    b. You wait until lunchtime, then have a few words with Mike, letting him know that you don't appreciate his comments.

    c. You walk away, thinking this isn't worth arguing about.

    d. You walk up to Mike and tell him that you're not going to put up with his insults.

_____ 2. This morning, your boss called you to the side and talked to you about something you did wrong yesterday. You made a few serious mistakes, and now you need to dismantle yesterday's work and do it all over again. He's patient with you and explains everything clearly, but he also says that you may need to work a few extra hours tonight to make up for lost time.

    Keeping the empathy rule in mind, evaluate how well your boss did his job and how you should react.

    a. Your boss was way out of line. If you were making mistakes, he should have told you about them yesterday. You have the right to be angry.

    b. Your boss did his job well, but it would have been better if he'd told you about your mistakes in front of a few other people. You should fix yesterday's mistakes but not have to work the overtime.

    c. Your boss took your feelings into account by talking to you privately instead of in front of other people. You should admit your mistakes and not complain about having to fix them or work overtime.

    d. Your boss has the right to point out your mistakes, but he didn't go about it the right way. You should dismantle the work you did yesterday, but he should get somebody more qualified to do the work properly.

_____ 3. You're a mellow person. You like to work at a nice, even pace—and you're pretty strict about putting away tools when you're done with them. You're mostly a quiet person—you talk occasionally, but you really concentrate when you're working. Today you got a new apprentice. By the end of the day, you realize that he's jittery, he drops things, and he talks a lot. He works really fast, and you can't keep track of where he is or what he's done. How would you assess the potential for conflict in this situation?

a. There's not likely to be much conflict, since young apprentices usually work too fast.

b. There may be some conflict over who puts away the tools, but other than that, you should get along fine.

c. There is potential for much conflict, so you should get the issues out into the open as soon as possible.

d. Due to the potential for conflict, you should change your working style so that it's more in line with the apprentice's style.

_____ 4. You're walking across the construction site, when two of your co-workers (Rob and Jorge) call you over. They're arguing because, Jorge says, Rob borrowed a pair of gloves from Jorge and never returned them. Jorge says to you, "Go ahead—tell Rob that everyone knows that he takes things and doesn't return them. That's why nobody wants to lend him anything." What should you do?

a. Tell Rob and Jorge that their argument is their business, and you don't want to get involved in it.

b. Tell Rob that Jorge is speaking the truth, and that he should return the gloves or buy Jorge a new pair.

c. Say that you'll send the foreman over to resolve the problem.

d. Tell Rob and Jorge to shut up and stop bothering you with their problems.

_____ 5. You and your co-worker, Mickey, have been arguing for a while about a small issue. You work together on a two-person job, and Mickey likes to take lunch from 11 A.M. to noon. You prefer a later lunch, and like to go from 12:30 to 1:30. But you both have to take lunch at the same time. Which of the following would NOT be a compromise that the two of you can reach?

a. You go to the foreman and complain that Mickey is too difficult to work with.

b. You both agree to take lunch from 12:00 to 1:00—later than Mickey wants, but earlier than you want.

c. You both agree that on Mondays and Tuesdays you'll both take lunch from 11 to noon, and on Wednesdays and Thursdays you'll both take lunch from 12:30 to 1:30. On Fridays, you'll flip a coin.

d. Each morning, you'll flip a coin to decide what time you'll both take lunch that day.

_____ 6. Yesterday you got really angry at Jose, one of the guys on your crew. You thought he was careless and that his mistakes caused a serious problem that will take you all of today to fix. You had a big argument and exchanged some rough words. Today, you found out that the mistake was actually caused by *you*. What should you do?

a. Just forget about the whole situation, but promise yourself that you won't lose your temper again.

b. Admit your mistake to Jose and apologize for your behavior.

c. Ask another co-worker to apologize to Jose for you, so that you don't have to feel embarrassed.

d. Let Jose continue to think the mistake was his fault, so that you can feel that you've won the argument.

_____ 7. You have a co-worker, Calvin, who drives you crazy. He has the annoying habit of laughing after everything he says and everything you say, whether it's funny or not. You can't stand talking to him because all he does is laugh nervously. Yet the two of you have to work together very closely, and you feel you have to say something. What approach should you take, and what should you say?

a. Be up front and open. "Calvin, do you realize that you laugh after everything you say? What's up with that?"

b. Use humor. "Hey, Calvin, did you know that you laugh like a hyena?"

c. Be tactful. "Calvin, I know you're a happy guy, but did you ever realize that the way you laugh drives me nuts?"

d. Be gentle. "Cal, I can't be as funny as you think I am. *No one can be that funny!* It's hard for me to concentrate on what we're saying and doing when there's so much laughing."

_____ 8. You need to talk to your foreman, Arnie. You really, really need to take next Tuesday off because your wife is having surgery. The company has a policy that everyone must ask for time off three weeks in advance. Arnie agrees to talk with you at lunchtime. What do you say to him?

a. "Look, I really need next Tuesday off—that's the bottom line."

b. "Arnie, is there any way at all I can take next Tuesday off? I know it's against policy, but this is an emergency—my wife is having surgery. I will make up the time whenever you want me to."

c. "I know you're going to give me a hard time about this, but I have to have next Tuesday off. My wife is having surgery. You may not care about this, but I do."

d. "Arnie, please, please give me next Tuesday off. It's the least you can do for me, after everything I've done for you."

Reading Skills I
The Basics

66 Reading is to the mind what exercise is to the body. 99
—Richard Steele, English writer (1672–1729)

The last few years have seen an explosion of technological advances. Technology has made it possible for you to chat on the phone while you walk down the street, to receive a fax at remote locations, and to check the weather conditions a world away. Cellular telephones, beepers, hand-held personal computers (sometimes called *PDAs,* short for *personal digital assistants*),[1] and mini fax machines have become common sights just about everywhere.

Despite all these advances, however, the business world still revolves around the *written word.* The construction industry is no different. Construction businesses of all sizes rely on written instructions, specifications, blueprints, correspondence, and progress reports to get the job done. As the Internet and the World Wide Web grow in importance, reading will become even more important.

In this module, you'll learn how to become a more effective reader. You'll find tips for improving your reading comprehension, whether you're skimming for information or making your way through a heavy procedures manual. The benefits of being a good reader are numerous. They include success on the job, greater efficiency, increased understanding of processes and procedures, and improved communication skills.

5.1 TIPS FOR READING EFFECTIVELY

The good news is: You've been reading for many years now, and reading is already second nature to you. The following general suggestions can help you better comprehend the wide variety of construction documents you'll encounter on the job.

READ WITH A PURPOSE.   Before you begin reading, understand what you're trying to accomplish. Are you looking for a specific piece of information in a blueprint or isometric? Are you reading a memo that outlines the company's policy regarding sick and vacation time? Are you reading an e-mail in which your foreman asks for specific information?

Knowing *why* you are reading will make you a much more active and effective reader. Everything is *written* for a purpose—so everything should be *read* with a purpose.

KNOW WHAT TO READ AND WHAT TO SKIP.   We live in a world jam-packed with information. At home, you receive a mailbox full of junk each day. The Sunday newspaper can run to hundreds of pages. Industry magazines, such as *Commercial Building, Concrete Construction,* and *Masonry Construction,* can be packed with more information than you can digest in one sitting.

To manage your reading load, quickly skim the reading material that comes your way. Ask yourself: How important is this material to my job, my safety, or my health? The most important material should be read first and in its entirety. Material that is interesting, but not important, can be put aside for later. Unimportant material (for example, advertisements and direct marketing letters for products you don't want or need) can be thrown out.

---

[1]For further discussion of PDAs, see Appendix A.

SKIMMING EFFECTIVELY AND SCANNING FOR INFORMATION

Skimming and scanning are two important techniques you can use to determine how much of something you need to read. They also can help you quickly and effectively find the information you're seeking.

Skimming means reading only for key ideas and ignoring nonessential material. You can generally get the key ideas of the piece (whether it's a memo, a magazine article, or a textbook chapter) by doing the following:

1. Read the title and the headings. These will provide much information regarding the contents.

2. Sometimes articles and memos have an introductory and/or concluding section that summarizes everything. Read the whole introduction and the summary if these are included.

3. Look for graphs, tables, and charts that summarize key ideas.

4. Notice material that is set off from the main text, either in *italics* or **boldface.** Also look for numbered lists (1, 2, 3, and so on) that summarize important material. Sometimes bullets (•) are used to indicate the items in a list.

5. Read the first sentence of each paragraph. Use your judgment to determine whether you should read the entire paragraph. Many times, the key ideas are found in the first sentence of each paragraph.

When you *scan*, you aren't really reading. Instead, you are looking for the answer to a particular question, such as: "Whom do I call to get this machine serviced?" or "What is the difference between a chain fall and a come-along?" To find the answer to your question, run your eyes down each page, paying closer attention to the following:

- Table of contents, including titles, headings and subheadings
- Index
- **Boldfaced** and *italicized* words
- Glossary
- Tables and graphics that summarize information
- Page tabs

TIP: You do not have to read everything that comes your way. Read selectively.

ONCE YOU'VE DECIDED WHAT TO READ CLOSELY, CONCENTRATE AND READ SLOWLY. On a construction site (and in many other places), it's easy to get distracted. Technical material is often crammed with information. Material that is dense with facts, figures, instructions, and diagrams requires you to *focus* and *concentrate* on what you're reading.

So, get rid of distractions that interrupt you while you're reading. Go to a quieter place. Don't try to read while you're listening to the radio, or while the people around you are talking. If you're reading at home, turn off the stereo, the

TV, and the telephone. Go into a quiet room and shut the door behind you. Don't attempt to do two things at once. In other words, don't try to chat on the phone while you're reading a safety manual. You'll miss important information.

> **TIP:** The more important the reading material, the more slowly you should read it. It's OK to read nonessential materials quickly, such as company newsletters or general-interest magazines (for example, *Time* or *Newsweek*).

TAKE NOTES OR HIGHLIGHT IMPORTANT MATERIAL.   Sometimes you are given a lot of information to read. For example, safety manuals can be hundreds of pages long. To help you remember what you've read, use a yellow highlighter to mark important material. Then, when you're done reading, you can go back and reread what you highlighted as a mini-review.

If you use a highlighter, make sure you do not highlight too much material. Too much highlighting is distracting. In general, highlighters should be used only for key points and important material, such as titles, key terms, definitions, dates, and essential facts. Be careful not to highlight trivia or minor details.

For example, suppose that you are reading a textbook about warning barricades. The following example shows the text marked with an appropriate amount of highlighting:

> Warning barricades alert workers to hazards but provide no real protection. Typical warning barricades are made of plastic tape or rope strung from wire or between posts. The tape or rope is color-coded:
>
> - Red means danger. No one can enter an area with a red warning barricade. A red barricade is used when there is danger from falling objects or when a load is suspended over an area.
> - Yellow means caution. You can enter an area with a yellow barricade, but be sure you know what the hazard is, and be careful. Yellow barricades are used around wet areas or areas containing loose dust. Yellow with black lettering warns of physical hazards such as bumping into something, stumbling, or falling.
> - Yellow and purple means radiation warning. No one may pass a yellow and purple barricade. These barricades are often used where piping welds are being X-rayed.[2]

Note that the highlighting touches on all the key points, but is not overdone.

As you read, you can also take notes in the margins or in a separate notebook. Taking notes and highlighting are excellent ways to remember new material.

USE VISUALIZATION.   When you *visualize*, you create a mental picture of what you're reading. Picture yourself performing the tasks you're reading about and you'll find them much easier to remember. Visualization can be particularly helpful when you're reading difficult material.

For example, suppose you're reading a procedures manual explaining how to check a 90-degree bend you've just made in a conduit. The manual might read as follows:

---

[2]National Center for Construction Education and Research, *Core Curriculum* (Upper Saddle River, NJ/Columbus, OH: Prentice Hall, 2000), Trainee Module 00101, pp. 1-24, 1-25.

Step One: With the back of the bend on the floor, measure to the end of the conduit stub-up to make sure it is the right length.

Step Two: Check the 90-degree angle of the bend with a square or at the angle formed by the floor and a wall. A torpedo level may also be used.[3]

As you read, visualize each step in your head. Picture yourself placing the back of the bend on the floor, then measuring to the end of the conduit. Then picture yourself using a square or torpedo level to check that the angle is exactly 90 degrees.

REREAD UNTIL YOU UNDERSTAND.   When you're reading technical material, don't expect to understand everything the first time. Rather, expect to read the material several times before grasping it completely.

Don't feel frustrated if you don't fully understand something, even after you've read it several times. Instead, write down questions to ask an expert, perhaps your foreman or another experienced person on the job.

TIP: A technical writer's job is to explain everything perfectly, but sometimes a demonstration is worth a thousand printed words.

Activity 5.1: Setting Reading Priorities

To be an effective reader, you need to separate what's important from what can wait. Imagine that you receive the following printed materials on Monday. Using the numbers 1–8, prioritize your reading load. Use 1 for the item you should read first, 2 for the item you should read second, and so on. Put an asterisk (*) next to any item you should read as soon as you get it. Briefly explain the order you chose.

___ The new issue of *Sports Illustrated*

___ A memo from your company's fire safety inspector outlining new safety procedures

___ A piece of mail from the National Arbor Day Society asking you to contribute money

___ A letter from your company's benefits department outlining changes in the tax law and how these changes will affect your pension

___ An e-mail from your brother in another state with attached electronic pictures of his new motorcycle

___ A revised blueprint of the project you're working on

___ An advertisement from a company offering stock in a start-up Internet company

___ An e-mail from your boss outlining the hours you're expected to work next week

---

[3]National Center for Construction Education and Research, *Electrical Trainee Guide* (Upper Saddle River, NJ/ Columbus, OH: Prentice Hall, 2000), Trainee Module 26102, pp. 2-6, 2-7.

Activity 5.2: Highlighting for Improved Comprehension

Highlighting can help you find information when you go back and reread. Two construction related passages are reproduced below. Use a highlighter to highlight the most important materials. (If you don't have a highlighter, use a pen to underline the key information.) Remember to highlight the appropriate amount—not too much, not too little.

Use what you learned in Section 5.1 to guide your highlighting. Specifically, remember to look for:

- The title, which gives you the key to what the passage is about
- Key words or important phrases, sometimes indicated by *italics* or **boldface**
- Bulleted or numbered lists that summarize information
- Important dates or numbers that you need to know or memorize

Passage A: The Nature of Soil[4]

To make use of the samples taken during subsurface exploration, it is necessary to understand something of the nature of soil, types of soil, and how they react under various circumstances. This topic, in all its facets, is a complete study in itself, and we deal here with the subject only as it pertains to construction.

For engineers and architects, *soil* denotes all the fragmented material found in the earth's crust. Included is material ranging from individual rocks of various sizes, through sand and gravel, to fine-grained clays. Whereas particles of sand and gravel are visible to the naked eye, particles of some fine-grained clays cannot be distinguished even when viewed through low-powered microscopes.

All soils are made up of large or small particles derived from one or more of the minerals that make up solid rock. These particles have been transported from their original location by various means. For example, there are notable deposits of *eolian soil* in western North America, which were deposited by wind. There are also numerous deposits of *glacial till*, a mixture of sand, gravel, silt, and clay, moved and deposited by glaciers. Other soils have been deposited by the action of water, whereas others, known as *residual soils*, consist of rock particles that have not been moved from their original location, but are products of the deterioration of solid rock.

Soil types, as determined by particle size, are as follows:

- *Cobbles and boulders:* Larger than 3 in. (75 mm) in diameter
- *Gravel:* Smaller than 3 in. (75 mm) and larger than #4 (5 mm) sieve (approximately 1/4 in.)
- *Sand:* Particles smaller than #4 (5 mm) sieve and larger than #200 sieve (40,000 openings per square inch)
- *Silts:* Particles smaller than 0.02 mm and larger than 0.002 mm in diameter
- *Clays:* Particles smaller than 0.002 mm in diameter.

For purposes of establishing the abilities of these soils to safely carry a load, they are classified as *cohesionless soils, cohesive soils, miscellaneous soils,* and *rock*.

---

[4]Cameron K. Andres and Ronald C. Smith, *Principles and Practices of Commercial Construction* (Upper Saddle River, NJ/Columbus, OH: Prentice Hall, 2001), pp. 3–4.

Cohesionless soils include sand and gravel—soils in which particles have little or no tendency to stick together under pressure. Cohesive soils include dense silt, medium dense silt, hard clay, stiff clay, firm clay, and soft clay. The particles of these soils tend to stick together, particularly with the addition of water. Miscellaneous soils include glacial till and conglomerate. The latter is a mixture of sand, gravel, and clay, with the clay acting as a cement to hold the particles together.

Rock is subdivided into *massive, foliated, sedimentary,* and *soft* or *shattered.* Massive rocks are very hard, have no visible bedding planes or laminations, and have widely spaced, nearly vertical or horizontal joints. They are comparable to the best concrete. Foliated rocks are also hard, but have sloping joints, which preclude equal compressive strength in all directions. They are comparable to sound structured concrete. Sedimentary rocks include hard shales, sandstones, limestones, and silt-stones, with softer components. Rocks in this category may be likened to good brick masonry. Soft or shattered rocks include those that are soft or broken but not displaced from their natural beds. They do not become plastic when wet and are comparable to poor brick masonry.

Passage B: The History of Paint[5]

Craftspersons in the painting trade have a long history. Paint has been used as a form of decoration since prehistoric times. Early cave dwellers used plants, clay, and water to make paint. They used this paint to decorate their bodies and the walls of caves. Most of what these early people painted were lines that formed pictures. The people of ancient Egypt used paint in tombs, palaces, and on temple walls using colors which they prepared from the soil. By 1500 B.C., they imported dyes such as indigo and madder. From these they made blue and red **pigments.** Pigments impart color and other properties to paint. The Egyptians were the first to use protective coatings. They applied forms of pitch and balsam to seal their ships. They also developed and used water-based paints produced from freshly-burned lime (*whitewash*) with milk curds as a **binder.** A binder serves to bind or cement the pigment particles together upon drying of paint.

The Greeks, Romans, and others copied Egyptian painting practices. The early Greeks developed painting into an art form. They not only decorated flat surfaces, but painted human beings, wood panels, and vases. Paint was widely used by the Romans, who are credited with the introduction of white lead as a pigment in 430 B.C. The ancient Romans used stencils to paint borders on wall surfaces. They also painted stone and plaster to look like granite and marble. The Roman Empire collapsed in the 400s A.D. After that, the art of paint-making became lost to the Western world until the Middle Ages (500 to 1450 A.D.), when the English and other Europeans began making and using paints to paint churches, public buildings, and the homes of the wealthy.

In Asia, the first pigments were developed before 6000 B.C. Coloring components included natural ores and organic pigments. Binders included color crayons sometimes made from boiled rice. **Vehicles,** the liquid part of paint in which pigments are dissolved or dispersed, were made from gum arabic, egg white (albumin), gelatin, and beeswax. The Chinese are credited with the use of lacquer as early as the Chou dynasty (1122 to 221 B.C.). During the Ching dynasty, the Chinese began using iron oxide to produce the color red.

Paint manufacturing began in Europe around the 1700s. Manufacturers ground pigments and oils on a stone table with a round stone. Their

[5]Adapted from National Center for Construction Education and Research, *Painting Trainee Guide, Level 1* (Upper Saddle River, NJ/Columbus, OH: Prentice Hall, 1997), pp. 5–9.

paints were made for limited private use. The Industrial Revolution in England changed this. In the late 17th century and early 18th century, power-driven machinery was brought into the paint-making process. At this time, **white lead,** a white pigment obtained from lead sulphate, became more widely available. These new machines and white lead allowed for the development and production of protective, anti-corrosion paints used for protecting metal structures such as bridges. The first varnish factories were started in Europe, beginning with England, in 1790.

In the 18th century, there was a general increase in the availability of vehicles and pigments. White lead was put to more uses. Also, there was an extensive extraction of linseed oil from the flax plant. Paint grade zinc oxide was also developed. By the 19th century, paint manufacturing changed. For the first time, the two basic ingredients, vehicle and pigment, were mixed together before distribution.

The evolution of materials technology throughout the 20th century has produced a proliferation of paint and related products. Today, linseed oil is found in only a few paints and in some putty and caulking compounds. After World War II, the dye and plastics industries also began extensive research and development of new painting-related products. The dye industry created new pigments, while the plastic industry developed new **polymers.** Polymers are substances in which the molecules, consisting of one or more structural units, are repeated any number of times. Synthetic **resins** were produced as new binders for paint that provided significant improvement in weathering, water resistance, toughness, elasticity, and resistance to chemical exposure. These binders included alkyds, phenolics, chlorinated rubbers, vinyls, latexes, and acrylics. Resins are natural or synthetic substances which, when heated, are soluble in drying oils and solvents.

Shortly after World War II, new paints containing epoxy and urethane resins and zinc-rich coatings began to be produced in the United States. Over time, these coatings were enhanced by the development of high-quality **solvents** and **additives** that improved their application and performance properties. Solvents are liquids used in paints to dissolve pigments and other materials. Solvents evaporate during drying. These high-performance materials became the main coatings for protecting steel in industrial environments. Waterborne (water-based) coatings using acrylic latex binders were first introduced in the early 1950s. Their use gained in popularity during the 1950s and 1960s because they were easy to use and nontoxic.

During the latter half of the 20th century and up to the present, advances in painting materials and methods of application have been driven by increased concerns about health, safety, and the environment. In the United States, the passage of the Clean Air Act in 1970, and its amendments in 1990, mandated the containment of all sources of air pollution including carbon-based solvents generally classified as **volatile organic compounds (VOCs).** Oil-based paints use VOC solvents such as mineral spirits to keep them liquid until they are applied. Upon evaporation into the atmosphere, VOCs react with nitrous oxides (combustion compounds from automotive emissions and the burning of fuels) and sunlight to form ozone and air pollutants. Ozone is an unstable form of oxygen that is highly reactive. Ozone in the Earth's upper atmosphere (stratosphere) protects the Earth and its inhabitants from harmful ultraviolet radiation. However, ozone trapped within the Earth's lower atmosphere (troposphere) contributes to smog that can be hazardous to humans, animals, and plant life. Emissions of VOCs from painting and various other sources can also contribute to poor indoor air quality.

Today, because the Environmental Protection Agency (EPA) is requiring the elimination of air pollution, the environmental laws and regulations that limit the amount of VOCs in paint are increasingly restrictive. This means that fewer VOC-type solvents can be used, causing the focus of most new materials technology to be toward the development of better waterborne paints. Today's waterborne paints and coatings are made in a variety of resin types, such as epoxy, alkyd, vinyl, latex, acrylic, and others. They are as effective on outdoor surfaces as they are on indoor surfaces. Special coatings are made to protect metal, concrete, and other industrial **substrates** (surfaces being painted) in mildly harsh environments. Other types developed to comply with the air pollution laws include high solids and 100% solid materials. These are often difficult to apply, resulting in a number of paint manufacturers offering training and licensing to painters to be exclusive applicators of their product(s).

Activity 5.3: Skimming for Main Ideas

Refer to Passage A in Activity 5.2, "The Nature of Soil." Follow the directions for "Skimming Effectively" in the box on page 105, and skim this passage. Answer these questions based on your skim.

1. **Read the title.**

   What is the general topic of the passage? _____

2. **Look for material set off from the main text.**

   The passage contains a bulleted list summarizing five types of soil, as determined by particle size. These five types are: (a) _____ , (b) _____ , (c) _____ , (d) _____ , and (e) _____ .

3. **Read the first sentence of each paragraph. By doing this, you can:**
   a. Define *soil*. _____
   b. Classify the five types of soil by particle size. Which is the largest type of soil? _____ The smallest? _____
   c. Classify soils by their abilities to carry a load. The four types of soil, classified by load-carrying ability, are: _____ , _____ , _____ , and _____ .

Activity 5.4: Scanning for Information

Refer to Passage B in Activity 5.2, "The History of Paint." Follow the directions for "Scanning for Information" in the box on page 105, and answer these questions based on your scan.

1. What are *pigments?*
   (*Hint:* Scan for the boldface term, **pigments.**)

   _____

2. In what years did the Chou dynasty rule China?
   (*Hint:* You know that you're looking for a date, so scan for numbers/years, then look for the words "Chou dynasty" near those numbers.)

   _____

3. What does "VOC" stand for?
   (*Hint:* Scan for a block of all capital letters to locate the definition of "VOC.")

   _____

4. Distinguish between *vehicles* and *white lead.*
   (*Hint:* Look to see if either of these terms appears in boldface or italics, to help you quickly locate the definitions.)

_____

5. What color is iron oxide used to produce?
   (*Hint:* Run your eyes down the page, looking for the word "oxide." This is a rare word, and would most likely "jump off the page" at you.)

_____

5.2 READING TO FIND INFORMATION

On the job, you'll sometimes need to consult a manual or book to find a specific piece of information. Because manuals and books are often complex, sometimes with hundreds or thousands of pages, knowing how and where to find specific information can save you a lot of time and energy.

Publishers and writers build special features and "shortcuts" into their books or manuals to help you locate information. Learn to use each of the following shortcuts effectively.

Table of Contents

The *table of contents* appears at the front of the book or manual. It lists the titles and contents of all the book's chapters or modules, along with the appropriate page numbers. Each chapter or module may be further subdivided into smaller sections, each with its own heading.

Suppose you are looking for information in your safety manual on the proper use of fire extinguishers. As you look at the table of contents, you may see that the title of Chapter 6 is "Preventing and Fighting Fires." You can assume that Chapter 6 includes material on fire extinguishers, and you can go right to that chapter.

Index

The *index* appears at the back of the book or manual. It is an alphabetical listing of all the topics included in the book, along with the pages on which those topics appear. So, if you need information on fire extinguishers, you can turn to the index and look under "F" for "fire extinguishers." You may see an entry that looks like this:

    Fire extinguishers
        Types of, 145
        Use of, 147–148

This index entry means that you can find information on the *types of* fire extinguishers on page 145, and information on the proper *use of* fire extinguishers on pages 147–148.

Sometimes books are not paginated beginning with page 1 and continuing through the end. Instead, each chapter may begin with a new page 1. The first page of Chapter 8 would be page 8-1, the second page of Chapter 8 would be page 8-2, and so on. To get a sense of how the book is paginated, flip through the table of contents and the book itself, and familiarize yourself with the system used by the publisher or author.

Glossary

Some manuals include a *glossary,* an alphabetical listing of key terms included in the book, along with their definitions. A glossary is like a mini-dictionary that is specific to one particular field of study. Here are some sample glossary entries:

Adhesive	A natural or synthetic material, generally in paste or liquid form, used to fasten or glue material together, install floor tile, fabricate plastic laminate-covered work, or otherwise attach work items together
Admixture	A substance other than portland cement, water, and aggregates included in a concrete mixture, for the purpose of altering one or more properties of the concrete; aids setting, finishing, or wearing of the concrete.
Aggregate	Hard, inert material, such as sand, gravel, and crushed stone, which is combined with portland cement and water to produce concrete; must be properly cleaned and well graded as required.[6]

The glossary usually appears at the end of the book or manual, just before the index. The glossary may also appear as an *appendix,* a section of important or reference information that also appears toward the end of the book. You will find a glossary of construction terminology in Appendix C of this book.

If you're unsure of a word's meaning, you can find it out quickly by looking at a glossary. For more general words, you can turn to a regular dictionary. (We discuss glossaries and dictionaries in more detail in Section 5.6.)

Tables of Information

Many books and manuals include *tables of information* that help you find important facts and figures at a glance. Tables can also be found in appendixes at the end of the book, or printed on the inside of the front and back covers.

An old saying goes "A picture is worth a thousand words." The same is true of tables. Tables often summarize facts and figures in a way that is much easier to read than long lists of facts and figures. For example, the following table compares silver, copper, and aluminum in wiring applications on three factors: cost per cubic inch, conductivity, and compatibility problems with other metals.[7]

Material	Cost per Cubic Inch	Conductivity (Using Copper as a Reference: Cu = 1)	Compatibility Problems
Silver	$41.60	1.05	No
Copper	$00.20	1.00	No
Aluminum	$00.08	0.61	Yes

This table condenses much information into an easy-to-read format. The table shows at a glance that aluminum is by far the cheapest, but that it suffers from compatibility problems with other metals. It also shows that silver is the most expensive, but that silver may be the best choice when superior conductivity is required (as in receivers that must pick up faint radio frequency signals).

---

[6]Ralph Liebing, *The Construction Industry: Processes, Players, and Practices* (Upper Saddle River, NJ: Prentice Hall, 2001), p. 189.

[7]Maris Roze, *Technical Communication: The Practical Craft,* 3rd ed. (Upper Saddle River, NJ: Prentice Hall, 1997), p. 39.

Page Tabs

In thick books, *page tabs* on the outside of the pages can help you find information quickly. Page tabs can be seen even when the book is closed, and they help you flip directly to the section you need. For example, you might need a quick overview of the OSHA regulations surrounding trench work. The code book you're using might have a page tab that says "OSHA." This tab will help you flip quickly to the OSHA part of the book.

TIP: You can add your own tabs to frequently consulted books by using Post-It Notes or other sticky notes.

Activity 5.5: Finding Information: Using a Table of Contents I

Reprinted below is a portion of the table of contents from a book titled *Construction Methods and Management*.[8] Use this table of contents to answer the questions that follow.

Contents

---

[8]S. W. Nunnally, *Construction Methods and Management,* 5th ed. (Upper Saddle River, NJ/Columbus, OH: Prentice Hall, 2001), pp. vi–vii.

QUESTIONS:

_____ 1. In which chapter would you find information on the production of concrete?
   a. Chapter 1
   b. Chapter 6
   c. Chapter 7
   d. Chapter 10

_____ 2. Suppose you're looking for information on rock ripping techniques. To which page should you turn?

    a. 21

    b. 46

    c. 195

    d. 215

_____ 3. Glancing through the table of contents, you see the term "clamshells" as the title of Section 3-5. You don't know what a clamshell is. To what part of the book could you turn to find a definition of *clamshell?*

    a. the glossary

    b. the index

    c. Chapter 5

    d. the page tabs

_____ 4. Chapters 3, 8, and 9 all begin with an "introduction" as the first section. What do you think these introductions might contain?

    a. A general overview of the material in that chapter

    b. Key terms that will be used in that chapter

    c. Background information necessary to understand the contents of that chapter

    d. All of the above

_____ 5. In which section of the text can you find material on safety precautions?

    a. 2-5

    b. 5-2

    c. 7-3

    d. 10-6

Activity 5.6: Finding Information: Using a Table of Contents II

Here is a good chance to preview other modules in this book. Turn to this book's table of contents and answer the following questions.

_____ 1. In which module or modules would you find information on improving your listening skills?

    a. Module 3

    b. Modules 3 and 4

    c. Modules 1 and 2

    d. Module 8

_____ 2. Your foreman has asked you to prepare a memo for distribution to your entire team. In which section would you find information to help you write an effective memo?

    a. Section 1.4.1

    b. Section 8.1.1

    c. Section 6.5.2

    d. Section 3.1

_____ 3. What is the topic of the third main section in Module 8?
   a. Writing for different purposes
   b. Formatting an e-mail properly
   c. Writing field and progress reports
   d. Handling bad news

_____ 4. You're about to embark on an interview for a better paying job. Which section of this book should you consult the night before?
   a. Module 2
   b. Section 5.4
   c. The glossary
   d. Appendix B

_____ 5. You have difficulty handling bad news. You tend to overreact and get very upset. On what page would you find some advice for handling bad news more effectively?
   a. Page 32
   b. Page 14
   c. Page 82
   d. Page 83

Activity 5.7: Finding Information: Using an Index

The following excerpt is taken from the index of *Tools for Success: Soft Skills for the Construction Industry*, a human relations manual for construction professionals.[9] Use the excerpt to answer the questions that follow.

Subject Index
   relaxation techniques, 119, 124-125
   respect
       for co-workers, 23, 24, 49-50
       for foremen, 32
   responsibility, taking, 7
   sexual advances, 181-183
   sexual harassment, 179-190
       complaints of, 183
       definition of, 181-182
       physical, 182-183
       prevention of, 182-183
       recognition of, 179-181
       understanding, 186-187
       verbal, 182
   shy people, working with, 50
   sickness, on the job, 5
   stereotyping, 50-51
       definition of, 50
       in the workplace, 50-51
   stool pigeon, 35

[9]Steven A. Rigolosi, *Tools for Success: Soft Skills for the Construction Industry* (Upper Saddle River, NJ/Columbus, OH: Prentice Hall, 2000), p. 220.

1. Place a checkmark next to the topics that you will find covered in *Tools for Success: Soft Skills for the Construction Industry.*

   _____ shy people

   _____ stress

   _____ social stigmas

   _____ time management

   _____ time cards

   _____ tobacco use

   _____ working with women

   _____ weather conditions on the job

2. To what page should you turn for a definition of stress? _____

3. True or false? You can find information on working effectively with women on page 186. _____

4. You're looking for information on alcohol and drug use on the job. On what pages might you find some information on this topic? (*Hint:* Look for words that imply the existence of drugs or alcohol.) _____

5. Suppose you're very interested in what makes your boss tick, and how you can better get along with her. From the following list, check all the topics that you can find in *Tools for Success* that are related to bosses.

   _____ Building a relationship with your supervisor

   _____ Getting your supervisor fired

   _____ Learning more about your supervisor

_____ Managing conflict with your supervisor

_____ Getting along with your supervisor

_____ Understanding the differences between male and female supervisors

---

Activity 5.8: Finding Information: Using a Glossary I

Appendix C of this book includes a glossary of construction terms. Use the glossary to complete the following exercises.

SET 1:   Match the terms with their definitions.

_____ 1. hose bibb	a. hole or slot near the bottom of masonry walls to allow the release of accumulated moisture
_____ 2. deflection	b. opening or slatted grille that allows ventilation while providing protection from rain, sight, sound, or light
_____ 3. weep hole	c. water faucet made for the threaded attachment of a hose
_____ 4. scuttle	d. amount of sag at the center of a horizontal structure member when subjected to a load
_____ 5. louver	e. opening in a ceiling or roof that provides access to an attic or roof

SET 2:   Match the terms with their synonyms. (_Synonyms_ are two words that mean the same thing, such as "slender" and "thin.")

_____ 1. notch	a. blacktop
_____ 2. bituminous concrete	b. datum point
_____ 3. bench mark	c. Western framing
_____ 4. steel lumber	d. open web joist
_____ 5. platform framing	e. three-sided slot

SET 3: TRUE OR FALSE

_____ 1. Prefabricated components are built in a factory and installed or assembled as a whole on the job site.

_____ 2. A mil is a standard unit of measure equal to one-millionth of an inch.

_____ 3. A quarry tile usually measures 8" x 8".

_____ 4. A concrete masonry unit usually is abbreviated CMU.

_____ 5. Bedrock has not been exposed to light.

SET 4: MULTIPLE CHOICE

_____ 1. Which of the following is not a common type of beam?
   a. continuous beam
   b. cantilevered beam
   c. simple beam
   d. arch beam

_____ 2. A butt joint can be accurately measured in all of the following ways, except:
   a. end to end
   b. back to front
   c. side to side
   d. edge to edge

_____ 3. Your foreman has asked you to bring him a plank. Which of the following wood measurements would not meet the criteria for a plank?
   a. 1/2" thick
   b. 8 inches wide
   c. 12 inches wide
   d. 4" thick

_____ 4. "Mesh" is another name for:
   a. weld-wire-fabric
   b. V-joints
   c. stucco
   d. spandrals

_____ 5. What is a synonym for fire-resistant?
   a. flammable
   b. incombustible
   c. inflammable
   d. extinguishable

5.3 STRATEGIES FOR IMPROVING YOUR COMPREHENSION

Sometimes it's easy to get lost in the details when you read. Noise or other distractions may prevent you from fully understanding what's before you. With practice, though, you can increase your comprehension and retention. Here are some strategies for improving your understanding.

USE TITLES AND HEADINGS TO HELP YOU FOLLOW THE MATERIAL.   If you flip through this book, you'll see that each module has a title, and that each module is broken into different headings and subheadings. This module is titled "Reading Skills I: The Basics," and it includes headings titled "Tips for Reading Effectively," "Reading Business Correspondence," "Understanding New Words," and so on.

One way to improve your comprehension is to notice the title and then flip through the chapter, previewing all the headings before you begin reading. Previewing the material gives you a sense of what you're about to read. It also helps your mind organize that material better. Previewing the headings always works to improve comprehension, whether you are reading a newspaper article, a textbook, a manual, or a business memo or e-mail.

TURN HEADINGS AND TITLES INTO QUESTIONS.   As you read the title and preview the headings, turn them into questions, then look for the answers to those questions as you read. For example, Section 2.1 of this book is entitled "Taking Notes." As you preview this section title, your question can become, "How do I take effective notes when I'm listening to someone?" As you read the section, you will find the answer to that question.

Think of this question-and-answer process as a conversation that you have with yourself while you read. Thinking this way turns reading into a conversation, rather than a solitary activity. The process works because it's easy to remember conversations you've had—because you actively participated in them!

WATCH FOR VISUAL CLUES THAT SIGNAL IMPORTANT MATERIAL.   As we saw in Section 5.1, writers often use **boldface** or *italics* to indicate words or information to which you should pay attention. To call attention to material that you should memorize, the author may use a *numbered list* (1, 2, 3, etc.) or a *bulleted list* (with each point in the list beginning with a "bullet," which looks like this: ●).

Consider the following excerpt from a construction textbook:

Housekeeping

In construction, **housekeeping** means keeping your work area clean and free of scraps or spills. It also means being orderly and organized. You must store your materials and supplies safely and label them properly. Arranging your tools and equipment to permit safe, efficient work practices and easy cleaning is also important.

If the work site is indoors, make sure it is well lighted and ventilated. Don't allow aisles and exits to be blocked by materials and equipment. Make sure that **flammable** liquids are stored in safety cans. Oily rags must be placed only in approved self-closing metal containers. Remember that the major goal of good housekeeping is to prevent accidents.

Here are some good housekeeping rules:

- Keep all scrap material and lumber with nails sticking out clear of work areas.
- Clean up spills to prevent falls.
- Remove all **combustible** scrap materials regularly.
- Make sure you have containers for the collection and separation of refuse. Containers for flammable or harmful refuse must be covered.
- Dispose of waste often.

Another way of explaining good housekeeping is pride of workmanship. If you take pride in what you are doing, you won't let trash build up around you. The old saying, "A place for everything, and everything in its place" may sound corny, but it's the right idea on the job site.[10]

Note the different visual cues that the author has provided. First, the title, "Housekeeping," lets you know what this section will be about. The author has also called your attention to three important terms by putting them in boldface: **housekeeping, flammable,** and **combustible.** These three words are defined in the glossary to that textbook—the boldface signals a glossary entry. Finally, the author has provided five bulleted points that offer simple, easy-to-follow, easy-to-read advice on the rules of good housekeeping.

STUDY DIAGRAMS THAT SUMMARIZE USEFUL INFORMATION.   Most books and manuals contain summary charts and diagrams. Pay close attention to these visual aids. Spend time studying them, and don't expect that you'll be able to understand the entire chart all at once. Study each diagram one piece at a time, and check the explanation in the book or manual for more information. (We look more closely at charts and diagrams in Section 6.1, "Reading Visual Materials.")

LOOK FOR TOPICS AND KEY IDEAS.   Two of the most important reading skills are (a) being able to understand what something is about, and (b) being able to distinguish what is important in the reading from what is less important.

The *topic* is the subject of the entire reading. Very often, the topic will be stated directly in a heading or subheading. So, for example, if you are about to read a section of a manual, and that section is titled "Daily Maintenance of the SU-2600," you will immediately know the topic of that particular section.

---

[10]National Center for Construction Education and Research, *Core Curriculum* (Upper Saddle River, NJ/Columbus, Ohio: Prentice Hall, 2000), Basic Safety—Trainee Module 00101, pp. 1-9, 1-10.

As you read, you will often find that writers frequently begin by making a direct *general* statement. They may then go on to give *specific* directions that follow from that direct statement, or give further examples. This is a hallmark of good, clear writing.[11]

General statement → Instructions

General statement → Additional examples

Notice how well this system works in the following passages:

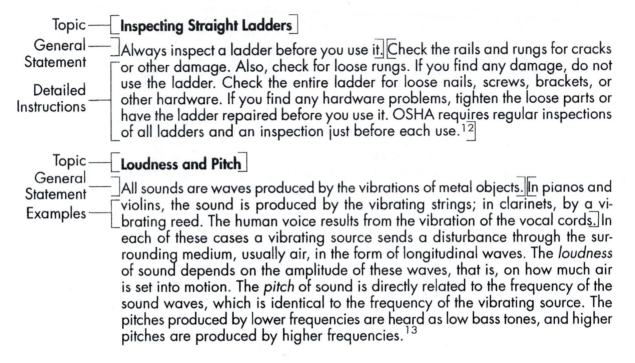

Topic — **Inspecting Straight Ladders**

General Statement — Always inspect a ladder before you use it. Check the rails and rungs for cracks or other damage. Also, check for loose rungs. If you find any damage, do not use the ladder. Check the entire ladder for loose nails, screws, brackets, or other hardware. If you find any hardware problems, tighten the loose parts or have the ladder repaired before you use it. OSHA requires regular inspections of all ladders and an inspection just before each use.[12]

Detailed Instructions

Topic — **Loudness and Pitch**

General Statement — All sounds are waves produced by the vibrations of metal objects. In pianos and violins, the sound is produced by the vibrating strings; in clarinets, by a vibrating reed. The human voice results from the vibration of the vocal cords. In each of these cases a vibrating source sends a disturbance through the surrounding medium, usually air, in the form of longitudinal waves. The *loudness* of sound depends on the amplitude of these waves, that is, on how much air is set into motion. The *pitch* of sound is directly related to the frequency of the sound waves, which is identical to the frequency of the vibrating source. The pitches produced by lower frequencies are heard as low bass tones, and higher pitches are produced by higher frequencies.[13]

Examples

Sometimes, though, the examples may come first, and the general statement will come last, as in the following passage:

Examples — A mixture of copper and tin in a molten state will cool to form a harder, stronger, and more durable solid than either copper itself or tin itself. This solid is bronze, historically the first of the materials we call *alloys*. Brass, a mixture of copper and zinc, is another alloy. Steels are alloys of iron with carbon, often with the addition of other elements for special purposes, like chromium for rustlessness and silicon for high permeability. Gallium arsenide is a newer alloy that is a semiconductor used in electronics for such solid-state devices as the light-emitting diodes in calculator readouts. All alloys are made by basically the same process, by mixing two or more molten metals in varying proportions and letting the mixture cool and solidify.[14]

General Statement

As you read, try to remain focused on the topic and on the key points the author wants you to remember.

---

[11]We discuss the principles of good writing in detail in Section 7.2.

[12]National Center for Construction Education and Research, *Core Curriculum* (Upper Saddle River, NJ/Columbus, Ohio: Prentice Hall, 2000), Basic Safety—Trainee Module 00101, p. 1-34.

[13]Paul. G. Hewitt, *Conceptual Physics,* 7th ed. (New York, NY: HarperCollins, 1993), p. 294.

[14]Paul. G. Hewitt, *Conceptual Physics,* 7th ed. (New York, NY: HarperCollins, 1993), p. 169.

TAKE A BREAK. If you're a slow reader or you find yourself getting bored or frustrated, take a break from reading. Take a walk or grab a bite to eat. If you're at home, you might even consider taking a nap, because it's hard to concentrate when you're tired. You'll be amazed at how a small break can help you maintain a positive approach to reading.

Activity 5.9: Looking for Keys to Comprehension

This activity will help you become better acquainted with the visual cues to meaning. Read Passage A, "The Nature of Soil," on pages 108–109, then answer the following questions.

_____ 1. Based on the title, what would you say is the topic of this selection?
   a. nature
   b. soil
   c. subsurface exploration
   d. the types of rock

_____ 2. Turning titles and headings into questions can keep you actively involved in what you're reading and help improve your comprehension. Which of the following is *not* a question that you could ask yourself to better understand "The Nature of Soil"?
   a. What exactly is soil?
   b. Are there different types of soil?
   c. How does the study of soil relate to the construction industry?
   d. How can I help preserve the natural environment?

_____ 3. Which of the following visual cues does the author of "The Nature of Soil" use to call your attention to key terms or important points?
   a. italics
   b. bulleted list
   c. both a and b
   d. neither a nor b

_____ 4. Reread the third paragraph of the passage, which begins "All soils are made up of large or small particles. . . ." Like most good writing, this paragraph offers both general statements and further examples. Which of the following sentences is the most general? (*Hint:* This will be the sentence that sets up the *topic* of that paragraph.)
   a. "All soils are made up of large or small particles derived from one or more of the minerals that make up solid rock."
   b. "For example, there are notable deposits of *eolian soil* in western North America, which were deposited by wind."
   c. "There are also numerous deposits of glacial till, a mixture of sand, gravel, silt, and clay, deposited by glaciers."
   d. "Other soils have been deposited by action of water, whereas others, known as *residual soils,* consist of rock particles that have not been moved from their original location, but are products of the deterioration of solid rock."

_____ 5. In the last paragraph, italics indicate the different types of rock. Which of the following is not a type of rock?
   a. shattered
   b. cohesive
   c. foliated
   d. sedimentary

Activity 5.10: Checking Your Comprehension I

Read Passage B, "The History of Paint," on pages 109–111. Then answer the following questions to check your comprehension of the material.

_____ 1. What is whitewash?
   a. a pigment
   b. a binder
   c. freshly burned lime
   d. a vehicle

_____ 2. From what is white lead made?
   a. whitewash
   b. polymers
   c. iron oxide
   d. lead sulphate

_____ 3. Which of the following is not a substance from which vehicles are produced?
   a. albumin
   b. egg white
   c. beeswax
   d. lacquer

_____ 4. When did water-based coatings using acrylic latex binders gain in popularity?
   a. with the ancient Egyptians
   b. in the 1950s and 1960s
   c. in 1970, as a result of the Clean Air Act
   d. when substrates were introduced in the second half of the 20th century

_____ 5. Based on the passage, which of the following is not true of ozone?
   a. The more ozone in the atmosphere, the better.
   b. VOCs react with nitrous oxide and sunlight to create ozone.
   c. Ozone trapped in the lower atmosphere can be hazardous to humans.
   d. Ozone is an unstable form of oxygen.

_____ 6. Which of the following gives color to paint?
   a. pigments
   b. binders
   c. polymers
   d. resins

_____ 7. When were vehicles and pigments mixed together before distribution for the first time?
   a. in the 18th century
   b. in the 19th century

        c. in the Chou dynasty (1122 to 221 B.C.)
        d. after the Clean Air Act

_____ 8. Which substance is used to produce the color red?
        a. white lead
        b. alkyds
        c. phenolics
        d. iron oxide

_____ 9. What is the general term for a surface that is being painted?
        a. VOC
        b. polymer
        c. substrate
        d. vehicle

_____ 10. In what year was the Clean Air Act amended?
        a. 1960
        b. 1970
        c. 1980
        d. 1990

Activity 5.11: Checking Your Comprehension II

Refer to the passage on "Housekeeping" on page 121. Read the passage and answer the questions that follow.

_____ 1. Which is not a component of good housekeeping?
        a. cleaning up spills
        b. disposing of refuse in appropriate containers
        c. keeping tools properly arranged
        d. keeping exit doors locked and inaccessible

_____ 2. In what type of receptacle should oily rags be placed?
        a. cardboard box
        b. self-closing metal container
        c. metal storage shed
        d. plastic bags

_____ 3. What is the chief goal of good housekeeping?
        a. to keep the workplace clean
        b. to keep supervisors happy
        c. to save money
        d. to prevent accidents

_____ 4. You've spilled oil in the area you're working. What should you do?
        a. Work around the spill.
        b. Clean it up immediately.
        c. Leave a rag over the oil to sop it up.
        d. Move to a different work area.

_____ 5. What is the best schedule for disposing of refuse?
        a. monthly
        b. as often as possible, several times a day
        c. weekly
        d. annually

Activity 5.12: Summarizing Information

Sometimes a lengthy description or set of information can be easily summarized in an easy-to-read table. Using "The Nature of Soil" and "The History of Paint" on pages 108–111, complete the following tables. Some examples are provided to get you started.

TABLE A   Soil Types by Particle Size

Soil Type	Size (in diameter)
cobble and boulders	Larger than 3 in.
gravel	
sand	
silt	
clay	

TABLE B   Types of Rock

Type	Description/Examples	Comparable to
Massive	very hard; no visible bedding planes or laminations; widely spaced, nearly vertical or horizontal joints	Excellent concrete

TABLE C   Timeline: Key Developments in the History of Paint

Period	Developments
Prehistory	Cave dwellers used plants, clay, and water to make paint; decorated bodies and cave walls with paint
Asia/6000 B.C.	
Egyptians/1500 B.C.	
Chinese/1122–221 B.C.	
Greeks and Romans/430 B.C.	
1700s/Europe	
19th century	
20th century through 1960s	
1960s through today	

TABLE D   Key Terms in Paint Production

Term	Definition
	Liquid part of the paint in which pigments are dissolved or dispersed
	Substances in which molecules, consisting of one or more structural units, are repeated any number of times
	Liquids used in paints to dissolve pigments and other materials; evaporate during drying
	Toxic substances used to keep paints liquid until they are applied
	Substances that give color to paint
	Substances used as binders to provide improvement in weathering, water resistance, toughness, elasticity, and resistance to chemical exposure
	White pigment made from lead sulphate
	Surfaces being painted
	Substance that helps bind or cement pigment particles together upon drying of paint

5.4 Reading Business Correspondence

On the job, you'll often be required to read material that has been prepared by someone within the company. You may also have to read material from people outside the company, such as suppliers, vendors, or clients. The most common types of business correspondence are memos and e-mail. You may also be lucky enough to work for a company that publishes a newsletter for its employees.

5.4.1 Memos

A *memo* (short for *memorandum*) is a brief note used to communicate within the company. Memos are sent only *within* an organization. For communication outside the organization, a business letter is used instead.

Memos serve many purposes. They can:

- give instructions
- ask or answer questions
- explain new policies
- call meetings
- summarize decisions
- request information
- remind people about upcoming tasks or events
- create written records of actions or events

Because memos are often short, it may seem convenient to avoid reading them. However, the day-to-day business of a company is often conducted through memos. For this reason, you should at least skim memos whenever you receive them. Use the tips provided in the "Skimming Effectively" box on page 105 to determine how important the memo is, then decide how closely you should read it.

A sample memo appears in Figure 5.1.

Note that the memo includes several components:

1. The word "Memo" or "Memorandum" near the top. If the memo is urgent, the word "Critical" or "Urgent" may also appear here. Those words are your key to drop everything and read the memo.

2. The person or persons who will receive the memo. Sometimes the names of people who will receive a copy of the memo are also included here. ("Cc" stands for "complimentary copy." "Bc" stands for "blind copy"—the recipients do not know that a copy is going to the person or persons whose names are listed as receiving blind copies.)

   Look to see who has received copies of the memo. In general, the more important a memo is, the more likely it is that higher-level supervisors and owners will receive a copy of it.

3. The sender's name.

4. The date of the memo—month, day, and year. The time may also be included.

5. The subject of the memo. Sometimes the term "Re:" is used to indicate the subject.

6. The body of the memo. The best memos get right to the point and are written in a conversational tone. However, long memos are becoming increasingly common, so you may need to be patient to read through the whole thing.

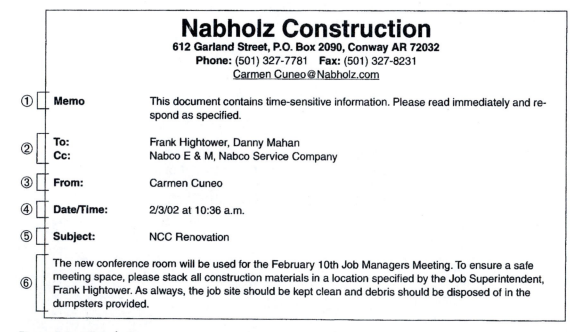

Figure 5.1: *Sample Memo*
Source: Courtesy of Nabholz Construction Corp., Conway, AR.

While reading the memo, ask yourself the following questions:

- Why am I receiving this memo? How does it affect me?
- Does this memo require me to do anything? In other words, must I respond in some way? If so, *what* do I need to do? *When* must I respond by? To *whom* must I respond?
- Is this memo clear to me? If you have questions, ask your supervisor for clarification.

> **TIP:** Business memos are important on-the-job documents. Be sure to read them. Don't just discard them.

5.4.2 E-Mail

The rise of computers has made *e-mail* (short for "electronic mail") extremely popular. By using computerized, sometimes wireless, e-mail accounts, contractors and owners in remote locations can communicate very rapidly. In fact, e-mail is often the most efficient way to communicate with people at distant sites.

E-mail is used for many of the same purposes as memos—especially to ask or answer questions and to notify people of upcoming events. Using e-mail can save time and paper, but it is not private.

A sample e-mail appears in Figure 5.2.

Note that an e-mail message contains many of the same elements as a memo: the names of the sender(s) and recipient(s), the date, a subject line, and the body of the message. As with memos, pay attention to the recipients and determine what is required of you.

Don Greenland
04/18/02 08:53 PM

To: Carmen Cuneo /Carmen_Cuneo@Nabholz.com
cc: Mark Seitler

Subject: Punchlist

Thanks to you, Frank, and the crew for getting the new Production Dept. ready for the move this weekend. Just a few "punchlist" items for your team to handle in my office:

- I should have my direct phone line moved to under my computer from my old office. This line bypasses the switchboard and is used to access Dodge reports, etc.
- My regular phone line was hooked up where the direct line should be. This needs to be moved to the other wall outlet.
- The trim around my table needs more stain and the legs need to be raised to match the millwork height.
- I would like an additional shelf for each cabinet on my side of the window. I'm short a few shelf brackets, too.
- Some of my file drawers are pretty stiff. Can they do something to make them pull in and out smoother?
- You know about the window blinds.

No big hurry on these ... just when you get time. Thanks.

Figure 5.2:   Sample E-Mail
Source: Courtesy of Nabholz Construction Corp., Conway, AR.

In general, e-mail falls into three categories:

- **Action e-mail:** These e-mails require a response or a reply from you. Perhaps someone needs information from you to continue or complete a job, or someone needs your approval to make a purchase or hire a subcontractor. To keep all members of the team working efficiently, reply to the e-mail as soon as you can. The e-mail reproduced in Figure 5.2 is an action e-mail, because it requires the recipient to take action on the punchlist.

> **TIP:** Some e-mail systems allow users to send e-mail with "Urgent Priority." These e-mails should be read and answered immediately.

- **FYI e-mail:** "FYI" stands for "For Your Information." These e-mails are generally copies of e-mails sent to other people. They may be sent to you to keep you "in the loop" or in touch with what's happening on a particular job. A response is optional.
- **General information e-mail:** These e-mails are sent to almost everyone who works for the company. They may offer information on things like vacation and sick policy, family or medical leave, or pension benefits. Or they might contain electronic copies of the company's newsletter. General information e-mail usually isn't urgent.

As with memos, you should read all your e-mail promptly. Most action e-mails are *time-sensitive*. That is, they require a quick or immediate response. In our electronic world, people have come to expect fast replies to their e-mail. For this reason, you should open all your e-mail promptly, and then prioritize it. Determine which messages need a response and which do not. Messages that don't require a reply can be read in detail later on, at your leisure.

5.4.3 Newsletters

Some companies publish a monthly, semi-monthly, or annual *newsletter* to inform employees of what's going on in the company. The newsletter usually offers a variety of features, including:

- Stories of new and upcoming projects
- Reports of recent successfully completed projects
- Profiles of or interviews with company personnel
- Employee benefits information
- "Fun" features such as photos from the company picnic
- Information about the company and its history

It may be tempting to simply discard the newsletter as another piece of unwanted mail. But resist the urge! A good team player should be aware of what's going on in the company. Also, the newsletter may provide excellent information that could be helpful to you in your career. For example, you might read about a new project in which you'd like to be involved. Your chances of being assigned to that project are much better if you volunteer early in the process.

The contents of a newsletter generally are not very "heavy," so the newsletter makes for perfect reading in the backyard or over a cup of coffee. Read the newsletter. You'll be glad you did.

Figure 5.3 reproduces the first page of the National Center for Construction Education and Research's Spring 2000 newsletter, which is aptly titled *Construction Education Newsline*.

construction education Newsline

National Center for Construction Education and Research

SPRING 2001   VOLUME 5 NO 1   One Industry... One Training Program

NCCER and American Petroleum Institute Develop Pipeline Curricula

On February 1, 2001, NCCER and American Petroleum Institute (API) entered into an agreement to develop skills assessments and training curricula to qualify pipeline personnel under the Department of Transportation's (DOT) new regulation for Pipeline Operator Qualification. API's Pipeliners Training and Assessment Program (PTAP) is setting the national industry standard for liquid pipeline operators. API develops and publishes technical standards relating to the petroleum and pipeline industry; and provides certification for workers that meet certain industry requirements.

"NCCER's relationship with API is exciting and presents many positive opportunities for both NCCER and our training sponsors," says NCCER Vice President of Training Operations and Program Development, Don Whyte. "Through this alliance, NCCER is diversifying its training operations by tapping into a new industry segment that

NCCER/API ALLIANCE SETS A NEW STAGE FOR OWNER INVOLVEMENT IN NCCER

has strong ties to our current maintenance and construction markets. The diversification will help NCCER sustain operations through economic swings. Of even greater importance, the NCCER/API alliance sets a new stage for owner involvement in NCCER."

Owners such as Equistar, BP-Amoco, CITGO, Chevron, Marathon Ashland, Enron, Williams Energy Services, Koch Industries, Unocal, and Texaco have been benefactors of NCCER training through contractors working for them and using NCCER programs. With the NCCER/API alliance, these owners, through their pipeline divisions and their contractors, will be direct participants in NCCER programs. Existing NCCER sponsors and accredited assessment centers will also benefit. Many of the pipeline owners and their

...continued on page 6

Fluor Global Services and PRIMEDIA Join Forces to Deliver Online Training

Fluor Global Services, a business enterprise of Fluor Corporation and PRIMEDIA Workplace Learning (PWPL), a PRIMEDIA company, announced the creation of a global strategic alliance that will develop and deliver 80 online courses to serve the continuing education needs of industrial maintenance and operations personnel.

In response to the growing demand for training delivery via the web, Fluor and PWPL will create the 80-program Maintenance Technician Training online series for the petrochemical, utility and general manufacturing sectors. The online courses will incorporate modules of NCCER's interactive construction and maintenance curricula.

"The alliance enables us to provide thousands of our employees essential technical skills training while reaping benefits offered by online learning," says J. William Leistner, President of Operations & Maintenance for Fluor Global Services.

More and more businesses around the world are turning to online learning as a flexible, cost-effective method to deliver training and to align growth strategies with business goals. The alliance between Fluor and PWPL will leverage their combined strengths to produce technical skills training that improves the customer's bottom line. ◆

SEE PAGE 7 FOR PRODUCT UPDATE!

Figure 5.3: Sample Newsletter

Source: NCCER *Construction Education Newsline*, Vol. 4, No. 1, Spring 2000.

Activity 5.13: Reading Memos

Refer to the memo in Figure 5.1 and answer the questions that follow.

1. Who wrote the memo? _____

2. On what date will the Job Managers Meeting take place? _____

3. What is the Job Superintendent's name? _____

4. Where should debris be disposed of? _____

5. In addition to the Job Superintendent, who else will receive a copy of this memo?_____

Activity 5.14: Reading E-Mail

Refer to the e-mail in Figure 5.2 and answer the questions that follow.

1. At what time was the e-mail sent? _____

2. True or false: The matters outlined in this e-mail are urgent. _____

3. In addition to Carmen Cuneo, who else will receive a copy of this e-mail?

_____

4. Which item in Mr. Greenland's office needs more stain? _____

5. What would Mr. Greenland like to have added on his side of the window?

_____

6. True or false: The file drawers are in good working order. _____

7. What type of report is the direct phone line used to access? _____

8. True or false: The legs of the table need to be raised. _____

5.5 READING (AND FOLLOWING) DIRECTIONS

Although creativity, problem solving, technological expertise, and craftsman-ship are all important tools in the construction professional's toolkit, there is no denying that construction is a procedure-based industry. While creative so-lutions are often welcome, there are clearly *right* ways to do things and *wrong* ways to do things.

The construction business's emphasis on efficiency and cost management requires that jobs get done correctly the first time around. Mistakes cost money and, more importantly, they cost time. For this reason, it's critical that construction workers be able to follow the instructions they receive to a "T."

Directions may be either written or spoken. We discussed how to follow spoken directions in Section 2.2. In this section, we focus on the procedures for following *written* directions.

Written directions generally come in two formats: either general guide-lines or step-by-step instructions. Regardless of the format, though, there is one simple rule for following directions:

> **TIP: When you're reading directions, read ALL of the directions completely through before you begin following them.** By reading all the directions first, you'll get a good sense of what needs to be accomplished. In those cases where advance planning is required, you'll be able to obtain and prepare all the tools you need before you begin a job. This is a good habit to get into, and it will save you many problems on the job and in your life.

5.5.1 General Guidelines

When learning safety procedures or other construction-related tasks, you may receive a set of *general guidelines*. These guidelines are often a set of "do's" and "don'ts" that outline the things you *should* or *should not* do. They're not necessarily listed in any particular order. To achieve the desired result, you need to be aware of all the guidelines, and you need to implement all of them simultaneously.

Consider, for example, the following list of "Tips for Getting Along with Your Co-Workers," from a human relations text for construction professionals:[15]

Do's

1. Realize that everyone works hard, not just you.
2. When appropriate, praise other people.
3. Share the credit, and take the blame.
4. Recognize the contributions of others.
5. Meet your deadlines.
6. Keep your personal problems at home.

Don'ts

1. Don't brag or act like a know-it-all.
2. Don't gossip about your co-workers.
3. Don't put other people down.
4. Don't shirk your responsibilities.
5. Don't be a stool pigeon.

To get along with your co-workers, you need to follow all these guidelines, but not in any particular order. The issues listed here are found on every job site all the time. They are not part of a step-by-step sequence for getting along with your colleagues.

Here are some tips for making the most of directions in this format:

- Numbered lists like the one above are so easy to read that it's tempting to read the entries quickly without stopping to think about them. So, as you read, force yourself to slow down. Read each point individually, and take the time to think about each one.

- Your retention and recall are always much stronger if you can associate the reading with your own life. So, for example, when you read "Don't brag or act like a know-it-all," you might think about a braggart you've worked with, someone who really got on your nerves. That memory could be a good reminder of how that sort of behavior affects co-workers.

- Pay as much attention to the *Do's* as to the *Don'ts*. It's often easier to remember what we *shouldn't* do than it is to remember what we *should* do. But success is not just a lack of the negative; it is a surplus of the positive. So be sure to concentrate on both the do's *and* the don'ts.

5.5.2 Step-by-Step Instructions

When learning how to operate a particular tool or machine, or when learning one of the many complex procedures found on a construction site, you will often receive detailed, step-by-step instructions. You will be expected to follow

---

[15]Adapted from Steven A. Rigolosi, *Tools for Success: Soft Skills for the Construction Industry* (Upper Saddle River, NJ: Prentice Hall, 2000), pp. 33–34.

these directions closely, in the *exact order* in which they are written. Any deviation from the directions could lead to serious problems or substantial delays.

Consider the following set of step-by-step instructions as an example:[16]

How to Use a Steel Tape

Step One	Pull the tape out to the desired length.
Step Two	Place the hook over the edge of the material you are measuring. Lock the tape if necessary (use the lock button on the holder).
Step Three	Mark or record the measurement.
Step Four	Unhook the tape from the edge.
Step Five	Rewind the tape by pressing the rewind button.

Note that these directions must be followed in order, beginning with Step 1 and moving sequentially through Step 5. It wouldn't make sense to begin with Step 3, then move to Step 1, then move to Step 4, and so on.

As you prepare to follow directions, keep the following in mind:

- Always read the *entire set of instructions* first, from top to bottom or front to back. Don't cut corners, and don't skip ahead. Don't assume that you know what the directions will say—you might be in for some nasty surprises later on.

- Reread the directions a second time, visualizing each step of the process. Picture yourself performing each step of the directions. This will make it much easier to perform the task in "real time."

- Prepare your work area before you begin. Assemble all the tools you will need.

- Don't skip steps or attempt to perform two steps at once. Take things one step at a time. Don't rush!

- Eliminate distractions, particularly when following detailed or intricate instructions. Don't listen to music or work in a noisy or congested area (unless doing so is unavoidable).

- If you've read the directions several times and still don't understand them, talk to your foreman or supervisor. It's better to ask questions than to make a mistake.

TIP: The engineers and other professionals who write directions are highly trained individuals. They have important reasons for preparing directions in a specific way. Don't second guess the directions; they have been carefully written, double-checked, verified, and proofread. Follow directions to the letter.

5.5.3 Reading Maps

An important part of the construction professional's job entails getting from Point A to Point B as quickly as possible. If you're working in an unfamiliar area, a road map can be an extremely helpful tool in making this possible.

[16]National Center for Construction Education and Research, *Core Curriculum,* Trainee Module 00103 (Upper Saddle River, NJ/Columbus, OH: Prentice Hall, 2000), p. 3-24.

Maps are easy to come by. They are sold at many gas stations across the country. In addition, free maps that give you specific directions from one place to another can be customized for you on free Websites, such as **yahoo.com** and **mapquest.com.**

Here are some pointers for reading and understanding road maps:

- *Familiarize yourself with the map's legend.* The *legend* is a list of symbols used on the map, along with an explanation of each. For example, local roads may be indicated by a thin black line, interstate highways by a thick red line, and county roads by a thin green line. If you have a long distance to travel, you'll probably want to use an interstate, which is designed for quick travel.

- *Understand distances.* Maps are drawn to scale. Depending on the map, one inch can stand for one mile, 50 miles, or 500 miles. Be sure to check out the scale so that you understand the distance and time required to complete your journey.

- *Be aware of north/south and east/west distinctions.* Learn how to tell north from south, and east from west. A compass can be helpful here.

- *Don't read a map while you are driving.* Taking your eyes off the road is dangerous. Rather, map out your course before you leave. Write out directions (for example, "Take Route 59 East to Exit 24 . . . end of ramp, make left . . . 2 miles down, make right onto Homestead Lane.") Keep your map with you for reference in case you get lost.

In general, when you embark on a road trip into an area you don't know, leave yourself some extra time to get lost. If you show up early, you can always kill a few minutes. But if you're late, you can never make up for the bad impression you may create.

5.5.4 Giving Driving Directions

A skill related to map reading is the art of direction giving. On the job, you may be asked to provide directions from one location to another. Some people are good at this task; others can benefit from some practice. Here are some suggestions:

- *Remember that others may not be as familiar with the area as you are.* If you grew up or live in a particular town, you may know its roads inside and out. But others will not be as familiar. So be sure not to assume that others have the knowledge you have.

- *Make your directions as specific as possible.* For example, don't say "Travel north a few miles until you see a gas station." It's much easier on the traveler if you say "Travel north approximately 3 miles until you see the Amoco station."

- *Give street names whenever possible.* Some people navigate by landmarks. That is, they know to turn right at the church, left at the school, and right again at the pond. But it is often helpful to tell people the names of the roads they'll be traveling on. This way, an unsure traveler can check on his progress from time to time just by looking at the street sign.

Activity 5.15: Following Directions

Use the lines on page 136 to follow this set of instructions:

1. On the bottom line, in the middle of the page, write your name.

2. On the fourth line from the top, about one inch from the left margin, write the sum of 2 and 2.

3. Draw a line connecting your name with the number 4.

4. In your mind, subtract 3 from 10. On the second line from the top, write the result as far to the right on the line as possible.

5. Place a circle between the sixth and seventh lines from the top of the page, in the center of the page. Place a square between the second and third lines from the bottom of the page, one-third of the distance from the left margin to the right margin.

6. Count the number of letters in the word *construction*. Place this number upside down on the eighth line from the top of the page, as far to the left side of the page as possible. Next to the 2, write the letter C, also upside down.

7. Using a straight line, connect the letter C to the number 7 somewhere on the page.

8. Turn this book upside down. Now, counting from the first line, move down to the sixth line. At the beginning of that line, write the time it is right now.

9. Ignore instructions 3 and 7.

10. Turn the book rightside up. At the left side of the page, on the third line from the top, write the smallest of these numbers: 357, 201, 695, 210, 306.

Activity 5.16: Following General Guidelines

Read the following set of general guidelines, then answer the questions that follow.

Wearing Rubber Gloves for Safety in Electrical Work[17]

Both high- and low-voltage rubber gloves of the gauntlet type are available in various sizes. To get the best possible protection and service life, here are a few general rules that apply whenever they are used in electrical work:

- Always wear leather protectors over your gloves. Any direct contact with sharp or pointed objects may cut, snag, or puncture the gloves and take away the protection you are depending on. Leather protectors are required by the National Fire Protection Association's

---

[17]National Center for Construction Education and Research, *Electrical Trainee Guide* (Upper Saddle River, NJ/Columbus, OH: Prentice Hall, 2000), Trainee Module 2610, p. 1-8.

Standard 70-E if the insulating capabilities of the gloves are subject to damage.

- Always wear rubber gloves right side out (serial number and size to the outside). Turning gloves inside out places a stress on the pre-formed rubber.

- Always keep the gauntlets up. Rolling them down sacrifices a valuable area of protection.

- Always inspect and field check gloves before using them. Always check the inside for any debris.

- Use light amounts of talcum powder or cotton liners with the rubber gloves. This gives the user more comfort, and it also helps to absorb some of the perspiration that can damage the gloves over years of use.

- Wash the rubber gloves in lukewarm, clean, fresh water after each use. Dry the gloves inside and out prior to returning to storage. Never use any type of cleaning solution on the gloves.

- Once the gloves have been properly cleaned, inspected, and tested, they must be properly stored. They should be stored in a cool, dry, dark place that is free from ozone, chemicals, oils, solvents, or other materials that could damage the gloves. Such storage should not be in the vicinity of hot pipes or direct sunlight. Both gloves and sleeves should be stored in their natural shape and kept in a bag or box inside their protectors. They should be stored undistorted, right side out, and unfolded.

- Gloves can be damaged by many different chemicals, especially petroleum-based products such as oils, gasoline, hydraulic fluid inhibitors, hand creams, pastes, and salves. If contact is made with these or other petroleum-based products, the contaminant should be wiped off immediately. If any signs of physical deterioration are found (e.g., swelling, softness, hardening, stickiness, ozone deterioration, or sun checking), the protective equipment must not be used.

- Never wear watches or rings while wearing rubber gloves; this can cause damage from the inside out and defeats the purpose of using rubber gloves. Never wear anything conductive.

- Rubber gloves must be tested every six months by a certified testing laboratory. Always check the inspection date before using gloves.

- Use rubber gloves only for their intended purpose, not for handling chemicals or other work. This also applies to the leather protectors.

_____ 1. For which type of gloves are the above instructions relevant?
   a. leather gloves
   b. cloth gloves
   c. rubber gloves
   d. all of the above

_____ 2. The guidelines above discuss all of the following facets of rubber glove use, except:
   a. storage of gloves
   b. twice-yearly inspections
   c. cleaning techniques
   d. disposal techniques for damaged gloves

_____   3. In which of the following situations are rubber gloves worn correctly?
　　　a. John's gloves show the serial number on the outside.
　　　b. Ray's gloves are inside out for added cleanliness and protection.
　　　c. Mabel is wearing her gloves over her wedding ring.
　　　d. Patti has rolled up the gauntlet to give her more freedom of movement.

_____   4. With which of the following substances should rubber gloves be washed?
　　　a. petroleum-based products
　　　b. hand creams
　　　c. water
　　　d. talcum powder

_____   5. Which of the following is not a sign that rubber gloves have been damaged?
　　　a. cool to the touch
　　　b. hardening
　　　c. stickiness
　　　d. swelling

Activity 5.17: Following Step-by-Step Instructions

Read the following set of step-by-step instructions and answer the questions that follow.

How to Use a Sledgehammer[18]

Obviously, a sledgehammer is a tool that can cause injury to you or to anyone working near you. You must use a sledgehammer in the right way and you must focus on what you are doing the entire time you use one. Follow these steps:

Step One	Wear appropriate personal protective equipment to protect your eyes and hands.
Step Two	Inspect the sledgehammer to ensure there are no defects.
Step Three	Ensure that no co-workers are standing in the surrounding area.
Step Four	Hold the sledgehammer with both hands (hand over hand).
Step Five	Stand directly in front of the object you want to drive.
Step Six	Lift the sledgehammer straight above the target.
Step Seven	Set the head of the sledgehammer on the target.
Step Eight	Begin delivering short blows to the target and gradually increase the length and force of the stroke.

---

[18]National Center for Construction Education and Research, *Core Curriculum* (Upper Saddle River, NJ/Columbus, OH: Prentice Hall, 2000), Trainee Module 00103, p. 3-8.

Precautions:
- Don't swing beyond your head.
- Don't swing behind you.

TRUE OR FALSE: Mark "T" if the statement is true, "F" if it is false.

_____   1. The order in which you follow Steps 1–8 doesn't matter, as long as you do each one carefully.

_____   2. The best technique is to hold the sledgehammer with one hand.

_____   3. A damaged sledgehammer should not be used.

_____   4. Using a sledgehammer requires you to focus closely on the task at hand.

_____   5. Co-workers should be cleared from the area before a sledgehammer is used.

_____   6. The best sledgehammer strokes begin from behind the person holding the sledgehammer.

_____   7. Protective eyegear is not required when driving wooden targets.

_____   8. An effective and safe sledgehammer swing should not move beyond the head.

_____   9. When using a sledgehammer, begin with large strokes, and end with smaller strokes as the target is driven deeper into the ground.

_____   10. Several of the steps in this set of directions could be skipped by workers who have a lot of experience with sledgehammers.

5.6 UNDERSTANDING NEW WORDS

Like all professional fields, construction has its own set of terms. People in the construction industry use terms like "HazMat" and "OSHA" everyday, but most people outside the industry would be stymied if they heard those words used in conversation.

In addition, there are words that mean one thing to the world at large and another to construction professionals. When a welder uses the term "flashback," he's referring to a welding flame that flares up and chars the hose at or near the torch connection. When a layperson uses the term "flashback," he's usually referring to a movie scene in which a character "flashes back" to a distant memory from the past.

As technology comes to play an even larger role in construction and you gain experience, you are likely to learn more new words with each passing year. Keeping up with the language of your field is important to your career. As the old saying goes, you have to "walk the walk" and "talk the talk."

Every so often, though, you may encounter words whose meanings you don't know. How can you find out their definitions? The easiest way is to simply ask someone you trust. But, if that person isn't sure, or there's no one around to ask, your best bet is to consult a dictionary or glossary.

Several construction dictionaries are widely available. Among them are the following:

Construction Dictionary, 9th Edition
Published by the National Association of Women in Construction
Greater Phoenix Chapter
P.O. Box 6142
Phoenix, AZ 85005

Construction Glossary, 2nd Edition
By J. S. Stein
Published by John Wiley and Sons, New York

Dictionary of Architecture and Construction, 2nd Edition
By Cyril M. Harris
Published by McGraw-Hill, New York

Means Illustrated Construction Dictionary
Published by R. S. Means Co., Inc.
100 Construction Plaza
P.O. Box 800
Kingston, MA 02364

5.6.1 Everyday Words—Use a Dictionary

Words fall into two categories: (1) words that are used by all people in every-day conversation, and (2) words that are used almost exclusively by the people in a particular industry.

If you're looking to find the meaning of an "everyday word," a *dictionary* is your best bet. Dictionaries are alphabetical listings of the words in the English language. You can purchase a good dictionary quite cheaply. Some paperback dictionaries cost as little as $5.00.

At the top of each dictionary page, you will find *guide words*. These represent the first and last word on that page. For example, suppose you're looking for the word "vicissitude." The guide words on that page might say "vial" and "vigor." You would know that the meaning of "vicissitude" can be found on this page, because alphabetically it falls between "vial" and "vigor."

Each dictionary entry shows the word's correct spelling, its pronunciation, and its various meanings. Many words have more than one meaning. (Think, for example, about how many things the word *run* can mean: I *run* three miles every day. Time is *running* out. There is a dog *run* in the back yard.) Some dictionaries also provide a history of the word, *synonyms* (words or phrases that mean the same), *antonyms* (words or phrases that mean the opposite), and examples of the word used in a sentence.

A sample dictionary entry follows:

vi·cis′-si-tude, noun. 1. [usually plural] Changes of circumstances; or the ups and downs of life. 2. Regular cycle of alternation, as of day and night. [Latin, *vicissitudo*, from *vix, vicis*, a turn] **Syn.** Ups and downs. **Ex.** When my daughter complains that she made the soccer team but not the track team, I tell her that these are the *vicissitudes* of life.

Buy an inexpensive dictionary and keep in handy. It will prove to be a valuable tool.

> **TIP:** Because words in the dictionary are listed alphabetically, you can run into difficulty if you don't know how to spell the word properly. Do your best to find the word. Experiment with different spellings until you get it right.

5.6.2 Jargon—Use a Glossary

To decipher the meanings of construction-related words that aren't used by the general population, a glossary is your best bet. Recall from Section 5.2 that a *glossary* is a mini-dictionary of the terms used in one specific field. Glossaries usually do not exist on their own. Rather, they are often found at the end of longer works, such as manuals or textbooks.

Glossary definitions can sometimes be circular. In other words, the definition found in the glossary may use a word you don't understand to define another word you don't understand. Consider the following glossary entry for masonry veneer:

masonry veneer
A single-*wythe*, non-load-bearing facing installed over a structural frame, e.g., brick veneer applied to a wood frame house.

This definition is somewhat helpful, but it could be problematic if you don't understand what "single-wythe" means. Note that *wythe* is in italics. This means that you can also find the word "wythe" in the glossary. Most glossaries offer this valuable feature.

Activity 5.18: Using a Dictionary

Use a dictionary to determine the meaning of the boldface words in the following passages. Each of these passages is taken from a construction-related textbook or document.

There are notable deposits of **eolian** soil in western North America.

_____ 1. **eolian**
   a. dry
   b. moist
   c. rocky
   d. deposited by the wind

Foliated rocks are hard, but have sloping joints, which **preclude** equal compressive strength in all directions.

_____ 2. **preclude**
   a. hinder
   b. contribute to
   c. allow
   d. verify

Coloring components include natural **ores** and **organic** pigments.

_____ 3. **ores**
   a. forms of plant life
   b. rocks
   c. natural combinations of minerals
   d. coloring agents

_____ 4. **organic**
   a. unnatural
   b. colorful
   c. derived from living organisms
   d. mineral-based

Everyone on the team must **forego** the thought that their work is **preeminent,** of the highest value, and worthy of reducing the work of others to **ancillary,** minor, or **inconsequential** status, of limited (if any) value to the project.

_____ 5. **forego**
   a. do without
   b. foster
   c. emphasize
   d. think

_____ 6. **preeminent**
   a. low-quality
   b. most important
   c. introductory
   d. technical

_____ 7. **ancillary**
   a. essential
   b. related to insects
   c. major
   d. subordinate

_____ 8. **inconsequential**
   a. penny-pinching
   b. unimportant
   c. serious
   d. effective

Behind and supporting the actual construction work is a massive **collaboration** of people of many talents, as well as an **elaborate** system of manufacturers who produce the systems, materials, modules, devices, clothing, tools, equipment, and other items required by the construction industry.

_____ 9. **collaboration**
   a. teamwork
   b. individuality
   c. talent pool
   d. management structure

_____ 10. **elaborate**
       a. simple
       b. capitalistic
       c. intimidating
       d. complex

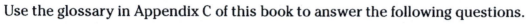

Activity 5.19: Using a Glossary II

Use the glossary in Appendix C of this book to answer the following questions.

TRUE OR FALSE?   Mark "T" if the statement is true, "F" if it is false.

_____ 1. Backfill is used to provide a slope for drainage away from a foundation wall.

_____ 2. A cupola is sometimes used for ventilation purposes.

_____ 3. Softwood is produced from deciduous trees.

_____ 4. Handcut aluminum shingles are often called shakes.

_____ 5. Tar is a common waterproofing agent.

_____ 6. A riser is the horizontal part of a stair step.

_____ 7. In galvanized iron, sheet iron is coated with molten cobalt to protect the iron against rust.

_____ 8. Bannister spindles are also called balusters.

_____ 9. Smokestack linings often make use of firebrick.

_____ 10. The term _pour_ is no longer used today.

Reading Skills II
Advanced Topics

66 A picture is worth a thousand words. 99

—Proverb

Module 5 explored the basics of effective reading on the job. That module offered a series of tips and strategies for improving your comprehension, reading to find information, and following directions. This module takes those basic skills one step further and shows you how to read a wide variety of more complex construction-related documents.

6.1 READING VISUAL MATERIALS

If you flip through the pages of any newspaper or magazine, you will see large numbers of photographs, graphics, and charts. The purpose of these visual materials is not simply to add "window dressing" or to make the material more visually appealing. Rather, visual materials often summarize pages of information, or huge amounts of data, in a relatively small amount of space.

The same is true of visual materials you will be asked to read on the job. Because visuals are an important part of construction-related reading materials, here we offer some specific tips for reading graphics and other visual materials.

As you read through the following sections, keep in mind that construction-related visual materials are generally used for two reasons:

- **To condense.** Pages of repetitious, detailed information are often summarized in a clean, easy-to-read format.
- **To clarify.** Machine parts, complex relationships, and procedures can be simplified and explained, piece by piece or step by step.

TIP: The first step in reading a graphic is reading its title. The title is the key to unlocking the graphic's meaning.

6.1.1 Illustrations

An *illustration* is a drawing designed to show you how something looks. Illustrations can be very useful the first time you are introduced to a concept, a tool, or some other item you're not familiar with.

Illustrations vary in complexity. Some simply show what things look like. For example, Figure 6.1 introduces the different types of trowels used in modern masonry work. Such a figure would be very useful to a new masonry apprentice not familiar with the tools of the trade.

Other illustrations show the different parts of a tool, machine, or system. Such illustrations can be useful in helping you learn the terminology of your chosen profession. Figure 6.2 is an illustration of oxyacetylene brazing equipment, which is used for brazing. (If you're not familiar with the term, *brazing*— also known as *hard soldering*—is the use of nonferrous filler metals to join base metals that have a melting point above that of the filler metals. It produces mechanically strong, pressure-resistant joints.)

Note that Figure 6.2 labels the different parts of the equipment, including the acetylene and oxygen cylinder valves, flashback arresters, and acetylene and oxygen regulators. Clearly, you will need to be familiar with *all* of these terms if you will be working with brazing equipment. A written explanation would explain what all these items *do,* but the diagram shows you *what* they look like and *where* you can find them on the equipment.

Some diagrams exist only to introduce or explain techniques or terminology. For example, all plumbers must know how to measure pipe accurately.

Brick

Plastering or Parging

Pointing

Margin

Tuck-pointer

Pointing

Buttering

Duck bill

Figure 6.1:   Trowels
Source: National Center for Construction Education and Research, *Masonry Trainee Guide* (Upper Saddle River, NJ/Columbus, OH: Prentice Hall, 1998), Module 28101, p. 33.

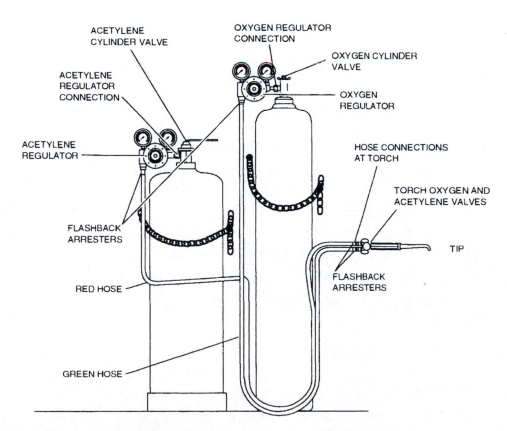

ACETYLENE CYLINDER VALVE

OXYGEN REGULATOR CONNECTION

OXYGEN CYLINDER VALVE

ACETYLENE REGULATOR CONNECTION

OXYGEN REGULATOR

ACETYLENE REGULATOR

HOSE CONNECTIONS AT TORCH

TORCH OXYGEN AND ACETYLENE VALVES

FLASHBACK ARRESTERS

TIP

RED HOSE

FLASHBACK ARRESTERS

GREEN HOSE

Figure 6.2:   Oxyacetylene Brazing Equipment
Source: National Center for Construction Education and Research, *Plumbing Trainee Guide* (Upper Saddle River, NJ/Columbus, OH: Prentice Hall, 1992), Module 02202, p. 14.

Pipe fitters must learn the difference between "end to end," "face to face," "end to face," and "face to crotch" measurements. An illustration like Figure 6.3 illustrates how each of these measurements would be taken.

Sometimes, textbooks and manuals may also use black-and-white or color photographs as illustrations.

TIPS FOR READING ILLUSTRATIONS:

- Don't assume that you already know everything in the illustration. Take a few minutes to look at each illustration closely. Then, either confirm your knowledge or adjust what you know on the basis of the illustration.
- If the illustration uses words you don't know, take the time to learn them. Check the text, manual, or glossary for further explanation of the terms, if need be.
- Use a Post-It note to mark key illustrations, and return to them periodically as necessary. An illustration can be the fastest way to find the information you need.

Activity 6.1: Reading Illustrations

Use Figures 6.1, 6.2, and 6.3 to answer the questions that follow.

SET A: FIGURE 6.1—TROWELS

1. Which trowel contains a long, flat, rectangular surface? _____
2. Which trowel is a handle attached to a thin narrow tube bent at a 90-degree angle? _____
3. The illustration shows two different styles of trowel that go by the same name. What is this type of trowel called? _____
4. Other than the pointing trowels, which trowel has the pointiest tip? _____
5. How do you think the duck bill trowel got its name? _____

SET B: FIGURE 6.2—OXYACETYLENE BRAZING EQUIPMENT

1. The illustration makes it clear that two substances are used in brazing, one in each tank. What are these two substances? _____ and _____
2. What color is the hose attached to the acetylene tank? _____
3. What color is the hose attached to the oxygen tank? _____
4. How many flashback arresters are used in this equipment? _____
5. Through what part of the system is the oxyacetylene combination discharged? _____

SET C: FIGURE 6.3—PIPE MEASURING TECHNIQUES

1. Which method of measurement is best used with a pipe with no elbow joints attached? _____
2. Which three methods of measurement are used with a pipe that has an elbow joint attached at both ends? _____ , _____ , and _____

(Continued on page 150)

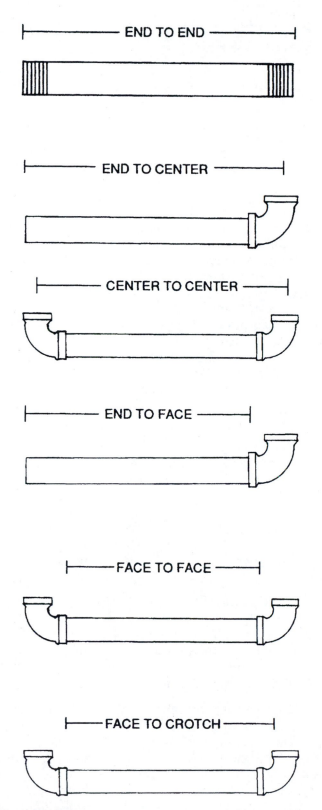

END TO END

END TO CENTER

CENTER TO CENTER

END TO FACE

FACE TO FACE

FACE TO CROTCH

Figure 6.3: **Pipe Measuring Techniques**
Source: National Center for Construction Education and Research, *Plumbing Trainee Guide* (Upper Saddle River, NJ/Columbus, OH: Prentice Hall, 1992), Module 02105, p. 3.

3. Which two methods of measurement are used with pipe that has an elbow joint attached at only one end? _____ and

_____

4. Based on the illustration, what does the term "center" mean?

_____

5. Based on the illustration, what does the term "crotch" mean?

_____

6.1.2 Diagrams

Unlike illustrations, which simply get you acquainted with the way something looks, *diagrams* explain how a system works or how a procedure must be done. For this reason, they are usually more complex than illustrations. This means that they usually take longer to read as well.

Diagrams must be studied with the text (words) that accompany them. In general, it is best to go back and forth between the text and the diagram. The text should make the diagram clear, and vice versa. The diagram is a visual aid to help you understand the text.

For example, look at Figure 6.4. This diagram shows how forced-air heat works. It may seem self-explanatory, but the system's workings are even more clear when you read the text that accompanies the drawing:

> Early humans burned fuel as a source of heat. That hasn't changed; what's different between now and then is the way it's done. We no longer need to huddle around a wood fire to keep warm. Instead, a central heating source such as a furnace or boiler does the job using the **heat transfer** principle. That is, heat is created in one place and carried to another place by means of air or water.
>
> For example, in a common household furnace, fuel oil or natural gas is burned to create heat, which warms metal plates known as heat exchangers (Figure 6.4). Air from living spaces is circulated over the heat exchangers and returned to the living spaces as heated air. This type of system is known as a forced-air system.[1]

By reading the text as you look at Figure 6.4, you can see how the furnace generates the heat and circulates it throughout the house.

As another example, look at Figure 6.5, "The Brickmaking Process." This diagram shows how bricks are made from clay, beginning with mining, continuing through forming, drying, firing, and shipping. But to get the full picture, you will want to read the accompanying text:

> Brick has been developed and improved upon for centuries. The modern age in brick manufacturing started with the first brickmaking machine. It was powered by a steam engine and patented in 1800. The process, shown in Figure 6.5, has not changed much. The clay is mined, pulverized, and screened. It is mixed with water, formed, and cut into shape. Some manufacturing plants extrude the clay, punch holes into it, then cut it into shape. Any coating or glazing is applied before the units are air dried. After drying, the brick is fired in a kiln. Because of small variations in materials and firing temperatures, not all bricks are exactly alike. Even bricks made and fired in the same batch have variations in color and shading. The

---

[1]National Center for Construction Education and Research, *Heating, Ventilation, and Air Conditioning Trainee Guide* (Upper Saddle River, NJ/Columbus, OH: Prentice Hall, 1995, 1999), Module 03101, p. 5.

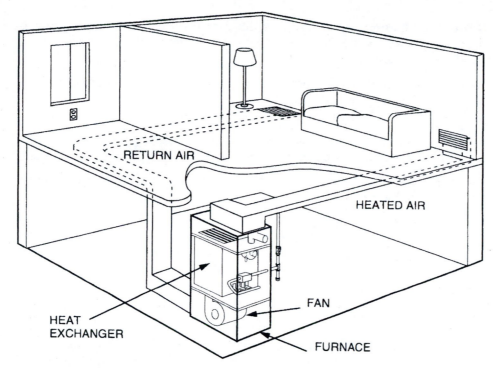

Figure 6.4:   Forced-Air Heat

Source: National Center for Construction Education and Research, *Heating, Ventilation, and Air Conditioning Trainee Guide* (Upper Saddle River, NJ/Columbus, OH: Prentice Hall, 1995, 1999), Module 03101, p. 5.

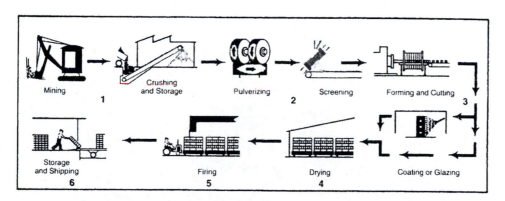

Figure 6.5:   The Brickmaking Process

Source: National Center for Construction Education and Research, *Masonry Trainee Guide* (Upper Saddle River, NJ/Columbus, OH: Prentice Hall, 1998), Module 28101, p. 15.

brick is slowly cooled to prevent cracking. It is then bundled into cubes and shipped. A **cube** traditionally holds 500 bricks, or 90 blocks, although manufacturers today make cubes of varying sizes.[2]

When reading a diagram that explains a procedure step by step, make sure you understand whether the diagram shows the *whole* process or only *part* of it. Look at Figure 6.6 on page 152, which shows how to install an anchor bolt in hardened concrete. Here is the accompanying text:

---

[2]National Center for Construction Education and Research, *Masonry Trainee Guide* (Upper Saddle River, NJ/Columbus, OH: Prentice Hall, 1998), Module 28101, p. 15.

Module 6

Here is an example of a typical procedure used to install many types of expansion anchors in hardened concrete or masonry. Refer to Figure 6.6 as you study the procedure.

Step One: Drill the anchor bolt hole the same size as the anchor bolt. The hole must be deep enough for six threads of the bolt to be below the surface of the concrete. Clean out the hole using a squeeze bulb.

Step Two: Drive the anchor bolt into the hole using a hammer. Protect the threads of the bolt with a nut that does not allow any threads to be exposed.

Step Three: Put a washer and nut on the bolt, and tighten the nut with a wrench until the anchor is secure in the concrete.[3]

Note that Figure 6.6 shows the procedure step by step. It is an excellent diagram to accompany the text. However, the diagram does *not* show cleaning the hole with a squeeze bulb. If you just look at the diagram without reading the text, you might miss this part of the process.

Before you look at Figure 6.7, read the following section on safety gear for masonry craftworkers:

In general, the employer is responsible to OSHA for making sure that all employees are wearing appropriate personal protective equipment whenever those employees are exposed to possible hazards to their safety. In turn, you are responsible for wearing the gear and clothing assigned to you.

Properly dressed masonry craftworkers are the workers who dress safely for the jobs they perform. It is important, for example, to take the following safety precautions when dressing for masonry work:

- Remove all jewelry, including wedding rings, bracelets, necklaces, and earrings. Jewelry can get caught on or in equipment, which could result in a lost finger, ear, or other appendage.

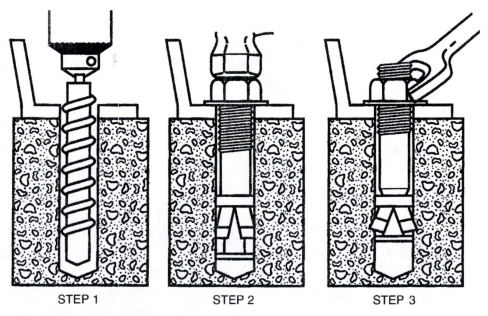

STEP 1   STEP 2   STEP 3

Figure 6.6: Installing an Anchor Bolt in Hardened Concrete
Source: National Center for Construction Education and Research, *Electrical Trainee Guide* (Upper Saddle River, NJ/Columbus, OH: Prentice Hall, 2000), Module 26103, p. 3–35.

---

[3]National Center for Construction Education and Research, *Electrical Trainee Guide* (Upper Saddle River, NJ/Columbus, OH: Prentice Hall, 2000), Module 26103, p. 3–34.

- Confine long hair in a ponytail or in your hard hat. Flying hair can obscure your view or get caught in machinery.
- Wear close-fitting clothing that is appropriate for the job. Clothing should be comfortable and should not interfere with the free movement of your body. Clothing or accessories that do not fight tightly, or that are too loose or torn, may get caught in tools, materials, or scaffolding.
- Wear face and eye protection if required or if there is a risk from flying particles, debris, or other hazards such as brick dust or chemicals.
- Wear hearing protection as required.
- Wear respiratory protection as required.
- Wear a long-sleeved shirt so as to provide extra protection for your skin.
- Protect any exposed skin by applying skin cream, body lotion, or petroleum jelly.
- Wear sturdy work boots or work shoes with thick soles. Never show up for work dressed in sneakers or gym shoes.
- Wear fall protection equipment as required.

Figure 6.7 shows a craftworker equipped with all appropriate personal protective equipment for most masonry jobs.[4]

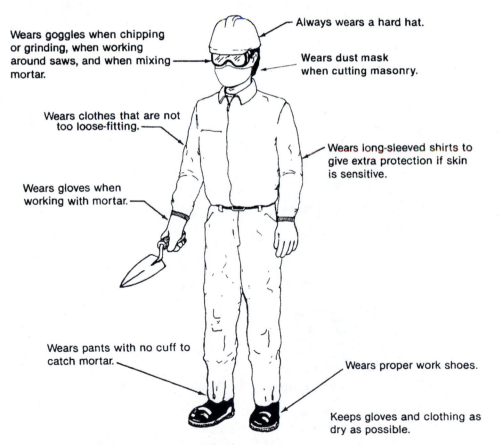

Figure 6.7: Personal Protective Equipment for Masonry Workers

Source: National Center for Construction Education and Research, *Masonry Trainee Guide* (Upper Saddle River, NJ/Columbus, OH: Prentice Hall, 1998), Module 28102, p. 26.

[4]National Center for Construction Education and Research, *Masonry Trainee Guide* (Upper Saddle River, NJ/Columbus, OH: Prentice Hall, 1998), Module 28102, p. 25.

Note that the figure gives a good overview of personal protective equipment, but it leaves out several important points. For example, it doesn't show that the worker has removed his jewelry or confined his long hair into a ponytail. To know all this information, you must read the text that goes along with the figure.

REMEMBER WHEN READING DIAGRAMS:
- Always read the text accompanying the diagram.
- Use the diagram to visualize the process in your head.
- Keep studying the diagram until you have a good sense of how the procedure or process works.
- Be aware of whether the diagram tells the full story, or only part of it.

Activity 6.2: Reading Diagrams

Use Figures 6.4 through 6.7 to answer the following questions. To answer the questions correctly, you have to read the text along with the diagrams.

SET A: FIGURE 6.4—FORCED-AIR HEAT

_____ 1. How many floors does the house in the diagram appear to have?
   a. one
   b. two
   c. three
   d. four

_____ 2. What principle does the system in Figure 6.4 operate under?
   a. the heated air principle
   b. the forced-air principle
   c. the heat transfer principle
   d. the heat exchange principle

_____ 3. What is the central heating source in Figure 6.4?
   a. a furnace
   b. a turbine
   c. a boiler
   d. a fan

_____ 4. Air from the living spaces is circulated over the
   a. heat exchangers
   b. fan
   c. ventilation system
   d. heat transfer plates

_____ 5. Heated air is brought into the room by a vent placed on the
   _____ , while air is returned back to the furnace through a
   vent placed on the _____ .
   a. ceiling, floor
   b. wall, floor
   c. wall, wall
   d. floor, wall

Set B: Figure 6.5—The Brickmaking Process

_____ 1. Which is not a stage of the brickmaking process?
   a. coating
   b. firing
   c. manipulating
   d. pulverizing

_____ 2. What is Stage 5 of the brickmaking process?
   a. mining
   b. screening
   c. firing
   d. storage

_____ 3. In the firing phase, the brick is fired in
   a. a brick oven
   b. a tandoori oven
   c. a pottery oven
   d. a kiln

_____ 4. How many bricks does a cube traditionally hold?
   a. 500 bricks
   b. 90 bricks
   c. 500 blocks
   d. 95 bricks

_____ 5. Stage 2 of the brickmaking process consists of:
   a. mining and crushing
   b. pulverizing and screening
   c. forming and cutting
   d. drying and firing

Set C: Figure 6.6—Installing an Anchor Bolt in Hardened Concrete

_____ 1. The material into which the anchor bolt is being installed in Figure 6.6 is:
   a. hardened concrete
   b. soft concrete
   c. brick
   d. asphalt

_____ 2. The tool used in Step 2 of the process is a:
   a. screwdriver
   b. hammer
   c. sledgehammer
   d. awl

_____ 3. The tool used in Step 3 of the process is a:
   a. hammer
   b. screwdriver
   c. wrench
   d. vise

_____ 4. In Step 1, how many of the threads in the anchor bolt must be below the surface of the concrete?

    a. three

    b. four

    c. five

    d. six

_____ 5. In Step 2, why is a nut used?

    a. To protect the anchor bolt

    b. To drive in the anchor bolt

    c. To chip away some concrete

    d. To help expose the bolt's threads

SET D: FIGURE 6.7—PERSONAL PROTECTIVE EQUIPMENT FOR MASONRY WORKERS

_____ 1. The diagram in Figure 6.7 is specifically aimed at:

    a. electrical workers

    b. masons

    c. carpenters

    d. HVAC specialists

_____ 2. Refer back to Figure 6.1. What type of trowel is the man in Figure 6.7 carrying?

    a. duck bill trowel

    b. parging trowel

    c. margin trowel

    d. brick trowel

_____ 3. When must goggles be worn?

    a. while chipping or grinding

    b. when working around saws

    c. when mixing mortar

    d. all of the above

_____ 4. If the man in Figure 6.7 is dressed appropriately, his clothes will be:

    a. close-fitting

    b. very tight

    c. loose

    d. torn

_____ 5. The worker in Figure 6.7 is not wearing:

    a. a hard hat

    b. a dust mask

    c. fall protection equipment

    d. work shoes

6.1.3 Tables of Data

Tables condense data (pieces of information) into an easy-to-read, easy-to-access format. Most tables are formatted into horizontal *rows* and vertical *columns.* Each row and/or each column has a label. You find the information you need by looking at the intersection of the row and column—that is, by looking at the points where the rows and the columns meet.[5]

As an example, consider Figure 6.8. This table summarizes which hacksaw blades should be used to cut various materials. Note the labels of each column. The first column lists the stock to be cut—machine steel, aluminum, brass, copper, conduit, and so on. The second column lists the required pitch of the hacksaw blade—that is, the required number of teeth per inch. The third column, titled "Explanation," offers some additional comments.

You can use this table in several ways.

- Suppose that you are about to cut channel iron, and you need to know what type of hacksaw blade to use. In that case, you would look for "channel iron" in Column 1, and you would find channel iron listed in Row 4. You would then look across Row 4 until you're under Column 2. There you will find the required information: You need to use a hacksaw blade that has 24 teeth per inch.
- Suppose you have a hacksaw with 14 teeth per inch. You are wondering what types of materials you can cut with this blade. So, you look in Column 2 until you find "14 teeth per inch." You find that number in Row 2. You then look back to Column 1 of that same row, and determine that you can use this blade to cut machine steel, cold rolled steel, or structural steel. The explanation (in Column 3) tells you that the coarse pitch of the blade makes the saw free and fast cutting—very good for simple projects.

	(1)	(2)	(3)
	STOCK TO BE CUT	**PITCH OF BLADE (TEETH PER INCH)**	**EXPLANATION**
(2)	Machine steel Cold rolled steel Structural steel	14	The coarse pitch makes the saw free and fast cutting.
(3)	Aluminum Babbitt Tool steel High-speed steel Cast iron	18	Recommended for general use.
(4)	Tubing Tin Brass Copper Channel iron Steel metal (over 18 gauge)	24	Thin stock will tear and strip teeth on a blade of coarser pitch.
(5)	Small tubing Conduit Sheet metal (less than 18 gauge)	32	Recommended to avoid tearing.

Figure 6.8: Hacksaw Blades for Various Materials

Source: National Center for Construction Education and Research, *Heating, Ventilating, and Air Conditioning Trainee Guide* (Upper Saddle River, NJ/Columbus, OH: Prentice Hall, 1995, 1998), Module 03103, p. 14.

---

[5]Note that electronic spreadsheets such as Microsoft Excel worksheets also use a row/column format, as do blueprints. For more information, see Section 6.3.2.

Just as illustrations and diagrams are often accompanied by textual explanations, the same is true of tables. Figure 6.9 outlines the nominal and actual manufactured dimensions for nominal brick sizes and actual dimensions for nonmodular brick sizes. But, when looking at the table, you may realize that you don't understand the difference between modular and nonmodular bricks. For this information, you should turn to the accompanying explanation, which reads as follows:

The Modular System

Today, brick is made for use on the modular system of grid building. The dimensions are based on a 4-inch unit of measure called the **module.** The grid system makes it easier to combine different materials in a construction job. The grid system allows the traditional measurements for different materials to intersect, so that different kinds of joinings can be measured or calculated easily.

In modular design, the **nominal dimension** of a masonry unit is the specified or manufactured dimension plus the thickness of the standard mortar joint to be used. That is, the brick size is designed so that when the size of the

(1)	(2)	(3)	(4)	(5)	(6)	(7)	(8)	(9)
	Modular Brick Sizes							
(1) Unit Designation	**Nominal Dimensions Inches**			**Joint Thickness Inches**	**Specified Dimensions Inches**			**Vertical Coursing Inches**
	w	h	l		w	h	l	
(2) Modular	4	2⅔	8	⅜	3⅝	2¼	7⅝	3C = 8
				½	3½	2¼	7½	
(3) Engineer Modular	4	3⅕	8	⅜	3⅝	2¾	7⅝	5C = 16
				½	3½	2¹³⁄₁₆	7½	
(4) Closure Modular	4	4	8	⅜	3⅝	3⅝	7⅝	1C = 4
				½	3½	3½	7½	
(5) Roman	4	2	12	⅜	3⅝	1⅝	11⅝	2C = 4
				½	3½	1½	11½	
(6) Norman	4	2⅔	12	⅜	3⅝	2¼	11⅝	3C = 8
				½	3½	2¼	11½	
(7) Engineer Norman	4	3⅕	12	⅜	3⅝	2¾	11⅝	5C = 16
				½	3½	2¹³⁄₁₆	11½	
(8) Utility	4	4	12	⅜	3⅝	3⅝	11⅝	1C = 4
				½	3½	3½	11½	
	Nonmodular Brick Sizes							
(9) Standard				⅜	3⅝	2¼	8	3C = 8
				½	3½	2¼	8	
(10) Engineer Standard				⅜	3⅝	2¾	8	5C = 16
				½	3½	2¹³⁄₁₆	8	
(11) Closure Standard				⅜	3⅝	3⅝	8	1C = 4
				½	3½	3½	8	
(12) King				⅜	3	2¾	9⅝	5C = 16
					3	2⅝	9⅝	
(13) Queen				⅜	3	2¾	8	5C = 16

Figure 6.9: Sizes of Bricks

Source: Roy Jorgensen Associates, Inc.

mortar joint is added to any of the brick dimensions (thickness, height, length), the sum will equal a multiple of the 4-inch grid.

For example, a modular brick with a nominal length of 8 inches will have a manufactured dimension of 7 ½ inches if it is designed to be laid with a ½-inch mortar joint. It will have a manufactured dimension of 7 ⅝ inches if it is to be laid with a ⅜-inch joint.

Figure 6.9 shows nominal and actual manufactured dimensions for nominal brick sizes and actual dimensions for nonmodular brick sizes. It includes the planned joint thickness of ⅜ of an inch or ½-inch. The last column shows the number of courses required for each size of brick to equal a 4-inch modular unit or a multiple of a 4-inch unit.[6]

Now look at Figure 6.9. Note that Figure 6.9 offers dimensions for seven types of modular bricks (modular, engineer modular, closure modular, Roman, Norman, engineer Norman, and utility), as well as five nonmodular brick sizes (standard, engineer standard, closure standard, king, and queen). The table provides a wealth of information on each type of brick. For example:

- Looking at Row 5, you can see that the nominal dimensions of a Roman brick are $4 \times 2 \times 12$ inches (Columns 2, 3, and 4). However, the manufactured size of the actual brick differs depending on the size of the intended mortar joint. If a ⅜-inch mortar joint is to be used (Column 5), the dimensions of the manufactured brick will actually be $3 \, ⅝ \times 1 \, ⅝ \times 11 \, ⅝$ inches (Columns 6, 7, and 8). If a ½-inch mortar joint is to be used, the manufactured brick's dimensions will be $3 \, ½ \times 1 \, ½ \times 11 \, ½$ inches. Finally, the last column (Column 9) shows that, with Roman brick, 2 courses will total 4 inches ($2C = 4$).

REMEMBER WHEN READING TABLES:

- Be aware of the units of measurement used in the table.
- Read the headings of all columns and rows.
- If a date is provided, check to make sure that the information is still accurate and up-to-date.
- You don't need to read every row and column of the table. Rather, use the table to find the specific piece of information you need.

Activity 6.3: Reading Tables

Use Figures 6.8 and 6.9 to answer the following questions. Mark "T" if the statement is true, "F" if it is false.

SET A: FIGURE 6.8—HACKSAW BLADES FOR VARIOUS MATERIALS

_____ 1. A hacksaw blade of 18 teeth per inch is recommended for general use.

_____ 2. To avoid tearing the stock being cut, a hacksaw with 24 teeth per inch should be used.

_____ 3. A relatively low number of teeth per inch makes a hacksaw free and fast cutting.

_____ 4. Babbitt should be cut with a hacksaw with 14 teeth per inch.

[6]National Center for Construction Education and Research, *Masonry Trainee Guide* (Upper Saddle River, NJ/Columbus, OH: Prentice Hall, 1998), Module 28104, p. 11.

_____ 5. Stock that is over 18 gauge should be cut with a hacksaw pitch of 32 teeth per inch.

SET B: FIGURE 6.9—SIZES OF BRICKS

_____ 1. Roman bricks are considered nonmodular.

_____ 2. With King size brick, four courses equal 16 inches.

_____ 3. The nominal dimensions of a Modular brick are as follows: 2 ⅔" width, 4" height, and 8" long.

_____ 4. The specified length of a Closure Standard brick is 8 inches.

_____ 5. Both Engineer Norman and Utility brick can be used with a joint thickness of either ⅜" or ½".

_____ 6. 1 course = 4 inches for both the Closure Standard and the Closure Modular bricks.

_____ 7. A Modular brick with a nominal length of 8 inches will have a manufactured dimension of 7 ½ inches if it is designed to be laid with a ⅜ inch mortar joint.

_____ 8. The nominal length of a Utility brick is 4 inches.

_____ 9. The specified dimensions of a brick are 3 ½ × 3 ½ × 11 ½. When designed to be laid with a half-inch mortar joint, the nominal dimensions of the brick will be 4 × 4 × 12.

_____ 10. The specified length of all nonmodular bricks shown in the table is 8 inches, except for the King brick.

6.1.4 Maps

A *map* shows a geographic area, whether large or small. For example, a map may show an area as small as a single plot of land, or an area as large as a country or continent.

Maps can show aspects of topography, distances between two points, and a wealth of other characteristics. Some maps show other, nonphysical characteristics of the region.

We discussed road maps briefly in Section 5.5.3. As we saw in that section, the first step is reading the title of the map. Next, you should look at the *legend*. The legend usually appears in a separate box and explains what is happening in the map. Finally, you should read any text that accompanies the map.

Figure 6.10 shows a sample map of the United States. The title, "Geographic Distribution of Building Codes," gives the key to what this map is all about. The legend shows which building codes are in effect in each state. Finally, the accompanying text offers a bit more information:

Codes

Model codes are technical documents written by the members of three code organizations. The codes are concerned with more than one subject, and more than one aspect of each subject. They are based on, or incorporate by reference, many standards published by ASTM [American Society for Testing and Materials] and other standards organizations. The codes also reference other codes published by industry associations. The model codes and standards documents are available for adoption by state and local jurisdictions.

Geographic Distribution of Building Codes

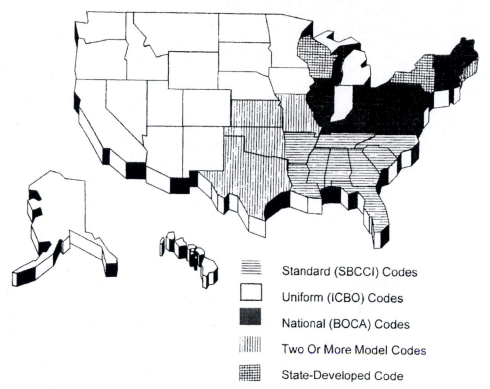

Standard (SBCCI) Codes

Uniform (ICBO) Codes

National (BOCA) Codes

Two Or More Model Codes

State-Developed Code

Figure 6.10:   Geographic Distribution of Building Codes
Source: Roy Jorgensen Associates, Inc.

If a jurisdiction adopts a model standard, it becomes a local, not a model, standard. In addition to the model contents, local codes also include local requirements, such as conformance with a zoning plan, or lot setbacks. Most local building codes in the United States are based on one of the following model codes:

- *The Southern Standard Building Code,* published by the Southern Building Code Congress (SBCC), is typically used throughout the Southeast.

- *The National Building Code,* published by the Building Officials and Code Administrators International (BOCA), is adopted mostly in the northeast and central states.

- *The Uniform Building Code,* published by the International Conference of Building Officials (ICBO), is used throughout the West.

The map in Figure 6.10 shows the areas of the United States where these codes are used.

These codes are used in different regions because they have different areas of concern. Western builders do not need to build against hurricane damage, but they must consider earthquakes. Southern builders must deal with higher humidity, but earthquakes are not as common as hurricanes. Local or regionally focused building codes take account of these differences in their contents.[7]

---

[7]National Center for Construction Education and Research, *Masonry Trainee Guide* (Upper Saddle River, NJ/Columbus, OH: Prentice Hall, 1998), Module 28104, pp. 40–41.

REMEMBER WHEN READING MAPS:

- Read the title first.
- Look at the legend to determine what the symbols stand for.

Activity 6.4: Reading Maps

Use Figure 6.10 to answer the following questions. Remember that you may need to read the accompanying text to answer the questions correctly.

Note: Before you complete this exercise, you may want to practice your geography. Use a reference text (such as an atlas) to make sure you can label all the states in the U.S. map shown in Figure 6.10.

_____   1. Which of the following states uses a state-developed code?
   a. New York
   b. Texas
   c. Alaska
   d. Maine

_____   2. The Uniform Codes are used mostly in:
   a. the southeastern United States
   b. New England
   c. The western states
   d. The Great Lakes region

_____   3. The Standard Codes are sometimes abbreviated as
   a. SC
   b. SBCCI
   c. ICBO
   d. BOCA

_____   4. Which of the following states does not use the National (BOCA) Codes?
   a. Maine
   b. Massachusetts
   c. New Jersey
   d. Florida

_____   5. Two states that use the same building codes are:
   a. Maine and New York
   b. Florida and California
   c. Utah and Minnesota
   d. Louisiana and Alaska

6.1.5 Web Pages

With the rise of the Internet and the World Wide Web, more and more companies are conducting business online. To keep up with the fast pace of business in the twenty-first century it is helpful to understand the basic components of Web pages on the Internet.

The *Internet* is a huge network that links hundreds of thousands of computers. The "Net," as it's called, allows you to access a large amount of information and services through the *World Wide Web* (WWW, or "Web"). All the documents on the Web have a similar format, and therefore can be read by just about any computer with an Internet browser. (A *browser* is a computer program that allows you to "surf" the Internet.)

Many companies and organizations have a *Web site,* a specific "place" on the Internet that includes and displays all their information. You get to the company's *home page* (the first page of its Web site) by typing the company's *URL* (short for Uniform Resource Locator) into your browser. On the company's home page, you will typically find basic information about the company, plus links to other important areas within the site. In essence, the home page is the "introductory" page from which you can navigate the whole site. For example, you can access the Associated Builders and Contractors home page by typing the following URL into your browser: *http://www.abc.org.*

This URL is broken down into the following components:

http://www.abc.org
  1   2   3   4

1. **http://** stands for "hypertext transfer protocol," which is the computer language that allows you to surf the Internet.

2. **www.** stands for "World Wide Web," the place on the Internet where the home page is housed.

3. **abc.** is the *domain name.* Generally, the domain name is the company's full name or an abbreviation. "abc" stands for "Associated Builders and Contractors."

4. **org** tells you the kind of organization whose home page you're accessing: "org" means a nonprofit organization, "com" means a for-profit business, "gov" means the U.S. government, and "edu" means an educational institution.

TIP: When you type a URL into your browser, you must type it 100% accurately. Every letter and period must be in the proper place. Otherwise, you will not be able to access the Web page.

Figure 6.11 on page 164 reproduces the home page for the National Center for Construction Education and Research (NCCER), a nonprofit educational foundation that publishes standardized construction training curricula. As you look at the Web page, note the following:

- Web pages are meant to be clicked on. If you roll your mouse cursor along the page, you will see the cursor turn into a hand whenever you can click on a particular word, phrase, picture, or box for more information. For example, you can get more information about any of the topics in the list on the left-hand side of the page by clicking on any of those topics.

- At the top of the page, below the "Welcome" bar, you can also get more information about NCCER, careers in construction, and craft skills assessment scores by clicking on those blocks. Usually, you can tell that more information is available about a subject when that subject is underlined, printed in color, or appears with an icon (a small graphic) or in a box.

- Note that the Web page also includes a paid advertisement from Delta Diversified Enterprises at the very top of the page. You can click on this

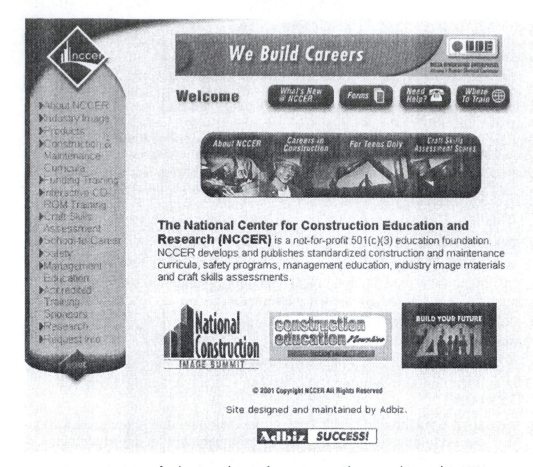

Figure 6.11:   Home Page for the National Center for Construction Education and Research (NCCER)
Source: *http://www.nccer.org.*

block for more information as well, but keep in mind that this is a paid advertisement, and is *not* part of NCCER's content.

> **TIP:** Many Web sites have a "Search" function that allows you to search for the specific information you need. This can be less time consuming than clicking all over the page until you find what you're looking for. To use the search function, just click on "Search," then enter a few words that correspond to what you're looking for. Or, you can use the "site map" that is included on many Web sites. The site map provides an overview of the contents of the entire Web site in one place.

If you're interested in viewing more construction-related Web sites, try the following:

Associated General Contractors of America	*http://www.agc.org*
Contractor Magazine online	*http://www.contractormag.com*
Engineering News Record	*http://www.enr.com*
Occupational Health and Safety Administration	*http://www.osha.gov*

For general sites that allow you to search the entire Internet for topics of interest to you, try the following *search engines*. When you type in the URL, you will be asked to provide a key word or words. Simply enter the topic you're looking for, and the search engines will search the entire World Wide Web looking for matches. You can find more tips on how to search effectively on the search engines' home pages.

Keep in mind that not all the material on the Internet is reliable or accurate. When looking at a Web site, you must actively evaluate its content to determine its reliability. (For more information on this topic, see Section 6.8.)

Alta Vista	*http://www.altavista.com*
DogPile	*http://www.dogpile.com*
Excite	*http://www.excite.com*
Web Crawler	*http://www.webcrawler.com*
Yahoo	*http://www.yahoo.com*

Construction Workers' Use of the Internet

The Internet explosion has truly come to the construction industry. Many companies are finding how effectively the Net helps them conduct their business. For example, some companies have begun keeping "project Web sites" that allow employees and clients to access key information and progress reports 24 hours a day.

Here are some other ways construction professionals are using the Net.

- To find addresses, phone numbers, driving directions, and maps.
- To order and get more information on tools.
- To obtain background information on a project or process.
- To research companies and their practices.
- To get current information about weather conditions and other important news.
- To receive additional training.
- To find and apply for jobs.
- To share ideas with other industry professionals.

Explore the ways in which the World Wide Web can help you.

Activity 6.5: Reading a Web page

Use the Web page in Figure 6.11 to answer the following questions. Mark "T" if the statement is true, "F" if it is false.

_____   1. NCCER is a not-for-profit organization.

_____   2. You can get more information about the topics on the left side of this home page by clicking on any of them.

_____   3. NCCER does not concern itself with safety programs.

_____   4. NCCER's home page offers a special section just for teenagers.

_____   5. NCCER offers interactive CD-ROM training.

Activity 6.6: Surfing the Net

Visit a construction-related Web site that interests you. (You may use one of the sites listed on page 164, or choose one of your own.) Answer the following questions about the site you've chosen.

1. What is the URL of the site you've chosen? What does each part of the URL mean?

2. What resources can be found on the organization's home page?

3. Do you think the Web site is well designed? That is, did you find it easy to read and follow? Were you able to find the information you were looking for?

4. How would you improve the Web site?

5. Does the Web site include advertisements? If so, from what kinds of companies or organizations? Were you interested in clicking on these "Web ads," or did you ignore them? Why?

6.2 READING MEASURING TAPES AND RULERS

Construction workers carry their rulers and measuring tapes everywhere. They are indispensable tools of the trade. For this reason, it's important that you be able to read them accurately.

Both steel rules and measuring tapes are divided into feet and inches. Keep the following equivalents in mind:

Twelve inches equals one foot.

Half a foot equals six inches.

One third of a foot equals four inches.

One quarter (or one fourth) of a foot equals three inches.

The abbreviation for *inch* or *inches* is ".

The abbreviation for *foot* or *feet* is '.

Steel Rules

Steel rules (and wood rules) are commonly only six or twelve inches long. In general, a steel rule is marked on both sides of the rule. Both sides carry the inch marks. These are the longest lines, and they appear at one-inch intervals (and are numbered accordingly). The inch lines generally start at the top of the ruler and go straight to the bottom.

Then, on one side of the ruler, each inch is divided into eight equal sections—that is, ⅛-inch intervals, along one edge of the ruler. On the other edge, the inch is divided into ¹⁄₁₆-inch intervals.

On the other side of the ruler, the inches are divided into thirty-seconds (along one edge) and sixty-fourths (along the other edge).

Usually, the lines for ¼, ½, and ¾ inches have different lengths to make counting easier. The larger the tick mark, the larger the unit of measurement. So, for example, the tick mark at ¾ inch will be longer than the tick mark at ½ inch, which will be longer than the tick mark at ¼ inch.

As you read your ruler, keep your basic math knowledge in mind:

1/4 inch = 2/8 inch = 4/16 inch = 8/32 inch = 16/64 inch
1/2 inch = 4/8 inch = 8/16 inch = 16/32 inch = 32/64 inch
3/4 inch = 6/8 inch = 12/16 inch = 24/32 inch = 48/64 inch

Also remember the following decimal equivalents:

1/4 inch = .25 inch
1/2 inch = .50 (or .5) inch
3/4 inch = .75 inch

Measuring Tapes

Measuring tapes are usually made of flexible, lightweight steel wound into metal cases. Often the tape will have a built-in lock that permits the tape to remain open for accurate measurements.

Unlike steel rules, measuring tapes are numbered only on one side. The primary unit of measurement is the inch. Each inch is then divided into thirty-seconds, sixteenths, or eighths. At the lower measurements, only the number of inches may be provided. At the higher measurements, both number of inches and foot/inch measurements may be provided. For example, at the 65-inch mark, the measuring tape may say both "65 inches" and "5 feet, 5 inches."

Keep the following mathematical principles in mind when working with measurements:

- To convert inches into feet, divide the number of inches by 12. The result is the number of feet. The remainder is the additional number of inches. For example, what is the foot/inch equivalent of 90 inches? 90 divided by 12 equals 7, with a remainder of 6. Thus, 90 inches equals 7 feet, 6 inches (or 7 ½ feet, or 7.5 feet).

- To convert feet into inches, multiply by 12. How many inches in 14 feet? Multiply 14 by 12. 14 × 12 = 168. Thus, 14 feet equals 168 inches.

Figure 6.12 shows the typical markings on a steel rule and on a measuring tape.

REMEMBER WHEN READING MEASURING DEVICES:

- The longer the tick mark, the larger the unit of measurement. The $\frac{1}{16}$th–inch mark will be the smallest, the $\frac{1}{8}$th–inch mark will be larger, the $\frac{1}{4}$–inch mark will be larger yet, and so on.

Figure 6.12: Steel Rule and Measuring Tape

- Always double check your measurement *at least* twice before you mark it down or act upon it.
- Learn the math equivalent measurements (pages 166–167) by heart.

A Note on Metrics

Throughout this book, we have been using the standard U.S. measurement system of inches and feet. However, the system in use in much of the world—and sometimes even in the United States—is the *metric system.* The basic unit of length measurement in the metric system is the *meter,* which is equal to approximately 3.28 feet. The basic unit of volume is called the *liter,* which is equal to about 1.05 quarts. The basic unit of weight is the gram, which is equal to about .03 of an ounce. In the metric system, temperature is measured in Celsius degrees, not Fahrenheit.

It is beyond the scope of this book to explain the metric system in detail. Here are a few key pointers.

- The metric system is based on units of ten, and can therefore be very easy to use. Keep the following equivalents in mind:

Distance:
1000 millimeters = 1 meter
  100 centimeters = 1 meter
  100 meters   = 1 hectometer
1000 meters   = 1 kilometer

Weight:
1000 milligrams = 1 gram
  100 centigrams = 1 gram
  100 grams   = 1 hectogram
1000 grams   = 1 kilogram

Volume:
1000 milliliters = 1 liter
  100 centiliters = 1 liter
  100 liters   = 1 hectoliter
1000 liters   = 1 kiloliter

- Just as there are standard rules and tape measures for inches and feet, there are rules and tape measures for the metric system.
- You will understand the metric system better when you can better understand the U.S. equivalents of metric measurements. To help you convert metrics to U.S. measures, or vice versa, you can use Table 6.1.

Activity 6.7: Reading Measuring Tapes and Rulers

Use your mathematical skills to answer the following questions about measuring.

_____ 1. 80 inches is equivalent to:
    a. 12 feet
    b. 8 feet, 8 inches
    c. 6 feet, 6 inches
    d. 6 feet, 8 inches

TABLE 6.1   Mathematical Conversion Tables for U.S./Metric and Metric/U.S.

How to Convert Units of Volume					
From	**Metric to English Multiply By**	**To Obtain**	**From**	**English to Metric Multiply By**	**To Obtain**
Liters	1.0567	Quarts	Quarts	0.946	Liters
Liters	2.1134	Pints	Pints	0.473	Liters
Liters	0.2642	Gallons	Gallons	3.785	Liters

How to Convert Units of Weight					
From	**Metric to English Multiply By**	**To Obtain**	**From**	**English to Metric Multiply By**	**To Obtain**
Grams	0.0353	Ounces	Pounds	0.4536	Kilograms
Grams	15.4321	Grains	Pounds	453.6	Grams
Kilograms	2.2046	Pounds	Ounces	28.35	Grams
Kilograms	0.0011	Tons (short)	Grains	0.0648	Grams
Tons (metric)	1.1023	Tons (short)	Tons (short)	0.9072	Tons (metric)

How to Convert Units of Length					
From	**Metric to English Multiply By**	**To Obtain**	**From**	**English to Metric Multiply By**	**To Obtain**
Meters	39.37	Inches	Inches	2.54	Centimeters
Meters	3.2808	Feet	Inches	0.0254	Meters
Meters	1.0936	Yards	Inches	25.4	Millimeters
			Miles	1,609,344	Millimeters
Centimeters	0.3937	Inches	Feet	0.3048	Meters
Millimeters	0.03937	Inches	Feet	30.48	Centimeters
Kilometers	0.6214	Miles	Yards	0.9144	Meters
			Yards	91.44	Centimeters
			Miles	1.6093	Kilometers

Source: National Center for Construction Education and Research, *Core Curriculum* (Upper Saddle River, NJ/Columbus, OH: 2000), Trainee Module 00102, p. 2–59.

_____ 2. 14 ½ feet equals
   a. 170 inches
   b. 172 inches
   c. 168 inches
   d. 174 inches

_____ 3. You are told to cut a piece of wood 24.5 inches in length. How long should this piece of wood be?
   a. 2 feet long
   b. 3 ½ feet long
   c. 2 feet, ½ inch long
   d. 2.25 feet long

_____ 4. Which of the following is not equivalent to ¾ of an inch?
   a. .75 inch
   b. ⅝ inch
   c. $^{24}\!/_{32}$ inch
   d. $^{16}\!/_{32}$ inch

_____ 5. On a steel rule, the longest vertical lines appear at the:
   a. inch-intervals
   b. ¾-inch intervals
   c. ½-inch intervals
   d. ¼-inch intervals

_____ 6. The difference between 3′ 6″ and 2′ 8″ is:
   a. one foot
   b. 10 inches
   c. 8 inches
   d. 6 inches

_____ 7. 46 feet, 6 inches can be abbreviated as:
   a. 46+6″
   b. 52″
   c. 46″ 6′
   d. 46′ 6″

_____ 8. On a measuring tape, the tick mark for ½″ would be the same length as the tick mark for:
   a. $^{8}\!/_{16}$″
   b. $^{8}\!/_{12}$″
   c. ⅝″
   d. $^{9}\!/_{12}$″

_____ 9. 72 feet equals how many inches?
   a. 864
   b. 684
   c. 6
   d. 12

_____ 10. Of the following, which is the smallest measurement?
   a. $^{1}\!/_{16}$″
   b. $^{1}\!/_{16}$′
   c. $^{1}\!/_{32}$″
   d. $^{1}\!/_{32}$′

6.3 READING BLUEPRINTS[8]

Few construction documents are more important than *blueprints,* the set of plans that detail what is to be built and what materials are to be used. In fact, because they include so much essential information, blueprints are incorpo-

---

[8]Blueprints are very complex. This section should be considered an introduction to blueprints, not an exhaustive discussion of them. For an excellent, in-depth look at blueprints, see James A. S. Fatzinger, *Blueprint Reading for Construction* (Upper Saddle River, NJ/Columbus, OH: Prentice Hall, 1998).

rated into building contracts "by reference," making them part of the legal documents associated with the project. Regardless of your construction specialty, an in-depth knowledge of how to read blueprints is essential to your success in the industry.

In the past, blueprints were drawn by hand. Today, they are usually produced using *computer-aided drafting (CAD)* systems. Table 6.2 outlines the six types of plans that are included in a complete set of blueprints for a project.

6.3.1 Key Blueprint Terminology

Blueprints can be very complex, filled with all kinds of abbreviations and specialized terminology. As you progress through your construction career, you will learn what all these abbreviations and words mean. However, there are some important terms you should know from the start.

- *Elevation (EL) drawings* are architectural drawings. They show side views. They're called "elevations" because they show height. *Exterior elevations* show the size and style of the building, as well as the placement of windows, doors, chimneys, and decorative trim. Figure 6.13 on page 172 shows the north, south, east, and west elevation (i.e., the four exterior sides) of a house. *Interior elevations* show details of designs and finishes in the individual rooms of the building.

TABLE 6.2   Types of Plans in a Complete Set of Blueprints

Type	Definition and Description
Civil plans	Civil plans are also called *site plans* or *survey plans*. Civil plans show the location of the building on the site from an aerial view, the natural contours of the earth, dimensions of the property, and natural features of the property (such as trees).
Architectural plans	Architectural plans are also called *architectural drawings*. Architectural plans include *floor plans*, which show the layout of each room from an aerial view, including stairways, doors, exterior and interior walls, and mechanical equipment. A floor plan of a house, for example, shows what the house would look like from above if the roof were removed. *Roof plans* show an aerial view of the roof of the building. Architectural plans usually also include *schedules* for the types of doors, windows, hardware, and fixtures to be used in completing the project.
Structural plans	Structural plans are engineered drawings used to support the architectural design. Structural plans include a *foundation plan*, which shows the lowest level of the building, including concrete footings and foundation walls, and a *roof framing* plan, which shows what kinds of roof rafters and ceiling joists are to be used and where trusses are to be placed.
Mechanical plans	Mechanical plans are engineered plans for such mechanical equipment as pumps, piping systems, and motors. *Piping and instrumentation drawings* show the process flow of a complete piping system. HVAC plans are also considered mechanical plans.
Plumbing plans	Plumbing plans are engineered plans showing the layout of the plumbing system and the location of the plumbing fixtures. These plans show the system that supplies hot and cold water, as well as the sewage disposal system.
Electrical plans	Electrical plans are engineered plans for electrical supply and distribution. These include the location of the electric meter, distribution panel, outlets, switchgear, and so forth.

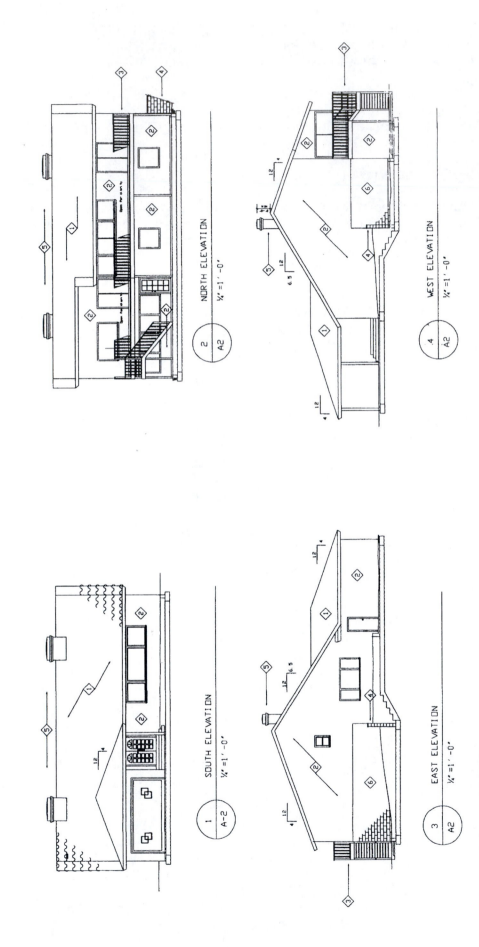

Figure 6.13: North, South, East, and West Elevations

Source: James A. Fatzinger, Blueprint set to accompany *Blueprint Reading for Construction* (Upper Saddle River, NJ/Columbus, OH: Prentice Hall, 1998).

- *Section drawings* are cross-sectional views that show the inside of an object or building. They show the construction materials used and how the various parts fit together. Figure 6.14 shows a section drawing.
- *Detail drawings* are enlarged drawings of specific features of the building. They are used to make the details clearer.
- Many architectural plans are drawn to *scale*. This means that everything in the plan is drawn in exact proportion to reality, with some smaller unit of measurement corresponding to a specific larger unit of measurement. For example, a scale of 1″ = 10′0″ means that every one inch on the drawing represents 10 feet, 0 inches. A scale of 1/4″ = 5′0″ means that every quarter inch on the drawing represents 5 feet, 0 inches in the finished project. Drawings that are not drawn to scale are labeled *NTS* ("not to scale").

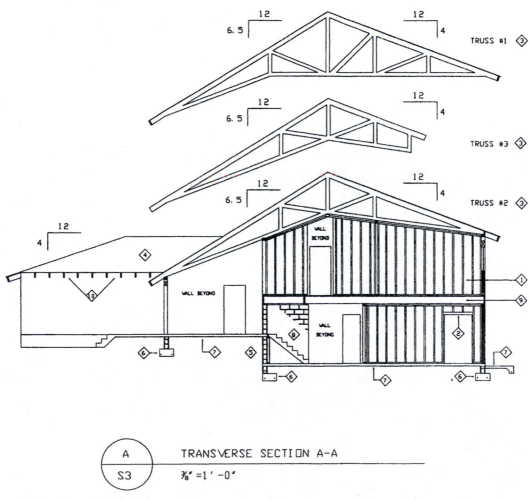

TRANSVERSE SECTION A-A

⅜″ =1′ −0″

Figure 6.14:   Section Drawing

Source: James A. Fatzinger, Blueprint set to accompany *Blueprint Reading for Construction* (Upper Saddle River, NJ/Columbus, OH: Prentice Hall, 1998).

Activity 6.8: Understanding Blueprint Terminology I

Match the term in Column A with its corresponding definition in Column B.

Column A	Column B
_____ 1. Plumbing plans	a. Show the natural contours of the earth from an aerial view and natural features of the property.
_____ 2. Floor plans	b. Show aerial views of the roof of a building.
_____ 3. Piping and instrumentation drawings	c. Show the layout of a room from an aerial view.
_____ 4. Civil plans	d. Show the location of the distribution panel, electric meter, outlets, and switchgear.
_____ 5. Schedules	e. Show the types of ceiling joists and roof rafters to be used and where trusses are to be placed.
_____ 6. Electrical plans	f. Show sewage disposal systems and water supply systems.
_____ 7. Foundation plans	g. Lists of the types of doors, windows, hardware, and fixtures to be used on a project.
_____ 8. Roof plans	h. Show the lowest level of a building, including foundation walls and concrete footings.
_____ 9. Roof framing plans	i. Show the process flow of a complete piping system.

Activity 6.9: Understanding Blueprint Terminology II

Place the terms in the box below into the correct categories in the table that follows.

> architectural drawings
> floor plans
> foundation plans
> HVAC plans
> piping and instrumentation drawings
> roof framing plans
> roof plans
> site plans
> survey plans

Civil Plans	Architectural Plans	Structural Plans	Mechanical Plans
(Also known as _____)	(Also known as _____)	_____	_____
(Also known as _____)	_____	_____	_____
	_____		

Activity 6.10: Working with Blueprints: The Basics

Using your knowledge of blueprints, answer the following questions.

SET A: MULTIPLE CHOICE

_____ 1. Suppose you are working on the construction of new luxury homes. You are looking for a drawing that shows the height of the living room, along with the design details of that room. The blueprint you would look for is called a(n):
   a. section drawing
   b. interior elevation
   c. exterior elevation
   d. detail drawing

_____ 2. You are looking at a particularly intricate blueprint. To make certain parts of the blueprint clearer, the architect has included enlarged drawings of those parts. These enlarged drawings are called:
   a. section drawings
   b. scale drawings
   c. exterior elevations
   d. detail drawings

_____ 3. You are looking for a drawing that shows what the inside of a chimney looks like, and how all of its parts fit together. Such a drawing is called a(n):
   a. chimney elevation
   b. interior chimney diagram
   c. section diagram
   d. exterior chimney elevation

_____ 4. Suppose an exterior elevation is drawn to a scale of 1″ = 35′0″. In this drawing, two inches would be the equivalent of:
   a. 17 ½ feet
   b. 35 inches
   c. 70 feet
   d. 35 feet

_____ 5. On one set of plans, certain components of the plumbing system are not drawn to scale. This set of plans would be labeled:
   a. EL
   b. 1″=10′0″
   c. NTS
   d. PS

SET B:

Use Figure 6.13 to answer the following questions. Mark "T" if the statement is true, "F" if it is false.

_____ 1. This blueprint shows four elevations: north, south, east, and west.

_____ 2. All of the elevations in Figure 6.13 are drawn to the same scale.

_____ 3. The east elevation shows two windows and a door.

_____ 4. The south elevation most likely depicts the rear of the house.

_____ 5. The elevations in this figure are all interior elevations.

Set C:

Use Figure 6.14, "Section Drawing," to answer the following questions. Mark "T" if the statement is true, "F" if it is false.

_____ 1. Four trusses are to be used in this building.

_____ 2. Pictured in this blueprint is a transverse section.

_____ 3. In this blueprint, 1/2″ is the equivalent of one foot.

_____ 4. Four doors are shown in this blueprint.

_____ 5. This blueprint is NTS.

6.3.2 The Components of a Blueprint

Although blueprints may look very different depending on the system being represented, all blueprints have certain elements in common. In this section, we look at those common elements: title blocks, legends, abbreviations lists, general notes, lines of construction, gridlines, and keynotes.

Title Block

The title block shows the blueprint's key identifying information, including a number that allows the blueprint to be easily filed and retrieved. The title block is usually found in the lower right-hand corner of the blueprint.

Title blocks vary from company to company, but most title blocks include the following information:

1. Company name and/or logo	Usually preprinted on the blueprint.
2. Sheet title	The type of blueprint.
3. Date	The date the blueprint was drawn, checked, readied, or issued.
4. Drawn	The initials of the draftsperson who drew the blueprint.
5. Drawing number	The code number assigned to the drawing.
6. Scale	The scale used in the drawing.
7. Revision block	Area for recording information on revisions, including the type of revision made, the date, and the person making the revision. All revisions must be indicated in this area.
8. Other information	Other identifying information may be included, as deemed appropriate by the company. Most of the time, the title block will specify the person or company for which the blueprints were drawn.

Figure 6.15 shows two sample title blocks. Note that the format of the title block varies from company to company.

Legends

A *legend* is a list of the symbols used in the blueprint, along with a description of what each symbol means. There are thousands of different symbols; you will come to understand them as you gain more experience in the industry. Figure 6.16 on pages 178–180 illustrates some of the most commonly used blueprint symbols.

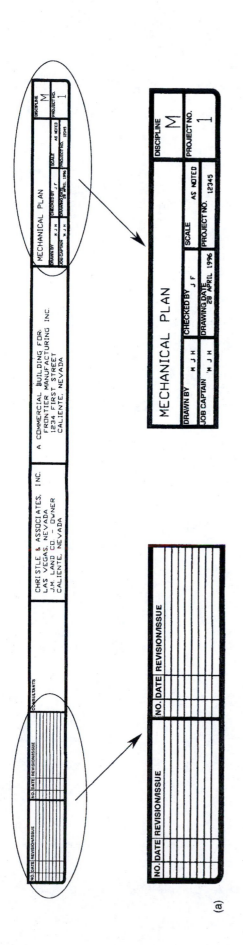

Figure 6.15: Title Blocks

Source: (a) James A. Fatzinger, Blueprint set to accompany *Blueprint Reading for Construction* (Upper Saddle River, NJ/Columbus, OH: Prentice Hall, 1998). (b) Blueprint set to accompany National Center for Construction Education and Research, *Masonry Trainee Guide* (Upper Saddle River, NJ/Columbus, OH: Prentice Hall, 1995, 1998).

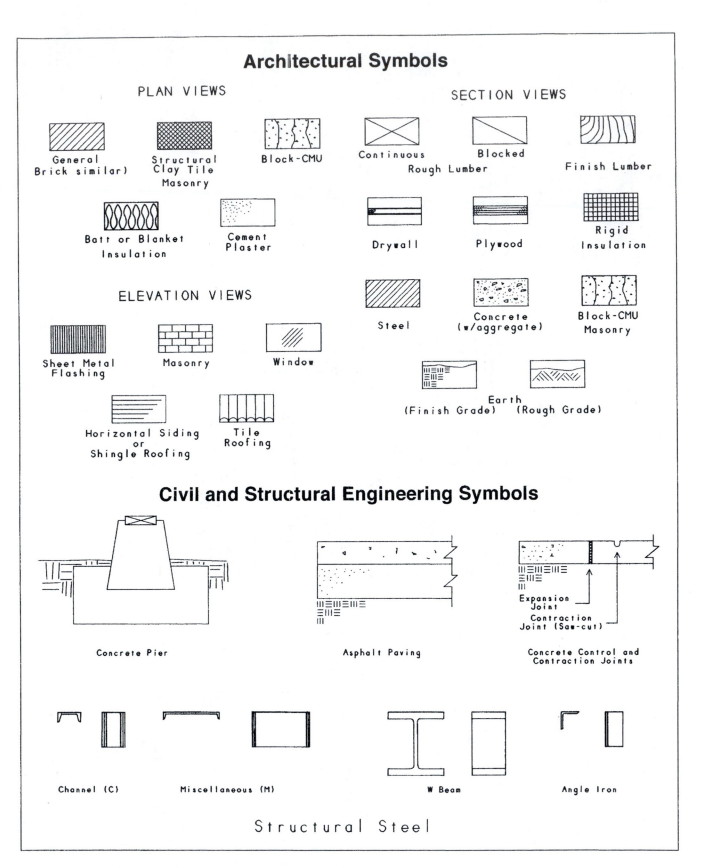

Figure 6.16: Common Blueprint Symbols

Source: James A. Fatzinger, *Blueprint Reading for Construction*. Reprinted by permission of Pearson Education, Inc., Upper Saddle River, NJ.

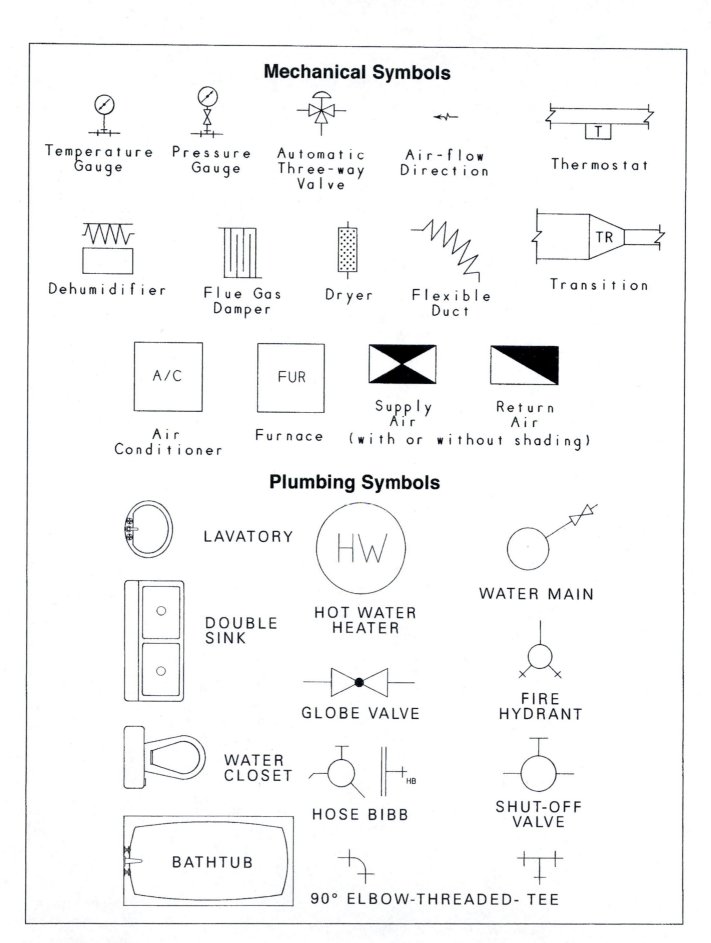

Mechanical Symbols

Temperature Gauge

Pressure Gauge

Automatic Three-way Valve

Air-flow Direction

Thermostat

Dehumidifier

Flue Gas Damper

Dryer

Flexible Duct

Transition

A/C — Air Conditioner

FUR — Furnace

Supply Air

Return Air
(with or without shading)

Plumbing Symbols

LAVATORY

DOUBLE SINK

WATER CLOSET

BATHTUB

HW — HOT WATER HEATER

GLOBE VALVE

HB — HOSE BIBB

90° ELBOW - THREADED - TEE

WATER MAIN

FIRE HYDRANT

SHUT-OFF VALVE

Figure 6.16: Continued

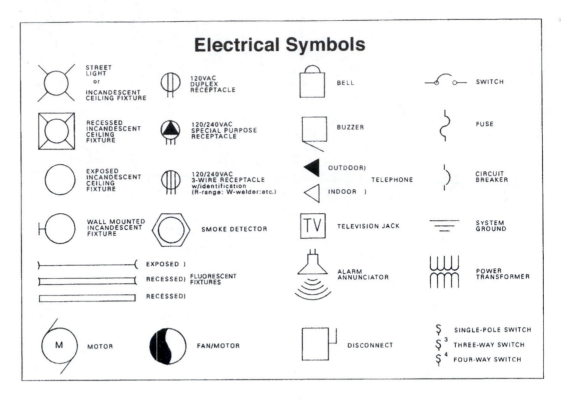

Figure 6.16:   Continued

Abbreviations List

Many blueprints include a list of all the abbreviations used in the blueprint. (*Note:* The letters in an abbreviation are always capitalized.) Figure 6.17 shows a list of commonly used electrical abbreviations.

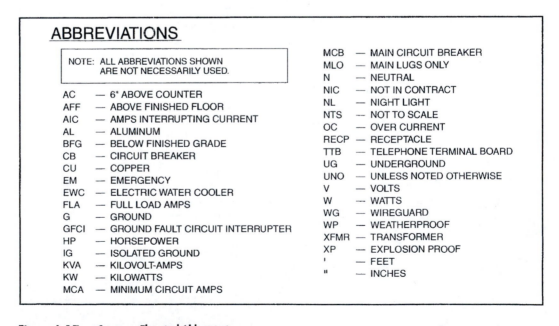

Figure 6.17:   Common Electrical Abbreviations

Source: National Center for Construction Education and Research, *Core Curriculum* (Upper Saddle River, NJ/Columbus, OH: Prentice Hall, 2000), Module 00105, p. 5–29.

General Notes

Many blueprints include a set of *general notes,* written descriptions that detail the materials to be used and the procedures to be followed in designing the system or building the structure. Figure 6.18 shows the general notes for an electrical plan.

Lines of Construction

Lines have very specific meanings on blueprints. Different lines mean different things. For example, *dimension lines* show the sizes of the parts of a structure, and they end with open or closed arrowheads. *Hidden lines* show a part of the

---

GENERAL NOTES (FOR ALL ELECTRICAL SHEETS)

1. COORDINATE LOCATION OF LUMINARIES WITH ARCHITECTURAL REFLECTED CEILING PLANS.

2. COORDINATE LOCATION OF ALL OUTLETS WITH ARCHITECTURAL ELEVATIONS, CASEWORK SHOP DRAWINGS AND EQUIPMENT INSTALLATION DRAWINGS.

3. COORDINATE LOCATION OF MECHANICAL EQUIPMENT WITH MECHANICAL PLANS AND MECHANICAL CONTRACTOR PRIOR TO ROUGH-IN.

4. PROVIDE (1) 3/4"C WITH PULL WIRE FROM EACH TELEPHONE, DATA OR COMMUNICATION OUTLET SHOWN, TO ABOVE ACCESSIBLE CEILING, AND CAP.

5. 3-LAMP FIXTURES SHOWN HALF SHADED HAVE INBOARD SINGLE LAMP CONNECTED TO EMERGENCY BATTERY PACK FOR FULL LUMEN OUTPUT. SEE SPECIFICATIONS.

6. SITE PLAN DOES NOT INDICATE ALL OF THE UG UTILITY LINES, RE: CIVIL DRAWINGS FOR ADDITIONAL INFORMATION. CONTRACTOR TO FIELD VERIFY EXACT LOCATION OF ALL EXISTING UNDERGROUND UTILITY LINES OF ALL TRADES PRIOR TO ANY SITE WORK.

7. THE LOCATIONS OF ALL SMOKE DETECTORS SHOWN ARE CONSIDERED TO BE SCHEMATIC ONLY. THE ACTUAL LOCATIONS (SPACING TO ADJACENT DETECTORS, WALLS, ETC.) ARE REQUIRED TO MEET NFPA 72.

8. ANY ITEMS DAMAGED BY THE CONTRACTOR SHALL BE REPLACED BY THE CONTRACTOR.

9. "CLEAN POWER" AND COMMUNICATION/COMPUTER SYSTEM REQUIREMENTS SHALL BE COORDINATED WITH COMMUNICATION/COMPUTER SYSTEMS CONTRACTOR.

10. REFER TO ARCHITECTURAL PLANS, ELEVATIONS AND DIAGRAMS FOR LOCATIONS OF FLOOR DEVICES AND WALL DEVICES. LOCATION WILL INDICATE VERTICAL AND/ OR HORIZONTAL MOUNTING. IF DEVICES ARE NOT NOTED OTHERWISE THEY SHALL BE MOUNTED LONG AXIS HORIZONTAL AT +16" TO CENTER.

11. ALL PLUGMOLD SHOWN SHALL BE WIREMOLD SERIES V2000 (IVORY FINISH) WITH SNAPICOIL #V20GB06 (OUTLETS 6" ON CENTER). PROVIDE ALL NECESSARY MOUNTING HARDWARE, ELBOWS, CORNERS, ENDS, ETC. REQUIRED FOR A COMPLETE SYSTEM.

12. ALL EMERGENCY RECEPTACLE DEVICES SHALL BE RED IN COLOR.

13. ALL BRANCH CIRCUITS SHALL BE 3-WIRE (HOT, NEUTRAL, GROUND).

14. COORDINATE EXACT EQUIPMENT LOCATIONS AND POWER REQUIREMENTS WITH OWNER AND ARCHITECT PRIOR TO ROUGH-INS.

15. ADA COMPLIANCE: ALL ADA HORN/STROBE UNITS SHALL BE MOUNTED +90" AFF OR 6" BELOW FINISHED CEILING, WHICHEVER IS LOWER. ELECTRICAL DEVICES PROJECTING FROM WALLS WITH THEIR LEADING EDGES BETWEEN 27" AND 80" AFF SHALL PROTRUDE NO MORE THAN 4" INTO WALKS OR CORRIDORS. ELECTRICAL AND COMMUNICATIONS SYSTEMS RECEPTACLES ON WALLS SHALL BE 15" MINIMUM AFF TO BOTTOM OF COVERPLATE.

16. COORDINATE ALL UNDERGROUND PENETRATIONS INTO THE BUILDING AND TUNNEL WITH STRUCTURAL ENGINEER, DUE TO EXPANSIVE SOILS.

17. ELECTRONIC STRIKES, MOTION DETECTORS AND ALARM SHUNTS ARE PROVIDED BY OTHERS. PROVIDE ALL NECESSARY ROUGH-INS FOR THESE ITEMS. COORDINATE WORK WITH SECURITY SYSTEM PROVIDER.

Figure 6.18:   General Notes for an Electrical Plan

Source: National Center for Construction Education and Research, *Core Curriculum* (Upper Saddle River, NJ/Columbus, OH: Prentice Hall, 2000), Module 00105, p. 5–27.

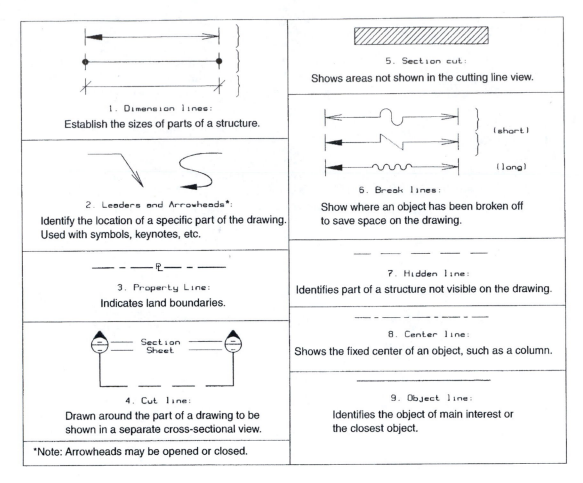

Figure 6.19:   Lines of Construction

Source: National Center for Construction Education and Research, *Core Curriculum* (Upper Saddle River, NJ/Columbus, OH: Prentice Hall, 2000), Module 00105, p. 5–35.

structure that isn't visible on the drawing; you may need to look at another drawing to see the detail of what's hidden. Figure 6.19 lists and explains more about the lines of construction.

Gridlines

Found at the top and sides of the blueprint, this system of letters and numbers helps you refer to specific parts of the blueprint. Across the top and bottom are letters of the alphabet (except for I, O, and Q, which are generally not used). Moving down the left and right sides are numbers. Sometimes, letters appear at the left/right, and numbers appear at the top/bottom.

The same way you would look for Section F6 on a highway map, you could look for (and refer to) section F6 on a blueprint. In a blueprint, these sections are called *bays*. You can see the gridlines in use in Figure 6.20.

Keynotes

Found directly on the blueprint, keynotes offer additional information about the items drawn on the plan. A *keynote* is a number or letter, usually in a square or circle, with a leader line and an arrowhead that is used to identify a specific object. The explanation of each keynote appears on the plan, as you can see in Figure 6.20.

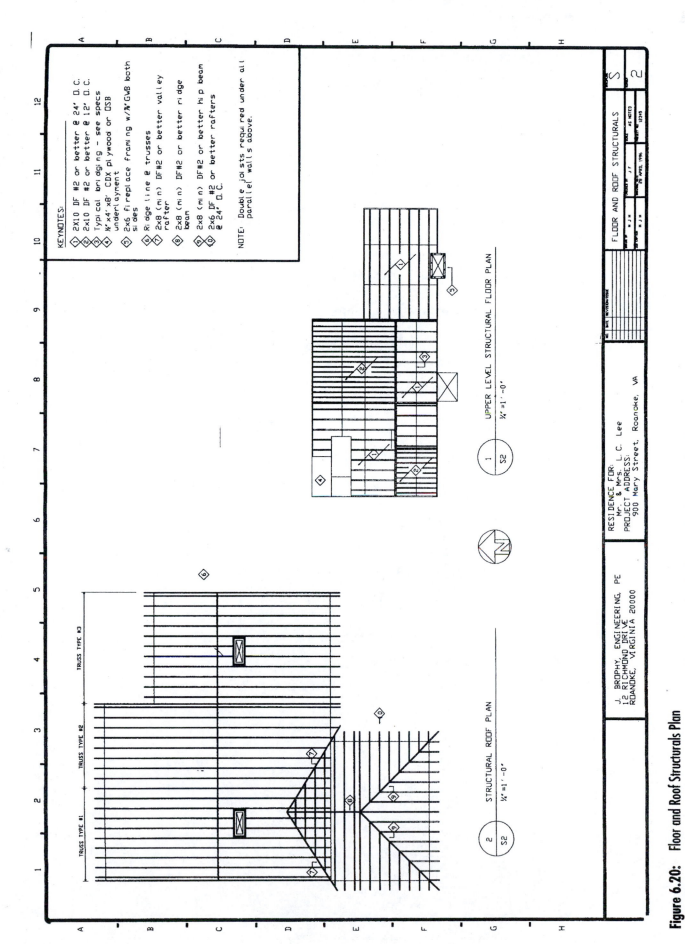

Figure 6.20: Floor and Roof Structurals Plan

Source: James A. Fatzinger, Blueprint set to accompany *Blueprint Reading for Construction* (Upper Saddle River, NJ/Columbus, OH: Prentice Hall, 1998).

REMEMBER WHEN READING BLUEPRINTS:

- Check the plans for inconsistencies. Two blueprints may offer inconsistent information. Call these inaccuracies to your supervisor's attention immediately.
- If you're unsure of the meaning of an abbreviation or icon, ask an expert.
- When reading the blueprint, visualize the building or system in your head. Visualizing will help you when it comes time to actually build the building or system.
- When a plan is not drawn to scale, you cannot measure dimensions on the drawing and use those dimensions to build from.

Activity 6.11: Reading Blueprints

Use Figures 6.15 through 6.20 to answer the following questions.

SET A: FIGURE 6.15—TITLE BLOCKS

Refer to Figure 6.15a.

1. What are the initials of the person who drew the blueprint? _____

2. On what date was the plan drawn? _____

3. From the title block, you can tell what type of plan is shown in the blueprint. What type of plan is shown? _____

4. What is the address of the commercial building being built for Frontier Manufacturing, Inc.? _____

5. How many times has this plan been revised? _____

Refer to Figure 6.15b.

6. How many sheets are there in the complete set of blueprints for this job? _____

7. What type of plan is shown in this blueprint? _____

8. On what date(s) was this blueprint revised or amended? _____

9. Who drafted this blueprint? _____

10. What type of building is shown in the blueprint: a commercial building or a residence? _____

SET B: FIGURE 6.16—COMMON BLUEPRINT SYMBOLS Specify whether each of the symbols shown here is architectural, civil/structural, mechanical, plumbing, or electrical.

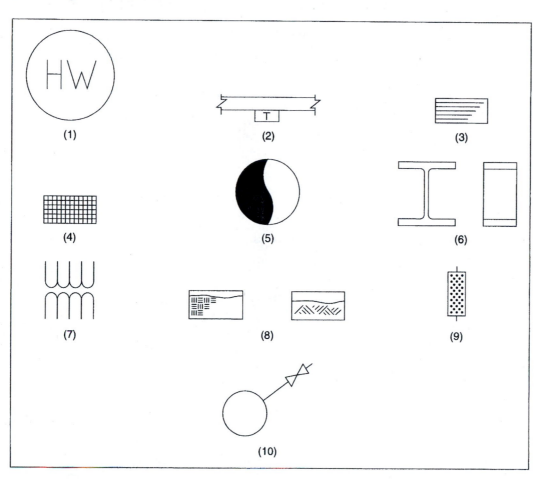

SET C: FIGURE 6.16—COMMON BLUEPRINT SYMBOLS Match each symbol with its definition below.

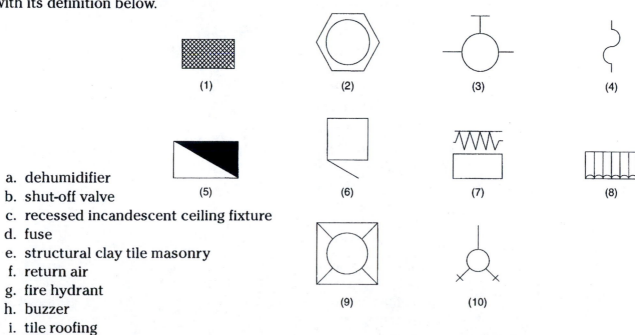

a. dehumidifier
b. shut-off valve
c. recessed incandescent ceiling fixture
d. fuse
e. structural clay tile masonry
f. return air
g. fire hydrant
h. buzzer
i. tile roofing
j. smoke detector

Set D: Figure 6.17—Common Electrical Abbreviations

Mark "T" if the statement is true, "F" if it is false.

_____ 1. "Watts" is abbreviated *W*.

_____ 2. *AC* means 6 inches above counter.

_____ 3. To indicate that something is explosion proof, use the abbreviation *XP*.

_____ 4. *UNO* means "unless noted outside."

_____ 5. To show that something is neutral, use the abbreviation *n*.

_____ 6. All the abbreviations shown in Figure 6.17 are used on every electrical blueprint.

_____ 7. Something marked *WP* is weatherproof.

_____ 8. Horsepower would be abbreviated as *hp*.

_____ 9. Either *TFMR* or *XFMR* can be used to abbreviate "transformer."

_____ 10. The presence of copper is noted by *CO*.

Set E: Figure 6.18—General Notes for an Electrical Plan

_____ 1. According to note 16, all underground penetrations should be coordinated with:
   a. the draftsman
   b. a structural engineer
   c. an architect
   d. the building designer

_____ 2. What color should be used to indicate all emergency receptacle devices?
   a. red
   b. yellow
   c. green
   d. blue

_____ 3. Who must replace any item damaged by the contractor?
   a. the builder
   b. the person responsible
   c. the contractor
   d. the subcontractor

_____ 4. According to note 17, with whom should motion detectors and alarm shunts be coordinated?
   a. the structural engineer
   b. the designer
   c. the security system provider
   d. the contractor

_____ 5. What series should all plugmolds shown be?
   a. V200
   b. GB06
   c. NFPA 72
   d. V2000

_____   6. In which note can you find information about ADA compliance?
      a. 3
      b. 6
      c. 10
      d. 15

SET F: FIGURE 6.19—LINES OF CONSTRUCTION

Match each line of construction with its definition below.

(1) ●————————————●

(2) ————————

(3) — — — — —

    a. hidden line
    b. property line   (4) —— · —— · —— · ——
    c. dimension line
    d. center line
    e. object line   (5) —— · — ₽ —— · ——

SET G: FIGURE 6.20—FLOOR AND ROOF STRUCTURALS PLAN

Use Figure 6.20 to answer the following questions about gridlines and keynotes.

1. In what row can you find information about the scale of the structural roof plan? ____

2. Which of the following bays is not empty: A7, H11, or F2? _____

3. Which bay shows the "North" direction arrow? _____

4. According to keynote 7, what is the minimum size of the valley rafter?

    _____

5. According to keynote 4, what size should the CDX plywood be? _____

6. Keynote 5 provides more information about which structural element? ____

6.4 READING ISOMETRIC DRAWINGS, ORTHOGRAPHICS, AND SCHEMATICS

Many blueprints and other construction documents make use of isometric drawings, orthographic drawings, and schematics.

Isometric Drawings

An *isometric drawing* is a three-dimensional representation of an object. Isometrics are very useful because they let you see all three dimensions—height, width, and length. Usually, isometrics are drawn to scale, but when scale is not practical, they are drawn proportionally.

In many isometrics, a reference point is established. Many draftspeople use a north symbol with a vertical line and an arrow showing up and down. With this reference point, people in different locations can all discuss the isometric from the same perspective.

Figure 6.21 shows an isometric illustration of a kitchen sink. Note that this illustration projects the illusion of three dimensions because vertical lines are drawn vertical, but horizontal lines are projected at 30 degrees.

Orthographic Drawings

Related to isometric drawings are orthographic drawings. *Orthographics* show straight-on views of the different sides of an object—top, bottom, sides. Such drawings are very useful when designers and craftspeople need to know what the object will look like from all directions.

Figure 6.22 on page 190 shows a sample orthographic drawing of the kitchen sink represented in Figure 6.21. All six sides of the object are represented.

Schematics

A third type of drawing, the *schematic,* is a single-line drawing that illustrates the scale and relationships among the project's components. Most plumbing and electrical sketches are schematics. In a plumbing schematic, the line represents the centerline of the pipe. In an electrical schematic, the line represents the electrical wiring routing or circuit.

Figure 6.23 on page 190 shows a schematic of a piping stack. The symbols (circles, triangles, lines) used in this schematic all have specific meanings in plumbing.

REMEMBER WHEN READING ISOMETRICS, ORTHOGRAPHICS, AND SCHEMATICS:

- The purpose of all these drawings is to help you "see" how the object will actually look when it's complete. As you look at each drawing, visualize the final product in your mind's eye.
- Understanding the intricacies of schematics often requires substantial knowledge of symbols, figures, and abbreviations. You will become more familiar with these as you learn more about your craft.

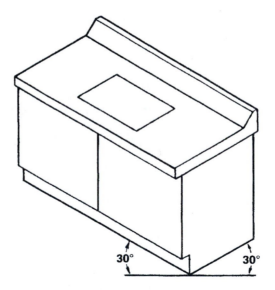

Figure 6.21:   Sample Isometric Drawing

Source: National Center for Construction Education and Research, *Plumbing Trainee Guide* (Upper Saddle River, NJ/Columbus, OH: Prentice Hall, 1992), Module 02106, p. 2.

FINISHED DRAWING

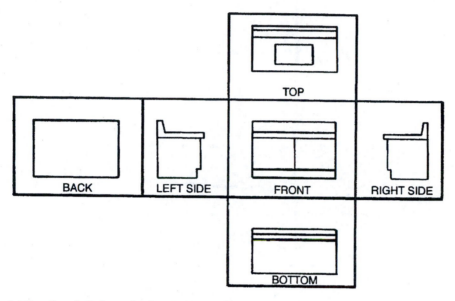

Figure 6.22: Sample Orthographic Drawing

Source: National Center for Construction Education and Research, *Plumbing Trainee Guide* (Upper Saddle River, NJ/Columbus, OH: Prentice Hall, 1992), Module 02106, p. 4.

Activity 6.12:
Reading Isometric Drawings, Orthographics, and Schematics

SET A:

Use Figures 6.21 through 6.23 to answer the following questions.

1. In the isometric drawing in Figure 6.21, the illusion of three dimensions is given by projecting horizontal lines at a(n) _____-degree angle.

2. How many views of the object are shown in Figure 6.22? _____

3. Have any views of the object in Figure 6.22 been omitted from the drawing? If so, which one(s)? _____

4. In addition to the basement, how many floors are there in the structure shown in Figure 6.23? _____

SET B:

Use Figures 6.24 and 6.25 (pages 190–191) to answer these questions.

1. What type of drawing is Figure 6.24? _____

   How can you tell? _____

2. What type of drawing is Figure 6.25? _____

   How can you tell? _____

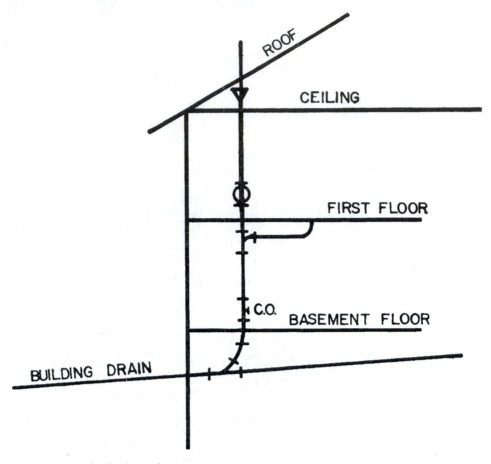

Figure 6.23: Sample Plumbing Schematic
Source: National Center for Construction Education and Research, *Plumbing Trainee Guide* (Upper Saddle River, NJ/Columbus, OH: Prentice Hall, 1992), Module 02106, p. 18.

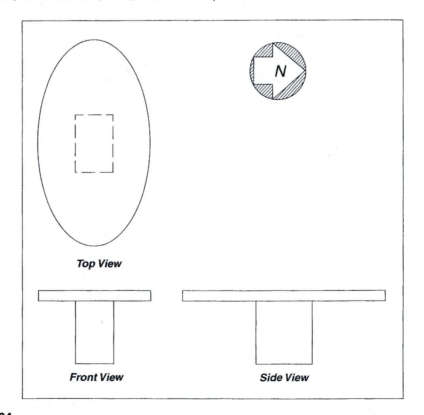

Figure 6.24
Source: Basil Wilber, *Construction Isometrics Drawing Workbook* (Madison, WI: Associated Builders and Contractors of Wisconsin), p. 104.

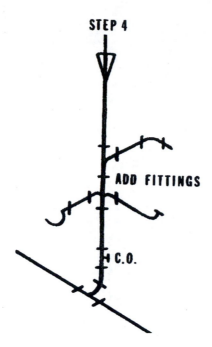

STEP 4

ADD FITTINGS

C.O.

Figure 6.25

Source: National Center for Construction Education and Research, *Plumbing Trainee Guide* (Upper Saddle River, NJ/Columbus, OH: Prentice Hall, 1992), Task Module 01206, p. 20.

6.5 READING JOB SPECIFICATIONS

In Section 6.3, we provided an overview of blueprints. While blueprints condense a huge amount of information into a visual format, they cannot show every aspect of an individual project. For example, blueprints do not spell out legal rights and obligations, or who is responsible for different parts of a project. And, while blueprints often include brief explanatory notes, much more detailed information is frequently needed. Such detailed information could not be included on blueprints without making them highly cluttered, difficult to read, and expensive to produce.

For all these reasons, it is common in the construction industry to prepare a Project Manual. The documents in the Project Manual support all the drawings in all the blueprints and spell out every aspect of the project in detail. The complete set of directions for the project are formalized in the project's *specifications,* or *specs* for short.

Specs are divided into two major parts. The *general conditions* cover the preliminary aspects of the job, such as contractual obligations, insurance arrangements, payments, responsibility for permits, supervision, and so on. The *technical sections* deal with the actual construction of the building and the tradework involved.

Figure 6.26 reproduces the table of contents of a set of specifications for a small house. Note several important features of this table of contents:

- The specs follow the format recommended by the CSI (Construction Specifications Institute).
- General conditions come first, followed by technical specifications.
- Several categories on this particular set of specs are not used (for example, Special Construction and Conveying Systems). These categories are not relevant to the building of a small house.

```
                      Small House
                    Sample Set of
                    Specifications
                Using the C.S.I Format


                    Table of Contents


General Conditions  . . . . . . . . . . . . . . . . . . . . . .ii—iii

Specifications

DIVISION  1—GENERAL REQUIREMENTS  . . . . . . . . . . . . . . . .1—4

DIVISION  2—SITE WORK . . . . . . . . . . . . . . . . . . . . .4—5

DIVISION  3—CONCRETE  . . . . . . . . . . . . . . . . . . . . .5—7

DIVISION  4—MASONRY . . . . . . . . . . . . . . . . . . . . . .7—8

DIVISION  5—METALS  (Not used)

DIVISION  6—WOOD & PLASTICS . . . . . . . . . . . . . . . . . .8—9

DIVISION  7—THERMAL & MOISTURE PROTECTION . . . . . . . . . . .10—12

DIVISION  8—DOORS & WINDOWS . . . . . . . . . . . . . . . . .12—14

DIVISION  9—FINISHES  . . . . . . . . . . . . . . . . . . . .14—16

DIVISION 10—SPECIALTIES (Not used)

DIVISION 11—EQUIPMENT (Not used)

DIVISION 12—FURNISHINGS (Not used)

DIVISION 13—SPECIAL CONSTRUCTION (Not used)

DIVISION 14—CONVEYING SYSTEMS (Not used)

DIVISION 15—MECHANICAL . . . . . . . . . . . . . . . . . . .17—18

DIVISION 16—ELECTRICAL . . . . . . . . . . . . . . . . . . .18—19
```

Figure 6.26: Table of Contents—Specifications for a Small House

Source: Edward J. Muller and Philip A. Grau, *Reading Architectural Working Drawings: Residential and Light Construction* (Upper Saddle River, NJ/Columbus, OH: Prentice Hall, 2000), p. 251.

- Though not obvious from Figure 6.26, the technical sections are frequently arranged in the same order as work completed. For example, "Excavation" would normally be placed early in the technical specs, while "Painting and Decorating" and "Landscaping" would be placed much later in the specs.

Figure 6.27 on page 194 reproduces a page from this particular set of specs. In this figure, detailed specifications for Division 9, "Finishes," are listed. Note several important features about the specifications themselves:

- The specs are set up according to a numbered format. "Finishes" is Division 9, so all the subsections within this main section begin with "09."
- Key terms are underlined to draw the reader's eye to them easily.
- While the pages are filled with information, white space is also included so that the pages do not appear jam-packed.

As you become more of an expert in your construction specialty, you will become quite proficient in reading specs. As you get started, however, keep in mind the following tips:

- To find the information you need in specs, look first at the table of contents, then flip to the correct pages.
- Use the skimming and scanning techniques you learned in Module 5 (Section 5.1) to locate information.
- To find information on general, nontechnical topics such as terms of the contract, supervisory responsibilities, and permits, look in the General Conditions section.
- By definition, specs are extremely detailed. They spell out everything in exhaustive detail so that there is no room for error. Therefore, read specs *slowly* to make sure you absorb all the information provided. In fact, it is a good idea to read relevant sections several times before you take any action.
- The word "shall" (see the last line of Figure 6.27) is commonly used to instruct the constructor to furnish something or do something.

Activity 6.13: Reading Specifications

Refer to Figures 6.26 and 6.27 to answer the following questions.

_____ 1. On what pages of the specifications can you find coverage of site work?
   a. ii–iii
   b. 1–4
   c. 4–5
   d. 10–12

_____ 2. In what division or section of the specs will you find information about doors and windows?
   a. Division 1
   b. Division 8
   c. Division 9
   d. Division 16

_____ 3. Which of the following divisions or sections of the specs are not used for this particular project?
   a. Equipment
   b. Mechanical
   c. Thermal and Moisture Protection
   d. Electrical

DIVISION 9—FINISHES

09250 GYPSUM WALLBOARD

This section includes the furnishing of $\frac{1}{2}$" "Drywall" for walls and ceilings as shown on drawings.

1. Materials:

   (a) $\frac{1}{2}$" thick gypsum wallboard, meeting Federal Specifications SS-51a and ASTM specifications C-36.

   (b) Use metal corner beads on all exterior corners. Metal bead trim shall be U.S. Gypsum No. 200-A metal trim.

   (c) Nails shall be GWB-54, $1\frac{5}{8}$" long annular ring, meeting the requirements of ASTM C-380.

2. Installation:

   (a) Apply Gypsum Wallboard first to ceilings and then to side walls; plan wallboard lengths to minimize end joints.

   (b) Space nails not more than 7" apart on ceiling panels and not more than 8" apart on walls. Dimple the nail heads slightly below surface of wallboard.

   (c) Finish joints, nail dimples, corners, and edges using the three-coat cement and tape system. Sand each coat after it is dry to a smooth, even surface.

   (d) Wallboard installation shall be done by experienced dry-wall applicators, normally engaged in the trade.

09300 CERAMIC TILE

This section includes furnishing and installing ceramic tile finish on all surfaces as indicated on drawings.

1. Material to be Mosaic Tile Co., American-Olean, or Cambridge Tile Co. manufactured tile.

2. Floor tile to be standard grade, factory mounted unglazed ceramic tile with square edges. Sizes, patterns, and colors to be selected from Harmonitone solid color or Velvetex mottled-color group. Set in 1:3 mix Portland cement bed at least $\frac{3}{4}$" thick with uniform joints not wider than $\frac{1}{16}$", with best waterproof white Portland cement.

3. Walls and Wainscot to be $4\frac{1}{4} \times 4\frac{1}{4}$ standard grade cushion edge, white nonvitreous body glazed tile in color selected from Harmonitone Satin or Bright Glaze group. Edges to have spacers to provide uniformly narrow joints. Provide all necessary trim shapes including 2" cap.

4. Bath accessories to be recessed nonvitreous body, glazed tile in same color as wainscot. Provide the following in each bath:

   (a) 1 paper holder, 1 soap dish, 1 grab bar.

   (b) 2–20" towel bars, 1–30" towel bar.

09650 CORK TILE FLOORING

Cork tile flooring, placed as shown on drawings, shall be $\frac{1}{8}$" thick, 9" × 9" as manufactured by Armstrong Cork Co. Color to be selected by Owner. Rubber base, 4" cove type, to be installed in all rooms having the cork tile floors. Installation shall be in accordance with the latest edition of the

Figure 6.27: Excerpt from Specifications for a Small House

Source: Edward J. Muller and Philip A. Grau, *Reading Architectural Working Drawings: Residential and Light Construction* (Upper Saddle River, NJ/Columbus, OH: Prentice Hall, 2000), p. 263.

_____ 4. In which section can material regarding general supervisory responsibilities and permits be found?
   a. the General Conditions section
   b. Division 1, General Requirements
   c. Division 2, Site Work
   d. Division 5, Metals

_____ 5. Which ASTM specification must the materials for gypsum wallboard meet?
   a. SS-51a
   b. C-36
   c. 200-A
   d. C-380

_____ 6. The cork tile flooring must be provided by which of the following manufacturers?
   a. Mosaic Tile Co.
   b. Velvetex
   c. Harmonitone
   d. Armstrong

_____ 7. When installing gypsum wallboard, what is the maximum space permitted between nails on walls?
   a. 1 ⅝″
   b. 7″
   c. 8″
   d. 4 ¼″

_____ 8. Which of the following companies may not supply ceramic tile for this job?
   a. Mosaic Tile Co.
   b. Cambridge Tile Co.
   c. Bright Glaze Tile Co.
   d. American-Olean

_____ 9. How many towel bars should be included in each bath?
   a. two 20″ towel bars and one 30″ towel bar
   b. one 20″ towel bar and two 30″ towel bars
   c. one 9″ × 9″ towel bar
   d. three towel bars, with the sizes to be determined by the contractor

_____ 10. By whom will wallboard installation be completed?
   a. apprentices
   b. available staff
   c. experienced carpenters
   d. experienced drywall applicators

6.6 READING MATERIALS LISTS

The materials used in large jobs are usually spelled out in detail in the Project Manual and its specifications. However, in some jobs, a simplified document called a *materials list* is also provided. Unlike specs, which include general conditions and instructions on how components are to be constructed, the materials list provides information only on the materials to be used.

Figure 6.28 reproduces a materials list used by the Federal Housing Administration (FHA). The materials lists used by other entities may differ, but the general format will be the same: Detailed information on the exact types of materials to be used are provided, with no alternates specified. As with specifications, read materials lists carefully, and always double check information before proceeding.

Activity 6.14: Reading Materials Lists

Refer to Figure 6.28 and answer the questions that follow.

_____ 1. Who is building the project?
    a. First National Bank
    b. Ace Construction Company
    c. G.I. Construction
    d. Celcure Construction

_____ 2. Which materials are not specified on the part of the materials list reproduced in Figure 6.28?
    a. Plumbing
    b. Floor framing
    c. Exterior walls
    d. Foundations

_____ 3. How many floors will this structure have?
    a. one
    b. two
    c. two, plus an attic
    d. three

_____ 4. What type of fireplace is to be installed in this structure?
    a. gas-burning
    b. circulator
    c. solid fuel
    d. No fireplace is to be installed in this structure.

_____ 5. How many coats of paint will be applied to the exterior walls of this structure?
    a. one
    b. two
    c. three
    d. four

_____ 6. In what proportion should the concrete for the foundation footings be mixed?
    a. 1:3:5
    b. 4:8:16
    c. 1:2:4
    d. 6:6:10

(Continued on page 198)

VA Form VB4–1852
FHA Form 2085
Jan. 1955

For accurate register of carbon copies, form may be separated along above fold. Staple completed sheets together in original order.

Form approved.
Budget Bureau No. 63-R085.10.

☒ Proposed Construction

☐ Under Construction

DESCRIPTION OF MATERIALS

No. ....
(To be inserted by FHA or VA)

Property address 1230 Pinedale Avenue   **City** Atlanta   **State** Georgia

Mortgagor or Sponsor First National Bank   Atlanta, Georgia
(Name)   (Address)

Contractor or Builder Ace Construction Company   Atlanta, Georgia
(Name)   (Address)

INSTRUCTIONS

1. For additional information on how this form is to be submitted, number of copies, etc., see the instructions applicable to the FHA Application for Mortgage Insurance or VA Request for Determination of Reasonable Value, as the case may be.

2. Describe all materials and equipment to be used, whether or not shown on the drawings, by marking an X in each appropriate check-box and entering the information called for in each space. If space is inadequate, enter "See misc." and describe under item 27 or on an attached sheet.

3. Work not specifically described or shown will not be considered unless required, when the minimum acceptable will be assumed. Work exceeding

minimum requirements cannot be considered unless specifically described.

4. Include no alternates, "or equal" phrases, or contradictory items. (Consideration of a request for acceptance of substitute materials or equipment is not thereby precluded.)

5. Include signatures required at the end of this form.

6. The construction shall be completed in compliance with the related drawings and specifications, as amended during processing. The specifications include this Description of Materials and the applicable Minimum Construction Requirements.

1. EXCAVATION:

Bearing soil, type ... Sand Clay ....

2. FOUNDATIONS:

Footings: Concrete mix (1:3:5)   2500#   Reinforcing 2 - #4 bars

Foundation wall: Material Concrete Block   Reinforcing ....

Interior foundation wall: Material ....   Party foundation wall ....

Columns: Material and size ....   Piers: Material and reinforcing Concrete Block

Girders: Material and sizes SYP 6" x 10"   Sills: Material SYP 2" x 6" – Celcure

Basement entrance areaway ....   Window areaways ....

Waterproofing ....   Footing drains ....

Termite protection G.I. Termite Shields, Soil Treatment

Basementless space: Ground cover Polyethylene Membrane   Insulation 4" Rock Wool   Foundation vents 4-8"x16" Cast Iron

Special foundations ....

3. CHIMNEYS:

Material Brick ....   Prefabricated (make and size) ....

Flue lining: Material Vit. Terra Cotta   Heater flue size 4" Dia.   Fireplace flue size 13" x 13"

Vents (material and size): Gas or oil heater Transite 4" Dia.   Water heater Transite 3" Dia.

4. FIREPLACES:

Type: ☒ Solid fuel; ☐ gas-burning; ☐ circulator (make and size) ....   Ash dump and clean-out None

Fireplace: Facing Brick ; lining Fire brick ; hearth Brick ; mantel None

5. EXTERIOR WALLS:

Studs: Douglas Fir #2

Wood frame: Grade and species Other: SYP #2 DIM.   ☐ Corner bracing. Building paper or felt ....

Sheathing Plywood ; thickness 1/2" ; width 4'-0" ; ☒ solid; ☐ spaced " o. c.; ☐ diagonal;

Siding Redwood ; grade Heart ; type Bevel ; size 10" ; exposure 9" "; fastening Alum. Nails

Shingles ....; grade ....; type ....; size ....; exposure "; fastening ....

Stucco ....; thickness ". Lath ....; weight lb.

Masonry veneer Brick, used   Sills Brick   Lintels ½" x 3" x 4" L

Masonry: Facing ....; backup ....   thickness ". Bonding ....

Door sills ....   Window sills ....   Lintels ....

Interior surfaces: Dampproofing, ... coats of ....; furring ....

Exterior painting: Material Exterior Latex ; number of coats 3

Gable wall construction: ☒ Same as main walls; ☐ other ....

6. FLOOR FRAMING:

Joists: Wood, grade and species #2 SYP ; other ....; bridging #2 SYP ; anchors ½" Bolts-6'-0" O.C.

Concrete slab: ☐ Basement floor; ☒ first floor; ☒ ground supported; ☐ self-supporting; mix 1:2:4 2500# ; thickness 4 ";

reinforcing 6 6/10 10 wire mesh ; insulation ....; membrane Polyethylene

Fill under slab: Material Gravel ; thickness 6 ".

7. SUBFLOORING: (Describe underflooring for special floors under item 21.)

Material: Grade and species Plywood, C-D grade ; size 4'-0" x 840" ; type Interior

Laid: ☒ First floor; ☒ second floor; ☐ attic ....   sq. ft.; ☐ diagonal; ☒ right angles.

8. FINISH FLOORING: (Wood only. Describe other finish flooring under item 21.)

LOCATION	ROOMS	GRADE	SPECIES	THICKNESS	WIDTH	BLDG. PAPER	FINISH
First floor	LR, Den, DR,Hall	Select	Oak	25/32"	2½	Yes	Fill, seal, varnish
Second floor	BR.1,2,3,4,Hall	"	Oak	25/32"	2½	"	" " "
Attic floor				sq. ft.			

Figure 6.28: Excerpt from a Materials List

Source: Edward J. Muller and Philip A. Grau, *Reading Architectural Working Drawings: Residential and Light Construction* (Upper Saddle River, NJ/Columbus, OH: Prentice Hall, 2000), p. 245.

_____ 7. Of what grade will the plywood for the subflooring be?
   a. Grade A
   b. Grade A or B
   c. Grade C only
   d. Grade C or D

_____ 8. How many bedrooms will this structure contain?
   a. one
   b. two
   c. three
   d. four

_____ 9. How many methods of termite protection will be applied to this structure?
   a. none
   b. one
   c. two
   d. three

_____ 10. Specs are provided for all of the following elements except:
   a. waterproofing
   b. foundation girders
   c. heater flue size
   d. water heater

6.7 MANAGING YOUR INFORMATION LOAD

As we saw in Module 5, information overload is an unavoidable fact of life in the twenty-first century. Each day, we are bombarded with more information than we know what to do with. On the way to work, we see hundreds of advertisements everywhere. At work, we receive memos, e-mails, manuals, and blueprints to read. At home, we get a mailbox full of junk mail almost every day. When we read a newspaper or watch the news on TV, we get even more information. But there are only 24 hours in the day. How do we process all this information? How do we decide what we should pay attention to, and what we can safely ignore?

Here are some tips to help you manage your information load.

PRIORITIZE.   Differentiate among what you should or must read, what you'd like to read, and what you can get away with not reading. Attend to "must read" items as soon as possible, and get to the "like to read" items when you have free time. Use the following table to help you figure out your priorities:

Must Read	Like to Read	Can Safely Ignore
Personal bills and bank statements	Daily newspapers	Junk mail
Renewal notices	Interesting magazines	Advertisements
Priority e-mails	Web sites of interest	Chain letters
Any work-related memos or manuals, especially safety-related materials or procedural memos	Company newsletters	Tabloids/gossipy newspapers
Information regarding your benefits, pension, and so forth	Industry/trade periodicals	
All job-related blueprints and drawings	Novels	

TIP: Don't fall into the trap of avoiding things you don't want to see—such as overdue bills or DMV renewal notices. They won't go away, and the longer you ignore them, the more stress you'll experience. But do feel free to throw out any junk mail unopened—you won't be missing anything!

WHEN APPROPRIATE, SKIM AND SCAN FOR INFORMATION.   Follow the tips in the box in Module 5, Section 5.1, to quickly locate the information you need, and ignore everything else. Remember that you can get much good information by looking closely at tables and graphics. If something is written in prose, you can often get a good sense of it by just reading the headings and the first sentence of each paragraph.

KEEP THE INFORMATION YOU NEED CLOSE AT HAND.   Make shortcuts to access the information you need. For example, if a project manual has a table to which you refer constantly, mark that page with a Post-It Note (or a scrap of paper, or something similar) so that you can quickly and easily find the table when you need it. Keep a metric conversion table in your wallet, so that you always have the information when you need it.

MAKE YOUR OWN PERSONAL FILING SYSTEM.   Paper can get overwhelming if it isn't sorted and stored properly. Whether at home or at work, keep file folders to store similar material. For example, you might keep all your car-insurance information in one folder, and all your medical plan information in another folder. Periodically review the folders and discard any material that is outdated or no longer useful. Alternatively, you might use binders with tabbed dividers rather than individual file folders.

USE A PERSONAL DIGITAL ASSISTANT (PDA).   Handheld PDAs can be remarkably efficient at helping you store all the information you need, from names and phone numbers, to conversion charts, to site plans. If you use such a device, keep the battery charged, and don't leave it on when you're not using it. (For more information on PDAs, see Appendix A.)

Activity 6.15: Managing Your Information Load

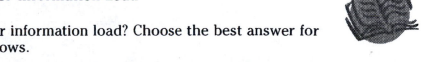

How well do you manage your information load? Choose the best answer for each of the questions that follows.

_____ 1. You've just read a piece of mail announcing the publication of a new magazine. You have no interest in the magazine. What should you do with the mail when you're done reading it?
   a. Hold onto it, in case you become interested in the magazine later.
   b. Throw it out.
   c. File it in your personal filing cabinet.
   d. Look for the company's Web site.

_____ 2. Which of the following should you read as soon as you get it?
   a. an industry magazine
   b. a memo about your retirement plan
   c. the company newsletter
   d. a new set of safety regulations

_____ 3. All of the following are good ways to create your own personal filing system, except:
   a. purchasing a small file cabinet and file folders to sort and keep track of important documents
   b. setting up a computerized system to help you remember when to pay your bills
   c. using a PDA or personal log to keep important information (such as phone numbers, conversion tables, measurements, and so on) accessible
   d. stacking piles of paper on a table or desk, then looking through them when you need to find something

_____ 4. Suppose you have a checking account with Bank A and a savings account with Bank B. In an effective personal filing/information retrieval system, you would have:
   a. two separate folders, one for Bank A and one for Bank B
   b. one folder marked "Finances"
   c. a separate folder for each month's bank statements
   d. There's no need to save any of your bank records, since the bank will have copies of them if you need them.

_____ 5. The best way to find information quickly in printed material is to:
   a. skim and scan for what you're looking for
   b. read every word
   c. read everything that comes your way
   d. ask a co-worker or friend to help you find the information

6.8 READING CRITICALLY

It's tempting to accept everything we read as "the truth." After all, we might think that if it's written down on paper it must be true.

In actuality, however, many written sources have hidden biases or hidden agendas. The letter that comes into your mailbox from a charitable organization has only one purpose: to get you to donate money to the cause. A newspaper, magazine, or TV ad also has only one purpose: to get you to purchase the product.

In addition, the rise of the Internet has brought up another problem: Much information is presented as fact, when it is really only opinion or *misinformation*. Many Web sites are not checked by experts in the field, so you need to be careful about relying on them. Also, many Internet and printed sources are poorly proofread, and they may contain errors that slipped past the publisher.

For all these reasons, it's important to approach everything you read with a critical eye. In this case, "critical" does not mean "finding fault with." Rather, it means actively *evaluating* everything you read, using your best judgment and experience to determine whether the material is reliable or not.

The good news is this: Your *critical reading* and *critical thinking* skills are more fully formed than you realize. Suppose you see a magazine ad for a product that promises to help you lose 50 pounds in one week. "Miraculous new drug!" the ad screams. "Guaranteed to take off the weight faster than any diet or exercise!"

What is your reaction? Most likely, you would think, "That's impossible. Nobody can lose 50 pounds in one week. If I bought that product, I'd be wasting my money."

You may not realize it, but you took several steps to reach this conclusion:

- First, you carefully read the advertisement, paying attention to the claims made by the ad.
- Second, you compared the ad's content to the knowledge that you already have. That knowledge can be based either on book learning or on personal experience.
- Third, you evaluated the truthfulness of the ad based on your knowledge.
- Finally, you made a decision: No product can help somebody lose 50 pounds in just one week—it's medically impossible.

By engaging in this thinking process, you have gone beyond recalling basic information from your memory. You haven't simply accepted what you've read as the truth. You also haven't automatically rejected it just because you didn't agree with it. Instead, you have *evaluated* the information before reaching a conclusion. Only after deeply thinking about the information did you make a decision.

The ultimate goal of critical reading is to make the best possible decisions. Thinking and reading critically can help you answer such questions as:

- Is it worth spending a lot of money on this new piece of machinery? (You'll want to do as much research as you can on the machinery, finding out what others have said about it. Do the experiences of users match the company's claims for what the product can do?)
- Can I believe this salesman when he quotes me such low prices on lumber? (You'll need to get those prices in writing, so that you're not overcharged later on.)
- Did the draftsman really mean to put this into the blueprints, or is it a mistake? (You'll want to check other parts of the blueprint for inconsistencies, and talk to other experts on the job site, to reach your conclusion.)

Critical Thinking Questions

The most important part of critical reading and thinking involves evaluating new information. Once you've evaluated the information, you can either accept it or reject it.

To evaluate the information that comes your way, ask yourself these questions.

1. What is the source of this information? Information that comes to you from your supervisor is usually reliable. The training manuals produced by, say, the National Center for Construction Education and Research are going to be very reliable sources of information about the industry. So are well-known trade publications such as *Contractor* magazine.

In contrast, gossip usually is not a reliable source of information. Think about the credibility of the source. For example, you're a lot more likely to get good information from *The New York Times* than you are from *The National Enquirer.*

2. How much expertise or experience does the information source have? Suppose you're an electrician, and you're having trouble figuring out the electrical schematic for a new building. Two people have offered you advice: another electrician and a carpenter. Whose advice do you think is better? While the carpenter may be skilled at electrical work, it's unlikely that he has the electrician's expertise. You'd be better off listening to the electrician.

3. How do I feel about this information? And why do I feel this way? Sometimes your personal feelings can get in the way of your evaluation. For example, if you don't like working with computers, you may be unwilling to believe that computers can draft blueprints better than a draftsman can. But all the evidence says that computers can be very helpful. So you should put your personal feelings aside and remain open-minded.

4. Does this information match my previous knowledge or experience? One of the best ways to evaluate information is to match it against what you already know. Don't underestimate yourself—you know a lot more than you think. If something goes against what you know, question it. For example, suppose you're reading a manual that says, "Workers shouldn't wear hard hats in the construction area." Everything you've learned on the job tells you that you *must* wear a hard hat. So there may very well be a misprint in the manual.

5. What do my co-workers, supervisors, and other trusted people think? When you're unsure about something, it pays to talk to other experts. It's often helpful to gather information from people you trust before making a decision.

Activity 6.16: Distinguishing Fact from Opinion

To think critically, it's important to distinguish facts from opinions. A *fact* is a statement that can be proven true or false. An *opinion* cannot be proven true or false. It is based on someone's personal point of view or interpretation of facts. Different people can have different opinions about the same fact.

For example, it is a *fact* that many people in the United States are killed each year by handguns. However, some people hold the *opinion* that citizens should not carry guns. Others hold the *opinion* that everyone has the right to bear arms.

To think critically, you should know when you encounter a fact and when you encounter an opinion. When someone expresses an opinion, you then need to evaluate that opinion and determine whether you agree with it or not.

This activity offers some practice in distinguishing between facts and opinions. In the spaces below, write "F" if the statement is a fact, and "O" if the statement is an opinion.

EXAMPLE:

F   a. HazCom guarantees workers' rights to know the specifics about
           any hazardous materials they may encounter on the job.

O   b. Most employers find it burdensome to deal with HazCom
           regulations.

_____ 1. New Jersey is the most densely populated state in the country.

_____ 2. New Jersey is a tough state to live in because it's so densely
           populated.

_____ 3. Wonder Tools makes the best tools available today.

_____ 4. I just got back from the supplier, and the Wonder Tools were
           almost twice as expensive as the Acme Tools.

_____ 5. The foreman's job is to manage costs and bring projects in on time.

_____ 6. Foremen are usually very opinionated people with strong
           personalities.

_____ 7. Mr. Robbins, I know that you've asked to have the walls painted red, but red walls aren't going to look good in this room.

_____ 8. Mr. Robbins, this room doesn't get much sun. Red walls will make the room appear very dark.

_____ 9. There are two ways to perform this procedure. Method A is cheaper but more time consuming. Method B is more expensive but takes less time to implement.

_____ 10. There are two ways to perform this procedure. Method A is better because it's cheaper. Method B is less desirable because it costs more.

Activity 6.17: Critical Reading I

You are reading a newspaper while waiting in line at the supermarket, and you come across the following write-up. Read this material, then use the critical thinking questions outlined in this module to determine how you should respond.

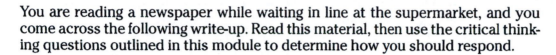

Advertisement*Advertisement*Advertisement*Advertisement*

MAKE HUNDREDS OF DOLLARS IN YOUR FREE TIME!

John McGee of Topeka, Kansas, worked every day of his life, 50 hours a week, from the time he was 17 until the time he was 55. And then he discovered a better way.

John sent for my free booklet, "How to Make Big Buck$$$ in Your Free Time," and before he knew it, he was bringing in hundreds of dollars a week in extra income. All he did was work a few hours on the weekends. Then he sat back and watched the money roll in.

And what is John doing today? He quit his back-breaking job several years ago. After toiling away, day after day, for so many years, John now gets up around 11 A.M. After a leisurely lunch, he spends a few hours working, then takes off for a round of golf in mid-afternoon. With only three hours of work a day, John pulled in almost $125,000 last year.

Now, John's secret is available to you. The booklet that got him started can be yours, FREE.

SEND NO MONEY

Would you like to be one of the thousands of Americans who shares our FAST-WEALTH system and climbs to the top of the economic ladder? Would you like to double, triple, or even quadruple your income, while working no more than ten hours a week? Would you like to tell your miserable, crabby boss to "shove it"?

If you answered yes to any of these questions, then you must send for our FREE booklet TODAY! We'll rush you a copy, and you can get started on the system that has helped so many people free themselves from unrewarding, low-paying jobs.

What are you waiting for? To get your free copy of "How to Make Big Buck$$$ in Your Free Time," send a self-addressed, stamped envelope to my attention at P.O. Box 123, Weston, Virginia, 32175. Please enclose $9.95 to cover the costs of postage and handling.   (continued)

The time to take advantage of this amazing opportunity is NOW! Don't Delay!

Peter Price-Jones
President, Independent Wealth Association

"Thank you, Mr. Price-Jones, for making all my dreams come true."

—Carolyn M., Winston-Salem, NC

"What an amazing system! So easy to learn, and so profitable. It's a miracle."

—Mike P., Boston, MA

"Send for this booklet today! I was skeptical, but now I see the light. I'm writing this letter from my brand-new house, which I bought after only one year of using your system."

—Terry P., Sacramento, CA

What is the source of this information?	
How much expertise or experience does the source of this information have? (Who is Peter Price-Jones? Does he even exist? What exactly is the "Independent Wealth Association"?)	
How do I feel about this information? Why do I feel this way?	
Does this information match my previous knowledge or experience? (Based on what I know, how much of this advertisement can I believe?)	
What do my friends, co-workers, and supervisors think? (What would other people say if I showed them this ad?)	

The final question: Should you send $9.95 to cover the costs of postage and handling for a copy of "Making Big Buck$$$ in Your Free Time"? _____

Activity 6.18: Critical Reading II

Put your critical thinking skills to work. The following safety tips for fire prevention appear in the employee manual. Read the tips, then answer the questions that follow.

Fire Prevention[9]

Obviously, the best way to provide fire safety is to prevent a fire from starting in the first place. The best way to prevent a fire is to make sure that the three elements needed for fire—fuel and heat—are never present in the

---

[9]Adapted from National Center for Construction Education and Research, *Core Curriculum* (Upper Saddle River, NJ/Columbus, OH: Prentice Hall, 2000), Trainee Module 00101, p. 1–46.

same place at the same time. Here are some basic safety guidelines for fire prevention:

1. Always work in a well-ventilated area, especially when you are using flammable materials such as shellac, lacquer, paint stripper, or construction adhesives.
2. Smoke or light matches when you are working with flammable materials.
3. Keep oily rags in approved, non-closing metal containers.
4. Store combustible materials only in approved containers.
5. Know where to find fire extinguishers, what kind of extinguisher to use for different kinds of fires, and how to use the extinguishers.
6. Make sure all extinguishers are fully charged. Remove the tag from an extinguisher—it shows the date the extinguisher was last serviced and inspected.

1. There are four mistakes in the passage above. By thinking critically and using your experience, you should be able to identify them. What are they?

   a. _____
   b. _____
   c. _____
   d. _____

2. Now that you've found these errors in the employee manual, what should you do?

   _____
   _____
   _____
   _____

Writing Skills I
The Basics

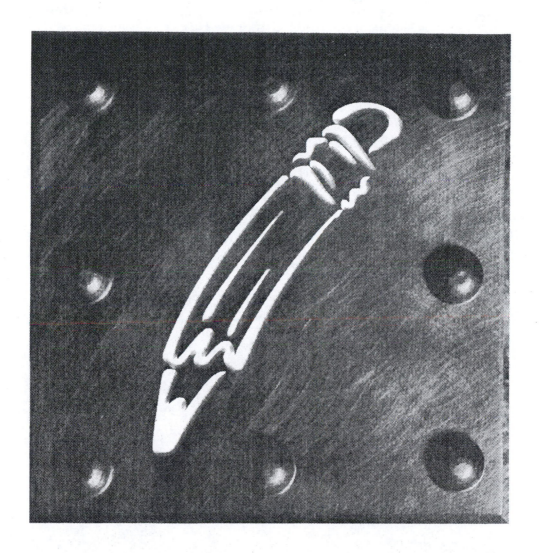

66 A common mistake in writing is lack of brevity. If this were not true, then there would be totally different meanings for 'beat around the bush,' 'get to the point,' and 'cut to the chase.' The first word taught in basic communication should be 'succinct.' 99

—Mike Watkins, Training Director, Encompass Mechanical Services

Over the past two decades, there has been a great increase in written communications in the construction industry. Some of it is related to OSHA (Occupational Safety and Health Administration) regulations, but much of it involves day-to-day correspondence that is needed to get the job done. The most common types of business writing are memos and e-mails, but you may also be asked to prepare progress reports, field reports, or job summaries.

In fact, you may be surprised at how much writing your job requires. You may think of yourself as a skilled craftsperson, an expert in carpentry, plumbing, electrical work, or HVAC—not as a professional writer. However, writing is an absolutely essential communication skill. Good writing fosters safety on the job site, keeps the job on budget and on schedule, and helps build teams. Poor writing leads to mistakes, morale problems, and wasted time, money, and effort.

Charles E. Dolce, manager of craft training at Halliburton Construction, summarizes the need for strong writing skills best in one simple statement: "If you can't communicate it, you can't build it." Similarly, if you can't write it, you can't build it. This is why so many construction projects generate thousands of pages of paper. A project simply can't be run on word of mouth. The written word lays out everything in detail and gives construction professionals a plan to follow.

7.1 BEFORE YOU WRITE: UNDERSTANDING YOUR AUDIENCE

Before you sit down to write anything—a letter, a memo, an e-mail, *anything*—you need to ask one important question:

Who is my audience? That is, who will be reading what I write?

The audience for your writing determines both *what* you should say and *how* you should say it.

Your audience might be composed of any of the following people:

- Your foreman
- The company's owner
- Land developers
- Architects, engineers, and designers
- Office personnel
- Government officials
- Draftspeople
- Contractors
- Subcontractors
- Co-workers who are as experienced as you
- Co-workers who have less experience than you
- Clients
- Homeowners
- Occupants or renters

Note that this list can be subdivided into two categories: (1) construction professionals and (2) *laypeople* (people who are not familiar with the construction business). Each group demands a different approach in your writing.

Writing for Construction Professionals

When writing for other construction professionals, you can safely assume that your reader will understand what you're saying. You can also assume a familiarity with a project and with procedures. This means that you don't need to explain every word you use.

Writing for Laypeople

You cannot assume that laypeople have a working knowledge of your business. Thus, when you write for laypeople, you need to spell things out clearly and define your terms. For example, you might know what a scupper or a scuttle is, but the homeowner may not. As a construction professional, it's your job to educate (and be patient with) people who are unfamiliar with the language of construction.

Here is a humorous example of what can happen when your audience doesn't understand the words you're using:

> A customer called an electric serviceman because his power was off. There are two types of electrical wires that enter a house: overhead wires (which are called *drops*) and underground wires (which are called *laterals*). The serviceman looked at the situation and wrote up the work order. The customer looked at the form and got angry. He called the boss and told him that the serviceman was rude.
>
> "What did the serviceman say?" the boss asked. He was surprised because the serviceman had always been friendly and good natured.
>
> "It's not what he said," the customer replied. "It's what he wrote."
>
> The serviceman had written in bold letters on the work order: INVESTIGATED POWER OUTAGE—DROP DEAD. The customer apparently took it personally, not realizing that the serviceman was being accurate![1]

Formal versus Informal Relationships

The list of people who will read your writing can also be divided in another way: those people with whom you have a *formal* relationship, and those with whom you have an *informal* relationship. Clearly, when you are writing to a boss, an owner, a foreman, or a client, you will be expected to write more "seriously." You'll want to watch your grammar, spelling, and punctuation. You'll want to be matter-of-fact and businesslike. But if you're writing to a friend or a co-worker, it is perfectly acceptable to be less formal. A friendlier tone is fine; so is the occasional joke (as long as it's tasteful).

> **TIP:** When in doubt, use a more formal tone. Sometimes your writing will be shared with other people without your knowledge. For example, your boss may decide to show a memo you've written to the company's owner. In these cases, a formal tone is better. It's always better to be too formal than not formal enough.

Here are some other things to consider when thinking about your audience:

- Do I need to take my readers' cultural backgrounds into account?
- How are my readers likely to react to my ideas? Do I need to persuade them that I am correct? (If you want to bring your readers around to your opinion, you'll need to give them strong reasons for doing so.)
- How busy are my readers? (If they are busy people—and they usually are—you'll want to keep your written communications short.)

---

[1]The author is grateful to Don Guminey of Electrical Concepts, Inc. (Waukesha, WI) for sharing this story.

- How will people use what I write? Have I been as informative as they need me to be?
- Have I used any "inside jokes" or terms that someone in my audience will not understand?

Activity 7.1: Writing for Laypeople

Rewrite each of the following sentences to make them understandable to someone who doesn't work in the construction business. Note that you may need to provide additional information to explain certain key terms to your audience. The following list may help familiarize you with unfamiliar terms:

- **CO:** carbon monoxide
- **NH$_3$:** ammonia
- **OSHA:** Occupational Health and Safety Administration; federal agency that oversees workplace safety
- **slag:** waste material from welding operations
- **spatter:** flying bits of solder or other molten material produced during welding

EXAMPLE: HazCom says that workers must be informed about the presence of dangerous substances on the job.

REWRITE: A federal law called the Hazard Communication Standard ("HazCom") says that workers must be informed about the presence of dangerous substances on the job.

1. Ensuring that workers comply with OSHA regs is an important part of every foreman's job.

_____

_____

_____

2. Don't move heavy equipment in crowded areas without a signaler.

_____

_____

_____

3. When working with gas-operated machinery, ventilate the area to avoid CO poisoning. Also make sure that you're careful when working with NH$_3$.

_____

_____

_____

4. The specs don't call for a window on the north wall.

_____

_____

_____

5. Mrs. Cowen, please be careful in this area. We're welding, and there's bound to be a lot of spatter and slag.

_____

_____

_____

Activity 7.2: Considering Your Audience

For this activity, assume the following situation. You need to write a letter to each of the people listed below. For each person, choose the most appropriate way to begin the letter.

_____ 1. Mark Peterson, the owner of the large corporation that employs you.
   a. Dear Mr. Peterson,
   b. Dear Mark,
   c. Mark,

_____ 2. Sally Steele, a homeowner who has asked you to bid on the cost of renovating her entire home, from top to bottom.
   a. Dear Ms. Steele,
   b. Dear Sally,
   c. Sally,

_____ 3. Robert Wong, a longtime friend you've known since grammar school.
   a. Dear Mr. Wong,
   b. Dear Bob,
   c. Dear Sir,

_____ 4. Linda Rodriguez, the Human Resources director of a company to which you're applying for employment.
   a. Dear Miss Rodriguez,
   b. Dear Ms. Rodriguez,
   c. Dear Linda,

_____ 5. John Thompson, a new apprentice with your company.
   a. Dear Mr. Thompson,
   b. John Thompson,
   c. John,

7.2 THE HALLMARKS OF GOOD WRITING

Regardless of the situation, all good writing shares several characteristics. Good writing is objective, economical, clear, simple, and legible.

Objectivity

Good writing presents the facts honestly, or _objectively._ Good writing also tells the full story—not just part of it. It's particularly important that foremen and other decision makers have the complete facts so that they can take the proper action.

If you are writing a recommendation—say, for Brand X cement instead of Brand Y cement—you should outline the pros and cons of each choice, and then make your final recommendation. In other words, you should show your reader that you have carefully considered the facts before coming to your decision. Here's an example of a good, objective piece of writing:

> I like Brand X cement because the price is right, it is very easy to work, and the supplier has always been reliable. Brand X has also proven to be sturdy. Brand Y has been known to crack after only a few months, and it's tough to work. It is true that Brand Y is 13 cents cheaper per unit than Brand X, but I believe that, overall, Brand X is the better choice.

Economy

Good writing gets to the point. It doesn't bore the reader with unnecessary details.[2] It presents the facts, makes a statement, and then ends. In other words, it doesn't ask for more of the reader's time than is absolutely necessary.

For example, say you're concerned because work is due to start on a new project, but the proper permits haven't yet been secured. You want to write an e-mail to your supervisor mentioning this. Which is the better way to begin your e-mail?

> OPTION A: Frank, I hope you read this e-mail soon. I'm writing about the new warehouse we're putting up on Industrial Way. As you know, my crew is scheduled to start working there next Friday. This going to be a big job, and we're facing a lot of challenges. Basically, I have everything under control and I think we're going to be OK on the schedule, but there are a few things worrying me. Probably what's worrying me the most is that we don't have the permits yet. Rita told me that we absolutely, positively cannot start until we have the permits.

> OPTION B: Frank, we're due to start on the Industrial Way project next Friday and we don't have the permits yet. I'm really worried about this—we can't start work without those permits.

In Option A, Frank would have to get through a lot of words before he found your main point. In Option B, he'll know what's on your mind almost as soon as he begins reading. Option B is the better way to go.

TIP: Sometimes you can convey information economically by spelling out your main points in a bulleted (•) or numbered (1, 2, 3, etc.) list, so keep these options in mind when you write.

Clarity and Simplicity

Good writing is clear and simple. Some people think that using big words or long sentences makes them look more professional or knowledgeable. This is not true. The best writing uses simple words and short sentences.

It is amazing how many long words and sentences can be replaced with simpler, clearer words or sentences. For example:

---
[2] Of course, the piece of writing should provide all the *necessary* details—just not the *unnecessary* ones.

Unclear: In order to prevent unwanted electrical shocks, workers should make sure they disconnect the main power supply before work commences.

Clear: To prevent shocks, disconnect the main power supply before beginning work.

In addition, whenever possible, use the active voice rather than the passive voice.

Passive voice (wordy, confusing): The main power supply should be disconnected by workers before work is begun.

Active voice (clear, concise): Workers should disconnect the main power supply before they begin work.

We offer more suggestions for achieving clarity and simplicity in Section 7.6.

Legibility

In our computer age, where many communications are handled electronically (through computers and Palm Pilots, for example), it's easy to forget that good writing is *legible*. Legibility is particularly important in filling out forms. Serious and costly mistakes can happen when your readers can't understand your handwriting.

Some people are blessed with good penmanship; others find writing a chore. If you're one of the unlucky people without good penmanship, here are some suggestions to help keep your writing legible:

- Write in block capital letters. Avoid cursive handwriting, which can be hard to read.
- Be particularly careful with numbers. Slow down when you have to write a number.
- After you've finished, ask someone to read the form before you hand it in. This way, if something is illegible, you can fix it before it goes too much further.

Activity 7.3: Writing Self-Assessment

In this activity, your goal is to assess your own writing abilities.

STEP ONE:
Read each of the statements that follow. Check each statement that you think applies to you. (*Note:* As in all self-assessments, complete honesty is essential.)

_____   1. I will sometimes leave out facts if they don't support my point.

_____   2. I tend to see things in black and white. If I like something, I really like it; if I don't like something, I really dislike it.

_____   3. When telling a story, I omit the details that might make me look bad or disprove my point.

_____   4. I tend to use too many words to get my point across.

_____   5. In conversations, I tend to ramble or monopolize the conversation.

_____   6. I have trouble separating what's important from what's not important.

_____ 7. When I'm trying to get my point across, I think it's better to keep hammering that point home, even after I've made it several times.

_____ 8. I think that big words are more impressive than small words.

_____ 9. My handwriting is a mess—hardly anybody can read it. Sometimes I can't even read my own handwriting!

_____ 10. I tend to write very quickly, and I sometimes skip things or miss things because of it.

STEP TWO: SELF-ASSESSMENT

- If you checked 1, 2, or 3 above, you might need practice in being more objective. Complete Exercise A in Activity 7.4 below.

- If you checked 4, 5, 6, or 7 above, you might need practice in being more economical in your writing. Complete Exercise B in Activity 7.4 below.

- If you checked 8 above, you might need to work on writing more clearly and simply. Complete Exercise C in Activity 7.4 below.

- If you checked 9 or 10 above, you might need to work on the legibility of your handwriting. Complete Exercise D in Activity 7.4 below.

Activity 7.4: Writing Objectively, Economically, Clearly, Simply, and Legibly

Use your self-assessment in Activity 7.3 to determine which exercise(s) to complete here. If you did not check any lines in Step 1 of Activity 7.3, choose two of the following exercises to complete.

EXERCISE A: WRITING OBJECTIVELY

THE SITUATION: You and the four other members of your team are working on a very large job site that covers nearly 25 acres. Communication has been a problem, because the walkie-talkies you've all been using to keep in contact are unreliable and full of static. Your team has nominated you to talk to the boss about getting cell phones for all five members of the team.

   You know that your boss will respond best to a request in writing. You also know that your boss will want to make sure that you've considered all the pros and cons of the request.

YOUR TASK: Write a one- or two-paragraph note to the boss in which you outline the pros and cons of purchasing cell phones for the team. Be sure to state your request directly, and support your request with strong reasons.

To get yourself started on this task, you might want to fill in the following grid:

Cell Phones for "Team B"

Pros

_____

_____

_____

Cons

_____

_____

_____

EXERCISE B: WRITING ECONOMICALLY

The following paragraph is written with far too many words and digressions. Rewrite it so that it is streamlined and economical. Put the terms and definition upfront, along with the most important information. Eliminate unnecessary details. Use an easy-to-read format.

There are so many areas on a construction site that require special safety precautions. Electrical safety is one area. Fire safety is another. Apprentices really need to know about working safely around trenches and excavations. For example, you shouldn't put tools within two feet of the trench. Why not? Because they could fall in and hurt people working down there. That happens way too often, and it can be avoided. So don't put tools near the edge of the trench. Another important thing is to never jump over or straddle the trench. That is bad! You should walk around it instead. It's way too easy to fall in and hurt yourself. And speaking of jumping, don't get into a trench by jumping into it. Well, OK, jump in, but only if you want a broken ankle. Seriously though, use a ladder to get into the trench. Much safer. And while we're on the subject of safety, you have to protect others, too. So put up barricades around the trench so that clueless people don't fall into them. By the way, an excavation is any man-made cut in the earth, formed by removing soil. A trench is usually a narrow excavation that is deeper than it is wide. Oh, and the maximum width of a trench is 15 feet. Last but not least, inspect the trenches daily to make sure they are properly shored up, and don't work in an excavation if there's water in it. Why not? Zap! You could get electrocuted.

EXERCISE C: WRITING CLEARLY AND SIMPLY

Each of the following sentences lacks clarity, simplicity, or both. Rewrite each sentence as simply and clearly as possible.

1. It is imperative that all workers don their hard hats before entering a construction site.

   _____

   _____

2. Confined spaces can be defined in the following manner: They are spaces that are actually big enough for a human person to work in. But even though they're big enough for a person to work in, they have limited means of entry or exit. There are several examples of confined spaces. Silos are one type. Another type is the tank. A third type is a hopper. A fourth type is a pit. A fifth type is a vault.

   _____

   _____

   _____

   _____

3. Personal protective equipment is really important on the job, in fact it is extremely important to your health, so always do four things with it, inspect it regularly, and care for it really good, and always wear it when you have to because that's the right thing to do, and don't change it or alter it or modify it or anything like that because that could be really problematic, and if you do all these things your

personal protective equipment, sometimes abbreviated PPE, will be your best friend.

_____

_____

_____

_____

_____

4. Any person who shows up inebriated for work will be summarily dismissed. This company does not tolerate dipsomaniacs. Nor are we inclined to continue the employment of kleptomaniacs or prevaricators.

_____

_____

_____

_____

EXERCISE D: WRITING LEGIBLY

Rewrite each of the following sentences in your most legible handwriting.

1. Pick up 697 units of Part Number 45-6122 at 8750 Vassar Street, Columbia, South Carolina.

_____

_____

2. Selma Jaczkova has been employed with our company for 15 years.

_____

_____

3. The quick brown fox jumped over the lazy dogs, while all good men came to the aid of their parties.

_____

_____

4. Construction is a multi-faceted industry that employs people from all walks of life. Construction jobs require many different talents and a good deal of training.

_____

_____

5. The foreman asked me to gather the entire team for a meeting at the home office this afternoon. If you have any questions about the meeting, call Jack at 201-555-7744.

_____

_____

_____

_____

7.3 WRITING TO CONVEY INFORMATION

In addition to considering your audience, you need to consider your *purpose* for writing. Unless you're writing a grocery list or a letter to a friend, most of the time you will be writing to convey information. For example, you may be writing an e-mail to let your supervisor know that you're running low on lumber. Or, you may be writing to outline the tasks that have already been completed on a job and what remains to be done.

How do you convey this information objectively, economically, clearly, and simply? You can do this simply by asking yourself the *journalist's questions,* also known as the 5 W's.

7.3.1 The Five W's

Journalists are experts at conveying large amounts of information in a small amount of space. They do so by getting the answers to five questions, known as *the 5W's,* about any given event. Then they summarize the answers to all these questions in one place.

You can use these same questions to ensure that you're providing all the necessary details in what you write. They are:

Who?	Who is the audience? Who is affected by the contents of your writing? Who needs to receive a copy of what you're about to write?
What?	What is the *specific* subject of your memo, e-mail, or letter? (All written material should be on one specific topic, with unnecessary details filtered out.)
Where?	Where did events happen? What construction site is being written about—which specific address, sector, floor, or other area is affected?
When?	When did events happen? When must your material be written by, or when do the readers need to respond by? Is time of the essence?
Why?	Why is this memo, letter, or e-mail being written? Is it to persuade, to summarize, to analyze, to evaluate, or to offer directions? (You need to be very clear and specific about your purpose, because that is the only way you'll get the desired response from your readers. We discuss the different purposes in more detail in Section 7.4.)

If you keep the answers to the five W's in mind as you prepare your memo or report, you will cover all the bases.

Let's look at an extended example to illustrate how you can use the five W's to gather information and then convey it in written format.

Because of some unexpected fires on the job site, your company is putting together a safety booklet. Your boss has asked you to help him prepare the booklet by writing the section that explains how fires start. The ultimate goal is to explain how to prevent fires from getting started in the first place. The booklet will be distributed to all company employees by the end of next week. Workers will be expected to read the booklet by the end of the month. Let's now use this information to answer the 5 W's:

Who?	The booklet will be distributed to all company employees. Because the information is intended for construction workers, you can assume that your *audience* is composed of

people who are familiar with construction terminology and basic construction concepts. Thus, you won't need to explain the words or terms that are used on the job site every day. However, you may need to explain words or terms that are unfamiliar or new.

What? The *specific subject* of your writing is obvious: how fires start. You will want to present all the specific facts necessary to convey this information, but you'll also want to make sure that you don't include any unnecessary information. For example, although the information may be interesting, you won't need to include material on the different types of fire extinguishers or the different classes of flammable materials.

Where? Clearly, the booklet is going to be aimed toward on-the-job safety, so you're going to present the information in a way that makes it useful *on the job site*. Of course, this same information may also be useful at home or in any other place, but for now you're primarily concerned with fire safety at work.

When? Your time frame is clear. If the booklet is to be distributed by the end of next week, you need to start writing *now*. Workers will have until the end of the month to read the booklet.

Why? The company has had some problems with unexpected fires. The purpose of the booklet is to prevent more fires from happening. To know how to prevent fires, workers must know how fires start. This is why you have to write an explanation of the process.

Based on the five W's, you can now write your part of the booklet, as follows:

How Fires Start

For a fire to start, three things are needed in the same place at the same time: fuel, heat, and oxygen. If one of these three is missing, a fire will not start.

Fuel is anything that will combine with oxygen and heat to burn. When pure oxygen is present, such as near a leaking oxygen hose or fitting, material that would not normally be considered fuel (including some metals) will burn.

Heat is anything that will raise a fuel's temperature to the flash point. The *flash point* is the temperature at which a fuel gives off enough gases (vapors) to burn. The flash points of many fuels are quite low—room temperature or less. When the burning gases raise the temperature of a fuel to the point at which it ignites, the fuel itself will burn—and keep burning—even if the original source of heat is removed.

Oxygen is a naturally occurring element that is always present in the air.

Together, these three elements make up what is known as the "fire triangle." All three elements—fuel, heat, and oxygen—must be present for the fire to start and continue. If any one element of the triangle is missing, a fire cannot start. If a fire has started, removing any one element from the triangle will put it out.[3]

Why is this description so effective in conveying the appropriate information? Note the following:

1. A title is included to introduce the topic.

2. Although written for a construction audience, the author was careful to define important terms: *fuel, heat, flash point,* and *oxygen.*

---

[3]This description is adapted from National Center for Construction Education and Research, *Core Curriculum* (Upper Saddle River, NJ/Columbus, OH: 2000), Module 00101, pp. 1-45–1-46.

3. The author has included all the required information on how fires start without using big words or adding unnecessary details. He has also kept in mind the ultimate purpose of the booklet: fire safety and the prevention of fires. So he closes by stating clearly that fires can be extinguished by removing one of the elements that started the fire.

Activity 7.5: Answering the Five W's

Two scenarios are presented below. After examining each scenario, prepare to write about it by answering the five W's.

SCENARIO A: You work for JP Construction, a small company that specializes in remodeling kitchens and bathrooms in private homes. Recently, the company's owner has been getting complaints from homeowners. It seems that the workers have not been cleaning up after themselves each day. They are bringing mud into the house, leaving coffee cups strewn about, and leaving sawdust all over the work areas.

The owner is quite upset that his employees are not following the rules of good housekeeping. He has asked you, the foreman, to write a memo to the employees who work in other people's homes. The memo will outline the problem and remind employees of the behavior expected of them as construction professionals. The owner has requested that you have the memo written by September 8th, so that he can include it with the workers' paychecks on September 15th.

Now, answer the five W's.

Who?	
What?	
Where?	
When?	
Why?	

SCENARIO B: You're in charge of ordering new tools for your company. Generally, when an employee needs a new tool, he or she simply asks you to order it. After you've decided whether or not the tool purchase is necessary, you place the order. However, a new system is being put in place. Workers must now follow a new procedure: They must go to their supervisor with a request for a new tool. The supervisor must then fill out a form, outlining the reason the purchase is needed. The supervisor then brings you that form. Each week, you bring all the forms you've collected to the site manager, who either approves or disapproves the request. Based on her decisions, you order the tools that are deemed necessary.

To explain the new procedure, you need to send an e-mail to all the supervisors in the company. It will be their job to explain the new procedure to their workers. Today is June 1. The new procedure will become effective on July 15.

Who?	
What?	
Where?	
When?	
Why?	

7.3.2 Main Ideas versus Details

As you write, you need to be aware of the important difference between *main ideas* and *details*. The main idea is the key point you want to make. The details are the materials or examples that support your key point. However, not all details are equally important. You must therefore ask yourself the following questions:

- How much do my readers really need to know?
- Do my readers need step-by-step instructions, or will a general overview be enough?
- How many examples do I need to give to prove my point?
- How much of this information is needed right now? How much of it can be provided later on?

Of course, the answers to these questions will differ on a case-by-case basis. Keep in mind, though, that unnecessary details are distracting. So are sentences that are irrelevant or off the topic.

As an example, consider the following introduction to fire safety, written for the same booklet we discussed above:

Introduction to Fire Safety

Fire is always a hazard on construction job sites. Many of the materials used in construction are flammable, and welding, grinding, and other construction activities create heat or sparks that can cause a fire. Of course, hard hats are an important part of job safety, too. Fire safety involves two elements: fire prevention and fire fighting.[4]

This paragraph provides good information, but one sentence is off the topic. The third sentence, which brings up hard hats, is irrelevant to the topic of fire safety. Hard hats would probably be dealt with in a separate part of the safety booklet, so they should be left out here.

As another example, look at the following e-mail message. Joe is writing to Harry about the need to hire a plumbing contractor to complete a house they're working on.

Joe,

We need to get a state-certified plumber to work on the Ramsey house. We're having trouble with the drains in the kitchen and bathroom, and I get the sense that there is some serious trouble there. I tried contacting Vincent Brothers Plumbing, our usual contractor, but they're booked solid. I really like the work they did for us on those two jobs over in Fort Lauderdale . . . they turned out great! One was a ranch, the other a bi-level. Plus they are good guys, easy to work with. One of them grew up with my sister, I think they even went to the prom together. So, since they're not available, try ABC Plumbing or Main Street Plumbing. If you call ABC, tell them that I gave you their name. It's really interesting, even though they're called "Main Street Plumbing," they're actually located on Elm Street.

Thanks,

Harry

The purpose of this e-mail is simple: Harry needs Joe to contact some plumbing contractors. But unnecessary details are getting in the way of the message. Joe *does* need to know that the Vincent Brothers aren't available, so that he doesn't waste time trying to contact them. But Joe certainly *doesn't* need to know, in this e-mail, the details of the Fort Lauderdale jobs or that one of the brothers used to go out with Harry's sister! Likewise, it's irrelevant to this e-mail that Main Street Plumbing is located on Elm Street. The e-mail would be much more concise and to the point without these unnecessary details, as follows:

Joe,

We need to get a state-certified plumber to work on the Ramsey house. We're having trouble with the drains in the kitchen and bathroom, and I get the sense that there is some serious trouble there. I tried contacting Vincent Brothers Plumbing, our usual contractor, but they're booked solid. So, since they're not available, try ABC Plumbing or Main Street Plumbing. If you call ABC, tell them that I gave you their name.

Thanks,

Harry

Your readers are busy people. Don't give them more information than they need.

---

[4]This description is adapted from National Center for Construction Education and Research, *Core Curriculum* (Upper Saddle River, NJ/Columbus, OH: 2000), Module 00101, p. 1-45.

Activity 7.6: Eliminating Irrelevant Details

Each of the following passages includes needless repetition or irrelevant details. In each passage, cross out the sentences or details that detract from the main idea. Be careful not to cross out relevant details that help support the main idea. Use the title of each passage to help determine which details are relevant.

Passage A: Alcohol and Drug Abuse on the Job

Alcohol and drug abuse costs the construction industry millions of dollars a year in accidents, lost time, and lost productivity. The true cost of alcohol and drug abuse is much more than just money, of course. Abuse can cost lives. Abusing alcohol and drugs really is not a good thing.

Using alcohol creates a risk of injury for everyone on the job site. And when I say everyone, I do mean *everyone*. Many states now have laws that prevent workers from collecting insurance benefits if they are injured while under the influence of alcohol or illegal drugs. Some think that this is not a fair system, while others find it very just and reasonable.

You don't have to be abusing illegal drugs like marijuana, cocaine, or heroin to create a job hazard. Many prescribed and over-the-counter drugs, prescribed for legitimate reasons, can affect your ability to work safely. Amphetamines, barbiturates, and antihistamines are only a few of the legal drugs that can affect your ability to work safely or to operate machinery. Horseplay can also cause job hazards.[5]

Passage B: The Importance of Teamwork in the Construction Business

More than any other industry, the construction industry relies on *teamwork*. There are very few, if any, construction projects that can be completed by one person. Teamwork is also important in other businesses as well, such as car manufacturing and assembly-line work. Ford Motor Company is very proud of the teamwork displayed by its employees.

Suppose you're putting up a skyscraper. How could you get the plumbing done without the plumbers? How could you get the electric lines installed without the electricians? How could the building be built without engineers, architects, and design professionals? How could you know how best to spend your time if you didn't have a foreman to direct you? Of course, you *couldn't* complete the project without the contributions of many people with different training and talents. This is why teamwork is so important. Cost management and savvy management skills are also important.

Teamwork entails more than simply working alongside other people. Much more, actually. Teamwork requires many things. For a team to be successful, *all* the workers must actively contribute. Teams don't benefit from loners or people who think they're above it all. Think about sports like hockey and basketball, where players help each other score goals or make baskets. Those individual players aren't playing for themselves. They know that winning the point for the team is more important than getting glory for themselves. Maybe someone should tell that to some of those hotshot NBA players who think that they're more important than their teammates.[6]

---

[5]Adapted from National Center for Construction Education and Research, *Core Curriculum* (Upper Saddle River, NJ/Columbus, OH: Prentice Hall, 2000), Module 00101, p. 1–7.

[6]Adapted from Steven A. Rigolosi, *Tools for Success: Soft Skills for the Construction Industry* (Upper Saddle River, NJ/Columbus, OH: Prentice Hall, 2000), p. 32.

7.4 Writing for Different Purposes

Information is conveyed in everything we write, from memos to e-mails to materials lists. Sometimes, though, in addition to providing information, our writing has an additional purpose. In this section, we examine some writing techniques to use when you are looking to:

- Persuade someone to do something
- Offer directions
- Summarize a large amount of information
- Synthesize, analyze, and evaluate a situation or set of circumstances

7.4.1 Persuasion

When you attempt to *persuade,* you're trying to bring someone around to your point of view. For example, you might need to write an e-mail in which you try to persuade your foreman to hire a specific contractor. Or, you might write a note in which you try to convince the materials department to purchase a specific type of lumber.

First and foremost, effective persuasion requires you to show the *benefits* of your suggestion to the reader. This means that your recommendation or choice must be supported by facts that will provide advantages for the reader—not the writer (you). Saying "You should hire Mary McMullen as our new HVAC specialist because she's a good friend of mine, and I'd really like to see her more often" is not persuasive at all. However, saying "You should hire Mary McMullen because she has fifteen years of experience, has worked on all types of construction projects, is an excellent team player, and is never late or sick" would be *very* persuasive to your boss.

As we discussed in Section 7.2, all good writing offers evidence and examples to support the points being made. But in persuasive writing, it's even more important that you offer detailed support for your recommendations.

Figure 7.1 shows a sample persuasive memo. In it, the writer (Don Gioretta) is making the case that Countryside Electronics should purchase the

---

Countryside Electronics

INTEROFFICE MEMO

TO: Linda Wilkins   FROM: Don Gioretta

    c: Sharad Jani   DATE: November 11, 1996

SUBJECT: Short Circuit Damage

An increasing number of manufacturers now use static-sensitive equipment in their plants. Accidental short-circuiting during our troubleshooting procedures can frequently be traced to the static sensitivity of these devices. By purchasing antistatic kits and supplying our field personnel with them, we can reduce the level of short-circuit damage.

    I recommend the RCA Antistatic Kit, which retails for about $54. It is the most effective and readily available kit on the market for its price. The kit is compact, easy to work with, and comes with a good set of instructions.

Figure 7.1: Persuasive Memo

Source: Maris Roze, *Technical Communication: The Practical Craft,* 3d ed. (Upper Saddle River, NJ: Prentice Hall, 1997), p. 72.

RCA Antistatic Kit, which helps reduce the level of short-circuit damage. Note the reasons that this memo is so effective:

- It is short and to the point.
- It begins by offering background information on the problem (accidental short-circuiting) so that the reader can place the recommendation in context.
- It closes with a recommendation for the RCA Antistatic Kit, along with several strong reasons for purchasing this kit: (1) it is effective and readily available, (2) the kit is compact and easy to work with, and (3) the kit comes with a good set of instructions.
- It states the price of the Antistatic Kit, $54. A good businessman, Don Gioretta knows that his supervisors are going to inquire about the price of the kit, so he includes this information in his memo.

REMEMBER WHEN WRITING PERSUASIVELY:

- Your *reliability* and *credibility* are critical. If your reader perceives that you are lying or withholding important information, your persuasive techniques will not work.
- A certain amount of *bias*—that is, feeling for or against something—is expected and acceptable in persuasive writing. It is important, though, that you openly admit your bias. For example, you could say something like "I admit that I prefer Acme Tools over Zenith Tools. Acme tools are ergonomic, sturdy, and reliable. Yes, Zenith tools are cheaper, but you get what you pay for."
- Your persuasive techniques will be much more reliable if you *anticipate* the questions your readers might have. In Figure 7.1, for example, Don Gioretta anticipated the question his boss would have—"How much does the kit cost?"—and provided the answer. Think about the information that your readers want and need, then give it to them.
- A certain level of enthusiasm is welcome in a persuasive note. If you feel strongly about something, it is perfectly acceptable to convey those strong feelings. Just be sure you do so professionally.
- You can make your recommendation even more effectively and strongly if you include a table or graph that summarizes your key points. (For more on including illustrations with your writing, see Section 8.2.)

Activity 7.7: Writing Persuasively

Your goal in this activity is to write a persuasive memo or letter. Choose one of the exercises from the two that follow. Keep the following tips in mind while you write:

- To be reliable, be aware of the pros and cons of your argument.
- To be credible, argue for your position reasonably and enthusiastically.
- To be respectful of your readers, anticipate any questions they might have.

For this activity, do not worry about using the proper format of a business letter or business memo. (We discuss proper formats in Section 8.1.)

EXERCISE A: PERSUASIVE LETTER
Over the last year or so, many of the workers in your company have been putting in a lot of overtime. At first, workers were happy to be earning extra money, but they are now working so many hours that they feel tired all the time. They are also becoming frustrated at not being able to spend time with their families and friends.

Write a brief letter to the president of your company in which you try to persuade him to adopt one of the following programs:

- Hiring contractors and subcontractors to do some of the extra work
- Instituting a system in which workers will not be required to put in any overtime for two weeks after they have worked 20 hours of overtime

Be sure to outline the pros and cons of each plan, and state your recommendations and desires strongly but respectfully.

EXERCISE B: PERSUASIVE MEMO

As a construction professional, you are very proud of what you do. You have three children, ages 15, 12, and 9, and you would like to have them visit your job site to get a better sense of what you do for a living. You like this idea so much, in fact, that you would like your company to sponsor a "Take Our Families to Work" day, in which all employees would be invited to bring family members to the job site to learn about construction work.

Write a memo to the personnel director in which you argue for the benefits of such a day. There are some possible drawbacks to such an idea—for example, lower productivity and possible safety issues—so be sure to include these in your memo.

7.4.2 Directions

Manuals, booklets, textbooks, and government regulations all offer directions on the proper procedures for getting things done. Why is it so important to have directions written down? The answer is simple: Directions given verbally can be confusing or hard to follow. If someone isn't listening, he or she might make serious errors. When directions are written, everyone gets the *same* set of procedures, and the proper way of doing things is established.

As with all good writing, directions should be clear, concise, and to the point. All relevant details should be provided, and unnecessary details should be left out. Whenever possible, illustrations should be provided to help the reader understand the process.

Before you sit down to write a set of directions, ask yourself: Exactly what kind of directions am I providing here? Do I need to spell out a process step by step, or am I offering general guidelines? The way you write depends on the answer to this question.

Writing Step-by-Step Directions

Step-by-step directions are required when a procedure must be followed *in a particular order* to be correct or effective. As an analogy, think of recipes. You must follow a recipe's directions in the order they're presented. Otherwise, strange things could happen.

In the past, directions were often written in a prose/paragraph format. Consider the following set of directions for using a claw hammer to drive a nail:

> Hold the nail straight, at a 90-degree angle to the surface being nailed. Grip the handle of the hammer. Hold the end of the handle even with the lower edge of your palm. Rest the face of the hammer on the nail. Draw the hammer back and give the nail a few light taps to start it. Move your fingers away from the nail and hit the nail firmly with the center of the hammer face. Hold the hammer level with the head of the nail and strike the

face squarely. Deliver the blow through your wrist, your elbow, and your shoulder.[7]

There is nothing wrong with these directions—they are complete and effective. All important details are included, and nothing irrelevant has been added. However, the format of these directions could be somewhat difficult to follow. For this reason, many manuals now offer step-by-step directions in a more vertical format that is easier on the reader's eyes. These vertical formats use bullets (•) or numbered steps (1, 2, 3) to make the material easier to follow. Here is the same set of directions, but in a vertical format:

Step One: Hold the nail straight, at a 90-degree angle to the surface being nailed.

Step Two: Grip the handle of the hammer. Hold the end of the handle even with the lower edge of your palm.

Step Three: Rest the face of the hammer on the nail.

Step Four: Draw the hammer back and give the nail a few light taps to start it.

Step Five: Move your fingers away from the nail and hit the nail firmly with the center of the hammer face. Hold the hammer level with the head of the nail and strike the face squarely. Deliver the blow through your wrist, your elbow, and your shoulder.

This step-by-step description is easier to read than the earlier description. Note that it could be improved even more by adding a diagram that shows the process. Such a diagram might look like the one shown in Figure 7.2.

REMEMBER WHEN WRITING STEP-BY-STEP DIRECTIONS:

- Use a format that is reader-friendly. Use strong, active verbs to give the directions.
- Visualize as you write. That is, break down each step in your mind's eye, and then write it down. Divide the process into sufficiently small steps to be easily followed. If a step seems to be too long, ask yourself: Can or should this be divided into smaller steps?
- Imagine that you are the person reading what you've written. Would you understand with no further explanations? Have all the steps been included?
- Ask several other people to read the directions you've written before you finalize them. The goal here is to test how well you have conveyed the information. Your readers can help you see what you may have

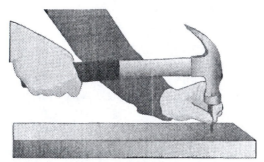

Figure 7.2: Proper Use of a Claw Hammer

Source: National Center for Construction Education and Research, *Core Curriculum* (Upper Saddle River, NJ/Columbus, OH: Prentice Hall, 2000), Module 00103, p. 3–3.

---

[7]National Center for Construction Education and Research, *Core Curriculum* (Upper Saddle River, NJ/Columbus, OH: Prentice Hall, 2000), Module 00103, p. 3–2.

missed. *Note:* One person is usually not enough to give you effective feedback. Always ask at least two or three people to check your writing.

- Use illustrations whenever possible. If you aren't a good artist, computer programs can help.

Writing Guidelines

Guidelines are sets of directions that don't necessarily need to be followed step by step. Rather, they offer basic instructions, or items to be aware of, during a specific process or procedure.

As you write guidelines, keep the tenets of good writing in mind. Keep your guidelines short, specific, and direct. Try to think of everything that someone should do to be effective at the assigned task, then list all those elements. Also think of things that could go wrong or mistakes that people could make, and list those as well. Remember: Doing something correctly means not only following the directions, but also not making mistakes!

As with step-by-step instructions, use a visually pleasing format. Bulleted lists and do/don't lists can be very effective. For example, here is a bulleted list that effectively offers safety guidelines on lockout/tagout systems:

- *Never* operate any device, valve, switch, or piece of equipment that has a lock or a tag attached to it.
- Use only tags that have been approved for your job site.
- If a device, valve, switch, or piece of equipment is locked out, make sure the proper tag is attached.
- Lock out and tag all electrical systems.
- Lock out and tag pipelines containing acids, explosive fluids, and high-pressure steam.
- Tag motorized vehicles and equipment when they are being repaired and before anyone starts work. Also, disconnect or disable the starting devices.[8]

The following set of guidelines uses a do/don't format to explain ladder safety.[9] Note that the writer has used capital letters for each "don't" to emphasize what not to do. Some alternatives to the do/don't format are the yes/no format and the always/never format.

Do's	Don'ts
Be sure your ladder has been properly set up and is used in accordance with safety instructions and warnings.	DON'T stand above the highest safe standing level.
Wear shoes with nonslip soles.	DON'T stand above the second step from the top of a stepladder and the 4th rung from the top of an extension ladder. You may lose your balance and fall.
Keep your body centered on the ladder.	DON'T climb a closed stepladder. It may slip out from under you.
Hold the ladder with one hand while working with the other. Never let your belt buckle pass beyond either ladder rail.	DON'T climb on the back of a stepladder. It is not designed to hold a person.

(continued)

---

[8]National Center for Construction Education and Research, *Core Curriculum* (Upper Saddle River, NJ/Columbus, OH: Prentice Hall, 2000), Module 00101, p. 1–23.

[9]National Center for Construction Education and Research, *Core Curriculum* (Upper Saddle River, NJ/Columbus, OH: Prentice Hall, 2000), Module 00101, p. 1–40.

Do's	Don'ts
Move materials with extreme caution. Be careful pushing or pulling anything while on a ladder. You may lose your balance or tip the ladder.	DON'T stand or sit on a stepladder top or pail shelf. They are not designed to carry your weight.
	DON'T climb a ladder if you are physically or mentally not up to the task.
	DON'T exceed the Duty Rating, which is the maximum load of the ladder. Do not permit more than one person on a single-sided stepladder or on any extension ladder.

Someone who reads these directions will have a good sense of ladder safety.

REMEMBER WHEN WRITING GENERAL GUIDELINES OR DIRECTIONS:

- Use a visually pleasing format. Use special typefaces (*italics,* **boldface,** icons) to emphasize particularly important procedures or warnings.
- Have a few people check your work. Have you left anything out? Have you been clear, concise, and to the point?
- Use illustrations whenever possible.
- Anticipate questions or problems that might arise, and address them in your list.
- If possible, set your work aside for a day or two. Then read it again to make sure that your document says what you want. If it doesn't, revise it accordingly. Taking some time between readings will help you catch your errors.

Activity 7.8: Writing Step-by-Step Directions

Write detailed, step-by-step directions for two of the following procedures. If you don't feel qualified to write on any of these topics, choose two of your own. If you are a good artist or have access to a good computer program, you might also create a graphic or visual aid to accompany your discussion.

Hint: Use a visually appealing format. Remember that many procedures can be broken down into Step 1, Step 2, Step 3, and so on.

1. How to shut off a water main
2. How to break away damaged drywall
3. How to remove a broken brick from a brick wall
4. How to seal a joint at a wall opening
5. How to seal a driveway
6. How to use a spirit level
7. How to use a crosscut saw
8. How to replace a tile in a tile shower
9. How to parallel park a car
10. How to grow a healthy, green lawn
11. How to change the oil in a car
12. How to make the world's best chili

Activity 7.9: Writing General Guidelines

Choose two of the topics below and write a set of general guidelines to follow for each topic. If you don't feel qualified to write on any of these topics, choose two of your own. If you are a good artist or have access to a good computer program, you might also create a graphic or visual aid to accompany your discussion.

Hint: Remember that guidelines can be formatted in different ways. You could use a bulleted list or a numbered list, or you might choose to use a do/don't, always/never, or yes/no format.

1. Getting along with your boss
2. Maintaining a positive attitude
3. Having a good time without spending a lot of money
4. Keeping your friendships strong and healthy
5. Keeping the workplace clean and neat
6. Developing a good working relationship with apprentices
7. Basic electrical safety
8. Giving constructive criticism
9. Dealing with difficult co-workers
10. Basic welding safety
11. Showing respect for the opposite sex
12. Sitting for a job interview
13. Filling out forms
14. Telephone etiquette
15. Controlling your temper

7.4.3 Summary

In Module 6, we talked about the huge amount of information that the average person deals with. Each day, we see more manuals, books, memos, advertisements, government regulations, and newspaper articles than we can count. It sometimes seems impossible to keep up with all of it. But the good news is: Summaries can help.

A *summary* has one simple goal: to reduce a large volume of information into an easy-to-read, brief format. A good summary covers all the main points of the original(s), but in many fewer words. Summaries don't waste any time. They state the bare-bones facts with no irrelevant information.

When might a summary be used in your construction job? Your boss might ask you to research the conductivity of different metals and prepare a one-page report summarizing your findings. Or she might ask you to investigate the reputations of several local electrical contractors and summarize your findings. In the second case, you'd need to talk with other people in your field. You'd need to take good notes during those conversations, then summarize the responses in your report. (We offer tips on note taking in Section 2.1.)

Prose Summaries

Sometimes a summary works best in a prose format. Figure 7.3 is an excerpt from *Tools for Success: Soft Skills for the Construction Industry,* a textbook designed to help construction professionals develop their teamwork and interpersonal skills. Assume that your boss is interested in learning more about stress management. He has asked you to read the relevant material in this textbook and give him a half-page summary.

Chapter 7   Managing Stress

Everyone has too much to do. At home, the lawn has to be mowed and the leaky faucet keeps dripping. Your spouse feels you don't spend enough time together. Your folks need you to help them paint the house this weekend. The car won't start in the morning. On the job, the foreman is cranky and the deadline for finishing the job is getting closer.

If you're like most people, the result of all these demands is stress. Stress is tension, anxiety, or strain that is caused by unexpected events or elements outside your control. Stress occurs when you believe that an event has the potential to demand more resources (such as money or time) than you have available. It can be caused by negative events (a divorce, getting fired, being evicted) or positive events (getting married, getting a promotion, buying a new house). If you don't handle stress well, you may find yourself suffering from headaches, irritability, exhaustion, or health problems such as ulcers or high blood pressure.

The bad news is that you can't completely avoid stress. It's a part of everyday life. But there is good news, also: There are ways to handle stress to help you perform your best.

Tips for Managing Stress

To cope with stress, you first need to be *aware* that you're experiencing stress. Sometimes it's obvious that you're feeling stressed out. Other times, it isn't. For example, you're probably aware of a higher stress level if you're being reprimanded by your foreman. But you may not realize the stressful effects of a series of small unrelated events.

You are probably feeling stress if you exhibit any of the following behaviors:

- Biting your fingernails
- Clenching your jaw
- Having trouble sleeping
- Losing your temper
- Massaging your temples
- Being unable to relax
- Having difficulty concentrating
- Feeling extremely tired
- Cracking your knuckles frequently
- Feeling tightness in your shoulder muscles
- Experiencing frequent headaches
- Having chest or back pain

The ways of coping with stress fall into two categories: (1) preventing stress from starting in the first place, and (2) taking steps to reduce stress when you experience it.

Preventing Stress

One of the best ways to deal with stress is to stop it before it gets started. Here are some tips for keeping stress out of your life.

1. Anticipate stress, and take steps to prevent it. If you know what causes stress in your life, you can find ways to stop that stress from happening. For example, suppose you are a contractor. You know that one of your subcontractors is always half an hour late. There are several possible ways to deal with this: (1) Rather than getting upset every time he shows up late, confront him with the issue.

Figure 7.3:   Managing Stress

Source: Adapted from Steven A. Rigolosi, *Tools for Success: Soft Skills for the Construction Industry* (Upper Saddle River, NJ: Prentice Hall, 2000), pp. 115–120.

Tell him that your time is precious, and that you need him to show up on time. Get a commitment from him that he'll show up on time from now on. (2) Change subcontractors. (3) If you need him to meet you at 7:00 a.m., tell him to be there at 6:30.

Some other examples: (1) Plan to wait on line in stores and banks, and you won't feel frustrated when you do. Bring your favorite magazine to read while you're waiting on line. This way, you'll be using the time to do something you enjoy. (2) Rather than waiting on line in a supply house, call ahead with your order. This way you'll be able to walk in, pick up your order, and leave quickly.

2. Keep things in good working order. There's nothing more stressful than a broken tool or a nonfunctioning piece of equipment. To prevent machinery from breaking down at critical times, keep everything in good working order. Do preventive maintenance—don't wait for things to break. When something does break, fix it immediately.

3. Be neat. A messy job site or work area makes it difficult to find what you need. It also causes stress for the people around you. Create a system, and work in an orderly fashion. Clean up your messes, and you won't have trouble locating what you need to get the job done.

4. Plan ahead. Before you start a project, think about what you'll need. Gather all the necessary tools and supplies, and put them in one place. This way, you won't have to stop what you're doing to go find more wood, more cement, more nails, more wire, and so forth. Constant starts and stops can be very stressful, so avoid them whenever possible.

5. Do the hardest part first. Thinking about a difficult task that awaits you can be very stressful. And, the longer you wait to do something difficult, the more stress builds up. So, whenever possible, do the hardest part of the job first. You'll be amazed at how much stress you can avoid by tackling the most challenging part of the project first.

6. Eat properly and exercise. The human body can handle stress much better when it's healthy. Avoid large amounts of caffeine—it makes many people jittery and nervous, and prevents them from sleeping well. Don't pig out on snack foods, which are high in fat and grease. Rather than consuming large amounts of sugar, try fruits and vegetables instead. Drink alcohol in moderation. Don't smoke or chew tobacco.

Most importantly, exercise to keep yourself in shape. Many construction workers think they get enough exercise on the job. This usually isn't the case—the body needs more aerobic activity than you get on the job. When stress gets to you, going to the gym or playing a good game of touch football can help you release tension. Also, exercising regularly helps you sleep better at night.

7. Get enough sleep. Many young people believe that they can "get by" on only four or five hours of sleep. This is not true. The construction industry is physically demanding, and it can take a lot out of your body. To be your best, you need enough sleep. On work nights, plan to get a minimum of eight hours of sleep.

8. Change stress-producing thoughts. Some people tend to look on the negative side of things. These people talk to themselves in a way that brings them down. This negative self-talk is often the product of low self-esteem or worrying, and it creates much unnecessary stress. Rather than worrying, try asking, "What's the worst thing that can happen?" Many times the "worst" isn't so bad, after all.

9. Be flexible. If you always expect everything to go perfectly, you'll always be frustrated, because things rarely go 100% according to plan. However, if you can roll with the punches and adapt to a changing situation, you'll experience much less frustration and stress.

10. Manage your money wisely. When asked what their number-one worry is, many people say "Money." There's nothing as stress-producing as not having enough money to pay your bills each month. So watch your money closely, and don't waste it. List your income and expenses for each month so that you know how much money you need to spend on essential items. Don't overuse credit cards—the interest alone can kill you. Shop for bargains. Before you buy something, ask yourself if you really need it. Each week, put some money in the bank so that you have it when you need it. (Many people have a special "vacation fund" for this purpose.) Be sure the monthly rent and bills are paid before you go out for meals.

A SPECIAL TIP: DON'T SWEAT THE SMALL STUFF! Some people worry excessively about small things that really shouldn't matter. So what if you have to wait on line for ten minutes? So does everyone else. So what if the car in front of you is going five miles under the speed limit? It will probably turn off the road soon anyway.

Notice when you get annoyed by small, insignificant things—and stop it from happening. Your stress levels will go down greatly.

Figure 7.3:   Continued

Coping with Unavoidable Stress

To help alleviate stress that you may be feeling, try one or more of the following techniques. As you read, you'll see that all these suggestions have one thing in common: They all require you to *take control of the situation.* People feel the most stressed when they feel like victims of circumstance. Taking steps to bring those circumstances under your control greatly decreases your stress level.

1. **Make a plan to deal with your problems.** Worrying about the events in your life or on your job only makes stress worse. The best way to eliminate this stress is to make a plan to alleviate the problem.

   For example, suppose you're an electrician, and you're having trouble making a three-way switch work properly. If you keep worrying about it, you'll only increase your stress level. But if you say to yourself, "OK, I'll call Tom now and ask him to take a look at this. He's an expert, and he'll be able to help me," you'll deal with your problem effectively. As a result, your stress level will decrease almost immediately.

2. **Control your anger and frustration. Don't let them control you.** Everyone experiences anger and frustration from time to time. But some people are much better at dealing with these emotions. It's essential that you control your anger at work. If you sense your anger level rising, close your eyes and count to ten. Doing so will take your mind off what's making you angry and help you refocus your energy elsewhere. If you feel like you're going to blow up, walk away.

3. **Use relaxation techniques.** An excellent way to reduce stress is to redirect your thoughts to another activity. Stress often feeds on itself—the more you think about your stressful situation, the more stressful it becomes. So, do something to take your mind off your problems. Some people prefer active physical exercise, such as competitive sports. Others prefer mellower techniques, such as listening to music or soaking in a bathtub. Do whatever works for you. Here are some additional relaxation methods you might want to try:

Active Methods	Passive Methods
Take a long walk	Meditate
Do some woodwork	Read
Chop wood	Take a hot shower
Cook a gourmet meal	Talk to a friend on the phone
Go running	Drink a cup of tea
Take a vacation	Listen to relaxing music
Go hiking	Take a nap
Go to a restaurant or local hangout	Rent a nonviolent movie
Play with the dog	Get a massage
Do volunteer work	

4. **Talk it out.** Some people are better at talking about their frustrations than others. On the job, though, it's particularly helpful if you can talk to co-workers or your supervisor about the stress you're encountering. You don't want to complain too much, of course. But if you really feel near the edge, you should talk to your supervisor about it. Sometimes he can take some of the pressure off while you attempt to regain some balance. Off the job, talking to friends and sharing your problems often helps to relieve stress as well.

5. **Learn to laugh.** Coping with stress is much easier if you can approach the situation with a sense of humor. It may be hard to laugh when you feel tension and anxiety, but laughter really is the best medicine. Many studies have shown the anxiety-relieving power of laughter.

6. **Breathe deeply.** When feeling stressed, people tend to breathe in short, shallow breaths. Such short breathing isn't healthy, because it only increases muscle tension. When you find yourself doing shallow breathing, relax all your muscles and take several slow, deep breaths. Your body will become more relaxed almost instantly.

7. **Do something to improve your appearance.** An old saying goes, "When you look good, you feel good." It's true. If you're feeling down or depressed, get a haircut, shave, or buy some new clothes. Looking better does wonders for making you feel better.

8. **Don't take work problems home with you.** Sometimes it's hard to separate your job from your life. But it's always a good idea to try to leave work problems at work. Your job is only part of your life—it's not your whole life. So enjoy your home, your family, and your friends while you're not working, and leave work problems at the job.

Figure 7.3: Continued

Making the Most of Your Time

Often, people who experience stressful lives think, "I wish there were more than 24 hours in a day. That's the only way I'd be able to get everything done."

In truth, 24 hours is usually enough time to meet all of your obligations. You don't need additional time in the day—you just need to manage your time better. You'll experience less anxiety if you attack each day with a game plan for getting your job done. Here are some tips to help you do just that:

1. **Make a plan, and stick to it.** A construction site is a busy place, and the final deadline for completing a project depends on everybody meeting their individual deadlines. As you leave work each day, plan what you'll do the next day. Identify your priorities—what are the most important tasks you need to accomplish tomorrow? The next day, attack those tasks with vigor.

Some people keep this plan in their heads; other people like to write everything down in a list format. Writing a list has many benefits, because you feel a sense of accomplishment each time you cross something off the list.

2. **Don't procrastinate.** Don't put off what you need to do. Not every task on a construction site is enjoyable, but they all need to get done on time. Each day, schedule the most challenging tasks first so that you can get them out of the way.

3. **Don't waste time.** Sometimes it's easy to get distracted on the job. You'd be amazed at how much time can be wasted just by talking with other people. Be aware of the activities that waste time, and see if you can become more efficient. For example, a job that would take one man three hours to do might be done by two men in an hour. The net gain is one full hour of time!

Figure 7.3:   Continued

As you write your summary, keep in mind that you need to answer one main question:

What are the most important points in what I've just read?

Because you won't have room to list all the examples and supporting details included in the original, your summary should focus on a definition of stress, how it can be prevented, and how it can be dealt with. So, as you read, follow the guidelines presented in Section 5.1 for highlighting key information. You can then use these highlights to summarize the main points in your summary. In Figure 7.3, the highlighting has already been done for you.

A good summary would appear as follows. Note that the writer has used varying formats and typefaces—including italics and numbered lists—to make the summary visually effective.

Summary of "Managing Stress"

Stress is anxiety, tension, or strain caused by unexpected events or events beyond our control. It can be caused by negative or positive events. We aren't always aware that we're experiencing stress.

We can cope with stress in two ways: by preventing it from happening in the first place, and by taking steps to reduce stress when it does happen.

To prevent stress:
1. Anticipate it, and take steps to prevent it.
2. Keep things in good working order.
3. Be neat.
4. Plan ahead.
5. Do the hardest part of the job first.
6. Eat properly and exercise.

7. Change stress-producing thoughts.
8. Be flexible.
9. Manage your money.
10. Don't sweat the small stuff—keep things in perspective.

To reduce stress:
1. Make a plan to deal with your problems.
2. Control your anger and frustration.
3. Use active or passive relaxation techniques.
4. Talk it out.
5. Laugh.
6. Breathe deeply.
7. Improve your appearance.
8. Keep problems at the job. Don't bring them home.
9. Make the most of your time—make a plan and stick to it, don't procrastinate, and don't waste time.

Tabular Summaries

Sometimes information can be quickly and effectively summarized in a tabular format rather than a prose format. We learned how to read tables of information in Section 6.1.3. Now let's see how to create them for use as a summary.

Remember that tables have both columns and rows of information. This format makes them very useful for summarizing specific aspects, qualities, or characteristics of a given set of items. For example, a table might lay out a series of abbreviations used in blueprints, along with what those abbreviations mean. Or it might list different kinds of woods, whether they are hard or soft, and specific characteristics of each type of wood.

So, when you see written explanations that compare and contrast products in a specific category (such as woods, metals, conductive devices, tools, and so forth), ask yourself: Could this material be summarized effectively in a table? The answer will almost always be "Yes."

Look at Figure 7.4. This excerpt from a construction textbook outlines the properties of several types of mortar admixtures used with cement and their effects on the workability, strength, and weather resistance of the cement. Your foreman has asked you to summarize this material in half a page or less.

Many materials or additives can be put into mortar to change its appearance or properties. Admixtures are additives put into cement before it is mixed with lime and sand to form mortar. Listed below are admixtures commonly used with cement and their effects on mortar.

- Air-entraining admixtures reduce water content and increase workability and freeze-thaw resistance. Bond strength may be reduced slightly. If air entraining is needed, it is recommended to use cements modified at the factory to include an air-entraining agent.
- Bonding admixtures increase the adhesion of masonry mortar to masonry units. Some organic modifiers provide an air-cure adhesive that increases bond strength of dry masonry.
- Plasticizers increase workability. Inorganic plasticizers, such as clay, clay-shale, and finely ground limestone, promote workability and water release for cement hydration. Organic plasticizers also promote workability; however, mortar may stick more to the mason's tools.

Figure 7.4: Mortar Admixtures
Source: Adapted from National Center for Construction Education and Research, *Masonry Trainee Guide* (Upper Saddle River, NJ/Columbus, OH: Prentice Hall, 1998), Module 28105, pp. 15–16.

- Set accelerators stimulate cement hydration and increase compressive strength of laboratory test mortars at normal temperatures. Nonchloride accelerators are preferred because chloride salts will deteriorate the cement in masonry.
- Set retarders delay cement hydration, providing more time for mortar to remain plastic without retempering. This is useful primarily during hot weather. Set retarders are also used in marketing ready-mixed, set-controlled masonry mortars. The effect of the modifier persists for up to 72 hours but dissipates when retarded mortar contacts absorptive masonry units.
- Water reducers lower the amount of water and potentially increase mortar strength. However, masonry mortar rapidly loses water in contact with an absorptive masonry unit. Water reducers may reduce the water below the level needed for cement hydration. Care must be taken to ensure sufficient water for the hydration process to take place. Water reducers increase weather resistance.
- Water repellents modify masonry mortar during the early period after construction. If persistent in their performance, rain penetration of the masonry may be reduced.
- Pozzolanic modifiers, because of their fineness and ability to combine with lime, will cause mortar to increase density and strength.
- Antifreeze admixtures are not recommended for use in mortar as the amounts needed to prevent freezing also significantly lower the compressive and bonding strength of mortar.

Figure 7.4: Continued

Note that the text specifically states (in the opening paragraph) that the list provides information on admixtures and their effects on mortar. Based on the descriptions listed in the reading, and by highlighting the key points as we go along, we can put together an easy-to-read tabular summary, as follows:[10]

Workability, Strength, and Weather Resistance of Mortar Admixtures

Admixture	Workability	Strength	Weather Resistance
Air-entraining agents	Increase	Decrease slightly	Increase freeze-thaw resistance
Bonding admixtures	—	Increase	—
Plasticizers	Increase	—	—
Set accelerators	Decrease	Increase	—
Set retarders	Increase	—	—
Water reducers	Decrease	Increase	Increase
Water repellents	—	—	Increase
Pozzolanic agents	Increase	Increase	—

Note: Do not use antifreeze admixtures.

This table summarizes the admixtures' properties at a glance, and is much faster to read than the original! (We discuss the creation of tables and other visual aids to support your writing in more detail in Section 8.2.)

KEEP IN MIND WHILE PREPARING SUMMARIES:

- Highlight the key points in the originals, then use your highlights to prepare the summary.
- Include only the most important main ideas in your summary. Do not include unnecessary details.

[10]National Center for Construction Education and Research, *Masonry Trainee Guide* (Upper Saddle River, NJ/Columbus, OH: Prentice Hall, 1998), Module 28105, p. 16.

- Make your summary visually appealing and easy to read. Remember that the purpose of a summary is to save time.
- If you're asked to summarize several readings or interviews in one place, organize your summary so that your key areas of comparison and contrast are highlighted.

Activity 7.10: Writing Summaries

Write a brief (no more than one paragraph) summary of the following article. To aid you in preparing the summary, use a highlighter (see Section 5.1) to indicate the key points as you read.

The Foreman's Job[11]

On a construction site, the foreman is not "one of the guys." In fact, the foreman's job differs from the average worker's job in several ways.

Most importantly, foremen are responsible for monitoring all aspects of a project, and making sure *all* the pieces come together. They must ensure that everyone on their team does his or her job well. They must deliver a quality job on time and on budget. They must coordinate various tasks, making sure that people are working together in the way that makes the most sense.

In contrast, the average worker's job is much more focused. For example, if you are a carpenter, you work on specific tasks, and you do what the boss asks you to do. What you do contributes to the final product. Your boss is the person responsible for that final product.

In general, supervisors have five main responsibilities. First, foremen are responsible for quality and productivity. They make sure that quality work gets done on time. They ensure that workers are using the most efficient tools, equipment, and procedures. They're always watching to make sure that workers aren't wasting time or supplies, and they're always looking for ways to do the job better or more efficiently. Second, foremen coordinate the team's efforts. Foremen make sure that a project runs smoothly. They assign different tasks to different workers, then make sure that all those tasks come together. Most of the time, foremen are both overseeing their own group of workers *and* working with people who are even higher up in the company. Third, foremen are responsible for cost control. Construction is a very profit-oriented industry. To be profitable, a job must come in at or under the budgeted costs. To this end, foremen make sure that no money is wasted, that contractors don't overbill and suppliers don't overcharge. Because time is money, foremen also watch to make sure that workers are reporting to work on time, taking reasonable lunch and coffee breaks, and putting in a full day's work. Fourth, foremen are responsible for their workers' safety. While safety is everyone's responsibility, the foreman is in charge of ensuring the safety of every worksite. Because of strict laws and legal responsibilities, foremen tend to be very, very strict about safety rules. Finally, foremen provide leadership. Foremen act as team leaders. Their job is to motivate workers and to make them feel like an essential part of the team. Foremen also serve as teachers, and sometimes as counselors if their workers are facing problems on the job (or at home).

---

[11]Adapted from Steven A. Rigolosi, *Tools for Success: Soft Skills for the Construction Industry* (Upper Saddle River, NJ/Columbus, OH: Prentice Hall, 2000), p. 19.

7.4.4 Synthesis, Analysis, and Evaluation

The summaries we saw in Section 7.4.3 all stuck strictly to the facts. They did not make any recommendations, nor did they draw on information from several different sources. However, sometimes you may be asked not only to summarize data or information, but also to synthesize, analyze, or evaluate it as well.

- *Synthesis* is the process of taking information from several different sources and putting it together into one well-organized whole. For example, your company may receive hundreds of pages of documents from the Occupational Safety and Health Administration. Professional writers take all those documents and read them closely. Then, by culling the most important information from them, they write employee safety manuals. This task is mostly one of synthesis.

- *Analysis* is the process of closely reviewing data or information to find commonalities and differences. While a summary stays on the surface, analysis looks below the surface for connections and insights. Architects and designers often rely on a wide variety of reports—for example, surveys, soil reports, and the like—to determine how buildings should be designed. The architect's job is to synthesize and analyze all the reports in order to design buildings safely.

- *Evaluation* is the process of thinking critically (see Section 6.8) about the information you've assembled, using various materials to make the correct decision. Synthesis and analysis always precede evaluation. Effective evaluation can occur only after you've organized and analyzed the information logically.

Several different formats exist to help writers synthesize, analyze, and evaluate. Specifically, you may choose any of the following methods to organize your writing: cause and effect, classification, and comparison/contrast.

Cause and Effect

The *cause and effect format* is useful for explaining why something is the way it is, or why something happened. Suppose that a brick wall has caved in on your job site. Your foreman wants to know why. In your written report, you will need to explain exactly what happened (the *effect*), as well as the *causes* of what happened.

TIPS FOR WRITING ABOUT CAUSES AND EFFECTS:

- Don't jump to conclusions. Conduct as much research as necessary to find the true causes.
- Be honest about causes. Do not assign blame, but do state the causes truthfully.

Classification

The *classification format* is useful for grouping data or items into categories. For example, if you were writing about the proper use of fire extinguishers, you would have to group fires into four categories (Class A, Class B, Class C, and

Class D), then explain the different types of fire extinguishers that are used to combat each fire. For example:[12]

Classes of Fires

Class	Materials and Proper Fire Extinguisher
Class A	Involves ordinary combustibles such as wood or paper. Class A fires are fought by cooling the fuel. Class A fire extinguishers contain water. Using a Class A extinguisher on any other type of fire can be very dangerous.
Class B	Involves grease, liquids, and gases. Class B extinguishers contain carbon dioxide (CO_2) or another material that smothers fires by removing oxygen from them.
Class C	Any fires near or involving energized electrical equipment. Class C extinguishers are designed to protect the fire fighter from electrical shock. Class C extinguishers smother fires.
Class D	Involves metals. Class D extinguishers contain a powder that either forms a crust around the burning metal or gives off gases that prevent oxygen from reaching the fire. Some metals will keep burning even though they have been coated with powder from a Class D extinguisher. The best way to fight these fires is to keep using the extinguisher so that the fire will not spread to other fuels.

TIPS FOR WRITING CLASSIFICATIONS:

- Define all your terms.
- Set up relevant categories. If you find that some of your items don't fit into the categories you've chosen, seek a category that does work for all the items.

Comparison and Contrast

A *comparison* shows how two things are similar. A *contrast* shows how two things are different. The comparison/contrast format is very useful when you need to choose among different options. Tables, such as the one shown for admixtures in Section 7.4.3 (page 235), can help convey your information succinctly.

Peter Rodriguez, a first-year apprentice in an electrical training program, was given the task of comparing and contrasting silver, copper, and aluminum in wiring applications. He was asked to determine which metal would be best used under different circumstances. After consulting several sources (including manuals, trade publications, and Web sites) to find the information he needed, Peter wrote the following evaluation, which synthesizes material from all the sources. Note that the memo includes a table comparing and contrasting the three metals on the basis of cost, conductivity, and compatibility problems.

Silver, Copper, and Aluminum in Wiring Applications[13]
by Peter Rodriguez

This report compares silver, copper, and aluminum to determine which is best for electrical wiring. The criteria used are cost, conductivity, and compatibility with existing electrical systems and wiring practices. Each metal is rated on these criteria in the following chart.

---

[12]National Center for Construction Education and Research, *Core Curriculum* (Upper Saddle River, NJ/Columbus, OH: 2000), Module 00101, p. 1–48.

[13]Adapted from Maris Roze, *Technical Communication: The Practical Craft*, 3d ed. (Upper Saddle River, NJ: Prentice Hall, 1997), p. 39.

Material	Cost per Cubic Inch	Conductivity (Using Copper as a Reference: Cu = 1)	Compatibility Problems
Silver	$41.60	1.05	No
Copper	$00.20	1.00	No
Aluminum	$00.08	0.61	Yes

An important fact in this comparison is that conductivity is increased by using thicker wire. Therefore, a thicker aluminum wire can conduct as well, or better than, a thinner copper or silver wire. According to the chart, aluminum wire twice as thick as copper or silver would give the best conductivity (1.22) at the least cost ($0.16). In fact, aluminum is used wherever possible, especially by the power companies. Many high-voltage wires are made of aluminum.

However, aluminum corrodes easily when it comes into contact with copper, brass, steel, or bronze, and it is difficult to solder. Thus, aluminum would pose problems in wiring homes where connectors are frequently made of these other metals, or in constructing circuits in a lab. In these applications, copper is the best choice because of its cost advantage over silver. Silver is used only when its slightly better conductivity is very important, as in receivers that must pick up faint radio frequency signals.

Peter's report is complete, yet brief. He shows the similarities between copper and aluminum (both are relatively cheap), as well as their differences (there are no compatibility problems with copper, but there are with aluminum). As part of his analysis and evaluation, he shows that cheaper materials can be used because thickness is a key factor in conductivity. He closes by showing the value of silver as a conductor in high-tech applications, while pointing out its high cost.

Tips for writing comparisons and contrasts:

- Some comparison/contrast reports can be effectively presented in a pro/con format. In a pro/con format, you spell out the advantages and disadvantages of all your options before making your final recommendation.
- Choose the areas to compare and/or contrast carefully. Note that Peter Rodriguez's report doesn't evaluate each metal on its beauty or shininess. These categories are irrelevant here.

Activity 7.11: Working with Cause/Effect, Classification, and Comparison/Contrast

From each of the three sets below, choose one activity to complete. If you don't feel qualified to write on any of the suggested topics, choose topics of your own.

Set A: Cause/effect
Write a brief e-mail (no more than three paragraphs) in which you explain one of the following sets of cause and effect.

1. The causes and effects of fires
2. The causes and effects of employee absenteeism
3. The causes and effects of pollution
4. The causes and effects of construction accidents
5. The causes and effects of workplace conflict

SET B: CLASSIFICATION

Write a brief bulleted list, numbered list, or table in which you classify the items in one of the topics below. Include a brief explanation for each item in the classification.

1. Types of blueprints (see Section 6.3)

2. Types of pliers

3. Types of power drills

4. Types of saws

5. Types of movies

6. Specialties within the construction industry

7. Types of music

SET C: COMPARISON AND CONTRAST

Write a brief memo (no more than three paragraphs) to your boss in which you compare and contrast one set of items below. Be sure to list both the similarities *and* the differences between the two items. For this exercise, do not worry about the proper format. (We discuss proper formatting of memos in Section 8.1.1.)

1. Working in a factory, working in the construction industry

2. Claw hammers, ball peen hammers

3. Foremen, non-managers

4. Copper, silver

5. Air conditioning, heating

Activity 7.12: Synthesizing, Analyzing, and Evaluating Information

Here is the situation. Your company is about to embark on a very large project with a very tight budget, and your boss has decided to hire one contractor to do all the electrical work on the project. He has narrowed his choices down to three possibilities: Acme Electric, Bradford Electric, or Calvin Electric.

He has asked you to do some research on these three companies, and then put together a formal report in which you recommend one of them for the job. You need to take into account such factors as cost and reliability. The results of your investigation follow.

TELEPHONE CALLS

You place three phone calls to people you trust, to ask their opinions of the three electrical contractors. Here is what people say to you:

MIKE HODGES—OWNER, HODGES CONSTRUCTION CO. "I've never worked with Acme, because their prices always seem to be pretty high. My sense is that they like to take on fewer jobs and charge higher prices—that's how they make their money. The guys at Bradford are great—fun to work with, good prices, but they're always really busy and not the greatest with deadlines. I only worked with Calvin once, on a small job. They were meticulous about every little detail, which I loved. Great with deadlines too. But the owner is really kind of a jerk. I didn't like dealing with him at all."

CAROL CHAMBLISS—MATERIALS BUYER, 323 CONSTRUCTION CO. "Hmmm . . . I think they all have their pros and cons. I worked with Calvin a bunch of times . . . very reliable; they'll get the job done. So are the people at Bradford, and their prices are really competitive. But some of their workers are hit or miss—I think they have high turnover because they don't pay their people that well. Acme does a great job . . . kind of high priced, but a classy outfit."

KEVIN CHAMBERS—FOREMAN, J&M CO. "Stay away from Calvin. That company can't be trusted. They tried to pull a fast one on me once, and I never really forgave them. I'd say go with Acme or Bradford. If you're looking for the right price, Bradford's your best bet. I'd say there's about a 50% chance that they'd finish up on time, which isn't bad these days. Acme is fine, too, but you'll definitely pay more. They're reliable and good in a pinch, though."

WEB SITES

While surfing the Internet for information about these three companies, you come across a Web site sponsored by a nonprofit construction trades group. For each region of the country, they compare contractors' costs, professionalism, quality of workmanship, and ability to get the job done on time. You check your state, and sure enough, there are rankings for all three of the companies you're researching. Here is a summary of the rankings:

	Cost	Professionalism	Quality	Timeliness
Acme	$$$$	+++	***	!!!
Bradford	$	++	**	!!
Calvin	$$	++++	****	!!!

Cost:

$$$$	Very expensive
$$$	Higher than average
$$	Average
$	Relatively inexpensive

Professionalism:

++++	Very professional
+++	Professional
++	Below average
+	Needs improvement

Quality:

****	Superior
***	Good
**	Average
*	Below average

Timeliness:

!!!!	Exceptional
!!!	Good
!!	Average
!	Below average

PERSONAL VISITS

You decide to go to each of the contractors' offices to scope the place out. You're trying to get a sense of the company and its owners, foremen, and workers. Here are the results of your visits:

ACME

A well-dressed secretary greets you politely and asks you to sit down. She asks if you'd like a cup of coffee. The office is very clean and well kept; it doesn't even look like a construction company. Very soon after you sit down, the owner,

George Coutros, comes out to greet you. He shakes your hand and welcomes you, and offers you a tour of the facility. On his office wall is a series of photos of projects on which the company has worked.

BRADFORD

Two secretaries in jeans and T-shirts are chatting when you walk in. They greet you in a very friendly way and ask if they can help. When you say that you'd like to talk to the owner, they say he's not available and they don't know when he'll be back. But if you leave your name, they will give him a message. The office is shabby but clean, with lots of pictures of babies and employees on the walls. The owner, Charlie Bradford, calls you back two days later and asks if you'd like to set up an appointment to meet.

CALVIN

Calvin is a small company run out of the owner's home. When you ring the doorbell, Frank Calvin answers the door. He brings you around to the back of the house, where he has a small office. He doesn't talk much; he's a business-man and he just wants to know who you are and what you want. When you explain that you're looking for a contractor, he becomes friendlier and offers to show you around the place. The house is extremely impressive in every detail, and Calvin tells you that he did all the work himself. As he's showing you around, a few workers walk past, and Calvin ignores them.

YOUR MISSION: Synthesize all the material you've gathered. Prepare a summary of all the pros and cons of each of the three companies, and then make a recommendation to your boss. You can use any of the writing techniques you've learned in this module to present your information.

7.5 THE WRITING PROCESS

Like the process of building a new structure, the writing process is one that requires careful planning, checking, coordination, and attention to detail. Follow these suggestions any time you sit down to write, and you can't go wrong.

Step One: Plan and outline. Before you begin to write, jot a few notes that will help you organize what you want to say. Think of an effective title and a way to lay out your material that will help your readers find your main points quickly. Many writers like to create an outline, and then write according to that outline. The outline provides structure and allows for a clear organization in the document.

Step Two: Draft. When you've figured out what you want to say, just start writing. Don't worry about grammar or punctuation at this stage. Just sit down and write. Let the ideas flow, and get everything down on paper. You will revise your work later in the process.

Step Three: Reread. After you've completed your draft, reread it. Does it say everything you want it to say? Are any sections unclear or incomplete? Does your writing have a logical flow? Think about ways to improve on your draft.

Step Four: Revise. Improve what you've written by revising it. Put into effect all the ideas you generated during the reread stage.

Step Five: Review. Ask someone to read what you've written before you finalize it. Can your reader follow what you've written? Is it clear and easily understandable? Ask your reader for suggestions on how to improve any section that needs work.

Step Six: Finalize. Using your reader's suggestions, finalize your work. When you're done, proofread it for mistakes (such as spelling errors, grammar problems, or punctuation issues) before sending it to its intended recipients. (We offer some tips on proofreading in Section 8.6.)

Working through this process each time you write will allow you to present your ideas in the clearest, most impressive manner possible.

Remember: Attention to detail is important in all aspects of construction. It is important in writing as well. Errors in printed material can lead to mistakes that cost lives, time, and money. Check all your facts, tell the complete story, and put your best foot forward.

Activity 7.13: Exploring the Writing Process

In this activity, you will proceed step by step through the writing process. The writing assignment is fairly simple so that you can focus more on the writing process than on the subject you're writing about. Choose one of the following topics:

- Should the death penalty exist in the United States? Why or why not?
- What is the most boring sport on earth, and why?
- Describe a news story you read or saw on TV recently. What happened?

Now, go through the writing process (on a separate sheet of paper):

1. *Plan and outline.* Think about what you will write. Jot down ideas that spring to mind. Make an outline if you'd like.

2. *Draft.* Write a paragraph in which you make use of the ideas you jotted down during the planning stage. Just write; don't worry about your writing being perfect at this point. Let the ideas flow!

3. *Reread.* Read what you've written. How can it be improved? Have you said everything you wanted to say? Is any part of it unclear?

4. *Revise.* Based on your reread, revise your paragraph to make it better, more interesting, or more clear.

5. *Review.* Ask a friend, classmate, or co-worker to read what you've written and to offer feedback. Does what you've written make sense? Can it be made even better?

6. *Finalize.* Based on your reader's suggestions, revise your paragraph one last time. Then go back and check to make sure all the words are spelled correctly and all the grammar is perfect. Notice how much better your final version is than the draft you created in Step 2!

7.6 TIPS FOR WRITING EFFECTIVELY

In Section 7.5, we focused on the "big picture"—the process that writers go through to effectively build their writing. But the details are important, too.

You may have heard someone say, "I like his style" or "I like her style." In a general sense, *style* refers to a set of personal qualities that create an overall impression. The same term is used in writing to describe the way a person's words work on the printed page (or, in the case of e-mail, a computer screen).

Developing a pleasing writing style takes some practice. In a nutshell, though, the writers with the most pleasing styles are those who (1) write clearly and directly, and (2) choose their words carefully.

7.6.1 Writing Clearly and Directly

As mentioned in Section 7.2, clarity and simplicity are two hallmarks of good writing. Big words don't make a good writer, but clarity and simplicity do.

Have you ever been around people who talk way too much? Don't they get boring and tiresome? Very long sentences, or unnecessarily long words or phrases, can have the same effect on a reader. For this reason, good writers strive to keep their words crisp and their sentences short. One professional editor has said, "There are very few sentences from which at least three words can't be cut."

Keeping your sentences crisp involves cutting out all distracters and stating the facts in as few words as possible. Consider the following wordy sentences and how they can be improved:

Wordy: We missed the deadline due to the fact that the contractor's supplier failed to deliver the appropriate materials in a timely manner.

Clear and direct: We missed the deadline because the supplier didn't deliver the materials on time.

Wordy: We are in the process of reviewing the bid.

Clear and direct: We are reviewing the bid.

Wordy: The point I am trying to make is that we should notify the supervisor in the case of any on-the-job injuries.

Clear and direct: Notify a supervisor whenever an injury occurs.

Note that the improved sentences remove bloated phrases like "in the process of" and "due to the fact that." Here are some other words or phrases that you can replace or eliminate to make your writing more direct:

Wordy	Better
A large number of	Many
Approximately	About
Are of the opinion that	Think, believe
At the present time	Now
At all times	Always
Aware of the fact that	Know
Bear in mind	Remember
Bring about	Cause
Close proximity	Near
Costs the sum of	Costs
Due to the fact that	Because
First of all	First
For the purpose of	For
Has a need for	Needs
Has the ability to	Can
In light of the fact that	Because
In order to	To
In the event that	If
In the month of December	In December
In the near future	Soon

Wordy	Better
In the neighborhood of	Approximately, about
In the vicinity of	Near
It is our opinion that	We think
Majority of	Most
Prior to	Before
Provided that	If
Second in a sequence	Second
Until such time as	Until
With the exception of	Except
Would be able to	Could

Activity 7.14: Writing Clearly and Directly

Rewrite the following sentences to make them more clear and direct.

1. We anticipate the need for more workers in the month of July.

   _____

2. At this moment in time, we are not in the process of hiring.

   _____

3. John is an excellent worker who has the capability of multi-tasking by performing many tasks simultaneously.

   _____

   _____

4. In our humble opinion, the material to be used should most likely be aluminum, not copper.

   _____

5. Marie's boss was aware of the fact that she had been tardy for several days—specifically, three.

   _____

   _____

6. In light of the fact that the days are shorter in winter, construction professionals tend to work fewer hours in the months of January, February, and March.

   _____

   _____

7. Until such time as we can hire more workers, our current employees will have the necessity of working overtime.

   _____

   _____

8. The hammer costs in the neighborhood of sixteen dollars.

   _____

7.6.2 Choosing Words Carefully

An old saying goes, "The pen is mightier than the sword." Words are an extremely strong force, and they can be used for good purposes or for bad ones. And, fortunately or unfortunately, many words lend themselves to various interpretations.

For all these reasons, good writers choose their words carefully. In writing, they need to consider both denotations and connotations, as well as concreteness and specificity.

Denotation and Connotation

A word's *denotation* is its neutral dictionary definition. A word's *connotation* is composed of the various associations, whether good or negative, that the word conjures up.

To get a better sense of connotation and denotation, look at the following lists of words. Each group has basically the same meaning:

Thorough

Detail-oriented

Conscientious

A nitpicker

Talkative

Loquacious

Chatty

Motormouth

Which of these words would you *not* want used to describe you? The words *thorough, detail-oriented,* and *conscientious* all connote positive qualities, but a *nitpicker* connotes someone who is annoyingly picky and small-minded. In a social situation, being *talkative, loquacious,* or *chatty* would be considered an asset, but being labeled a *motormouth* would be a definite liability.

When writing anything for the workplace, consider the effect that your words would have on the reader. Writing a memo to your boss in which you describe a contractor as "bottom-line oriented" would lend one impression. Describing that same contractor as "a penny pincher" would give quite another impression.

CONCRETENESS AND SPECIFICITY

Because so many words are open to interpretation, depending on the circumstances and context, construction documents need to use words that are as specific as possible. In any document that you prepare, your goal is to ensure that your readers don't misunderstand anything you say.

Suppose you're reading a manual, and you come across the following instruction:

- Adjust the thermostat.

If you're visualizing the process as you read—a technique we discussed in Section 5.5—this line is going to stop you dead in your tracks. Why? The word "adjust" could mean one of several things. Are you supposed to turn the thermostat *up,* or are you supposed to turn the thermostat *down?* Doing one when you should do the other could cause a serious mistake.

Here's another example. You are reading a project guide and come across the following instruction:

• Fold a piece of paper in half.

Again, you are likely to become confused by the lack of specificity. What details are missing here? The instruction would be much better if it answered these questions: How large a piece of paper? What color? In which direction should the paper be folded—from top to bottom, or from left to right?

> **TIP:** Be wary of using words like *adjust, alter,* and *change,* all of which could be open to interpretation. Similarly, watch for vague time references, such as *later in the day, sometime next week,* or *in a few days.* Instead, be as specific as possible.

Activity 7.15: Choosing Words Carefully

SET A: CONNOTATIONS
In each set of words below, choose the word with the most positive connotation.

1. a. hardworking   b. workaholic   c. driven   d. relentless
2. a. prudish   b. backward   c. conservative   d. uptight
3. a. body-obsessed   b. health-conscious   c. exercise nut   d. gymrat
4. a. respectful   b. fawning   c. obsequious   d. brown-noser

In each set of words below, choose the word with the most *negative* connotation.

5. a. different   b. uncommon   c. abnormal   d. distinctive
6. a. friendly   b. gregarious   c. welcoming   d. pushy
7. a. mongrel   b. mutt   c. mixed breed   d. hybrid
8. a. quiet   b. uncommunicative   c. shy   d. introverted

SET B: SPECIFIC LANGUAGE
Rewrite each of the following sentences to make them less vague and more specific.

1. Do not subject this material to heat for more than several seconds.

   _____

2. We should ask the contractor to submit the bid by sometime next week.

   _____

3. We're all meeting in the conference room in the late afternoon, mid-week.

   _____

4. Employees aren't permitted to take vacation days in the fall.

   _____

5. Brickmakers make their bricks in a very hot kiln that is heated to at least several hundred degrees.

   _____

   _____

6. Please ask Joe and a couple of the guys to meet me in the morning, before work.

_____

_____

7. Mary is allergic to several items, all of which could have very serious effects on her health.

_____

_____

8. The coffee tasted bad.

_____

9. Please divide these 100 nails into four batches.

_____

10 For emergencies, dial a special number.

_____

7.7 FILLING OUT FORMS

While they don't usually require much creative writing, *forms* are a fact of life in every industry. Before you even get your first construction job, for example, you'll need to fill out applications and give the company and government some personal information. On the job, you'll frequently be asked to fill out forms. For example, you may have to fill out a form to request time off, to order supplies, to account for your time, or to purchase a new piece of equipment.

The following tips can help you complete forms clearly and accurately.

1. Always read through the whole form *before* you begin filling it out.

2. Be particularly careful the first time you fill out a form. When you become familiar with the form, you will be able to move through it more quickly.

3. Follow the directions *exactly.* For example, some forms ask you to write your first name first. Others ask you to write your last name first.

4. Think before you write. Mistakes look terrible on a form.

5. Until you're familiar with the form, use a pencil so that you can easily correct any mistakes. If you have to complete the form in ink, use a pencil first. Then, after you've checked for accuracy, write over the pencil with ink.

6. Write legibly. Use block capitals if your penmanship is less than perfect.

7. Be particularly careful when writing numbers.

8. Do not leave spaces blank. If you don't know the required information, find a way to get it.

Activity 7.16: Filling Out Forms

Figures 7.5, 7.6, and 7.7 are all forms used by Roberts Construction Associates of Madison, Wisconsin. Using the following information, complete each form. Be sure to read each form carefully before filling in the blocks.

APPLICATION FOR EMPLOYMENT
(PRE-EMPLOYMENT QUESTIONNAIRE)   (AN EQUAL OPPORTUNITY EMPLOYER)

PERSONAL INFORMATION

DATE _____

NAME _____   SOCIAL SECURITY
　　　　　　LAST　　　　　　　FIRST　　　　　　　MIDDLE   NUMBER _____

PRESENT ADDRESS _____
　　　　　　　　　STREET　　　　　　　　　　CITY　　　　　STATE　　　ZIP

PERMANENT ADDRESS _____
　　　　　　　　　　STREET　　　　　　　　　　CITY　　　　　STATE　　　ZIP

PHONE NO. _____   ARE YOU 18 YEARS OR OLDER   YES ☐   NO ☐

SPECIAL QUESTIONS

DO NOT ANSWER **ANY** OF THE QUESTIONS IN THIS FRAMED AREA UNLESS THE EMPLOYER HAS **CHECKED A BOX PRECEDING A QUESTION,** THEREBY INDICATING THAT THE INFORMATION IS REQUIRED FOR A BONA FIDE OCCUPATIONAL QUALIFICATION, OR DICTATED BY NATIONAL SECURITY LAWS, OR IS NEEDED FOR OTHER LEGALLY PERMISSIBLE REASONS.

☐　Height _____ feet _____ inches　☐　Are you prevented from lawfully becoming employed in the U.S.? _____ Yes _____ No

☐　Weight _____ lbs.　☐　Date of Birth * _____

☐　What Foreign Languages do you speak fluently? _____ Read _____ Write _____

☐　Have you been convicted of a felony or misdemeanor within the last 5 years?　Yes _____　No _____　Describe:

* The Age Discrimination in Employment Act of 1967 prohibits discrimination on the basis of age with respect to individuals who are at least 40 but less than 70 years of age.
** You will not be denied employment solely because of a conviction record, unless the offense is related to the job for which you have applied.

EMPLOYMENT DESIRED

POSITION _____   DATE YOU
　　　　　　　　　　　　　　　　　CAN START _____   SALARY
　　　　　　　　　　　　　　　　　　　　　　　　　　　　DESIRED _____

ARE YOU EMPLOYED NOW? _____   IF SO, MAY WE INQUIRE
　　　　　　　　　　　　　　　　　OF YOUR PRESENT EMPLOYER? _____

EVER APPLIED TO THIS COMPANY BEFORE? _____   WHERE? _____   WHEN? _____

EDUCATION	NAME AND LOCATION OF SCHOOL	* NO. OF YEARS ATTENDED	* DID YOU GRADUATE?	SUBJECTS STUDIED
GRAMMAR SCHOOL				
HIGH SCHOOL				
COLLEGE				
TRADE, BUSINESS OR CORRESPONDENCE SCHOOL				

* The Age Discrimination in Employment Act of 1967 prohibits discrimination on the basis of age with respect to individuals who are at least 40 but less than 70 years of age.

GENERAL

SUBJECTS OF SPECIAL STUDY OR RESEARCH WORK _____

_____

U.S. MILITARY OR
NAVAL SERVICE _____   RANK _____   PRESENT MEMBERSHIP IN
NATIONAL GUARD OR RESERVES _____
(CONTINUED ON OTHER SIDE)

Figure 7.5:　Employment Application
Source: Roberts Construction Associates, Madison, Wisconsin.

FIGURE 7.5—EMPLOYMENT APPLICATION

- Use your personal information to complete this employment application.
- Under "Special Questions," complete the questions that ask for your height, weight, date of birth, and language proficiency.

FORMER EMPLOYERS (LIST BELOW LAST FOUR EMPLOYERS, STARTING WITH LAST ONE FIRST)

DATE, MONTH AND YEAR	NAME AND ADDRESS OF EMPLOYER	SALARY	POSITION	REASON FOR LEAVING
FROM				
TO				
FROM				
TO				
FROM				
TO				
FROM				
TO				

REFERENCES: GIVE THE NAMES OF THREE PERSONS NOT RELATED TO YOU, WHOM YOU HAVE KNOWN AT LEAST ONE YEAR.

NAME	ADDRESS	BUSINESS	YEARS ACQUAINTED
1.			
2.			
3.			

PHYSICAL RECORD:

DO YOU HAVE ANY PHYSICAL LIMITATIONS THAT PRECLUDE YOU FROM PERFORMING ANY WORK FOR WHICH YOU ARE BEING CONSIDERED?

☐ Yes   ☐ No

IF YES, WHAT CAN BE DONE TO ACCOMMODATE YOUR LIMITATION? _____

PLEASE DESCRIBE: _____

IN CASE OF EMERGENCY NOTIFY _____
                              NAME   ADDRESS   PHONE NO.

" I CERTIFY THAT THE FACTS CONTAINED IN THIS APPLICATION ARE TRUE AND COMPLETE TO THE BEST OF MY KNOWLEDGE AND UNDERSTAND THAT, IF EMPLOYED, FALSIFIED STATEMENTS ON THIS APPLICATION SHALL BE GROUNDS FOR DISMISSAL.

I AUTHORIZE INVESTIGATION OF ALL STATEMENTS CONTAINED HEREIN AND THE REFERENCES LISTED ABOVE TO GIVE YOU ANY AND ALL INFORMATION CONCERNING MY PREVIOUS EMPLOYMENT AND ANY PERTINENT INFORMATION THEY MAY HAVE, PERSONAL OR OTHERWISE, AND RELEASE ALL PARTIES FROM ALL LIABILITY FOR ANY DAMAGE THAT MAY RESULT FROM FURNISHING SAME TO YOU.

I UNDERSTAND AND AGREE THAT, IF HIRED, MY EMPLOYMENT IS FOR NO DEFINITE PERIOD AND MAY, REGARDLESS OF THE DATE OF PAYMENT OF MY WAGES AND SALARY, BE TERMINATED AT ANY TIME WITHOUT ANY PRIOR NOTICE".

SIGNATURE _____ DATE _____

DO NOT WRITE BELOW THIS LINE

INTERVIEWED BY _____ DATE _____

HIRED ☐ Yes ☐ No _____ POSITION _____ DEPT. _____

SALARY/WAGE _____ DATE REPORTING TO WORK _____

APPROVED: 1. _____   2. _____   3. _____
            EMPLOYMENT MANAGER   DEPT. HEAD   GENERAL MANAGER

This form has been designed to strictly comply with State and Federal fair employment practice laws prohibiting employment discrimination.

Figure 7.5: Continued

- Under "Former Employers," note that you are asked to list your most recent employer first.
- Under "References," note that family members cannot be listed.

FIGURE 7.6—TIME CARD (PAGE 251)

- Use your name. Your employee number is 15358.
- The name of the project is "Orchard Beach Condominiums."
- The project number is 988-C.
- The time card is being completed for the week ending Sept. 15, 2001.

TIME CARD

DESCRIPTION:	CODE	M	T	W	T	F	S	TOTAL
Employee Name:								
Employee #:								
Week Ending Date (Saturday):								

Project Name:
Project#:

DESCRIPTION:	CODE	M	T	W	T	F	S	TOTAL
Supervision								
Demolition Clean Up								
Construction Clean Up								
Final Clean Up								
Demolition								
Floor Prep & Patch								
Hand Excavation/Backfill								
Concrete Patch								
Concrete (Walls) (Slabs)								
Concrete (Sidewalks) (Stoops)								
Masonry								
Structural Steel								
Miscellaneous Metal								
Wood Stud Walls								
Wood Blocking (Walls) (Roof)								
Wood Trusses & Bracing								
Field Frame (Roof) (Soffit) (Fascia)								
Sheathing (Walls) (Roof)								
Other Carpentry (Please list):								
Finish Soffit and Fascia								
Inter. Trim (Jambs, Trim, Casing, Base, Handrails)								
Custom Woodwork & Millwork								
Prefab (Cabinets) (Tops)								
Damp-Proofing								
Drain Tile								
Insulation (Rigid) (Fiber)								
Roofing & Felt								
Caulking								
Metal (Doors) (Frames) (Hardware)								
Wood (Doors) (Hardware)								
Windows (Wood) (Aluminum) (Interior)								
Drywall (Hanging) (Finishing)								
Toilet (Partitions) (Accessories)								
Misc. Specialties (Please list):								
Meeting								
Travel (Job to Job only):								
Punch List Items: (Please list if other than above)								
TOTAL HOURS:								

	Mon.	Tues.	Wed.	Thurs.	Fri.	Sat.	
Daily - Job Time In:							
Daily - Job Time Out:							
DAILY - Job Superintendent's Initials:							
NOTES/COMMENTS:							

Figure 7.6: Time Card

Source: Roberts Construction Associates, Madison, Wisconsin.

- Your hours are 7 A.M. to 4 P.M., Monday through Friday. You have one hour for lunch, which means you work an eight-hour day.
- On Mondays, Tuesdays, and Thursdays, the job superintendent is Marcia Raven. On Wednesdays and Fridays, the job superintendent is Daniel Marcus.

Here is a summary of your weekly activities:

- On Monday, you spent the full day doing masonry work.
- On Tuesday, you spent three hours doing concrete patch and five hours doing demolition.
- On Wednesday, you spent five hours doing drywall, two hours doing concrete patch, and one hour doing damp-proofing.
- On Thursday, you spent the whole day doing damp-proofing.
- On Friday, you spent four hours doing masonry work and four hours doing floor prep.

The relevant codes are as follows:

- concrete patch—960
- damp-proofing—555
- demolition—840
- drywall—680
- floor prep—390
- masonry—420

On the time card, you would like to ask for a vacation day on December 8, 2001.

FIGURE 7.7—LETTER OF TRANSMITTAL (PAGE 253)

- Use today's date.
- The job name is Newark Shopping Plaza and the job number is 8950.
- The documents should go to the attention of Roger MacAlester of Meyerson Development Corp., 550 State Blvd., Trenton, NJ 08609.
- Enclosed with the letter will be 4 complete sets of specifications and 6 complete sets of shop drawings. These will be hand delivered with the letter.
- The specs are dated February 16, 2001, and the shop drawings are dated February 18, 2001.
- These documents are being sent for approval purposes.
- Copies of the transmittal letter should go to Monica Sluzak and Ethel Johnson.

LETTER OF TRANSMITTAL

Roberts Construction Associates, Inc.

849 East Washington Avenue
Madison, Wisconsin 53703
Office: (608) 257-0500   Fax: (608) 257-4374

RE: _____   DATE: _____
                                    JOB NO.: _____
ATTN: _____

TO: _____

WE ARE SENDING YOU: ☐ Attached   ☐ Hand Delivered   ☐ Specifications

            ☐ Shop drawings   ☐ Prints   ☐ Plans   ☐ Samples

            ☐ Copy of letter ☐ Change order ☐ Cut Sheets   ☐ _____

COPIES	DATE	NO.	DESCRIPTION

THESE ARE TRANSMITTED as checked below:

☐ For approval   ☐ Approved as submitted   ☐ Resubmit _____ copies for approval

☐ For your use   ☐ Approved as noted   ☐ Submit _____ copies for distribution

☐ As requested   ☐ Returned for corrections   ☐ Return _____ corrected prints

☐ For Technical Review   ☐ Reviewed   ☐ For Bids Due _____ 20 _____
   and Comment

☐ RETURN ORIGINAL TO:

REMARKS:

cc: _____

_____

                            SIGNED: _____

Figure 7.7:   Letter of Transmittal
Source: Roberts Construction Associates, Madison, Wisconsin.

Writing Skills II
Advanced Topics

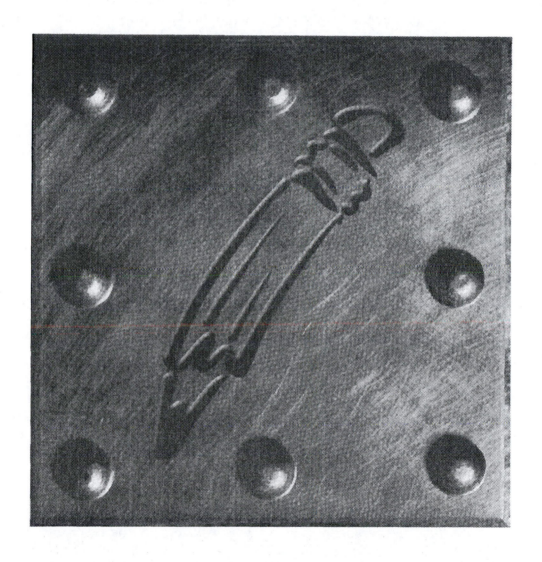

> People who don't take time to actually read what they have written, or spell-check the results for accuracy, are my pet peeve. Nothing says 'Don't pay attention to my thought—because I certainly don't!' more than an error-filled letter or presentation.
>
> —Marcy Anderson, Manager, Craft and Supervisory Development,
> Zachry Construction Corp., Laporte, TX

Module 7 explored the basics of effective on-the-job writing. In that module, we emphasized the importance of writing for a specific audience and purpose. We saw that good writing is objective, simple, clear, and economical.

This module discusses further writing-related topics. Because many audiences expect a specific format, it explains how to properly format your memos, letters, and e-mail. It also shows how to use illustrations effectively in your writing and how to prepare professional field and progress reports.

8.1 FORMATTING YOUR DOCUMENTS PROPERLY

As noted in Module 5, the past two decades have seen a great increase in written communication in the construction business. The written communications that most workers are expected to prepare fall into three categories:

- Memos
- E-mail
- Business letters

Workers at all levels of the company write memos and e-mail, while business letters are usually written by managers and office workers. Foremen and other supervisors are often asked to write progress reports, which we discuss in Section 8.3.

Each of these types of written communication requires a specific format. In other words, you must prepare your memo, e-mail, or business letter according to a pre-established template.[1]

8.1.1. Memos

Recall from Section 5.4.1 that a *memo* (short for *memorandum*) is a brief note written to give instructions, to ask or answer questions, to explain new policies, to call meetings, to summarize decisions, to request information, to remind people about upcoming tasks or events, or to document decisions. For example, a safety inspector might notice several safety violations on a job site. He might then issue a memo to supervisors reminding them of the proper safety procedures, as shown in Figure 8.1.

Memos are sent only *within* an organization. For communication outside the organization, a business letter is used instead.

Note that the memo in Figure 8.1 includes several components. Any memo you write should include these components as well:

1. **Memo:** The word "Memo" or "Memorandum" near the top or side of the page.

2. **To:** The person or persons who will receive the memo. If others are to receive a copy of the memo, their names are listed under **Cc:** (which stands for "complimentary copy" or "carbon copy"). Sometimes the **Cc:** line appears directly under the **To:** line. Other times, the **Cc:** line appears at the bottom of the memo. There may also be a **Distribution** list at the end of the memo.

   The **To:** line should contain the names of the people who are directly affected by the memo. In general, the **Cc:** line is used for managers and

---

[1]Note that Module 5 provided tips for reading memos and e-mail. This module explains how to *write* good memos and e-mail. Reading and writing are two sides of the same coin. Good readers are usually good writers, and good writers are usually good readers.

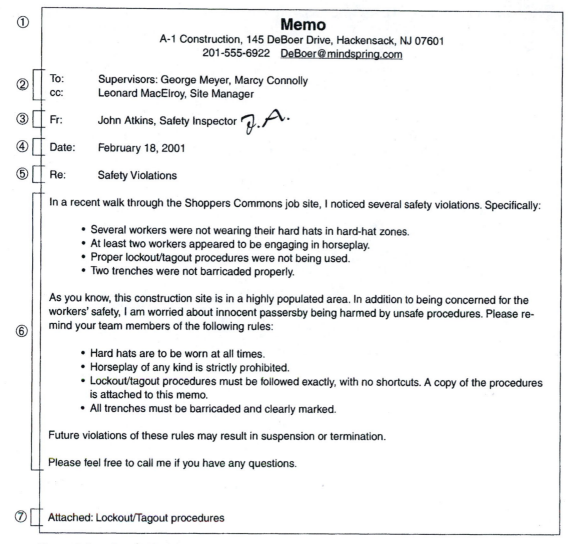

①

Memo
A-1 Construction, 145 DeBoer Drive, Hackensack, NJ 07601
201-555-6922   DeBoer@mindspring.com

② To: Supervisors: George Meyer, Marcy Connolly
   cc: Leonard MacElroy, Site Manager

③ Fr: John Atkins, Safety Inspector *J.A.*

④ Date: February 18, 2001

⑤ Re: Safety Violations

⑥ In a recent walk through the Shoppers Commons job site, I noticed several safety violations. Specifically:

- Several workers were not wearing their hard hats in hard-hat zones.
- At least two workers appeared to be engaging in horseplay.
- Proper lockout/tagout procedures were not being used.
- Two trenches were not barricaded properly.

As you know, this construction site is in a highly populated area. In addition to being concerned for the workers' safety, I am worried about innocent passersby being harmed by unsafe procedures. Please remind your team members of the following rules:

- Hard hats are to be worn at all times.
- Horseplay of any kind is strictly prohibited.
- Lockout/tagout procedures must be followed exactly, with no shortcuts. A copy of the procedures is attached to this memo.
- All trenches must be barricaded and clearly marked.

Future violations of these rules may result in suspension or termination.

Please feel free to call me if you have any questions.

⑦ Attached: Lockout/Tagout procedures

Figure 8.1:   Sample Memo

supervisors, or other people who need to remain "in the loop" regarding events on the job site.

> **TIP:** Be careful about whom you include on the cc: line. Some people think that you are reporting them to their supervisors and could be offended.

3. **From:** The sender's full name. If you are typing or word processing the memo, sign your initials here in pen.

4. **Date/(Time):** The date the memo was written—month, day, and year. Because so many projects are time-sensitive, this information is very important. The time is sometimes included.

5. **Subject:** When receiving a memo, your readers like to have an idea of what the memo is about quickly and at a glance. This is the purpose of

the **subject** line, sometimes abbreviated "**Re.**" It's best to keep the subject line short and to the point. For example, the subject of the safety inspector's memo in Figure 8.1 is "Safety Violations."

6. **The body of the memo:** The body of the memo is the "nitty gritty." It conveys the information you want to communicate.

   Most memos should be brief, no more than two or three paragraphs. The best memos get right to the point and are written in a conversational tone. They focus on main ideas and provide just enough detail to get their point across. Bulleted and numbered lists are sometimes used. If a memo is too long, people may choose not to read it.

   Note that memos are not signed at the end.

7. **Other information:** Some memos may also include the name and address of the company, phone or fax numbers, e-mail addresses, or attachments. An *attachment* is a separate sheet of paper (or several sheets of paper) that is usually stapled or paper clipped to the memo. Attachments are usually documents that workers must refer to later on. For example, the safety inspector who wrote the memo in Figure 8.1 decided to include a copy of the company's lockout/tagout guidelines as an attachment to the memo.

Activity 8.1: Writing Memos

Using the template shown in Figure 8.1 and the explanations in Section 8.1.1, write a memo that includes the following information. Either fill in the template on page 259, or create your own memo on a separate sheet of paper.

- You are the writer.
- Today's date is October 7, 2000.
- The memo is going to Christopher Daniels, the company owner.
- The time is 3:30 P.M.
- Copies of the memo will go to (1) Mike Elias, the personnel director, and (2) Barbara Kennedy, the company's payroll clerk.

In this memo, you will provide information on lateness. The owner has asked you to list the workers on your team who have been late for work more than once in the past thirty days, and how many days they have been late. Here is the information you have collected on the eight people who work for you:

Name	Days Late in the Last 30 Days
Mary Draper	0
Peter Fallow	3
Mike Gregorio	1
Jake Larrone	2
Shelly Minichetti	0
Laurie Rowen	5
Wayne Sellers	0
Terrence Washington	1

MEMO

To:

cc:

Fr:

Date:

Subject:

8.1.2 E-Mail

A few years ago, no one would have predicted how popular *e-mail* (short for "electronic mail") would become. In many circumstances, e-mail has become a replacement for printed memos and phone calls.

Like memos, e-mail is used to ask or answer questions and to notify people of upcoming events. Because e-mail volume can be overwhelming (some managers now get more than 100 e-mails a day), it's extremely important that you keep e-mails short and to the point. (For tips on achieving simplicity and clarity, see Sections 7.2 and 7.6.1.)

A sample e-mail message appears in Figure 8.2.

Note that an e-mail message contains many of the same elements as a memo:

- name(s) of the sender(s)
- name(s) of the recipient(s)
- date and time
- subject line

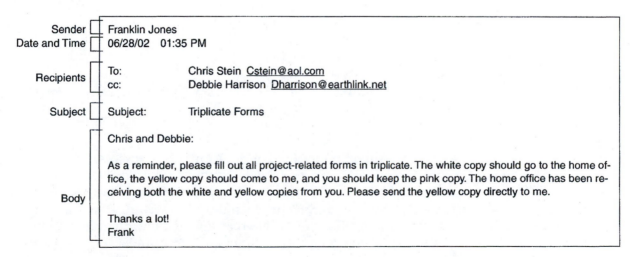

Figure 8.2:   E-Mail Message

- body of the message
- electronic attachments—these are often documents that have been prepared in well-known software programs, such as Microsoft Word or Microsoft Excel[2]

If you have an e-mail account, your name will appear automatically as the sender, so you don't need to type it in every time. The date and time are also recorded automatically. However, you do need to type the recipients' names, the subject line, and the body.

> **TIP:** When typing an e-mail address, you must type the address 100% accurately. If you don't, the e-mail may be bounced back to you as "undeliverable."

The same way a memo's subject line summarizes the memo at a glance, an e-mail's subject line should do the same. *Never send an e-mail with an empty subject line!*

Like memos, e-mails should be short and to the point. Keep them to a few sentences or paragraphs—the shorter, the better. State your main point, main concern, or main question up front, then use the rest of the e-mail to explain or offer suggestions.

REMEMBER WHEN YOU WRITE E-MAIL:

- **E-mail can become public knowledge.** In today's fast-paced, Internet-based world, e-mail can be circulated to thousands of people with the click of a button. So don't include private, sensitive, or confidential information in business e-mail.
- **Don't send junk e-mail to business addresses.** It's tempting to send jokes and other nonbusiness material to friends' e-mail addresses. But such e-mail only distracts people from their work, and many companies frown on their workers receiving this kind of e-mail. Save private e-mail for private e-mail addresses.
- **E-mail is not a substitute for face-to-face interaction.** Never convey bad news through e-mail, and don't use e-mail to avoid your responsibilities.
- **Be careful how you phrase your sentences.** Because e-mail tends to be informal, it is easily misinterpreted. Watch how you phrase your thoughts. Never use obscene or offensive language. Though they may seem silly, "emoticons" such as :) or :-) (which look like smiley faces when rotated 90 degrees to the right) can help you indicate when you're being lighthearted and shouldn't be taken too seriously.
- **Use both uppercase and lowercase letters in your e-mail messages.** Using only uppercase letters makes it appear as if you're shouting. HOW WOULD YOU FEEL IF YOU GOT A MESSAGE FROM YOUR SUPERVISOR THAT WAS WRITTEN IN ALL CAPITAL LETTERS?
- **If you need to document an important decision, use a memo rather than e-mail.** E-mail is too easily erased or deleted. Important decisions need to be communicated person to person and on paper, rather than via e-mail.
- **Think twice before you attach a document electronically.** Although many e-mail programs allow you to open attached electronic documents, there are still many compatibility problems. Attempting to open an in-

---

[2]There are no attachments shown in Figure 8.2.

compatible document can cause the machine to crash. Attachments can also introduce viruses into someone's computer. So, if you do send an attachment, scan it for viruses beforehand.

- **Be careful when you reply.** Some e-mail programs let you reply to everyone included on the original distribution list. This is a valuable option, but it should be used sparingly. Send e-mail only to those people who really need to see what you've written. Don't clog up co-workers' e-mailboxes (in other words, don't waste their time) with things they don't need to see.
- **Respond to urgent e-mail immediately.** When you receive e-mail that is marked as urgent (usually indicated by an exclamation point), respond as soon as possible. These days, an urgent e-mail message is the equivalent of an urgent phone call.

Activity 8.2: Writing E-Mail

Using the e-mail template below, compose an effective e-mail message based on the following information.

- The sender of the e-mail is you.
- Today's date is November 15, 2001.
- The time now is 9:15 A.M.
- This e-mail is of urgent importance.
- The e-mail is addressed to Hal Franklin. Hal's e-mail address is hal.franklin@jjconstruction.com. Benjamin Mahwah and Maxine Wyckoff should receive copies of the e-mail. Their e-mail addresses are ben.mahwah@jjconstruction.com and maxine.wyckoff@jjconstruction.com.

This urgent e-mail concerns an incorrect delivery that was made late yesterday. Your company ordered 5000 units of Part #6755 from Allendale Plumbing Supply. Your foreman, Mark Green, signed for the delivery. However, while unpacking the materials today, the crew found that Allendale actually delivered 6755 units of Part #5000. The correct parts are needed by next week to keep the project on schedule. You have tried to reach Hal Franklin (the owner of your company) on the phone, but the line is busy. Because this matter is urgent, you

From:
Date and Time:

To:
cc:

Subject:

☐ Normal Priority   ☐ Urgent Priority

decide to send him an e-mail. Hal is friendly with Jeff Sommers (the owner of Allendale Plumbing Supply), so Hal should be able to solve the problem quickly.

8.1.3 Business Letters

All companies have letterhead paper for *business letters,* their formal written communications to outside companies. In general, letters are written in a much more formal tone than memos and e-mail. When you begin writing letters for your employer, you'll know that you've reached management status!

Business letters contain many of the same elements as memos and e-mail. However, because they are going to people outside the company, they tend to

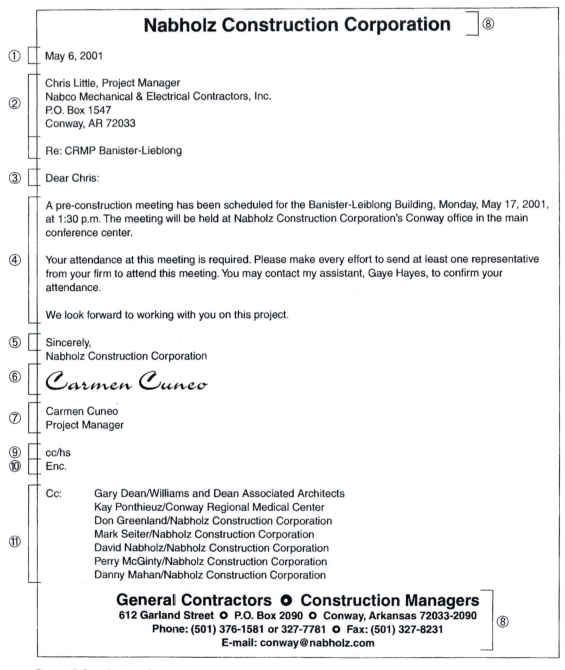

Figure 8.3: Business Letter

Source: Courtesy of Nabholz Construction Corp., Conway, AR.

be printed on more expensive stationery. A sample business letter appears in Figure 8.3.

The business letter includes the following elements, in the following order:

1. The **date**—month, day, and year, at the top of the page.

2. The **inside address,** giving the name, title, and complete address of the receiver. Make sure you spell the receiver's name properly, and be sure his or her title is correct. You might want to call the intended recipient to verify his or her name and title before you send the letter.

   Sometimes a **subject line** is included after the inside address.

3. A **salutation,** or greeting. In business letters, the salutation is usually in the form "Dear Mr. Robinson:". Note that a colon [:] follows the name, not a comma [,].

4. The **body.** While some business letters require a few pages, readers always appreciate brevity. Give all the necessary details, but don't make the letter longer than it needs to be.

5. The **complimentary close,** usually in the form of "Sincerely yours," or "Regards,".

6. The **writer's signature.**

7. The **writer's complete name and title.**

8. The company's **letterhead,** which gives the company's full name, address, phone and fax numbers, and e-mail address. A company logo may also be included in the letterhead. (Letterheads may appear at the top or bottom of the company's stationery, or even at the sides.)

9. The initials of the **writer** (first) and the **typist** (second). Often, the writer's initials will be in capital letters, and the typist's initials will be in lowercase letters. If the writer has typed the letter himself, he uses the abbreviation "hs" ("himself") for the typist's initials.

10. The abbreviation **"Enc."** (short for "enclosures") if additional documents are enclosed.

11. The abbreviation **"cc"** or **"xc"** if copies of the letter are going to other people ("cc" stands for "complimentary copy" or "carbon copy," "xc" for "Xerox copy").

REMEMBER WHEN WRITING A BUSINESS LETTER:

- Follow all the suggestions provided in Section 7.2 for writing clearly, directly, simply, and economically. Make your main points easy to find.

- While the format of a business letter is standard, you should still make it as easy to read as possible. It is acceptable to use bulleted and numbered lists within a business letter.

- Business letters represent your company's communications with the outside world. For this reason, be sure that all your letters are carefully proofread and double-checked before you mail them. Typos, grammatical mistakes, and errors make a poor impression. (Tips for proofreading are covered in Section 8.4.)

- Tone is very important in a business letter. Informal communications are fine in e-mail, but the tone of a business letter should be formal. Don't use slang or inappropriate language.

Activity 8.3: Writing a Business Letter

Suppose you are the director of surveying at a small construction company called SouthWest Construction. Your offices are based in Albuquerque, New Mexico. Your phone number is 505-555-5487.

While reading *Surveying Quarterly,* a construction trade magazine, you come across an interview with a man named Jason Dell. Mr. Dell, whose title is Survey Director, has pioneered a new system of surveying difficult terrain. His company, New England Surveying, is based in Boston. Its address is 3937 Commonwealth Avenue, Boston, Massachusetts 02118.

You will be visiting Boston next month, and you would like the opportunity to meet with Mr. Dell, because you feel that you can learn a lot from him. Because surveying is also your field of expertise, you feel that both you and Mr. Dell could benefit from a meeting.

You will be in Boston on Tuesday, October 22, 2001, and could find time to meet with Mr. Dell that day. Write him a letter as the representative of your company, asking if he would be able to meet with you during your visit to Boston. You can use the template below to get started. Today's date is September 15, 2001. Be sure that the president of your company, Jack Zilsky, receives a copy of your letter to Mr. Dell.

SouthWest Construction
4751 Gallegos Blvd., Albuquerque, NM 87114
Phone: 505-555-5487 Fax: 505-555-9087
E-mail: southwestconst@aol.com

8.2 USING VISUAL AIDS IN YOUR WRITING

In Section 6.1, we discussed how to read the many types of visuals—illustrations, diagrams, tables, and so on—that are commonly encountered in construction-related materials. Visuals can easily summarize pages of information into a user-friendly format.

As you write, you may find that your presentation would benefit from an added visual. Consider using visuals in the following ways:

- When many numbers have been presented in a small amount of space, summarize them in a table. Other ways to summarize numbers are bar graphs and pie charts.
- When explaining relationships between people or processes, use a flow chart or summary diagram.
- When identifying the parts of a machine or the stages in a process, use an illustration of that machine or process, with each part or stage clearly labeled. Photos can also be used for this purpose.

Don't worry if you don't have a lot of artistic talent. Using computer software, it is simple to create easy-to-read tables and diagrams. For example, Figure 8.4, which summarizes owner-managed construction, was created by a common word processing system. For more complex figures, you may need to call on a professional artist or a computer professional for assistance.

Visual Aids to Accompany Text

Sometimes, a visual aid works best when it is accompanied by text that provides the same information in writing. Note how well Figure 8.4 illustrates and clarifies the concepts laid out in the following paragraph:

> Many large industrial organizations, as well as a number of governmental agencies, possess their own construction forces. Although these forces are utilized primarily for performing repair, maintenance, and alteration work, they are often capable of undertaking new construction projects. More frequently, owners utilize project directors in their construction staffs to manage their new construction. The work may be carried out by workers hired directly by the owner (hired labor force), by specialty contractors, or by a combination of these two methods.[3]

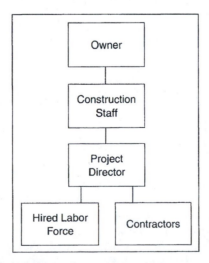

Figure 8.4: Owner-Managed Construction
Source: S. W. Nunnally, *Construction Methods and Management*, 5th ed. (Upper Saddle River, NJ: Prentice Hall, 2001), p. 6.

---

[3]Adapted from S. W. Nunnally, *Construction Methods and Management*, 5th ed. (Upper Saddle River, NJ: Prentice Hall, 2001), p. 5.

Combining the text with the diagram, we can create an effective memo that summarizes owner-managed construction:

MEMO

To: John Rosen
Cc: Mary Johnson, Martin Davidson, Richard Garcia
Fr: Elizabeth Conant
Date: September 15, 2001
Subject: Summary of Owner-Managed Construction

What exactly is *owner-managed construction?* In a nutshell:

Many large industrial organizations, as well as a number of governmental agencies, possess their own construction forces. Although these forces are utilized primarily for performing repair, maintenance, and alteration work, they are often capable of undertaking new construction projects. More frequently, owners utilize project directors in their construction staffs to manage their new construction. The work may be carried out by workers hired directly by the owner (hired labor force), by specialty contractors, or by a combination of these two methods. So, in other words, *owner-managed construction* means the use of a company's construction staff, plus hired contractors and subcontractors, to take on new construction projects.

The following diagram summarizes owner-managed construction:

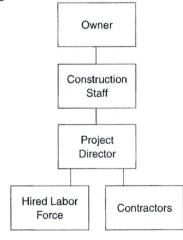

Visual Aids Instead of Text

There may be times when a visual aid can take the place of a large amount of text. When choosing this option, be sure that your diagram conveys *everything* you need it to convey. Because you won't have text to back you up, your diagram must include all essential details.

Suppose you work for a professional construction association, such as the National Association of Home Builders. NAHB is putting together a brochure to show how the demand for building materials has increased over the last few years. As part of the brochure, it wants to explain how many construction materials are used in building a typical single-family house. The person writing the brochure *could* write a bulleted list spelling out exactly how much concrete, plastic piping, gypsum wall board, copper wiring, and nails are needed to build the house. This would be an effective way of presenting the information. However, a diagram might work equally well *instead* of the written explanation.

Figure 8.5 shows a diagram that would work well in this situation. Notice that it is easy to read and clearly labeled, and could be understood by just about anyone (both construction professionals and laypeople). This diagram could be very effective on the first page of the brochure, because it grabs the reader's interest and summarizes much relevant information.

REMEMBER WHEN USING VISUALS IN YOUR WRITING:

- Always make your visual aids large enough so that they're easy to read.
- Give each visual aid a title that clearly identifies its purpose.

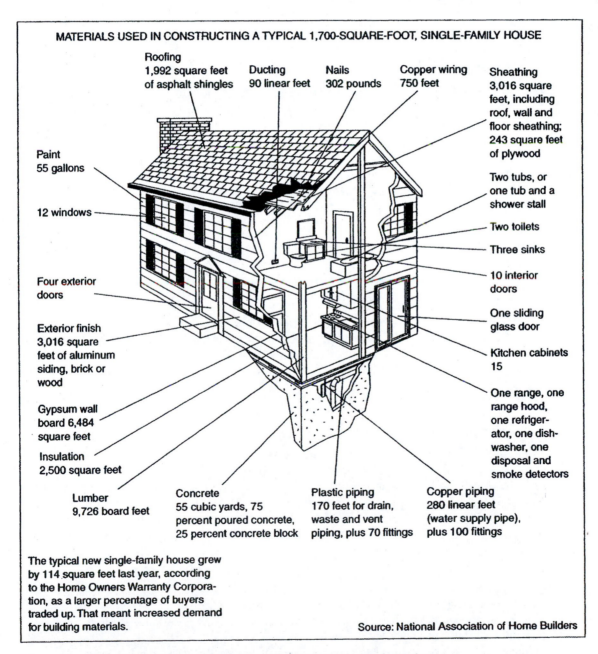

Figure 8.5:   Materials Used in Constructing a Typical 1,700-Square-Foot, Single-Family House

Source: National Association of Home Builders.

- Determine when a visual aid should *accompany* text and when a visual aid should *replace* text. It's often best to present information in two different ways, because repeated exposure to the material makes it easier to learn and remember.
- Place your visual aids as close to the relevant text discussion as possible.
- When planning your visual aids, be creative, but make sure the final table, graph, or diagram conveys the information accurately. Don't be afraid to enlist the help of a trained artist to help you with your task.
- Use more than one visual aid when presenting large amounts of information. Don't cram too much information onto one visual aid.

Activity 8.4: Using Visual Aids in Your Writing

Create visual aids to accompany two of the passages below.

Passage A: Using Straight Ladders Safely[4]

It is very important to place a straight ladder at the proper angle before using it. A ladder placed at an improper angle will be unstable and cause you to fall.

The distance between the foot of a ladder and the base of the structure it is leaning against must be one-fourth of the distance between the ground and the point where the ladder touches the structure. For example, if the height of the wall against which the ladder will be leaning is 16 feet, then the foot of the ladder should be 4 feet from the base of the wall. If you are going to step off a ladder onto a platform or roof, the top of the ladder should extend at least 3 feet above the point where the ladder touches the platform or roof.

(Hint: Draw a diagram.)

Passage B: Design Professionals' Activities[5]

Design professionals provide a variety of services. In general, designers divide their time as follows: 40% of their time is spent on creating construction documents, 20% of their time is spent on design development, and another 20% is spent on construction services. Schematic design takes 15% of their time, while bidding takes up the remaining 5%.

(Hint: Use a pie chart.)

Passage C: Installing Steel Piping[6]

Although piping drawings should be available for every piping system that is installed, this is not always the case. Therefore, the HVAC installer often has to select the best route and install the piping. This is known as field-fabricating or field-routing a pipe run. In this case, the HVAC installer has to determine the placement of the pipe hangers, based on the size, weight, and type of pipe being run. In order for a hanger system to do its job, it must support the pipe

---

[4]National Center for Construction Education and Research, *Core Curriculum* (Upper Saddle River, NJ/Columbus, OH: Prentice Hall, 2000), Trainee Module 00101, pp. 1-35–1-36.

[5]Adapted from Ralph Liebing, *The Construction Industry: Processes, Players, and Practices* (Upper Saddle River, NJ/Columbus, OH: Prentice Hall, 2001), p. 73.

[6]National Center for Construction Education and Research, *Heating, Ventilating, and Air Conditioning Trainee Guide* (Upper Saddle River, NJ/Columbus, OH: Prentice Hall, 1999), Module 03106, pp. 20–21.

at regular intervals. Evenly spacing the hangers prevents any individual hanger from being overloaded.

Recommended maximum hanger spacing intervals for carbon steel pipe are as follows: For pipe size up to 1¼" with a rod diameter of ⅜", use maximum spacing of 8 feet between hangers. For pipe size of 1½" and 2" with rod diameter of ⅜", use maximum spacing of 10 feet. For pipe size of 2½" to 3½" with rod diameter of ½", use a maximum spacing of 12 feet. For 4" and 5" pipe with rod diameter of ⅝", use maximum spacing of 15 feet. For 6" pipe with rod diameter of ¾", use 17 foot maximum spacing. And for 8" to 12" pipe with rod diameter of ⅞", use 22 foot maximum spacing.

(Hint: Create a table to summarize the data.)

Passage D: Screwdrivers[7]

A screwdriver is used to tighten or remove screws. It is identified by the type of screw it fits. There are six types of screw heads.

The most common screwdrivers are slotted (also known as straight-blade or standard tip) and Phillips head screwdrivers. There are also specialized screwdrivers such as clutch-drive, Torx, Robertson, and Allen head (hex). Each is described below:

- *Slotted*—This is the most common type of screwdriver; it fits slotted screws.
- *Phillips*—This is the most common type of cross-head screwdriver; it fits Phillips head screws.
- *Clutch-drive*—This screwdriver has an hour-glass-shaped tip that is especially useful when you need extra holding power, as in cars and appliances.
- *Torx*—This screwdriver has a star-shaped tip that is useful for replacing such parts as tailgate lenses; it is widely used in automobile repair work. Torx screws are also used in household appliances as well as lawn and garden equipment.
- *Robertson (square)*—This screwdriver has a square drive that provides high torque power. Usually color coded according to size, it can reach screws that are sunk below the surface.
- *Allen (hex)*—This screwdriver conforms to screws that can also be operated with hex keys; it is suitable for socket-head screws that are recessed.

(Hint: Draw an illustration showing each kind of screw head.)

8.3 WRITING PROGRESS AND FIELD REPORTS

As we saw in Section 8.1, memos and e-mail communications are basically informal. They deal with one topic at a time, and they're most effective when they are short.

In almost all large jobs, however, there is a need for formal written reports on a regular basis. On a construction site, these formal reports usually fall into two categories: (1) progress reports and (2) field reports.

[7]National Center for Construction Education and Research, *Core Curriculum* (Upper Saddle River, NJ/Columbus, OH: Prentice Hall, 2000), Trainee Module 00103, pp. 3-4–3-5.

Progress Reports

Suppose that you're the owner of a new shopping mall that is being erected in a highly populated suburb. The mall will cover 500 acres and include more than 125 stores. The time scheduled for completion is twelve months.

The amount of work that will go into such a project is mind-boggling. Contracts must be drawn up. Contractors and subcontractors must be hired. Traffic consultants must ensure that the construction project affects residents of the town as little as possible. Millions of dollars worth of construction materials need to be ordered, delivered, stored, and accounted for.

As the owner, wouldn't you want reports from your staff on a regular basis? You need to make sure that everything is happening on schedule, and you need to be alerted to potential problems and what the solutions might be. You need all this information in one place, rather than in a series of hundreds of memos or e-mails, so that you can see the "big picture." In other words, you need a *progress report*.

Progress reports inform managers of the work completed on a project and the work that is yet to be finished. Most of the time, the progress report assesses progress against schedule and estimates the time required for completion. Progress reports may be required weekly, biweekly, monthly, or at any other time determined by management.

While different companies have different requirements for progress reports, the following all-purpose format always works.

> **Progress Report**
> Prepared by: [Name]
> Date:
>
> I. Subject: Identify the project and the schedule
> II. Background: Discuss previous work completed
> III. Present status
> A. Present work
>   1. Work completed (organized by task, or time, or both)
>   2. Work started but not complete
> B. Problems encountered
>   1. Problem definitions/explanations
>   2. Problem solutions found
>   3. Unresolved problems awaiting resolution
> IV. Work remaining (organized by task, or time, or both)
> A. Work planned next, plus time frame for completion
> V. Summary: Assessment of progress
> A. From start of project to now
> B. During the period covered by this status report
> C. From now through completion
> D. Overall evaluation of project and schedule

Like memos, progress reports may include attachments that offer additional documentation or verification.

Figure 8.6 reproduces a progress report.

REMEMBER AS YOU WRITE YOUR PROGRESS REPORTS:

- Your tone should be formal. These reports will be read by *your* managers and *their* managers.
- As in all forms of business writing, clarity is essential. Strive to keep your report as short as possible so that managers don't spend their time reading unnecessary details.

 **ABCo**

INTEROFFICE MEMORANDUM

To: Pat Drynan   From: James DeCarlo

Subject: June Progress Report   Date: July 1, 2002
         K-9820 User's Manual

In May, we completed the following steps per the project plan authorized in February:

1. Interviewed R & D (Hodges, Klein, Metzger, and Alvarez) to gather technical information on the K-9820.
2. Interviewed Marketing staff (Roberts, Bender) on projected sales, dealer training program, and customer characteristics.
3. Drafted a preliminary outline and graphics plan for the manual.
4. Developed a working version of the table of contents.

Current Activity

This month, we made final assignments to the writers and editors (see Table 1) and to the art department, and completed drafts of sections 2.1, 2.2, and 3.1. These are now in editing.

Work in progress includes first drafts of sections 3.2, 3.3, 4.2, and Appendix A. Also, photos of the main K-9820 subassemblies were taken and are in processing. Of the projected 13 schematic diagrams, we have been able to obtain sketches of only 7, which are being redrawn in the art dept.

The remaining six schematics have been delayed pending "design improvements" in R & D. I am attempting to determine the extent of these changes and to estimate the length of the delay.

Figure 8.6: Progress Report

Source: Maris Roze, *Technical Communication: The Practical Craft,* 3rd ed. (Upper Saddle River, NJ: Prentice Hall, 1997), p. 81.

- Honesty is crucial. You must report on your progress accurately. If you have made good progress, say so, but don't overstate the case. Likewise, don't underplay problems that could have serious negative consequences for the project. Managers need to have a realistic sense of what is happening on the project.

- Progress reports reflect strongly on you, so they should be expertly proofread and double-checked. They should be printed on good paper.

- Always hand in your progress reports on time.

Field Reports

If you work for a public utility or private business—say, a plumbing company or an electrical company—part of your job may involve driving to different locations to assess problems and find solutions. As part of your duties, you may be required to write *field reports* that summarize the different situations you encounter in different locations. Field reports help supervisors keep track of what their workers are doing in the field.

Unlike progress reports, which are quite a bit longer than most e-mail messages and memos, a field report is often a slip of paper with various blocks to be filled in. Brevity is the key to an effective field report. You should summarize the situation as simply and clearly as possible.

What might a sample field report look like? Consider the following situation:

Frank Cilento works for a power company. One stormy night, a power outage is reported in the 5700 block of LaGrange Street, and Frank is sent to investigate.

North Carolina Gas and Electric

Description of Problem
Live wire down. Safety hazard for bystanders.

Action Taken to Correct Problem
Ordered bystanders inside. Turned power off. Called for repair crew.

Date: August 18, 2001   **Location:** 5700 block, LaGrange   **Technician:** FC

Figure 8.7:   Field Report

> When he arrives at the scene, he sees a group of people milling around a truck that has crashed into a utility pole. The driver appears to be in shock, and one bystander tells Frank that an ambulance has been summoned.
>
> The utility pole is listing, with a severed voltage line dangling from it. The line is flapping wildly in the street, sending showers of sparks and loud electrostatic cracks through the air.
>
> Frank orders all bystanders back into their houses, then uses his cell phone to call the police for backup. He then places a call back to headquarters asking to have all power turned off on the 5700 block of La-Grange. He also asks for a repair crew to get to LaGrange Street as quickly as possible.[8]

When the situation is under control, Frank needs to write a field report of this incident. The utility company's completed field report form is shown in Figure 8.7.

REMEMBER AS YOU WRITE FIELD REPORTS:

- Be as specific and concise as possible. Your job is to reduce the information to its essentials. However, do not omit any important details.
- Fill out all sections of the report.

Activity 8.5: Writing a Progress Report

Using the outline shown in Section 8.3 (page 270), prepare a brief progress report for the general manager of your company, Frank Torres. The information you need to write the report follows.

NAME OF PROJECT: Your company is building Cedarwood Townhomes, a residential community of 850 two- and three-bedroom condominiums on 50 acres of land in Statesboro, Georgia.

TIMETABLE AND DEADLINES: Your goal was to begin this project in January, 2001, and end by December 30, 2001. The project started on time on January 2, 2001.

Along the way, you were to meet several interim guidelines, as follows:

- Ten model units complete by February 15, 2001—successfully completed on February 13

---

[8]Adapted from Maris Roze, *Technical Communication: The Practical Craft,* 3rd ed. (Upper Saddle River, NJ/Columbus, OH: Prentice Hall, 1997), p. 74.

- Buildings A, B, and C complete by June 15, 2001—successfully completed, but one week late: June 22
- Landscaping for Buildings A, B, and C complete by August 15, 2001
- Buildings D, E, and F complete by October 15, 2001
- Buildings G, H, and I complete by November 30, 2001

PROGRESS THIS MONTH: Today's date is August 17, 2001. Your report will cover the period from July 15th to August 15th. A summary of the progress during this period:

- Landscaping for Buildings A, B, and C is not yet finished, but should be complete by August 23. The work is 90% complete, but the nursery that was to deliver arbor vitae bushes ran out of stock. The nursery has promised to deliver them to you by August 20th.
- Next main deadline is completion of Buildings D, E, and F. All buildings have been framed out and filled in, and all plumbing systems are in place. Work on finishing interiors is expected to be complete by October 1, and all roofing will be complete by October 15.
- Final deadline is November 30 for Buildings G, H, and I. Buildings G and H have been framed out, but you have run into problems with the soil for Building I. Soil analysis is being conducted; results are expected August 30th. Depending on results, engineers, architects, and designers may have to be consulted. You anticipate that Buildings G and H will be complete by the November 30 deadline, but that Building I could lag behind by as much as a month.

Activity 8.6: Writing Field Reports

Based on the following two scenarios, complete the field reports.

SCENARIO A: PLUMBING CONTRACTOR   Today is May 23, 2001. You have been called to the offices of Marine Bank in Fort Lauderdale, Florida. The company is encountering a problem with its plumbing. You find the toilet in the men's room overflowing, so you quickly plunge the toilet. After further exploration, you determine that one of the pipes leading from the toilet into the sewer system is seriously clogged. You apply chemicals to break up the clog, and you are successful. For these services, you bill the bank $175.

MID-STATE PLUMBING, INC.

Company and Location:

Description of Problem:

Action Taken to Correct Problem:

Date: **Plumber:**   **Fee:**

SCENARIO B: SMITH BROTHERS HEATING AND AIR CONDITIONING   You receive a call from a homeowner in Newark, New Jersey. Her central air conditioning unit is making a buzzing sound, and the air conditioning has stopped working. When you arrive at the house, you see that the unit outside is indeed buzzing. The unit appears to be on, but the fan is not turning. Clearly, a new motor is needed. You have the needed model in your truck and replace it. You then test the system, and everything is fine. Time spent on the call: two hours. Today's date: March 3, 2002.

SMITH BROTHERS HEATING AND AIR CONDITIONING
BELLEVILLE, NJ

Location of Call:

Description of Problem:

Action Taken to Fix Problem:

Hours spent on call: **Technician:**   **Date:**

8.4 PROOFREADING WHAT YOU'VE WRITTEN

As emphasized in this module and the last, it is essential that you *proofread* all memos and reports before submitting them. You should also proofread any forms you complete to ensure that they're filled out completely and accurately.

Proofreading involves a careful, line-by-line reading of what you've written. While this process may seem tedious, it is very rare for a writer to find no mistakes as he or she proofreads. Even if you catch only one error, the time it took you to proofread was well spent.

Here are some tips for proofreading your work.

WAIT BEFORE YOU PROOFREAD.   Writers are often a bit tired when they've just completed their report or memo. If they proofread it immediately, they are likely to miss some of their mistakes. When possible, wait until the next day to proofread. When waiting that long isn't possible, give yourself a break of at least 15 minutes before proofreading and finalizing your writing.

PROOFREAD IN A QUIET PLACE.   If you're distracted by noise, you won't be able to devote your full attention to the proofreading process.

WHEN WRITING ON COMPUTER, BE CAREFUL WITH SPELL CHECKERS AND GRAMMAR CHECKERS.   Most word processing systems allow you to run an automatic "spell check" or "grammar check" of your documents. While these functions are often helpful, they rarely catch everything. For example, spell checkers can't tell the difference between words that are spelled correctly but used improperly. "Their is two much light in this room" is incorrect, but the spell checker will not catch the errors because "their" and "two" are real words, and they are spelled correctly. Grammar checkers are also of limited use.

The bottom line: After running your spell check or grammar check, you still need to proofread with your own eyes.

ASK A FRIEND OR CO-WORKER TO PROOFREAD YOUR WORK.   Sometimes, a separate set of eyes will catch errors that you might not catch on your own. You can return the favor by helping your friend or co-worker proofread something later on! When relevant, give your proofreaders clear directions on what they should be looking for.

WHEN PROOFREADING, READ LINE BY LINE AND WORD BY WORD.   Proofreading is a painstaking task. You can't skip over anything, because the errors might be found in the material you decided to skip. Start at the very top of your document and read every word, one at a time, until you reach the end. This is the only way to ensure that you've checked your entire document. Another option is to read your document out loud or to read backwards, from last sentence to first. Both these techniques can help to catch errors.

ALWAYS DOUBLE-CHECK NUMBERS.   Throughout this book, we've emphasized the importance of accurate numbers. When proofreading, take the time to verify that all your numbers are 100% correct.

WHEN PROOFREADING FORMS, MAKE SURE YOUR HANDWRITING IS LEGIBLE.   Also, keep in mind that "legibility" applies to more than just handwriting. Ensure that all boxes are checked properly, and that you have indeed checked off the correct boxes. By checking the wrong box, you could turn yourself from a "Mr." into a "Mrs." instantly.

WATCH FOR COMMON PROOFREADING MISTAKES.   Some common mistakes can be avoided by asking yourself the following questions when you proofread:

- Are all dates, times, and days consistent and correct?
- Are the details regarding addresses and locations accurate?
- Are all personal names and company names spelled correctly?
- Are all decimal points in the right places?

Activity 8.7: Practicing Proofreading Skills

Document A on page 276 is completely accurate in every way. Document B on page 277 has 15 mistakes. Proofread Document B against Document A, making corrections so that B resembles A in every way.

DOCUMENT A: ACCURATE EXCERPT FROM A PROJECT MANUAL[9]

SECTION 16471
TELEPHONE SERVICE ENTRANCE

PART 1 GENERAL

1.01 SUMMARY

    A. This section covers the work necessary to provide and install a complete raceway system for the building telephone system. The system shall include telephone service entrance raceway, equipment and terminal backboards and empty 3/4 inch conduits to telephone outlets.

1.02 RELATED SECTIONS OF THE PROJECT MANUAL

    A. <u>Section No.</u>   <u>Item</u>

Section No.	Item
09900	Painting and Staining
16111	Conduit
16130	Boxes
16195	Electrical Identification

1.03 QUALITY ASSURANCE

    A. Telephone Utility Company: Southwestern Bell Telephone Company

    B. Install work in accordance with Telephone Utility Company's rules and regulations.

PART 2 PRODUCTS

2.01 TELEPHONE TERMINATION BACKBOARD

    A. Material: Plywood.

PART 3 EXECUTION

    B. Size: 4 × 8 feet, 3/4 inch thick.

3.01 EXAMINATION

    A. Verify that surfaces are ready to receive work.

    B. Verify that field measurements are as shown on the Drawings.

    C. Beginning of installation means installer accepts existing conditions.

3.02 INSTALLATION

    A. Finish paint termination backboard with durable enamel under the provisions of Section 09900 prior to installation of telephone equipment. Color to match wall.

    B. Install termination backboards plumb, and attach securely at each corner. Install cabinet trim plumb.

    C. Install galvanized pull wire in each empty telephone conduit containing a bend of over 10 feet in length.

    D. Mark all backboards and cabinets with the legend "TELEPHONE" under the provisions of Section 16195, ELECTRICAL IDENTIFICATION.

END OF SECTION 16471 - TELEPHONE SERVICE ENTRANCE

[9]Courtesy Nabholz Construction Corp., Conway, AR.

DOCUMENT B: INACCURATE EXCERPT FROM A PROJECT MANUAL
There are 15 errors that must be fixed.

SECTION 16741
TELEPHONE SERVICE ENTRANCE

PART 1 GENERAL

1.00 SUMMARY

   A. This section covers the work necessary to provide and install a complete pathway system for the building telephone system. The system shall include telephone service entrance raceway, equipment and terminal backboards and empty 3/8 inch conduits to telephone outlets.

1.02 RELATED SECTIONS OF THE PROJECT MANUAL

   A. <u>Section No.</u>   <u>Item</u>

Section No.	Item
09900	Painting and Staining
16111	Conduct
16130	Boxes
16159	Electrical Identification

1.03 QUALITY ASSURANCE

   A. Telephone Utility Company: Northeastern Bell Telephone Company

   B. Install work in accordance with Telephone Utility Company's rules and regulations.

PART 2 PRODUCTS

2.01 TELEPHONE TERMINATION BACKBOARD

   A. Material: Plywood.

   B. Size: 4 × 6 feet, 3/4 inch thick.

PART 3 EXECUTION

3.01 EXAMINATION

   A. Verify that surfaces are read to receive work.

   B. Verify that field measurements are as shown on the Drawings.

   C. Beginning of installation means installer excepts existing conditions.

3.02 INSTALLATION

   A. Finish paint termination backboard with durable enamel under the provisions of Section 09090 prior to installation of telephone equipment. Color to match wall.

   B. Install termination blackboards plumb, and attach securely at each corner. Install cabinet trim plumb.

   C. Install pull wire in each empty telephone conduit containing a bend of over 10 feet in length.

   D. Mark all backboards and cabinets with the legend "TELEPHONE" under the provisions of Section 16195, ELECTRICAL.

END OF SECTION 6741 - TELEPHONE SERVICE ENTRANCE

8.5 Tips on Writing with a Computer

Just as computers have made drafting blueprints—and many other construction-related jobs—so much easier, they have also greatly simplified the writing and editing process. Using a word processing program (such as WordPerfect or Microsoft Word) to write your memos and reports can greatly facilitate the process. With a word processor, you can:

- Quickly fix typographical errors
- Cut and paste material into different parts of the document
- Move sections of your document around
- Use different typefaces and features (such as bullets) to make your documents visually appealing
- Check your spelling (but see the warning in Section 8.4)
- Add photos, graphics, and illustrations to your documents

If you haven't used a word processing program before, or if you're a little uncomfortable with this method of writing, here are some tips to help you get started.

SAVE YOUR WORK FREQUENTLY.   Computers are subject to power outages and occasional "crashes" (in which the machine freezes up). Saving your work every few minutes will ensure that you don't lose anything you've worked hard on. In fact, most word processors have an "auto save" feature that will automatically save your work at the interval you set.

USE THE HELP FUNCTION.   Almost all computer programs have a "Help" option on their menu bar. If you can't figure out what to do, the "Help" function can be very useful.

DON'T OVERDO THE TYPEFACES.   Because word processing programs have so many interesting typeface options, it's tempting to use as many of them as possible. However, too many changes in typefaces (also called *fonts*) can be distracting to your reader. Try to use no more than two or three typefaces in one document. Also, don't overuse italics and boldface, which work best when used sparingly.

REMEMBER THAT YOUR E-MAIL PROGRAM HAS MANY OF THE SAME FEATURES AS YOUR WORD PROCESSOR.   This means that you can also use spell checks, different fonts, and cutting and pasting features to make your e-mails professional and clear.

PRACTICE, PRACTICE, PRACTICE.   If you're using a word processing program for the first time, it may take a while to get used to all the options, buttons, and icons. Never fear: The more you write, the easier it will get. Within a couple of weeks, you'll be a computer pro.

Activity 8.8: Writing with a Computer

Take this short quiz to sharpen your understanding of the "do's and don'ts" of writing on a computer. Mark T if the statement is true, F if it is false.

_____   1. If you have a question about your word processing program, you can probably find the answer in the HELP menu.

_____   2. E-mail programs offer many of the same features as word processing programs.

_____ 3. Automated spell checkers on word processing programs can be counted on to find all errors.

_____ 4. The more boldface you use in a document, the better.

_____ 5. If you use a computerized grammar checker to double-check your writing, you won't have to worry about learning the basic rules of grammar.

_____ 6. A "crash" is another name for a word processor's auto-save feature.

_____ 7. When writing on computer, it's a good idea to save your work every few minutes.

_____ 8. Most word processing programs can be mastered in a single sitting.

_____ 9. Word processors allow you to format documents with bulleted lists and numbered lists.

_____ 10. A font and a typeface are the same thing.

8.6 TIPS ON SPELLING, GRAMMAR, AND PUNCTUATION

To write effectively, you don't need to be an expert on the English language. Rather, you just need to know some basic rules. Because most writing errors are the result of common mistakes, this section focuses on the most common errors and how to avoid them.

Spelling

Spelling errors usually fall into two categories: (1) misspelled words, and (2) confusion between sound-alike words.

Table 8.1 (page 280) lists the correct spellings of commonly misspelled English words. Table 8.2 (page 281) lists the differences between sound-alike words. Study these tables to improve your spelling abilities.

Table 8.3 (page 282) shows words or forms that are not correct or not acceptable in formal written English. Use the correct form as shown in Table 8.3, instead.

Grammar and Punctuation

Many people think grammar and punctuation are boring and tiresome. But good grammar is essential to effective writing. Grammatical errors are distracting, and in a formal report they reflect poorly on you.

The following pages offer some tips on the basics of grammar and punctuation. For more information, consult any grammar handbook. These handbooks are widely available in bookstores for about $10.

CAPITAL LETTERS

- Capitalize the first word of a sentence and the first word of a quotation within a sentence. _I said to my foreman, "Have you seen the bill of materials?"_
- Capitalize proper names. _John and Henry are brothers._
- Capitalize titles if they are accompanied by a specific name, but do not capitalize generic titles. _I went to see Dr. Brown on Friday. My sister is a doctor._
- Capitalize the days of the week and the months of the year. _I work Monday through Saturday, January through December. I take a vacation in July._

TABLE 8.1   Correct Spellings of Commonly Misspelled Words

absence	decision	friend	muscle	quantity
accidentally	definite	fulfill	necessary	questionnaire
accommodate	description	grammar	neighbor	receive
acknowledge	desperate	guarantee	neither	recognize
acquaintance	develop	guidance	ninety	recommend
acquire	disappear	height	ninth	repetition
across	disappoint	hindrance	nucleus	rhythm
address	discipline	hoping	occasion	ridiculous
against	dissatisfied	hypocrisy	occurred	sacrifice
all right	doesn't	immediately	omission	schedule
amateur	easily	independent	opinion	scissors
analysis	efficiency	indispensable	opportunity	secretary
apparent	eighth	intelligence	paid	seize
approximately	eligible	irrelevant	parallel	sensible
argue	embarrass	irresistible	particularly	separate
article	environment	knowledge	perform	significance
auxiliary	equipment	library	permanent	similar
basically	erroneous	license	permissible	sincerely
believe	especially	literature	persistent	statistics
benefit	exaggerate	maintenance	personally	strength
breathe	excellent	management	persuade	succeed
business	except	maneuver	practically	supposed to
category	exercise	marital	preferred	suppression
committee	existence	marriage	prejudice	surprise
competent	fascinating	mathematics	prevalent	therefore
courteous	February	meant	privilege	thought
criticism	finally	medicine	probably	through
criticize	foreign	mileage	procedure	truly
curiosity	fortunately	mischievous	proceed	usually
deceive	forty	misspell	psychology	used to
				vacuum
				valuable
				Wednesday
				weird

- Capitalize the names of races, nationalities, religions, and languages. *Many people in Spain are Catholics; many Israelis are Jewish; and many people who speak French are Protestants.*
- Capitalize holidays and historic events. *The Fourth of July celebrates the founding of our country. My grandfather fought in the Vietnam War.*
- Capitalize the names of specific places and school subjects. Don't capitalize general directions, general places, or general subjects. *I took Masonry 101 and Mathematics 202. I live on Fourteenth Street, just south of the highway. My favorite subjects were art and history.*

TABLE 8.2   Commonly Confused Words

accept/except	• To *accept* is to receive. *"I accept your compliment. Thank you."* • *Except* means excluding. *"Everyone is a good worker, except Rich."*
advice/advise	• You get or give *advice*. *"Thank you for the good advice."* • *Advise* means "to give advice to." *"I advise you not to be late for work again."*
affect/effect	• *Affect* is a verb. It means *to influence*. *"How does the vacation policy affect you?"* • An *effect* is a result. *"The effect of the strike has been disastrous for the workers."*
among/between	• Use *among* for groups of three or more. *"How can I choose my favorite among all my friends?"* • Use *between* for groups of two. *"I can't decide between the screwdriver and the pliers."*
dessert/desert	• *Dessert* comes after dinner. *"Would you like ice cream for dessert?"* • The *desert* is the arid, sandy environment. *"We were caught in the Gobi Desert with no water."*
eminent/ imminent	• *Eminent* means distinguished. *"She is an eminent surgeon."* • *Imminent* means about to happen. *"The snow is imminent."*
imply/infer	• *Imply* means to suggest. *"Are you implying that I'm lazy?"* • *Infer* means to extract an implied meaning from a statement. *"From your statement, I am inferring your belief that I'm lazy."*
it's/its	• *It's* means *it is*. *"It's about time you showed up for work."* • *Its* is the possessive form of *it*. *"The dog wandered around, looking for its bone."*
lose/loose	• To *lose* something is to misplace it. *"I fear I may lose my T-square."* • *Loose* means not tight. *"This hard hat is too loose."*
passed/past	• *Passed* is the past tense of pass. *"I passed the exit on the interstate."* • Use *past* to describe time or place. *"I drove past the exit off Route 95."*
principal/ principle	• A *principal* is the head of a school, or it can refer to money. *"The principal of Wilson School had quite a bit of principal in the bank."* • A *principle* is a rule or truism. *"The same principles of safety apply on every job site."*
right/write	• *Right* means correct. *"Do you have the right measurements?"* • *Write* means to take pencil to paper. *"Did you write your progress report yet?"*
site/sight/cite	• A *site* refers to a place. *"This is our new job site."* • *Sight* is one of the five senses. *"He has a keen sense of sight."* • To *cite* something is to refer to it. *"She always cites the OSHA regulations during her safety inspections."*
than/then	• *Than* is used for comparison. *"Jane works harder than Joan."* • *Then* refers to time. *"First, we worked. Then, we broke for lunch."*
there/their/ they're	• *There* refers to a place, or is used as part of the phrase *there is/there are*. *"There are many new construction projects in Monroe County. We hope to work there."* • *Their* is the possessive form of *they*. *"Their work is exceptionally good."* • *They're* means *they are*. *"They're two excellent masons."*
threw/through	• *Threw* is the past tense of *throw*. *"Did you see the way he threw the ball?"* • *Through* means *by way of*. *"He drove through town on the way to the construction site."*
to/too/two	• *To* is a preposition used in phrases. *"Would you like to go to the store?"* • *Too* means *also*. *"Let's bring along the carpenters, too."* • *Two* is the number 2. *"There are two electricians on the job."*
weather/ whether	• *Weather* is the state of the atmosphere. *"The weather forecast calls for rain."* • *Whether* means if. *"We'll work today, whether it rains or not."*
who's/whose	• *Who's* means *who is*. *"Who's that reading the blueprints?"* • *Whose* is the possessive form of *who*. *"I thanked Jack, whose jacket I had borrowed."*
you're/your	• *You're* means *you are*. *"You're one of the best workers on the team."* • *Your* is the possessive of you. *"Do you have your hard hat with you?"*

TABLE 8.3   Incorrect and Correct Usage

Incorrect	Correct	Incorrect	Correct
ain't	is not/are not	off of	off
alot	a lot	supposably	supposedly
alright	all right	suppose to	supposed to
anyways	anyway	theirselves	themselves
could of	could have	thru	through
everywheres	everywhere	thusly	thus
hisself	himself	use to	used to
irregardless	regardless	would of	would have

COLONS [:]

- Use a colon to introduce a list. *The following workers are particularly good: Frank Reed, Tamara Lizst, Jose Garcia, and Isaiah Washington.*
- Use a colon after the greeting in a business letter. *Dear Sirs:*
- Do not use a colon after *is* or *are*. *Three variations on blue are navy blue, sky blue, and royal blue.*

COMMAS [,]

- Use a comma before an introductory phrase. *As I've said before, it's very important to be on time for work.*
- Use a comma before a linking word such as *and, but, or* if there is a full sentence before and after the linking word. *I work for Fred McElwee, and I find him to be an excellent foreman.*
- Use a comma to separate items in a series. Use a comma before the final element in the series. *The American flag is red, white, and blue.*[10]
- Use a comma between city and state. *I live in Chicago, Illinois.* If a zip code follows the state, do not use a comma between the state and the zip code. *I live in Boston, Massachusetts 02118.*
- Use a comma between the day and the year in a specific date. *I was born on January 17, 1966.*
- Avoid unnecessary commas. Do not use a comma in a very short introductory phrase. *In September I begin my apprenticeship.* Do not use a comma to separate the subject from the verb.

  Incorrect: I really think that, I should take a refresher course in computers.
  Correct: I really think that I should take a refresher course in computers.

- Do not connect complete sentences with a comma. This incorrect usage of the comma is called a *comma splice.* Incorrect: *I live in Washington, my sister lives in Oregon.* Use a semicolon instead. Correct: *I live in Washington; my sister lives in Oregon.*
- In general, place commas inside quotation marks. *"That is a beautiful house," I said.*

EXCLAMATION POINTS [!] AND QUESTION MARKS [?]

Use a question mark to indicate a question, and an exclamation point to indicate a particularly strong statement.

---

[10]Some experts recommend omitting the comma before the final item in the series. However, you can't go wrong by adding a comma here.

What do you mean by that?

I have never seen such behavior!

In general, place question marks and exclamation points inside quotation marks.

"How are you?" my cousin asked.

The client said, "You have done a fabulous job!"

Never use more than one exclamation point or question mark in a sentence.

Incorrect: Can you believe that????
Correct: Can you believe that?

Incorrect: We're number one!!!!
Correct: We're number one!

SEMICOLONS [;]

- Use a semicolon to join two sentences that are not joined by a connecting word such as *and, but, or. I enjoy working for Sandra Petty; she is a good and fair boss.*
- Use a semicolon for clarity when too many commas might interfere with comprehension. *My company has offices in Juneau, Alaska; Honolulu, Hawaii; Austin, Texas; Salt Lake City, Utah; and San Francisco, California.*

SENTENCE FRAGMENTS

Always write in complete sentences. A *fragment* is a collection of words that doesn't express a complete thought.

Incorrect: I went to the shore. In July.
Correct: I went to the shore in July. ("In July" is a fragment. It doesn't express a complete thought.)

Incorrect: The foreman fired Marty. Which he deserved.
Correct: The foreman fired Marty, which he deserved.

Incorrect: Ate a huge amount of food.
Correct: The children ate a huge amount of food.

Activity 8.9: Correcting Commonly Misspelled Words

In each of the following sentences, circle the correct spelling of the word in parentheses.

1. We should be able to (accommodate, acommodate) your request.

2. Please have the lumber delivered to the site by (Wendsday, Wednesday).

3. Be sure the circuits are kept (parallel, parrallel).

4. That is a serious (ommission, omission) from the specs.

5. I (reccommend, recommend) that we hire the foreman from JLS Construction.

6. Joe just got his plumber's (license, liscence).

7. To (suceed, succeed) in the construction business, you need excellent communication skills.

8. There are two (separate, seperate) manuals for this project.

9. If we don't finish this job by Friday, the homeowner is going to be very (dissapointed, disappointed).

10. Good workers are (niether, neither) lazy nor dishonest.

11. That old truck has a lot of (mileage, milage) on it.

12. A serious accident (occurred, ocurred) when the crane malfunctioned.

13. I've known her (practically, practicly) my whole life.

14. Wearing jewelry is not (permissible, permissable) on the job.

15. I'm not going to meet this deadline. (Therefore, Therefor), I need to let the foreman know.

16. I'll be 25 years old in (Febuary, February).

17. The owner asked if we could speed up the (schedule, scedule).

18. There is some extremely heavy (equiptment, equipment) on the site.

19. The materials haven't shown up, and we're getting (desperate, desparate).

20. I like to work with a team, but Joe prefers to work (independantly, independently).

Activity 8.10: Distinguishing Between Commonly Confused Words

In each of the following sentences, circle the correct phrase in parentheses.

1. The construction (sight, site) is located in Mobile, Alabama.

2. The black clouds told me that a thunderstorm was (eminent, imminent).

3. Good housekeeping is a basic (principle, principal) of a well-run construction site.

4. (It's, Its) too early to tell whether the subcontractor is going to make the deadline.

5. The wiring in that house is way too (loose, lose).

6. When I was traveling on the highway, I (past, passed) the town I used to work in.

7. Mark works every day (accept, except) Sunday.

8. (Their, There) isn't much work left to do on this job.

9. The foreman said, "Mike, I think (you're, your) the man for the job."

10. The workers couldn't find (their, there, they're) tools.

11. I suggested that he talk to the foreman, but he wouldn't follow my (advise, advice).

12. I can't decide (among, between) copper, steel, or aluminum for this job.

13. The (affect, effect) of all the rain was a serious delay in the schedule.

14. I have more (than, then) 20 years with this company.

15. From her statement, I (inferred, implied) that there would be layoffs.

16. After lunch, I decided to have some chocolate cake for (desert, dessert).

17. Our company (accepted, excepted) the lowest bid for the job.

18. (Who's, Whose) ruler is this?

19. We need to run that piping directly (thru, through, threw) the center of the structure.

20. I'm not sure where the supplies are, but I think (there, their, they're) in the office.

Activity 8.11: Practicing Proper Usage

In each of the following sentences, circle the correct phrase in parentheses.

1. I could see (alot, a lot) of people gathering on the street.

2. If she had known about the concert, she definitely (would have, would of) attended.

3. Marcy was (supposably, supposedly) out sick, but someone saw her in the mall.

4. When Walt fell off the ladder, I asked him if he was (alright, all right).

5. I didn't really like that brand of concrete (anyway, anyways).

6. Mike always showed up for work, (regardless, irregardless) of the weather.

7. The tool works much better if you hold it (thus, thusly).

8. We are (suppose to, supposed to) have this job done by the end of next week.

9. John saw a reflection of (hisself, himself) in the mirror.

10. Amazingly, the cat didn't hurt itself when it jumped (off, off of) the roof.

Activity 8.12: Practicing Grammar Skills: Capital Letters

In each of the following sentences, correct the capitalization errors. There may be more than one error per sentence. In some cases, lowercase letters should become capital letters, and in other cases capital letters should become lowercase letters. If the sentence is correct as it is, place a "C" on the line that precedes it.

_____ 1. My favorite co-workers are Sally, bill, and terry.

_____ 2. I just read a book about the civil war in america. That was the War that ended Slavery in the united states.

_____ 3. Three of the people on my team were born in September.

_____ 4. This year, the company is giving everyone a week's vacation between Christmas and new year's day.

_____ 5. I go to a catholic church, but my neighbors attend the baptist church in the next town.

_____ 6. The address of the new construction site is 1440 Paddington Lane, Mahwah, NJ.

_____ 7. The foreman asked, "has anyone seen the blueprints?"

_____ 8. My favorite subject was always Math, because I was never any good at english.

_____ 9. In all jobs, it pays to be bilingual. If you work in texas, it helps to speak spanish.

_____ 10. After I hurt my back on the job, I went to see a Doctor.

Activity 8.13: Practicing Grammar Skills: Colons and Commas

SET A: COLONS

In each of the following sentences, correct the colon errors. There may be more than one error per sentence. In some cases, a colon may need to be added, and in other cases a colon may need to be deleted. If the sentence is correct as it is, place a "C" on the line that precedes it.

_____ 1. My favorite months are: May, October, and November.

_____ 2. I would recommend the following course of action Send in a letter of inquiry, then call to ask for an interview.

_____ 3. We offer sand in six colors: natural, yellow, brown, blue, green, and red.

_____ 4. What I can't decide is: whether or not to ask for a promotion.

_____ 5. These are the best workers on my team Mary Washington, Karl Jeffries, and Tony Gold.

SET B: COMMAS

In each of the following sentences, correct the comma errors. There may be more than one error per sentence. In some cases, a comma may need to be added, and in other cases a comma may need to be deleted. If the sentence is correct as it is, place a "C" on the line that precedes it.

_____ 1. It seems to me that, everyone deserves a second chance.

_____ 2. The deadline is May 15 2002.

_____ 3. I would rather work in Florida, than in Georgia.

_____ 4. I'd like to bid on the government project, the mall project, and the housing development project.

_____ 5. She lives at 3890 Tamara Lane, Woodcliff Lake, IL 60077.

_____ 6. As noted in my letter of June 17 your bill is three months overdue.

_____ 7. I really enjoy working as a carpenter but I also enjoy the masonry aspect of construction.

_____ 8. Would you ask Oliver Beth and Lily to meet with us at four o'clock?

_____ 9. Alyce has never missed a day of work, and as a result she got promoted.

_____ 10. October 30, 2001 is a day I will never forget.

Activity 8.14: Practicing Grammar Skills: Exclamation Points, Question Marks, and Semicolons

In each of the following sentences, correct the errors. There may be more than one error per sentence. You will be looking for errors in exclamation points, question marks, and/or semicolons. If the sentence is correct as it is, place a "C" on the line that precedes it.

_____ 1. How many people plan to attend the picnic?

_____ 2. Frank asked for volunteers to attend the convention, Zeke and Josh raised their hands.

_____ 3. I didn't expect him to do something like that!!!

_____ 4. This year Christmas falls on a Sunday, and that's the day I leave for New Orleans.

_____ 5. Do you think we have enough money in the budget to purchase new tool belts for the staff.

_____ 6. The tower came crashing down, I ran as fast as my legs could carry me.

_____ 7. There are 14 million people in New York City. Isn't that amazing????

_____ 8. Tom is a rapid talker and a slow worker, Jim is a slow talker and a rapid worker.

_____ 9. You expect me to pay fifty dollars for a pair of shoelaces? That's ridiculous!

_____ 10. Are you free to work overtime on Friday night.

Activity 8.15: Correcting Sentence Fragments

On the lines below, indicate whether each group of words is a sentence (S) or contains a fragment (F). If the words form a fragment, complete the thought to form a full sentence.

_____ 1. The sun rose at 10 A.M.

_____ 2. On the way to work, seeing the fire engine racing through the streets.

_____ 3. Please come to my office. On Friday.

_____ 4. I finally bought a new pipe wrench. Which I desperately needed.

_____ 5. The truck came to a dead stop.

_____ 6. Falling to the ground.

_____ 7. Life goes on.

_____ 8. I saw the foreman. Jack.

_____ 9. Ted called in sick three times last month. On the 8th, the 12th, and the 17th.

_____ 10. Check to see if the power has been shut off, please.

Working with Technology

> 66 What do you mean we don't communicate? Just yesterday I faxed you a reply to the recorded message you left on my answering machine. 99
>
> —*The Wall Street Journal*

With each passing year, technology becomes a more vital part of the construction industry. Jobs that used to take days or weeks to complete, such as drafting blueprints, can now be accomplished much more quickly and accurately with computers and computer-enhanced equipment.

Throughout this text, we offered suggestions for making the most of today's technology. In Section 6.1.5, we saw how to read Web pages, for example. And in Sections 2.5.1 and 4.4.3, we examined proper and courteous use of cell phones on the job. This appendix offers some additional tips on working with technology.

A.1 TECHNOLOGY: THE DRIVING FORCE BEHIND CHANGE

Technology is the most important force driving change in the construction industry today. Advanced computer-aided design and drafting tools allow more sophisticated and refined types of construction, while financial reporting and management programs help owners and managers keep a tight rein on a project's profitability.

It would be impossible in this appendix to outline every type of technology used in the construction trades. Rather, it is more helpful to offer some suggestions on how to make technology work for you.

- **Embrace technology.** Technology is all around you, and its role will only become more significant. When confronted with change, it may be tempting to think, "Oh, but I like doing things the old way. . . . I'm comfortable with the old systems." Avoid that temptation. Be open to new technology and what it can do for you.

- **Keep learning.** The more you know about technology, the more valuable you will be. So take advantage of any and all technology training opportunities that come your way. If the boss needs someone to learn a new process or how to operate a new computer program, volunteer. Take classes at local community schools and read trade magazines to stay in touch with advances in your field. If possible, attend local conventions, where new computerized systems and equipment are often demonstrated.

- **Be patient.** Getting used to a new way of doing things—especially when the old way was so comfortable—may take some getting used to. Remain patient. Look forward to long-term benefits.

- **Understand technology's support role.** Workers sometimes feel threatened by technology. They think that it will take their jobs and put them out of work. While this has happened in the case of some extremely repetitive jobs on assembly lines, it will never happen in construction. Technology is never a substitute for a team of skilled tradespeople. Instead, technology exists solely to help construction professionals do a better job.

- **Discuss, discuss, discuss.** There's no better way to determine which technology will work best for you than to discuss the latest developments with friends and co-workers. Technology and computer-related discussions should become common topics of conversation. The same way you'd ask around about a particular type of car or truck before purchasing it, you can learn much about new technology by talking to the people who have developed or worked with it.

A.2 PERSONAL DIGITAL ASSISTANTS (PDAs)

An increasingly common device on construction sites is the *personal digital assistant* or PDA. Much smaller than a laptop computer, the PDA is a miraculous little machine. By utilizing the benefits of wireless technology, PDAs can allow users to:

- Connect to the Internet
- Access and answer e-mail
- Take electronic notes
- Store databases of personal contacts, with phone numbers and other contact information
- Transmit information or programs from PDA to PDA, with no physical connections
- Keep track of appointments
- Access huge documents (such as regulations and specifications)

This list includes just a small sample of the tasks a PDA can handle. PDA technology is developing quite rapidly, and more new features are becoming available almost daily. Though PDAs are not yet common on the job site, they are likely to become more common as the technology continues to develop.

If you use a PDA, keep the following tips in mind:

- *Keep the battery freshly charged.* PDAs are electronic devices that need a source of power—in this case, batteries. If you want your PDA always ready when you need it, be sure to replace or charge the batteries regularly.
- *Keep the PDA in a safe place.* PDAs are still fairly expensive. Because they're compact and portable, they're easy targets for theft. Keep your PDA close to you, and lock it up when it's not in use. Be especially careful with it in public places, such as airports and restaurants.
- *Don't tune the world out when using your PDA on a construction site.* Computers and PDAs can be almost hypnotic—when we're working on them, it's easy to tune out the world. But on a construction site, for safety purposes you must always be aware of your surroundings.
- *Use the PDA's security features.* PDAs have a security function that allows you to block others from accessing your information. Always use these features, and don't share your access passwords with anyone.
- *Back up your information.* Most PDAs allow you to save their contents externally—that is, in a different location. It is a good idea to save all your PDA files externally and to back them up occasionally. This way, you're covered if your PDA is damaged, misplaced, or stolen.

A.3 FAX MACHINES

A fax (short for *facsimile*) machine can now be found in just about every office in America. This technology has become so popular and affordable that many people even have fax machines in their homes.

Some quick tips on using fax machines:

- *Don't send more pages than necessary.* Long faxes clog up the receiver's fax machine and increase the sender's phone bill. Before sending a very long fax, ask yourself if overnight delivery via an express mail service (such as UPS or FedEx) would be more effective.

- *Include a cover sheet or sticker.* The cover sheet or sticker should include the sender's name, the sender's phone number and/or e-mail address, the date, the subject, and the number of pages in the fax (including the cover memo).

- *After you've sent a fax, call the receiver.* Sometimes faxes can go unclaimed for days because people don't know a fax is waiting. So call the receiver to let her know that you've sent one.

- *Be aware of readability issues.* A faxed document is always more difficult to read than the original. Even the best fax machines make the letters slightly fuzzier than the original. This can be a big problem if the correspondence uses small typefaces or includes many numbers. Again, the U.S. mail (or e-mail) may be the better way to go.

- *Check to make sure the fax has gone through.* Most faxes print out a confirmation report once the fax has gone through. Check the printout to make sure that your fax has been received. If it hasn't, resend it.

A.4 A FINAL WORD ON COMPUTERS

When used properly, computers can make your job incredibly easy. Here are just a few final tips for working with computers on the job.

- *Keep business computers strictly business-oriented.* Don't send personal e-mail from your business e-mail address, and don't load games onto your work computer. Most companies have policies that allow managers to read your e-mail at any time, with or without your knowledge or permission.

- *Keep your files organized and backed up.* Periodically, review what's on your computer and get rid of the files or programs you don't need. Back up all your most important work at least once an hour and at the end of each day. Many people use computer "autosave" programs to save their work every five minutes. Anyone who has ever experienced a power blip knows the value of a good autosave program!

- *Use the "Help" function.* Most computer programs have a "Help" function that can help you answer any questions you may have. The "Help" function can be a valuable resource for you, especially when you're first learning a program. Many software applications also have phone numbers for technical support, though it can be expensive and difficult to get through to these numbers.

- *When working on a computer, take breaks.* Staring at a computer screen too long, or typing for an extended period, can cause health problems. Every ten minutes or so, look away from the screen. You might even take a short walk. Make sure your keyboard, mouse, trackballs, and other peripherals are all comfortably within reach while you work. Sit at a height and angle that are comfortable for you.

Managing Your Construction Career

Whether you're looking for your first construction job, seeking a promotion, or looking to work for a new company, it pays to have some career-management skills under your belt. In Modules 1–8, we focused on the four key communication skills: listening, speaking, reading, and writing. The materials in this appendix are a natural extension of those four activities.

It's true that most construction professionals are hired because they have the technical know-how to get the job done. But technical expertise is only one side of the coin. The other side of that coin is the worker's self-presentation, attitude, and communication skills. The people who get the best jobs—and the people who are most often promoted—are those who present themselves most successfully during a job interview and who work the hardest once they get the job.

How can you get the job that's right for you? This appendix offers suggestions for the three key phases of the job search: compiling your résumé, writing a cover letter, and sitting for the interview. We close with some suggestions for ways to present yourself as a team player (and a candidate for promotion) once you've gotten the job.

B.1 COMPOSING A RÉSUMÉ

A *résumé* is a summary of your personal information, career goals, education and training, and job experience. Essentially, it is a one- or two-page snapshot that summarizes your entire working life.

In general, résumés are not required for entry-level construction jobs or apprenticeships. Rather, you will most likely be asked to fill out an application form (see Figure 7.5), and you'll then attend a series of interviews. When filling out the application form, be sure to follow the suggestions outlined in Section 7.7. To get through the interviews successfully, see Section B.3 below.

For higher-level supervisory or technical jobs, a résumé may be required. Figure B.1 shows a sample résumé for a construction professional. Note that the résumé contains several key sections. Follow this format exactly when compiling your résumé.[1]

1. **Personal information:** At the top of the résumé, include your full name and address. You may also include your day and evening phone numbers, as well as your e-mail address, cell phone number, fax number, or beeper number—anything that will help prospective employers reach you.

2. **Objective:** State the general type of job you are looking for, in two sentences or less. Include a reference to the personal and technical skills you possess that make you particularly well suited for the job.

3. **Education or training:** Summarize the training you received, including both your school-based education (high school, college) and your technical training. Outline the degrees or certificates you received and the years(s)

---

[1]There are many acceptable résumé formats. However, you can never go wrong by using the format shown in Figure B.1.

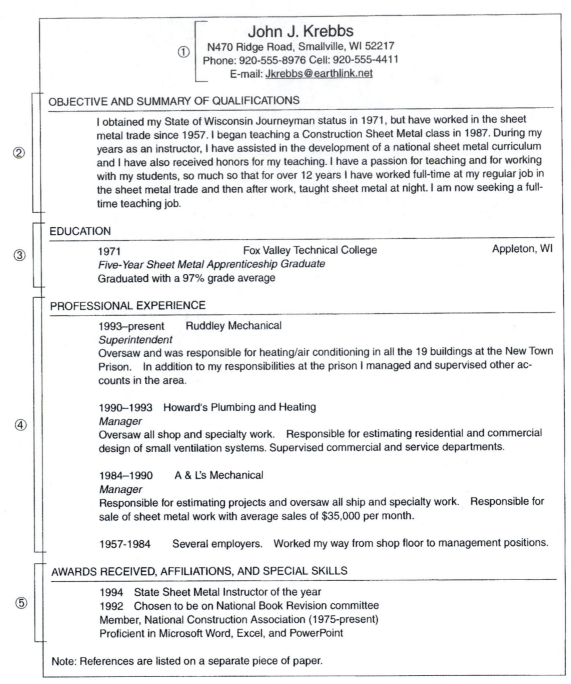

Figure B.1: Sample Résumé
Source: Courtesy of Wayne Belanger

you received them. Include dates of apprenticeship and other relevant information.

4. **Experience:** Use this section to impress your prospective employer with your work experience. Starting with your most recent job first, provide the name and location of the company you worked for, your job title, and a summary of your job responsibilities. Use active verbs such as "managed," "handled," "supervised," and so on to describe your job activities. Figure B.2 (on page 294) lists some additional action verbs. If you were promoted while on the job, be sure to say so. It is also appropriate (and desirable) to list military experience here. (Many employers are impressed by the teamwork training received by members of the military.)

accomplished	designed	maximized
achieved	drafted	operated
aided	earned	ordered
analyzed	excelled	painted
applied	handled	participated
assessed	helped	performed
assisted	implemented	rated
built	improved	received
calculated	maintained	recommended
contracted	managed	trained

Figure B.2: Action Verbs

5. **Awards, skills, licenses, and affiliations:** Summarize any awards or special training you have received or any skills that are particularly strong. For example, if you have operated specialized equipment or know the ins and outs of particular computer programs, list them here. Also list any licenses you hold, as well as memberships in professional associations. The more skills the employer sees, the more likely the company will be to hire you.

6. **References:** Your references are the people with whom or for whom you've worked in the past who can vouch for your excellence as an employee. Type a list of your references on a separate sheet of paper and provide the list to the interviewer upon his or her request. Your list should include at least four names. For each reference, provide the person's title, company, phone number, and e-mail address (if known). Be sure to ask your references for permission to list them.

When preparing and finalizing your résumé, keep the following suggestions in mind:

- Print the résumé on clean, heavy, durable bond paper. Fancy colors are nice but not necessary.
- Be sure that the résumé is free of inaccuracies and typographical errors. Never lie on a résumé.
- Proofread your résumé before finalizing it, or ask a friend to proofread for you.
- Résumés should say much in a small amount of space. No résumé should be longer than two pages.
- Résumés do not need to include hobbies, vital statistics (such as age and height/weight), or marital status.
- Remember that it is the résumé's job to sell you and your skills to prospective employers. If you've done things worth bragging about, list them proudly!

B.2 WRITING A COVER LETTER

Most of the time, résumés are sent through the mail and are accompanied by a cover letter. Even when sending a résumé through e-mail, a cover letter is appropriate.

The purpose of a *cover letter* is to introduce yourself and clearly state your interest in the job. For many people, the cover letter seems like a dull

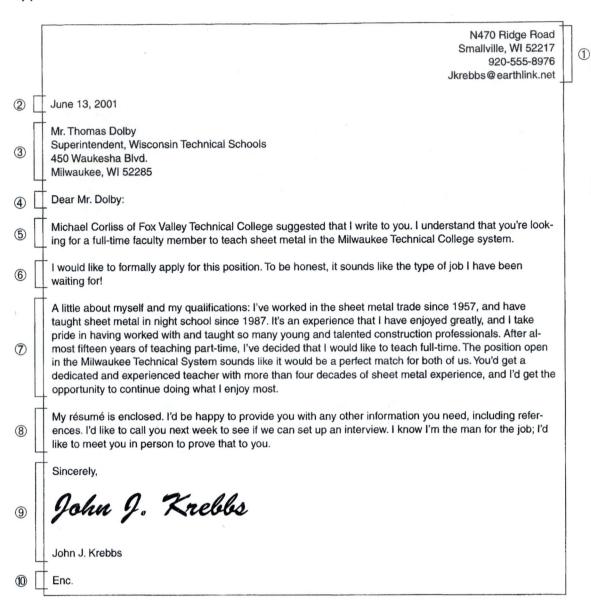

Figure B.3:   Sample Cover Letter

and useless item, merely a formality. But in reality, the cover letter is an excellent opportunity for you to make a positive first impression.

In general, a good cover letter has four paragraphs plus several additional elements. Figure B.3 provides an example of an effective cover letter. If you always follow this format, you can never go wrong!

Note the following elements in Figure B.3:

1. **Return address:** As on your résumé, include your key contact information: address, phone numbers, e-mail address, beeper number, and so on. Note that your name does *not* appear here.

2. **Date:** Use the date on which you plan to mail the letter.

3. **Inside address:** This is the person to whom you are applying for the job. Include his or her full name and title, as well as the street address. Call the company to make sure you are spelling the name right, getting the job title correct, and have the right address.

> **TIP:** Always direct the cover letter to a specific person. Addressing it to "Human Resources Department" or "Staffing Department" will not get it much attention.

4. **Greeting:** Use a formal greeting. The "Dear Mr. X:" or "Dear Ms. Y:" format is appropriate here. Do not use first names.

5. **Introductory paragraph:** Use this paragraph to introduce yourself and get the reader's attention. Say something that will interest the reader right from the start. Perhaps you can use the name of someone you both know. Or you might name an accomplishment you are particularly proud of.

6. **Interest paragraph:** Use the second paragraph to state your interest in the job, industry, or promotion. Be enthusiastic about the opportunity you're seeking.

7. **Summary paragraph:** Use the third paragraph to briefly summarize your qualifications. That is, provide a very quick overview of the material on your résumé. But do more than just list your experience and qualifications. Here is your chance to present yourself so positively that the reader feels that he simply must call you for an interview.

8. **Action paragraph:** End the letter by stating the action you will take to follow up on the cover letter. Will you call to set up an interview? Will you send an e-mail? Spell out clearly what action you will take.

9. **Complimentary close and signature.** "Sincerely" or "Sincerely yours" is most effective for a cover letter.

10. **Attachments:** Be sure to include a copy of your résumé with the cover letter.

    While preparing the cover letter, keep the following hints in mind:

- The best cover letters demonstrate what you can do for the company, not what the company should do for you.
- An error- and typo-free cover letter is as important as an error- and typo-free résumé. Print both documents on the same type of paper.
- A positive attitude and a sense of enthusiasm are essential in a good cover letter. However, do not exaggerate or stretch the truth.

B.3 INTERVIEWING SKILLS

Many people are terrified by interviews. They are fearful of making mistakes or saying the wrong thing. This is the wrong approach to take. Instead, you should consider the interview your chance to demonstrate your positive outlook, winning attitude, and technical skills.

The good news is: A company calls you for an interview only when it's interested in hiring you! So, just by getting called for the interview, you're halfway there. You can ace an interview by practicing beforehand and by following some simple suggestions.

> **TIP:** Be sure to bring plenty of copies of your résumé to the job interview. You may be asked to talk to several people, and you'll want to give a copy of your résumé to each.

Research the company. Interviewers are always impressed when interviewees know something about the company. It pays to do some research into the company and the successful projects it has completed. A little research will also yield excellent information about the personality of the person who's interviewing you.

Your research need not be formal. If the company has a Web site, visit it to see what the company is all about. You can also ask friends in the industry for information.

Be on time for the interview. In fact, try to arrive 5 to 10 minutes early, just to be on the safe side. If you're late, you're unlikely to get the job.

Be enthusiastic. Show how much you want the job. Emphasize your ability to work as part of a team. Smile. Describe your qualifications for the job with enthusiasm.

Be proud of your accomplishments. An old saying goes, "The only time it's OK to brag is at a job interview." List your accomplishments and explain why you're proud of them. If you can take the credit for any innovative solutions or creative ideas, talk about them in detail.

Be courteous. Shake hands when you meet the interviewer. Sit at attention—don't slouch. Listen to what the interviewer says. Don't interrupt. Let the interviewer finish her questions before you reply. Usually the interviewer will ask all the questions first, then ask if you have any questions. Wait your turn. It helps to prepare your questions the night before. Don't miss this opportunity to learn about the job—ask about the job's responsibilities, opportunities, and so on.

Be clear. Speak clearly. Use proper grammar.

Be clean and neat about your appearance. Your physical appearance makes a strong impression at a job interview. Get a good night's sleep before the interview and show up well groomed. It's always better to be overdressed than underdressed at an interview. If you're a man:

- Wear a long-sleeved shirt.
- Be well-groomed. If necessary, get a haircut before the interview.
- Be clean-shaven (or keep facial hair well trimmed).
- Don't have things dangling from your belt.
- Don't chew gum or tobacco.
- If you're a smoker, don't carry a pack of cigarettes in your shirt pocket.
- Wear a belt.
- Wear a watch.
- Coordinate your colors. If colors aren't your strong suit, ask someone for help.

Follow up. Send a thank-you note to the person who interviewed you and re-express your interest in the job. This will make an excellent impression. If you're not comfortable writing a note, call to thank the interviewer.

Ask for the job if you want it. If you think this is the job for you, don't be shy about asking for the job. It's appropriate to say, "I would love to work here, and I hope you'll give me the job."

Remember: At the interview, your goal is to impress not only with your technical skills and know-how, but also with your interpersonal and communication skills.

B.4 DEVELOPING YOUR CAREER

If you'd like to be a supervisor someday, you can do several things to help others see you as a future foreman. In fact, the following suggestions can help you be perceived as a valuable, hard-working team member no matter what your job or career aspirations. Think of the following as general tips for success in the construction industry.

Be willing to explore multiple facets of the business. Actively seek to learn about different areas of construction. Never turn down an opportunity to learn a new side of the business. For example, don't say, "I'm a carpenter. Why do I need to know about fuse boxes?" The more you know, the more you're worth. And the more you're worth, the more you get paid, and the more likely you are to get promoted.

Keep learning. Always look for ways to increase your knowledge, technical expertise, and abilities. Don't wait for training or learning opportunities to come to you. Rather, actively seek them out and make them happen.

Keep up with industry. It's an excellent idea to know what's going on in the world beyond your job. Reading industry magazines will give you insight into how other companies do things. (Many of these magazines offer free subscriptions. See Figure B.4 on page 300.) Also, most newspapers routinely carry stories about the construction industry in their business sections. Read these stories and discuss them with your co-workers. And, of course, there is a wealth of information at your disposal on the Internet.

Take on additional work. In every industry, one thing is true: The people who work the hardest and smartest are the people who get promoted. Be willing to work overtime and to go that extra mile when the boss asks you to. Volunteer to do the tasks that no one else wants to do. Your boss will thank you for it.

Join professional and trade associations. By joining professional and trade associations, you make contacts with other professionals in your specialty. These contacts can be valuable sources of information, resources, and job opportunities. There are dozens of trade associations in the United States, from the Aluminum Association (AA) to the Woven Wire Products Association (WWPA). Join any and all that are of interest to you.

Ask for the promotion. When you feel ready, talk to your supervisor about applying for a promotion. At that point, she'll tell you whether she thinks you're ready or not. If she thinks you need more experience before you can be promoted, ask her how you can improve your skills. Don't sulk if she says you need to wait a while before getting promoted. Remember, there are many qualified people who will want the job, so you'll need to prove yourself. This takes time. In the meantime, keep learning.

Best of luck in your construction career!

Publication	Address	Fee
Commercial Building	P.O. Box 1888, Cedar Rapids, IA 52406-1888	Free
Concrete Construction	The Aberdeen Group, P.O. Box 3246, Northbrook, IL 60065-9502	$24 per year
Engineering News Record (McGraw-Hill Construction Information Group)	P.O. Box 516, Hightstown, NJ 08520-9467	$74 per year; published weekly
Job-Site Supervisor	P.O. Box 31108, Raleigh, NC 27690-8260	$161 per year
Masonry Construction	The Aberdeen Group, P.O. Box 3245, Northbrook, IL 60065-9500	$30 per year

Web Sites:

Associated Builders and Contractors: *http://www.abc.org*

Associated General Contractors of America: *http://www.agc.org*

Contractor Magazine online: *http://www.contractormag.com*

Engineering News Record: *http://www.enr.com*

National Center for Construction Education and Research: *http://www.nccer.org*

Occupational Safety and Health Administration: *http://www.osha.gov*

Figure B.4:   Construction-Related Magazines and Web Sites

Glossary of Construction Terms

A

Acoustic materials Composition board installed on ceilings or walls for the purpose of reducing sound reflection (or echo); board is generally the same as that used for ordinary insulating purposes, or can be specially manufactured material for added acoustic capabilities; acoustical tile for ceilings is often perforated or fissured to increase the area of sound-absorbing surface; may be boards, batts, blocks, foam, spray-on, panel, sheets, pads, or tile materials.

Adhesive A natural or synthetic material, generally in paste or liquid form, used to fasten or glue material together, install floor tile, fabricate plastic laminate-covered work, or otherwise attach work items together.

Admixture A substance other than portland cement, water, and aggregates included in a concrete mixture, for the purpose of altering one or more properties of the concrete; aids setting, finishing, or wearing of the concrete.

Aggregate Hard, inert material, such as sand, gravel, and crushed stone, which is combined with portland cement and water to produce concrete; must be properly cleaned and well graded as required.

Angle (steel) A piece of rolled structural steel bent to form a 90-degree angle; may have equal or unequal legs; identified by the symbol "L".

Approved Term used to indicate acceptance of condition, material, system, or other work or procedure; reflects action by design professional or other authorized party, but does not relieve basic responsibility of party seeking such approval, as written in other binding documents and provisions.

Arch A curved structure that will support itself, and the weight of wall above the opening, by mutual pressure.

Asphalt A mineral pitch insoluble in water and used extensively in building materials for waterproofing, roof coverings, shingles, floor tile, paints, and paving.

Asphalt expansion joint material A composition strip of felt and asphalt material made to specified thickness and used to take up the expansion in concrete floor and sidewalks.

Asphalt roofing On a flat surface the roofing is composed of alternate layers of roofing felt and hot-applied asphalt (called built-up roof). Asphalt is the most widely used material for covering roofs because it possesses the characteristics needed for protection against weather and is easily applied, at a relatively inexpensive cost.

Asphalt shingles Composition roof shingles made from asphalt-impregnated felt covered with mineral granules, reinforced with strands of fiberglass; available in several weights.

Assemblies Portion of a building in combination; for example, a roof/ceiling assembly, or a ceiling/floor assembly, where different materials are combined, installed, and interfaced to form protectives and other aspects of construction for an entire building.

Attic The space/area between the roof and top ceiling of a building.

Source: Ralph Liebing, *The Construction Industry: Processes, Players, and Practices* (Upper Saddle River, NJ/Columbus, OH: Prentice Hall, 2001), pp. 189–200.

B

Backfill   Coarse earth or granular material used to fill in and build up the ground level around the foundation wall to provide a slope for drainage away from the foundation wall.

Backup   A material, usually not in view, which acts as a support, filler, or rigidity reinforcement for another material (example—concrete masonry units act as "backup" to face brick).

Balcony   A deck projecting from the wall of a building above ground or at floor level.

Ballast   A heavy material (usually gravel or stone) installed over a roof membrane to prevent wind uplift and to shield the membrane from sunlight and aid water evaporation.

Balloon framing   Name of a system of light-wood or house framing characterized by the studs extending in one piece from the foundation sill to the roof plate; not widely used because it requires applied fire blocking and a let-in ribbon for the second floor framing, and; utilizes long pieces of lumber, not readily available; also called Eastern framing.

Baluster(s)   Small vertical posts supporting a handrail; more commonly known as bannister spindles.

Bar   Small rolled or drawn steel shape, round, square or rectangular in cross section; a deformed steel shape used for reinforcing concrete.

Bar joists   Structural framing units made from bar- and rod-shaped steel and other lightweight members, for supporting moderate roof and floor loads; also known as open-web steel joists, or steel lumber.

Barrier-free design   Providing layout and design that affords accessible routes for all persons; meets requirements of ADA regulations and local codes.

Base   The bottom part of any unit on which the entire thing rests; can be a separate concrete pad under equipment; slang for "baseboard."

Baseboard   Interior wall trim at the floor line to cover the joint between wall and floor materials; strip of wood placed along the base of a wall or column to protect the finish from damage by shoes.

Base cabinet(s)   The lower, floor mounted cabinets that support the work- or countertop, in offices, laboratories, kitchens, or other work areas.

Base plate   A steel plate forming the bottom or base of a steel column; usually larger than the column to disperse the imposed load, to allow proper anchorage to the bearing surface.

Batt insulation   Flexible blanket-like roll of insulating material (usually faced or unfaced fiberglass) used for thermal or sound insulation by being installed between framing members in walls, floors, or ceilings.

Batten   Narrow strip of wood or other material used to cover joints in sheets of decorative materials, plywood, or wide boards.

Bay window   Any fixed window space projecting outward from the walls of a building, either square or polygonal in plan.

Beam   A structural member that is normally subject to bending loads, and is usually a horizontal member carrying vertical loads (an exception to this is a purlin); three types are
1. Continuous beam—has more than two points of support.
2. Cantilevered beam—supported at only one end, and restrained against rotation and deflection by design and connection.
3. Simple beam—freely supported at both ends.

Bearing plate   Steel plate set on grout bed (nonshrinking) under the end of a beam or other structural member; distributes the load carried on the member over a greater area of the wall; may also be a "pad" made of a block of plastic or synthetic rubber which cushions point at which members meet.

Bearing wall or partition   Wall that supports all or part of the floors, roofs, or ceilings in a building; partition that carries the floor joists and other partitions above it.

Bed rock   Unweathered (never exposed to light) solid stratum of rock; excellent bearing surface for foundation systems.

Bench mark (B.M.)   A fixed point used as the basis for computing elevation grades; identified by marks or symbols on stone, metal or other durable surveying items/matter, permanently affixed in the ground and from which differences of elevation are measured; also referred to as a "datum" or "datum point."

Blacktop   An asphaltic compound with small aggregate placed in a thick liquid which hardens into a paving surface, also called "bituminous concrete."

Blocking   Method of bonding two adjoining or intersecting walls not built at the same time; also, various wood members sized and shaped and used as fillers.

Board measure   A system for specifying a quantity of lumber; one unit is one board foot, which is the amount of wood in a piece 1" × 12" × 12".

Braced framing   Supported framework of a house, especially at the corners; diagonal or let-in braces (wood or metal) form a triangular shape to make the frame rigid and solid; plywood sheets at corners provide the same function.

Bracing   Support members in framing that are used to make the major structural members more rigid.

Brick   Masonry unit(s) composed of clay or shale formed into a rectangular prism while soft, then burned or fired in a kiln; can have voids or recessed panel to reduce weight and increase bond to mortar. There are many types of brick, face brick being most familiar (can be exposed—many colors, textures and sizes).

Brick veneer   Single wythe (thickness) of brick facing applied over wood frame construction, or masonry other than brick; this facing is nonstructural.

Bridging   (1) Method of bracing floor joists to distribute the weight over more than one joist; joins joists to act as a diaphragm unit and not individually; prevents displacement and wracking; usually two wood (1" thick) or light metal pieces crisscrossed between joists; also can be wood stock same size as joists and is called "solid bridging"; must be installed continuously from end wall to end wall. (2) Also, a newer method of project delivery which involves an owner's separately contracted design professional, and a design/build contract.

Btu (British thermal unit)   The amount of heat required to raise the temperature of one pound of water one degree Fahrenheit (F).

Building line   Lines established and marked off by a surveyor which denote the exterior faces of a proposed building; used by tradespersons as guidelines; surveyors get their information from the plans, specifications, and official records; building line is generally extended and marked on batter boards placed about 6 feet outside the corners/lines of the building excavation.

Building paper   Heavy sheet material used between sheathing and siding/facing for insulation and windbreaking purposes; four types: (1) red rosin paper, (2) sisal paper, (3) plain asphalt felt paper (tar paper), and (4) plastic sheeting.

Built-up roof   A roof covering made of alternate layers of building (roofing) felt and hot liquid asphalt, with a final surfacing of gravel; laid on a low-slope or comparatively level roof.

Butt   Type of door hinge that allows the edge of a door to butt into the jamb of the frame.

Butt joint   The junction of two members in a square-cut joint, end-to-end, or side-to-side (edge-to-edge).

C

Caisson   A deep shaft drilled into ground down to adequate bearing soil, then filled with concrete; used to support a column or to provide other structural foundation.

Callout   A note on a drawing with a leader line to the feature, location, material, or work item involved.

Cant strip   An angular board installed at the intersection of the roof deck and a wall, curb, or other penetrating item; used to avoid sharp right angles when the roof covering is installed.

Cantilever   Projecting beam or slab supported at one end only.

Casement window   A side-hinged window that opens outward by a crank device or push-bar.

Casework   Manufactured or custom built cabinetry, including shelves, cabinets (base or wall), countertops, and ancillary equipment; can be metal, wood, laminate covered, etc.

Cast-in-place (concrete)   Current and proper term for the placing of concrete into its forms on the job site; also called "site-cast," which replaces the word "poured," which has negative connotations relating to a watery mix inappropriate for construction use.

Caulk(ing)   A waterproof material used to seal cracks and various types of joints between materials or building parts; *see also* Sealants.

Cavity wall   A masonry wall made of two or more wythes of masonry units joined with ties, but having an air space between them.

Cement, portland   A gray, powdery material which will harden when mixed with water; used with aggregate of various sizes in concrete and mortar.

Centerline   Actual or imaginary line through the exact center of an object.

Center-to-center   Measuring distance from centerline to centerline of adjacent units; term meaning "on center," as in the spacing of joists, studding, or other structural parts.

Channel   Structural section, steel or aluminum, shaped like a rectangle, but with one long side missing; "C"-shaped.

Chase   In masonry a channel cut or built in the face of a wall to allow space for receiving pipes, conduits, etc.; also a recess in any wall to provide space for pipes and ducts.

Chimney   A vertical shaft for drawing smoke from a heating unit, fireplace, or incinerator, and venting it to the outside.

Clear dimension; Clear opening   Designation used to indicate the distance between opposing inside faces of an opening, frame, room, etc.

Column   A vertical structural member supporting horizontal or sloped members; can also be purely decorative.

Common bond   Brick laid in a pattern consisting of five courses of stretchers, followed by one "bonding" course of headers.

Common rafter   Rafter extending from the top of the wall to the roof ridge.

Composite wall   A masonry wall that incorporates two or more different types of masonry units, such as clay brick and concrete masonry units (CMUs).

Concave joint   A mortar joint tooled into a curved, indented profile.

Concrete   A thick, pasty (but plastic/formable) mixture of portland cement, sand, gravel, and water; can be formed into any shape which it retains when hardened and cured; mixes may be varied in proportioning, strength, and other attributes.

Concrete block   See concrete masonry unit (CMU).

Concrete brick   A solid concrete masonry unit the same size and proportions as a modular clay brick.

Concrete masonry unit (CMU)   Units of hardened concrete formed to varying profiles, sizes, and strengths, some solid, others with hollow cores (voids); designed to be laid in same manner as brick or stone to form walls, partitions, etc.

Concrete slump test   A test to determine the plasticity of concrete. A sample of fresh concrete is placed in a cone-shaped container 12″ high. Concrete is compacted with 25 rod strokes at ⅓, ⅔, and completely full. The container is then slowly lifted; the concrete will "slump" as the form is removed. The flattened concrete is then measured to ascertain how much lower than the 12″ original height remains, i.e., how much the concrete has "slumped" down from the 12″ cylinder height. This "slump" will be specified and the actual test results note the acceptability of the concrete (for use in the project). This test is completely site-accomplished. Usually a slump of 3–5 inches is required or acceptable; it varies as required to meet the various job conditions.

Conduit, electrical   A pipe, usually metal or plastic, in which wire is installed for electrical service.

Contour line(s)   Lines on a survey plan, site plan, or topographic map which connect points of like (same) grade elevation above/below sea level or other datum point(s).

Control joint   An intentional, linear discontinuity in a structure or component, designed to form a plane of weakness where cracking can occur in response to various forces so as to minimize or eliminate cracking elsewhere in the structure.

Crawl space   A space beneath a house or structure that lacks a basement, but which allows access to utilities; may also refer to the space in an attic that is too low to walk in, but high enough to crawl through or store in.

Cubic foot   Measure of volume that has three 12″ dimensions—width, height and depth; contains 1,728 cubic inches (12″ × 12″ × 12″).

Cubic yard   Measure of volume that is 3 feet on each side—width, depth, and height; contains 27 cubic feet (3′-0″ × 3′-0″ × 3′-0″).

Cul-de-sac   A street or court with no outlet, but providing a circular turnaround for vehicles.

Cupola   Small, decorative structure built on a roof of a house; often placed over an attached garage; may be utilized for outside air intake for ventilation purposes.

Curb   Linear edging, raised or partially concealed around paved areas, at walks, around other areas; also, a raised box installed around roof openings for passage of equipment, piping, devices, and the watertight mounting of same.

Curing   The slow chemical process that takes place in concrete after it is placed, and as it attains its load-bearing strength over a period of time.

Curtain wall   Non-loadbearing wall placed over the structural skeletal frame construction of a building; an exterior "skin" (a relatively thin wall).

Cut stone   Decorative, natural stone of various types, cut to given sizes and shapes (veneers, sills and copings, for example).

D

Damper   Movable plate that regulates the draft of air in a stove, fireplace, or furnace.

Damproofing   Layer of impervious material, spread or sprayed on walls, usually to prevent moisture from passing through.

Datum (point)   *See* Bench mark.

Dead load   Load on a structure imposed by its own weight, i.e., the weight of the materials of which it is built, and other fixed loads.

Decibel   Unit used to measure the relative intensity or loudness of sound; higher numbers indicate greater sound.

Deck   Exterior floor, similar to a concrete slab, patio, or porch; usually wood and extending out from building wall; usually slightly elevated above ground surface.

Deed   Legal document indicating that ownership of a parcel of land has been transferred from one party to another; gives legal description of the land, and may contain applicable restrictions as to the use of the land (easements, for example).

Deflection   Amount of sag at the center of a horizontal structural member (between supports) when subjected to a load.

Dimension lumber   Framing lumber that is 2 inches thick and from 4 to 12 inches wide (nominal sizes).

Directed   Term which reflects action(s) of design professional or other authorized party; used in same manner as "requested," "authorized," "selected," "approved," "required," and "permitted."

Door jamb   Two vertical pieces of the door frame (wood or metal) held together by the head (top, horizontal piece), forming the inside lining of a door opening, into which the door itself is set.

Dormer   A rooftop projection built out from and above a sloping roof to provide greater headroom inside.

Double glazing   Making a sealed glass unit of two or more panes of glass, with air space between panes, to provide added insulating value; also called "insulated glass."

Double header   Two or more structural members joined together for added strength; also, the shorter framing, of two members, to create an opening in structural framing.

Double-hung window   A window unit having a top and bottom sash, each capable of moving up and down, independently, by-passing each other.

Double-strength glass   Glass that is approximately ⅛ inch (3 mm) in thickness.

Downspout   A tube or pipe of plastic or sheet metal, for carrying rainwater from the roof gutter to the ground, or to a sewer connection; also called a "leader," or "conductor."

Drainage   Flow or removal of water.

Drip   A projecting construction member or groove in the underside of a member, to throw-off rainwater.

Drywall construction   Interior wall construction other than plaster; usually referred to as "gypsum board," "wall board," or "plasterboard"; sheets of material are applied to a stud framework.

Duct   In a building, usually round or rectangular metal pipes for distributing warm or conditioned air from the air handling units to the various rooms; also may be made of composition materials.

E

Earth-sheltered dwelling (building)   A structure which is totally or partially underground; uses soil coverings to reduce heat loss (or gain).

Eaves   The projecting lower edges of a roof overhanging the walls of the building.

EIFS (Exterior Insulation Finish System)   A material, usually a polymer, used as an exterior finishing material applied over insulation foam; stucco-like coating in several colors which conforms to any profile cut and constructed in the foam backing; adds thermal performance and decreases air infiltration.

Engineered fill   Earth compacted in such a way that it has predictable physical properties, based on field and laboratory tests; produced using specified, supervised installation procedures.

Erect   To raise or construct a building frame; generally applied to prefabricated materials, such as structural steel, as they are installed on the job site.

Erector   The subcontractor who raises, connects, and accurately sets (plumb and level) a building frame from fabricated steel or precast concrete members.

Erosion control   Temporary or permanent facilities installed to prevent/minimize erosion during construction; silt fences, straw bale lines, sheet plastic barriers used temporarily; permanent area for temporary storage of water (retention and detention ponds); rip-rap, swales, drainage ways, culvert pipes, etc.

Excavation   A cavity or pit produced by digging and removing the earth in preparation for construction.

Expansion bolt   A combination of a bolt and a sleeve used when an ordinary bolt is unsuitable; sleeve is inserted in predrilled hole, bolt is then inserted and turned to expand a "V" shaped piece into the sleeve and forces sleeve to become wider at bottom; tightened until assembly is firmly anchored in material.

Expansion joint   Joint in walls, floors, or other materials to permit and take up expansion caused by temperature changes without damage to surrounding surfaces; all materials expand in warm/hot weather and contract in cold; joint provided for resultant cracking at the joint where it is not noticeable and with least damage.

Exposed aggregate finish   Concrete surface in which the top of the aggregate (usually "pea gravel") is exposed; can be used in walks or wall panels.

F

Fabricator   Company that prepares materials or members (such as structural steel) for erection and installation to specific project conditions by cutting, fitting, punching, coping, and otherwise making ready for specific installations.

Face brick   Brick of higher quality, made specifically for exposure to weather; usually hard-burned and frostproof; available in large array of colors, textures, sizes, and combinations.

Facing   Any material attached to the outer portion of a wall and used as a finished surface.

Fascia   Vertical member that runs horizontally on the edge of a roof or overhang; closes off ends of rafters/trusses and is backing for gutter.

Fasteners   General term for metal devices, such as nails, bolts, screws, etc., used to secure materials and members within a building.

Fiberglass   Glass spun into fine threads, and made into batting which is used as an insulation material; can also be pressed into rigid board insulation; and can be fashioned into intricate shapes.

Fill   Clean sand, gravel, or loose earth used to bring a subgrade up to desired level around a building, in a trench, etc.

Finish carpentry   Carpentry work which will be exposed to view in the final project; casing of openings, running trim (base, chair rail, crown molds, etc.), bookshelves, panelling, and so forth (see Rough carpentry for contrast).

Finish floor (covering)   The floor material exposed to view as differentiated from the subfloor, which is the load-bearing floor material beneath.

Finish hardware   Devices and features of door hardware; in particular, knobs, rosettes, escutcheons, push/pull plates, closers, hinges, etc., which are exposed and which have decorative finishes (see Rough hardware for contrast).

Finish lumber   Good quality lumber used to form surfaces that will be finished (often in natural finish) and exposed to view.

Firebrick   A refractory brick that is especially hard and heat resistant; for use in fireplace fire boxes, and as smokestack linings.

Fireproofing   Material to protect portions of buildings, primarily structural members, against fire; can be stiff material (brick, concrete, tile, gypsum) or flexible (spray-on, wraps, paints).

Fire protection system   An interconnected system of devices and equipment installed throughout a structure (or in specific hazardous areas) to detect a fire, activate an alarm, suppress or control a fire, or any combination thereof; fire alarm systems, sprinkler systems, and smoke detectors are examples.

Fire-rated doors   Doors designed to resist the passage of fire from one side to the other; constructed to match those tested in standard fire tests, and subsequently awarded an hourly rating and label.

Fire-rating   The comparative resistance of a material to failure, as stated in hours, when subjected to fire testing; ratings are standardized by fire underwriters (the Underwriters' Laboratories/UL for example), who publish full data on tests, results, and material performance.

Fire-resistant   Incombustible; slow to be damaged by fire; forming a barrier to the passage of fire.

Fire-separation wall/partition   Wall required by building codes to separate two areas of a building as a deterrent to the spread of fire.

Fire-stop   Any material, even wood, placed to prevent the rapid spread of fire; used to block the passage of flames or air currents upward or across and in concealed building parts; includes draft-stops.

Fire-stopping system   Installation of a combination of fire-resistant wraps, packing, and sealants in holes around piping, etc. in walls and floors, to preclude the passage of fire and smoke.

Fire wall   Walls designed and constructed to remain in place, despite collapse of structure on either or both sides of the wall, to resist the spread and passage of fire from one portion of a building to another for extended period of time (up to 4 hours).

Fixed window   Unit of glass mounted in an inoperable frame, mounted in a wall opening.

Flange   Horizontal bottom and top portions of an I-beam, wide-flange beam, or channel member.

Flashing   Sheet metal or rubberized plastic material used for making joints, openings, and connections in roofs and walls watertight; used in roof valleys, at dormers, chimneys, and other vertical penetrations through roofs; also at window and door openings; usually covered, at least in part, by finished material such as siding or roofing so water is directed away from the areas in which leaks could occur.

Flat-slab construction   Type of reinforced concrete floor/roof construction having no beams, girders, or joists below the underside; requires thick slabs, moderate spans, and special reinforcement at columns.

Flue   Space or passage in a chimney through which smoke, gasses, and fumes ascend; each fuel-burning appliance requires its own flue.

Flue lining   Special, high-temperature fire clay or terra-cotta pipe, round or square, usually made in all ordinary flue sizes and in 3-foot lengths; used for inner lining of chimneys with brick or masonry work surrounding; runs from above the smoke chamber to several inches above the top of the chimney.

Flush door   A door with two flat faces (no panels), resembling a "slab"; can have a hollow or solid core; can have glass or louvered openings; can be fire-rated.

Footing   Lowest part of a structure, generally of reinforced concrete; spread out flat to distribute the imposed load of the wall, column, grade beam, chimney, foundation wall, or other feature it supports, over sufficient area of earth to provide stability.

Form (work)   Temporary framing, basically a "mold," into which concrete is placed; serves to give shape to cast-in-place concrete, and to support it and keep it moist as it cures; built of wood, plywood, or metal for holding and shaping concrete.

Form tie   Mesh, strap or heavy wire/rod used to hold wall forms in place, but of proper length to provide specified width; spaced at intervals over the entire area of forms, as necessary.

Foundation   Lowest portion of structure, fully or partially below grade; substructure of building, consisting of foundation system (walls, grade beams, etc.) and supports (caissons, footings, etc.).

Framing   Process of putting the skeletal part (beams, columns, studs, etc.) of a building together; rough lumber, steel, or concrete frame including floors, roofs, and partitions; in light wood framing there are "Platform" and "Balloon" systems.

Furring   Narrow strips of wood or other material (metal channels) attached to a surface to provide a level, true-to-line, and plumb plane for attachment of finish wall or ceiling materials; provides some added insulation space.

G

Gable   End wall of a building where the roof slopes on only two sides; gable is that triangular shaped part of the wall between the eaves and ridge.

Galvanized iron   Sheet iron (steel) which has been dipped into, and coated with, molten zinc to protect it against rust.

Gauge   A uniform standard of measure for wire diameters and thicknesses of sheet metal, plates, etc.; also a measure of other materials in regard to spacing or thickness.

Girder   Larger of principle structural members of wood, steel, or concrete used to support concentrated loads at isolated points along its length, e.g., at the bearing points of a series of supported beams.

Glass block   Hollow masonry units made of glass; usually square, and made of diffused or molded glass; translucent.

Glass fiber batt   Thick, fluffy, nonwoven insulating blanket of filaments spun from glass.

Glazing   Placing glass or other similar materials (acrylic plastic, for example) into windows and doors, or tubular grid curtain wall systems.

Glue-laminated (Glu-Lam) timber   Timbers and rigid frames (arches) built-up from a large number of small strips (laminations) of wood, glued together; used where solid wood timbers are not available for the loads and spans involved.

Grade   (1) Construction/building trade term used in referring to the ground level around the building; (2) lumber term to denote the quality and classification of the pieces related to their adaptability for different uses; (3) the slope or gradient of a roof, piece of land, ramp, etc.

Grade beam   Concrete foundation (wall) formed into a beam configuration (by pattern of reinforcement), which spans across isolated footings, piles, or caissons spaced at intervals; used where soil bearing pressure is inadequate for continuous support.

Grade, wood   Designation given to indicate quality of manufactured lumber.

Gradient   Inclination or slope of a road, piping, ramp, ground level, etc.

Grain   In wood, the direction of the longitudinal axes of wood fibers, or the figure formed by the fibers.

Granite   Igneous rock with visible crystals of quartz and feldspar.

Gravel stop   Metal (usually) strip or piece formed with a vertical lip used to retain the gravel on the roof surface around the edge of a built-up roof; can be enlarged to act as the fascia also.

Grout   A thin cement mortar used for leveling bearing plates and filling masonry cavities; usually a nonshrinking type is preferred.

Gunnable sealant   A sealant material of any formulation that is extruded in thickened liquid or mastic form under pressure from a caulking gun.

Gusset plate   Plywood or metal plate used to overlay adjacent/intersecting members in a truss joint to connect and strengthen the joint; plate is nailed in place.

Gutter   A U-shaped trough, along roof line of buildings, of metal or plastic to receive and carry off various types of drainage, usually nonsanitary; flat areas out from street curb for drainage.

Gypsum (wall) board   Sheet material having a gypsum core laminated between layers of heavy paper (exposed face is manilla in color—the back [concealed] face is gray); also called "drywall" and "plasterboard"; available in varying thicknesses, edge treatments, finishes (some prefinished), and fire-ratings; overall usually 4' × 8', 10', or 12'.

H

Hanger   Wire, rod, or bar (or other shape required for loading) suspended from roof or other structural members used to support and carry piping, balconies, runways, etc.; stirrup-like drop support attached to wall to carry ends of beam.

Hardware   A wide variety of items, in both rough and finished form, which provide various functions such as attachment, operation, etc.; *see* Rough hardware, and Finish hardware for further distinction.

Hardwood   Wood cut from broad-leaved trees or trees that lose their leaves annually; examples include oak, maple, walnut, and birch; utilized in a number of construction and architectural items, primarily as finish carpentry.

H-beam   Another name or designation for steel beam shapes; most often refers to an I-beam used as a column—"H-column"; *see* I-beam, and Wide-flange.

Head   The top of a frame at a door, window, or other opening; also, a standing depth of water which exerts downward pressure.

Header   (1) Doubled members installed perpendicular to trimmer joists on each end of openings for stairs, chimneys, or other features for attachment of joists cut short to allow the opening; also wood lintels; (2) in masonry, units laid on the large flat face with small end exposed.

Head room   Vertical clear space in a doorway, or in the height between a stair tread and the ceiling overhead.

Hearth   The incombustible floor or covering extension in front of and in a fireplace (actual floor of firebox); can be brick, stone, or tile.

High-tension bolts   Steel bolts designed to be tightened with calibrated wrenches to high tensile strength; used as a substitute for conventional rivets in steel frame construction.

Hip roof   Roof that rises by inclined planes from all four sides of a building.

Hollow core door   Door consisting of two wood veneer panels separated by a lightweight core (grid, eggcrate, strips) installed to reinforce and stabilize the faces; solid wood members for stiles and rails.

Hopper window   Window with sash pivoted along the sill; opens by tilting the top inward.

Hose bibb   A water faucet made for the threaded attachment of a hose; exterior bibbs should be frostproof.

I

I-beam   Rolled structural steel section with a cross section resembling the letter "I"; often called "H-column" when used vertically; usually higher than it is wide; can be made of wood in similar profile; used for larger spans across openings, etc.

Indicated   Term refers to graphic representations, notes, or schedules on the drawings, or to paragraphs and schedules in the specifications; used to help locate references and information in manner similar to "shown," "noted," "scheduled," and "specified."

Insulating board   Material in rigid board form of various sizes and thicknesses for insulating purposes; usually manufactured from vegetable fibers or synthetic chemicals, and pressed or caused to "foam" into finished profile.

Insulating concrete   Concrete with vermiculite added to produce lightweight concrete, with insulating properties, used for sub-floor and roof fills.

Insulating glass   Multiple panes of glass, separated by air spaces (for insulation purposes), and sealed in a single frame/unit.

Insulation   A variety of materials designed and manufactured for protection from heat or cold, protection against fire, or reduction of sound transmission; usually paper, composition board, fiberglass, wools, foam products are good insulators (poor conductors).

Interior finish   Term applied to the total effect produced by the inside finishing of a building; includes not only the material used, but the fashion of their installation and decoration.

Interior trim   General term for all finish moldings, casings, baseboards, cornices, and other applied running and isolated trim pieces inside a building; installed by finish carpenters for fine fitting, finishing, and decorative expression.

Intumescent coating   Paint or mastic that expands to form a stable, foam-like, insulating char when exposed to fire, that acts as an insulating agent (against the fire) for surfaces to which applied.

J

Jalousie   Type of window with a number of long, narrow, hinged glass panels, which operate in unison—outswinging; can be used in doors, or as isolated window units.

Jamb   Lining or frame mounted in a rough opening for installation of a door or window; side of an opening.

Joint   Line, point, or position where two items meet or adjoin each other; in masonry, the layer of mortar between the horizontal courses of units (tooled to raked, flush, weeping, concave, tooled, or V-shape).

Joist   Horizontal member used with others as a support for floor, ceiling, or roof; identified by location/placement; usually smaller than a beam, and rests on same; can be wood, steel or concrete.

Junior beam   Smaller, lightweight rolled structural steel sections similar to an I-beam; used for short spans and light loads, bracing, etc.

K

Keene's cement   White finish plaster which produces a very durable and moisture-resistant surface; used in bathrooms around bath tubs and showers, and in areas of high pedestrian traffic wear or abuse.

L

Lag screw   Large wood screw with hexagonal or square head for turning/tightening with a wrench.

Lally column   A steel pipe column, with or without concrete/sand fill; used for loads up to moderate sizes, including residential floor loads.

Laminated beam   Beams, arches, and other members formed by pressure-gluing multiple layers or strips (laminations) together to form the shapes and size desired; substitute for solid wood members due to limited availability of same (*see* Glue-laminated timber).

Landing   Platform between two flights of stairs where they end or change direction as they run between floors of a building.

Lath   Material secured to framing on which plaster is applied; can be gypsum lath (solid or perforated) or metal lath, each providing a mechanical or chemical bond for the plaster.

Lattice   Framework of crossed wood or metal slats; lightweight, usually, but can be heavy where used as bracing in structures.

Leader   Vertical pipe—downspout—that carries rain water drainage from roof gutter to ground or storm sewer.

Level   (1) On a perfectly flat, horizontal line or plane; (2) tool used by workers to determine such level plane or line; (3) surveyor's instrument, similar to or a function of a transit, for establishing grade elevations.

Lift slab   System of construction where the various floor slabs are poured at ground level, and then subsequently lifted into proper position by hydraulic jacks, working simultaneously at each column; cast-in, steel collars are welded to steel columns to hold slabs in place.

Light   A pane of glass.

Light steel framing (LSF)   Construction method utilizing light gauge steel members for the structure; also called cold-formed metal (steel) framing.

Lintel   Structural member (wood, steel, concrete, stone, etc.) placed horizontally across the top of an opening, to support the wall above.

Live load   All furniture, persons, and other movable loads not included as a permanent part of the structure.

Load-bearing wall   Wall designed to support the weight (load) imposed on it from walls and structural members.

Louver   Opening or slatted grille that allows ventilation while providing protection from rain, sight, sound, or light.

M

Masonry   General term applied to construction made of brick, stone, concrete masonry units, and similar materials; sometimes called "unit masonry."

Masonry cement   Factory-made mixture of portland cement and admixtures specially designed to increase the workability of mortar; usually better than site mixing, due to control available at plant.

Masonry unit   A brick, stone, concrete masonry unit, glass block, or hollow clay tile intended to be laid in courses and embedded in mortar.

Masonry veneer   A single-wythe, non–load-bearing facing installed over a structural frame, e.g., brick veneer applied to a wood frame house.

Mastic   A thick, paste-like adhesive or other coating material used for attachment, dampproofing, etc.

Member   Individual element of structure such as a beam, girder, column, joist, piece of decking, stud, truss chord, brace, etc.

Membrane   Sheet or mastic material which is impervious to water or water vapor.

Metal lath   Steel mesh created by slitting sheet steel and pulling it out until it forms a grid or mesh; used primarily as an excellent plaster base due to mechanical "keying" of plaster around mesh wires.

Metal wall ties   Strips of corrugated sheet metal (galvanized) used to anchor (tie) brick veneer construction to the structural frame behind.

Mil   Unit of measure (thickness) for very thin sheets; one thousandth part of an inch (.001″).

Millwork   General term for interior woodwork and trim which is machined to profile, size, and finish; usually does not include flooring, ceiling and siding materials; finished carpentry work, as opposed to rough carpentry (framing).

Mineral wool   Type of batt insulation consisting of many fine threads of a wood by-product; also used for fireproofing and acoustical treatment.

Modular housing   Buildings (usually small in size or made of several units) fully constructed, built, and assembled in a factory and then transported to the site for final attachment and connections.

Moisture barrier Material—plastic or specially treated paper—that retards the passage of moisture or vapor into walls, and prevents condensation; *see* Vapor barrier.

Molding Single strip/piece or series of pieces of material cut, shaped, and finished to serve as an ornament; can be made of various materials—wood, stone, fiberglass, plaster, etc.

Monolithic Term used for concrete and other materials placed or installed without joints; as one-piece, or a unit.

Mortar A mixture of masonry cement, sand and water, used by masons as the bonding agent between masonry units; the "joint material" in masonry.

Mosaic Small colored tile, glass, stone, or similar material, regular or irregular in shape but arranged to produce a decorative surface; used on walls or floors.

N

Nail-base sheathing Sheathing material, such as wood boards, panels, or plywood to which siding can be attached by nailing; such nailing is not provided by fiber board or plastic foam materials used as sheathing (primarily for better insulation).

Nailer Wood member shaped to fit in any of several places used to provide a nailing base for other members or materials; called "blocking" in some locations.

Needling Series of steel or wood beams (called "needle beams") threaded through a bearing wall to support it while its foundation is underpinned.

Nominal size Size of material before final working and dressing; not the actual size; as a 2×4 (nominal) is $1\frac{1}{2}'' \times 3\frac{1}{2}''$ (actual).

Nonbearing partition wall Term used for space dividing partitions or other walls which carry no imposed floor or roof load.

Nosing Portion/edge of stair tread which projects beyond the riser below it; any other similar projections.

Notch A three-sided slot, groove, or opening cut into a piece of material, usually along an edge.

O

On-center (o.c.) Method of indicating spacing of framing members or other items; measurement is from center of one object to the center of each of those adjacent.

Open web (steel) joist Prefabricated, light steel truss-like member with a welded lattice-like web; closely spaced for moderate spans; also called "bar joist" or "steel lumber."

Ordinary construction Building type with exterior masonry-bearing walls, and an interior structure of wood framing.

Orientation (1) Direction in which a building or structure faces; (2) relationship to a direction or bench mark/line; (3) relating contract drawings to the actual structure.

Oriented-strand board (OSB) Building panel composed of long shreds of wood fiber oriented in specific directions and bonded together with an adhesive matrix under pressure.

Overhang Area or portion of upper story, building part, or roof at the eave, which projects beyond the wall below.

P

Pad Extra concrete slab installed on top of a floor slab, as the mounting surface for mechanical or other equipment; adds some strength, but mainly provides a better, slightly elevated surface for mounting the unit(s).

Panel (1) A fabricated section of a wall, ceiling framing; (2) a sheet of material; (3) an electrical box device for current distribution, etc.

Panel door   Door constructed with thin panels installed between solid rails and stiles (perimeter frame).

Panelling   Thin sheet material of composite, synthetic, or wood composition which is used as a lining or interior wall finish; can be nailed or glued into place over various subsurfaces.

Parapet   The portion of a wall that extends above the top of the roof; usually in exterior walls, or interior fire walls.

Particle board   Composition board made from wood chips or particles bonded together in an adhesive matrix under pressure.

Partition   Interior wall, full or part-high for dividing, separating, or screening spaces one from another, or for directing traffic.

Party wall   Single wall between and common to two adjoining buildings owned by different owners; also common walls between row houses.

Patio   Paved, open area outside a house; also called a terrace, and can be a structure such as a deck.

Paver   Clay masonry (brick) made specifically for finish floor surfaces, walks, drives, and terraces, etc.; must be frostproof and serviceable for heavy traffic.

Paving   Concrete or asphaltic material (or composites) used as installed ground cover as a hard-stand for vehicle access or parking; usually asphaltic concrete (blacktop) or cast-in-place concrete over a compacted gravel fill; can be light duty or heavy duty depending on traffic requirements and construction.

Penthouse   A relatively small structure/enclosure, usually roof mounted, usually to enclose mechanical and/or elevator equipment without taking up valuable interior floor space.

Pier   Vertical structural member, usually of concrete or masonry; also, short foundation columns, between window/door openings; also mass, masonry supports such as for bridges, gates, and girders.

Pilaster   Rectangular pier engaged in a wall, for the purpose of strengthening it; also can be decorative, or act as a beam support (expanded bearing area at the wall).

Pile (Piling)   Concrete, wood, or steel member driven into the ground to act as an undergrade column to support the building; used to carry building load to sufficient bearing soil.

Pitch   Slope of roof or other inclined/sloped surface(s).

Plank   Long, flat wood members 2–4″ thick and 6+ inches wide.

Plaster   A cementitious material usually applied to gypsum or metal lath or masonry surfaces; formed of a gypsum or portland cement mixture; applied in paste form, which hardens into a hard smooth surface (or other finish desired).

Plastic laminate   Composite material made from compressing kraft paper into phenolic resin layers to form a decorative material; usually has a melamine exposed (decorated) surface; used for covering doors, countertops, wall panelling, cabinets, etc.

Plat   Drawing of a parcel or parcels of land based on and giving its legal description, and perhaps other survey data; may be filed as an official record of the land.

Plate   Horizontal members at top (doubled) and bottom of stud walls (sole plate); also, refers to bearing, top, and base plates for structural steel members.

Plate glass   Glass of high optical quality produced by grinding and polishing both faces of the glass sheet; glass with parallel faces and minimal distortion.

Platform framing   System of light-wood framing for housing where each story is built on top of the one below, but framed independently (upper story rests on flooring decking applied to top of first floor ceiling joists); also, called "Western framing"; *see* and contrast with Balloon framing.

Plot   Lot, parcel, or other piece of land (real estate) with specific dimensions; potential building/construction site.

Plumb   Absolutely vertical; straight up and down; a plumb line is created when a weight (plumb bob) is tied on a cord and held vertically.

Plywood   Wood panel, of many varieties and types, composed of a number of thin veneers bonded together, glued under pressure; normally 4 feet wide by 8 feet, although longer lengths are available; has various face finishes and can be used as a finish or rough material.

Portland cement   Very fine, powder-like, gray-colored limestone material (crushed and pulverized) made from burning compounds of lime, silica, and alumina together; is the bonding agent in concrete, grouts, etc.

Post-and-beam construction   Wall and roof construction system using widely spaced posts and beams as the frame; plank decking applied transversely across the beams for stability and roof structure; a wood version of a rigid frame, in concept.

Pour   Outdated term, meaning to place concrete, casting concrete in place without interruption; not used today, because of negative impression of a thin, watery, inadequate substance.

Precast   The shaping of structural members in a factory, which are then transported and installed in a building; includes concrete joists, beams, tee-slabs, as well as nonstructural terrazzo, stair treads and risers, and miscellaneous trim, such as copings, sills, etc.

Precut   Cutting wood stock to exact dimensions at a mill, yard, or job site, before using/installation; for standardizing building components and minimizing errors.

Prefabricated   Sections or component parts of a building built in a factory and installed/assembled as a whole on the job site; *see* Modular housing.

Pressure-treated lumber   Lumber that has been impregnated with chemicals under pressure, for the purpose of retarding rot, decay, vermin, or fire.

Professional association/society   Organization usually representing a given profession which combines single efforts (by members) into a larger and more extensive voice; presents educational, informational efforts, information and document sales, and other combined services to individual members; somewhat of a lobbying group which acts on behalf of members.

Q

Quarry tile   Unglazed, machine-made tile used for floors with sanitary requirements and open to wet conditions; usually red or tan color, and 6″ × 6″.

Quarter round   Small molding whose profile is a quarter circle.

Quarter sawn   Lumber, usually flooring or veneer, that has been sawn so that the medullary rays showing on end grain are nearly perpendicular to the face.

Quoins   Large squared stone pieces, or slightly projected panels of brick, set in the corners of masonry walls for decorative purposes.

R

Rafter   A sloped/inclined structural roof member running from the wall to the ridge or top of the roof; designed to support the roof deck, roofing, and other loading; such rafters for a flat roof are called "joists."

Rake   An incline or slope, as in a pitched roof.

Ramp   A sloped surface for walking, or rolling equipment for easier access than stairs; required as access under the ADA regulations for disabled persons; can be utilized with stairs.

Raze   To demolish or wreck work, usually to provide place for new construction.

Re-bars   Contracted term indicating "reinforcing bars" (rods/steel); *see* Reinforcing steel.

Reinforced concrete   A composite material in which steel bars are placed in the concrete to reinforce its tensile strength; material bonded together to act in unison with a combined capacity that exceeds that of either material alone; various design principles utilize varying amounts of reinforcing.

Reinforcing steel   Steel bars (rods) formed with projecting ridges to ensure bonding, placed in concrete to add tensile strength; bars are bent or straight as required, and tied in shapes, grids or other configurations as required for concrete member comes in various diameters; most are round, but some are square in cross section.

Resilient flooring   Manufactured sheet or tile flooring material of asphalt, vinyl, vinyl composition, polyvinyl chloride, rubber, cork, or other similar resilient materials; installed with adhesive.

Retaining wall   Wall that holds back an earth embankment; usually concrete, but can be wood, stone, or masonry.

Return   Change in direction of a molding, cornice, or other design feature, without breaking the continuity of the profile.

Reveal   Side of an opening for a window or door in a masonry or wood structure; margin to which the casing is set on the jamb for appearance, and to accommodate the door hinges.

Ridge/Ridge board   The top edge of a roof where two slopes meet; also, the vertical board running horizontally between, and to which opposing rafters are attached, running the length of the roof structure.

Rise   In stairs, the vertical height of a step, or a flight of stairs; also, distance from one floor to the next for stair design is called "total rise"; also, vertical height of a roof above the surrounding walls.

Riser   In general, the vertical part of a stair step; in plumbing, a vertical water supply line.

Roof sheathing   Boards or sheet material fastened to the roof framing (rafters/trusses, etc.) and to which the shingles or other roof covering is attached; also called "roof deck or decking."

Rough carpentry   That work of the carpenter trade which is for the most part concealed, such as framing, blocking, etc.; usually involves dimensioned lumber, and rough hardware.

Rough hardware   All devices such as nails, screws, bolts, hangers, etc., which aid in the construction of the framing and rough construction of the project; also called "builders' hardware"; *see* Finish hardware.

Rough opening   Framing around a window or door opening that has been sized to accept the finished units with allowances for fitting, shimming, and leveling.

Roughing-in   The erection of the framing of the structure; in plumbing the installation of the underground lines and all associated plumbing piping, but not the fixtures themselves.

Rowlock   Method of laying brick on the side so the vertical ends appear in the face of the wall; a vertical header.

Run   Horizontal distance of a flight of stairs; also, the horizontal distance from the top of the sidewall to the ridge of a roof.

Running bond   Brick bonding pattern consisting entirely of stretchers overlapping by half a brick; i.e., vertical joints centered over brick below.

S

Safing insulation   Fire-resistant material inserted into space between piping, ducts, curtain wall, conduit, beam, column, wall, floor, etc., where fire might pass through; packing behind fire penetration sealant used to close top of such openings and retard passage of fire and smoke.

Sandwich panel   Panel consisting of two outer faces of wood, metal, or concrete bonded to a core of insulating material.

Sash Individual frames around glass in windows; movable part of window.

Scale Use of proportional measurements, i.e., using a small increment of measure to represent one foot (usually); also a drafting tool with markings at different intervals to permit measuring using different increments.

Scupper Opening through a wall for drainage of water from floor or roof into a downspout; requires careful and extensive flashing for watertight installation.

Scuttle Opening in a ceiling or roof that provides access to an attic or roof.

Sealant Thickened liquid or paste substance used to seal cracks, joints, and porous surfaces; must adhere to surrounding material and permit expansion and contraction without rupture; many varieties, chemical compounds, types, colors, and uses involved; may also be in tape or gasket form.

Seismic load Load on a structure caused by movement of the earth relative to that structure during an earthquake; varies by locale and history of earthquake incidents.

Select lumber Lumber without knots or other deformities. It is the best lumber. In hardwood it refers to a specific grade.

Set The change in concrete and mortar from a plastic (semi-liquid) to a solid (hardened) state.

Setback A required minimum distance from the property line to the face of a building.

Shakes Handcut wood shingles.

Sheathing The rough covering over the framing of a house; not exposed in complete building.

Sheet metal Flat rolled metal less than ¼ inch (6.35 mm) in thickness.

Shoring The placing of a series of supports under formwork; also refers to the bracing or sheeting used to hold back an earth bank.

Sidelight A tall, narrow glass panel on either or both sides of a door.

Siding Boards placed over the outside wall of a frame building and nailed to the sheathing. Although wood or plywood is generally used, composition board is also popular. Wood siding is made in several different patterns, as are vinyl and aluminum.

Signage The entire coordinated system or pattern of signs used on, around, and throughout a building, interrelated and color coded or coordinated.

Silicone A polymer used for high range sealants, roof membranes, and masonry water repellant.

Sill General: the lowest part of an opening in a wall such as a door or window sill. Frame construction: the bottom rough structural member that rests on the foundation.

Sisal kraft paper A paper reinforced with strands of sisal fibers. The strands of sisal are placed between two layers of paper stuck together with a coat of pitch. This paper has many uses in construction because of its toughness and durability.

Site-cast (Cast-in-place) concrete Concrete placed and cured in its final position in a building.

Skylight A window built into a roof or ceiling.

Slab A thick slice of stone or other masonry material; word generally used when referring to a concrete floor; concrete pavements and sidewalks are also concrete slabs.

Slab-on-grade A concrete surface lying upon, and supported directly by, the ground beneath.

Slope Ratio between rise and run of a roof; amount of incline on any nonlevel surface.

Smoke chamber The portion of a chimney flue located directly over the fireplace.

Softwood   Wood produced from coniferous trees, or trees that bear cones. Most commonly used are the pines, but also included are such trees as fir, spruce, redwood, and cedar. The term has no reference to the actual hardness or softness of the wood.

Soil boring   Holes drilled into subsurface soil for the purpose of investigating the load-bearing and stability characteristics of the earth under a building.

Solid core door   A flush door with no internal cavities.

Span   The horizontal distance between supports for joists, beams, trusses, and other structural members.

Spandral   The wall area above a window.

Splash block   A small precast block of concrete or plastic at the bottom of a downspout used to divert water away from the foundation.

Splice   The joining of two members to form one piece.

Spread footing   A concrete footing larger than the structural member it supports, constructed for the purpose of spreading the load over the bearing soil; used under piers, columns, and foundation walls.

Sprinklers   *See* Fire protection systems

Square   A unit of measurement used by roofers that designates 100 square feet. Generally roof area estimates are expressed in the number of squares of material required for application. Also indicates perpendicular.

Stair well   A compartment extending vertically through a building, into which stairs are placed.

Steel joist   A light steel truss made from bars, rods, or angles welded into rigid units.

Storefront construction   System of light aluminum tubular sections interconnected to form a network of glass frames utilizing large glass panels; usually includes the entrance complex, and acts as both wall and fenestration.

Storm sewer (drain)   A sewer, pipe, or other feature (natural or man-made) used to carry away surface water but not sewage.

Story   Space between two floors of a building; top of floor to top of floor.

Straightedge   Used to strike off the surface of a concrete slab using screeds and a straight piece of lumber or metal.

Stringer   General construction: the member of each side of a stair that supports the treads and risers. Reinforced concrete construction: horizontal structural member supports.

Strip flooring   Wood finish flooring in the form of long, narrow tongue and groove boards.

Structural glazed (clay) tile   Hollow clay tile with glazed faces; used for constructing interior partitions where sanitation or cleanliness are concerns.

Structural shapes   "H", "I", "T"   beams, angles, channels, and plates.

Structural tubes   Usually welded-seam, hollow tubular sections of various sizes used as light columns, struts, and bracing; also, other structural and sometimes decorative installations; can be square or rectangular.

Stucco   Most commonly refers to an outside plaster made with portland cement as its base.

Stud   In building, an upright member, usually a piece of dimension lumber, 2 × 4 or 2 × 6, used in the framework of a partition or wall.

Subcontractor   A company (or individual) who enters into an agreement with a general contractor. The subcontractor usually agrees to do certain specific skilled work on a building. Plumbing, heating, electrical work, and other portions of construction work are sublet to contractors who specialize in that one kind of work.

Subfloor   Carpentry: a term applied to flooring laid directly on the joists and serving that purpose during construction. When all rough construction work is completed, the finish floor is laid over the subfloor.

Subgrade   A fill or earth surface upon which concrete is placed.

Substructure   Foundation system, and portion of structure/building below grade line; lowest support for superstructure.

Superstructure   The above ground portion of a building.

Suspended ceiling   A ceiling hung below the underside of the building structure. Wire and channel section are commonly used to support the ceiling material.

T

Tee   A metal or precast concrete member with a cross section resembling the letter T.

Tempered glass   Glass that has been heat treated to increase its toughness and its resistance to breakage.

Tension   A stretching force; to stretch.

Testing agency   Entity, separate from any of the contractual parties on a project, engaged to perform specific inspections, tests, and analysis either at the site, in a laboratory, or elsewhere; reports results to proper project party, and interprets results if required; may function to meet specifications or to investigate problems which arise; building codes list some such agencies which are approved and acceptable because of their impartiality, reliability, and past performance.

Threshold   A strip of wood or metal with beveled edges used over the joint between finish floor and the sill of exterior doors.

Tile   A fired clay product that is thin in cross section as compared to a brick; either a thin, flat element (ceramic tile or quarry tile), a thin, curved element (roofing tile), or a hollow element with thin walls (flue tile, tile pipe, structural clay tile); also a thin, flat element of another material, such as an acoustical ceiling unit or a resilient floor unit.

Tilt-up construction   A method of constructing walls, and sometimes floors, by pouring concrete or putting wooden walls together in flat panels. When complete, they are moved to the building site where they are tilted into permanent place.

Timber   Construction lumber larger than 4″ × 6″ (102 × 152 mm) in cross section.

Tinted glass   Glass that is colored with pigments, dyes, or other admixtures.

Toilet room accessories   Various items of equipment such as towel dispensers, soap dispensers, waste receptacles, napkin and seat dispensers, robe hooks, tissue holders, etc., for installation in restrooms.

Tongue and groove   A continuous projection on the edge of a board that fits into a groove formed on another board.

Transom   A window placed above a door or permanent window which is hinged for ventilation.

Tread   The horizontal board in a stairway on which the foot is placed.

Trim   The finished woodwork of a structure. The term is also used in reference to painting and decorating.

Truss   Structural steel or wood members fastened together to make a framework that will span long distances; utilizes principle of rigid triangular panels.

Two-way ribbed slab   Structural concrete slab with ribs (joists) running in two directions between supports; also called "waffle slab"; can be left exposed and unfinished as a decorative texture/pattern for the ceiling of space below; light fixtures can be mounted in the voids, if desired.

Two-way slab   A concrete slab in which the reinforcing steel is placed in perpendicular directions; usually a structural floor or roof slab.

Type-X gypsum board   A fiber-reinforced gypsum board used where greater fire resistance is required; fire-rated board.

U

Underlayment Floor covering of plywood or fiberboard used to provide a smooth, level surface for carpet or other resilient flooring.

Underpinning The process of placing new foundations beneath an existing structure.

V

Valley A depression in a roof where two parts of a roof at different slopes come together.

Vapor barrier (retarder) A watertight material used to prevent the passage of moisture or water vapor into and through walls and slabs.

Veneer (1) A thin sheet of wood or other material. The outside sheet is generally of superior quality, chosen for its beauty. Plywood is made by gluing sheets of wood veneer together. (2) Brick veneer consists of one row of brick placed around a framework. Most brick houses have wood frames covered by veneer.

Vestibule An open area at an entrance to a building.

V-joint A joint between two pieces of a material. The corners are beveled to form a joint profile resembling the letter "V."

Void Air space between material or between substance in material.

W

Waferboard A building panel made by bonding together large, flat flakes of wood.

Waffle slab A two-way concrete joist system (ribbed slab), formed with square pan forms; *see* Two-way ribbed slab.

Wainscot The lower section of a wall made of different material from the upper part; usually composed of wood, tile, or wall covering.

Wall board A general term used to refer to large rigid sheets used to cover interior walls. It can be made of wood fibers, gypsum, or other material.

Wall tie A small metal strip or steel wire used to bind wythes of masonry in cavity-wall construction or to bind brick veneer to the wood-frame wall in veneer construction.

Warp To bend or twist out of shape.

Waterproof To render a material or surface impervious to water. This is generally done by coating it with another material that will not let water pass through it. Tar, asphalt, mortar parging, and heavy-body cementitious paints are common waterproofing agents.

Weatherstripping A strip of fabric or metal fastened around the edge of windows and doors to prevent air infiltration; can be interlocking or spring fit.

Weep hole Holes or slots (usually in vertical joints) near the bottoms of masonry walls to allow the release of accumulated moisture; important in brick veneer work.

Weld A joint between two pieces of metal formed by fusing the piece together, usually with the aid of additional metal melted from a rod or electrode.

Weld-wire-fabric (WWF) Steel wires welded together to form a grid for concrete slab reinforcing; commonly called "mesh."

Wide-flange section Any of a wide range of steel sections rolled in the shape of a letter I or H, with different dimensions than I-beams.

Wind brace A diagonal structural member whose function is to stabilize a frame against lateral (wind) forces.

Wind load Lateral forces acting against a building that, in particular, must be considered in the design of high-rise buildings.

Wired glass Glass in which a large-gauge wire mesh has been embedded during manufacture.

Wood shakes (shingles) Individual wood roofing pieces, made of cedar (usually) which are hand split, or machined to useable size; can be fire-rated for added protection.

Work The tasks, construction, installation, etc., that must occur to build, finish, and produce the project anticipated and under contract; comprises the complete scheme of construction required by the contract documents including all labor, material, systems, tests, ratings, devices, apparati, equipment, supplies, tools, adjustments, repairs, expendables, aids, temporary work or equipment, superintendency, inspection/approvals, plant, release, and permissions required to perform and complete the contract in an expeditious, orderly, and workmanlike manner.

Wythe A section of a masonry wall (in plan) which is 4 inches wide; pertains to the number of 4-inch sections in the full width of a masonry wall.

Y

Yard Usually that area of a lot from the building to the property lines; in zoning, the minimum prescribed distance back from the property lines where building cannot occur (also called setbacks).

Z

Zoning Government regulations which control the use of land, so adjacent uses are compatible and not intrusive; also regulates access, open areas, setbacks; creates a positive, general atmosphere or environment in neighborhoods.

Suggested Answers to Activities

MODULE 1

Activity 1.1: Understanding the Communication Process

1. The communication channel
2. Feedback
3. Two-way communication
4. Noise
5. One-way communication

Activity 1.2: Applying the Communication Process

Mini-Case #1

Sender(s)	Receiver(s)	Communication Channel(s)	Is Noise Present? If so, what is it?	Is This One-Way or Two-Way Communication?
Billy Hutchins	Mark Singer and his five teammates	Team meeting	No noise appears to be present, because Billy has chosen a quiet place	Two-way; Billy asks if the workers have any questions after he demonstrates the procedure

Mini-Case #2

Sender(s)	Receiver(s)	Communication Channel(s)	Is Noise Present? If so, what is it?	Is This One-Way or Two-Way Communication?
Carol Mayfield	Rachel Bennington, Steve Franklin, and Gregg Kastell	Memo	Yes—all the paperwork on Rachel's desk is a distraction	One-way; Rachel's memo doesn't allow for feedback

Mini-Case #3

Sender(s)	Receiver(s)	Communication Channel(s)	Is Noise Present? If so, what is it?	Is This One-Way or Two-Way Communication?
Melanie Harkness	Julie Gold	Face-to-face meeting	Yes, the ringing telephone	Two-way; Melanie's job is to answer any questions Julie might have

Activity 1.3: Active Listening Quiz

1. c, 2. a, 3. d, 4. a, 5. b

Activity 1.4: Listening Actively

SET 1:

1. brown
2. Mrs. Johnson
3. Tuesday

SET 2:

1. 10%
2. Roosevelt, NJ
3. No
4. terra cotta, burnt red, or Arizona cactus

SET 3:

1. Morrison Road
2. Exit 95
3. Michaels Road
4. 59

Activity 1.5: Understanding Body Language

1. b, 2. b, 3. a, 4. c, 5. d, 6. a

Activity 1.6: Interpreting Body Language

Answers will vary. Clearly, though, the foreman is the most likely to consider Pete the best worker, because Pete shows all the signs of listening closely and carefully. Bob, Sally, and Charlie all need to work on their listening skills. It seems that this crew isn't going to get the job done very effectively.

Activity 1.7: Differentiating Noise

1. I, 2. P, 3. I, 4. P, 5. P, 6. P, 7. I, 8. I, 9. P, 10. I

Activity 1.8: Self-Assessment: Identifying Bad Listening Habits

Answers will vary.

Activity 1.9: Eliminating Barriers to Effective Listening

MINI-CASE #1:
Dave is in an awkward position. Whether they realize it or not, the younger workers are undermining the foreman by ignoring him and talking to Dave. Dave should advise the younger workers to respectfully ask questions of the foreman. They should ask him to speak more slowly and to explain the words he uses. They should also make the effort to hear past his accent, though it would be acceptable to ask the foreman (again, respectfully) to repeat what he's said if they can't understand him. In a nutshell, the younger workers need to open their minds and to listen more carefully. Clearly, Gary would not be a

foreman if he was not a very skilled worker, and the young people can learn as much from him as they can from Dave.

MINI-CASE #2:
Both Darlene and Fran should become more open minded, because each can benefit from their working relationship. Fran should be discouraged from talking too much, out of respect for Darlene's working style. But Darlene should be encouraged to have a more open communication channel with Fran, and to be more open-minded about listening to Fran's ideas and suggestions.

MODULE 2

Activity 2.1: Taking Notes

Suggested responses:

LECTURE #1

HIST. OF PLUMBING

sunlight → water → evap. → clouds → cold air → condens. & precip. → into earth or into bodies of water

plumber, from Latin word meaning "lead"

4000 yrs ago, Crete, 1st toilet
400 BC, Greeks, bath house
312 BC, Roman aqueducts
Dark Ages—neglect, disease
1721—water supply in London
1775—Cummings, valve toilet
1870s—Twyford, 1st washout toilet → indoor plumbing
1937—Moen, double valve faucet
1950s—stainless steel fixtures
1958—cent. pipe casting machines
1961—compression gaskets
1964—hubless couplings

Today—emphasis on sanitation

LECTURE #2

RESPECT F/CUSTOMERS

Residential work—faith in workers

Don't smoke
Protect area, dropcloths, rags
Don't bring in dirt
Clean up
Be on time, call if late
Bring right tools, pack neatly
Do job efficiently
Avoid gen. conversation

Show positive attitude! Respectful, apologize for problems

Activity 2.2: Following Spoken Directions

SET #1:

Carpenters

Activity 2.3: Responding to Criticism

Responses will vary, but here are suggested answers.

1. I would like to be a better team player. What can I do to accomplish that?

2. Can you give me a specific example? I really am very dedicated to doing a good job.

3. I hadn't realized that you prefer not to talk while working. I'll clam up.

4. I'm sorry, I will make every effort to clean up my work area. I just get distracted, but I will really try to improve.

5. I admit that I'm inexperienced, but I want to do a good job. What am I doing wrong?

6. This is tough on me . . . you're right, I can't seem to figure it out. Some additional training would really help. Thanks.

7. I am having trouble getting this. It's frustrating me. Can you suggest any ways for me to get more practice?

8. I am incredibly sorry, and I won't make any excuses. I promise: It will never happen again.

9. It was my pleasure. I'm happy to do anything I can to help.

10. I didn't think of that—I was just so hungry! I'll put a stop to it.

Activity 2.4: Converting Destructive Criticism into Constructive Criticism

1. [Answer provided in text.]

2. We need everyone working at 100% efficiency. What can we do to help you be a full member of the team?

3. Please pay better attention. Listening is important. This is a mistake that could have been avoided.

4. You're a talented guy, but there are a lot of things going on around here that I'm not pleased with. Everyone who works for me is expected to tell the truth, take responsibility for their mistakes, and not blame other people.

5. Losing things must be as frustrating for you as it is for me. One way I keep track of things is always putting the tool down in the exact same place, so it's there the next time I look for it. Have you ever tried that? It works.

Activity 2.5: Self-Assessment: Handling Bad News

Answers will vary.

Activity 2.6: Speaking on the Telephone

Dialogue #1

Suggested responses (answers will vary)

Operator: Hello, New England Electric.

You: Hi, this is Frank Torres with Valerian Brothers Plumbing. I need to place an order for six units of Part Number 7—8—3—3.

Operator: You need the order department. I'll put you through. Hold on, please.

[ring, ring]

Voice: This is Joe in Electrical Supply.

You: Hi, this is Frank Torres with Valerian Brothers Plumbing. I need to place an order for six units of Part Number 7—8—3—3.

Joe: OK, let me see if we have those in stock. . . . Yup, looks like we do. When do you need 'em by?

You: Can you have them to me by 4:00 tomorrow afternoon?

Joe: That should be no problem. Address?

You: I'm at 9894 Paddington. That's 9—8—9—4 Paddington in New Orleans.

Joe: OK, the total comes to $325.50. Anything else I can help you with today?

You: That's it for today. If you need me, I'm at 504-555-7494. That's 5—0—4—5—5—5—7—4—9—4.

Dialogue #2

Suggested response

You: Hello, Total Remodeling, Inc. This is Freddy Washington speaking.

Ms. Wiggins: Hello, my name is Janice Wiggins. I live over on Elm Street, and I've been thinking about redoing my kitchen and bathroom. I heard good things about your company from my friend, Mary Ellen Grabonski.

You: That's great to hear, Ms. Wiggins. I'm the owner here. What kind of work were you looking to do on those rooms?

Ms. Wiggins: Well, basically, both the kitchen and the bathroom are really, really old. The house was built in 1940, and it still has the original kitchen and bathroom. I want all new cabinets in the kitchen, plus a big new sink. The bathroom has a really old bathtub and fixtures, and I'd like all those replaced. The tile is falling apart, so I'd like all new tile in there as well.

You: That's our specialty . . . I really think we could do a great job for you. Could I send our guy over to your house to give you an estimate?

Ms. Wiggins: I would really love to see some samples of your work. You did a great job for Mary Ellen, but you only did her kitchen. Have you done any bathrooms in the area?

You: As a matter of fact, we just did a bathroom in your area. The owners were very pleased and let us use them as a reference. Their names are Jack and Mindy Garcia, and they are at 801-555-0851. That's 801-555-0851.

Ms. Wiggins: Great, thanks. When would you be able to come by and give me the estimate?

You: Our estimator, Perry Knight, works Monday through Friday, 8 A.M. to 4 P.M. Do any of those times work with your schedule?

Ms. Wiggins: Well, I work during the week, and it's really hard for me to get away during the day.

You: OK, we can work with that. Perry also does estimates on Wednesday nights from 6 to 9. Could we stop by on a Wednesday?

Ms. Wiggins: Sure, this Wednesday would be fine. Can you make it around 7 P.M.?

You: Sure. This Wednesday it is, October 17, at 7 P.M. Can I have your address, please?

Ms. Wiggins: Yes, it's 2123 Elm Street—that's 2—1—2—3 Elm, near the corner of Prospect.

You: OK—2123 Elm, got it. Can I take your number in case any emergencies come up?

Ms. Wiggins: Sure, my work number is 801-555-7766, and my home number is 801-555-4297.

You: Thank you, Ms. Wiggins. We'll see you on Wednesday, and we look forward to working with you!

Ms. Wiggins: Thanks, I'll see your guy on Wednesday!

Activity 2.7: Taking Phone Messages

PHONE MESSAGE #1:

PHONE MESSAGE				
To: Joe Nahanic				
Caller: Marty Fredericks		**Date:** 12/3	**Time:** 10:15 am	
Phone: ( )				
Message: Will be late picking you up tomorrow—look for him at 6:45 a.m.				
			Initials: _SR_	

☑ Urgent   ☐ Please Call Back   ☐ Wants to Meet
☐ Sent a Fax   ☐ Check Your E-Mail   ☐ No Need for Return Call

PHONE MESSAGE #2:

```
                         PHONE MESSAGE
To:    Marcy
Caller:   Jackie                              Date:  4/18   Time:  1:00 pm
Phone:  (    ) work: 555-6166, home: 555-8432
Message:   Is losing her job, wants referral to owner for a new job!
_____
_____
_____
                                             Initials:  SR
_____
☐ Urgent            ☑ Please Call Back        ☐ Wants to Meet
☐ Sent a Fax        ☑ Check Your E-Mail       ☐ No Need for Return Call
```

Activity 2.8: Practicing Meeting Etiquette

1. b, 2. d, 3. a, 4. a, 5. c, 6. c, 7. a, 8. d, 9. b, 10. c

MODULE 3

Activity 3.1: Talking with Different Audiences

1. b, 2. c, 3. a, 4. b, 5. d, 6. b, 7. d, 8. a, 9. c, 10. c

Activity 3.2: Changing Slang to Formal English

Suggested answers (responses will vary):

1. My boss was very upset when half the crew came down with the flu.

2. Joe was very sick. He spent half the night vomiting.

3. I was used to seeing mostly white men on construction sites. But lately I have been seeing many women also.

4. I told the supplier I wasn't going to pay his inflated prices.

5. The client was really angry when her new roof blew off in the thunderstorm.

6. Matt and Casey drank too much on Saturday night and got out of control.

7. We had a job in a predominantly African-American and Latino neighborhood.

8. I got the best price because I was the first person in line. A friend of mine showed up late. I said, "You have to be here early to get the good prices."

9. The speed limit was 55, but Janet was going a lot faster than that.

10. Southerners like to take their time, but Northerners often seem rushed.

Activity 3.3: Preparing Your Message

What is your goal for the meeting?	You have two goals: (1) to inform workers of the new store, and (2) to entice workers to volunteer to work at the new store instead of the existing location.
How is your audience likely to react?	There may be mixed reactions. While you are giving good news, and offering new opportunities and higher salaries, some workers may worry that they will be forced to work in the new location. So you must be sure to anticipate and allay any fears they have.
When would be a good time to have the meeting?	A good time might be at the end of the day, perhaps on a Friday, so that the workers can discuss their options with their families over the weekend.
What will be your main points? In what order will you present them?	One way of ordering your points effectively would be: (1) announce the new location, (2) talk about the need for staff at the new location, (3) present the benefits of working at the new location, (4) reassure workers that working at the new location is completely voluntary, (5) ask for volunteers by the end of the month, and (6) answer any questions that arise.
What specific information will you provide to entice workers to sign on as staff members of the new store?	You will want to emphasize the higher salary ($2 more per hour), as well as the additional vacation time, to compensate people for the longer drive to and from work each day.
How much time do you think you will need for this meeting?	This meeting shouldn't take very long, because the information being presented isn't very complex. Half an hour or so should be enough.

Activity 3.4: Speaking Clearly

(Oral exercise—No answers.)

Activity 3.5: Choosing Words Carefully

1. African-American, 2. works us very hard, 3. women, 4. workers, 5. inexpensive, 6. senior citizens', 7. fastidious, 8. Asian-Americans, 9. biracial, 10. profit-oriented.

Activity 3.6: Avoiding Distracters While Speaking

The following should be avoided:

- Running your hand through your hair
- Speaking very softly
- Wearing bracelets that make jingle/jangle sounds
- Speaking in the same tone throughout the discussion
- Using nonwords like "Um" or "Uh" to pace the discussion
- Chewing tobacco or gum while speaking
- Speaking at great length
- Cracking your knuckles
- Wearing a holographic tie that shines light directly into your listeners' faces

Activity 3.7: Distinguishing Fact from Opinion

1. Opinion. Most people would not disagree with the fact this is good news, but the sentence still states an opinion.

2. Fact.

3. Opinion. The clue words are "I think . . ."

4. Fact. The clue words are "Our research has shown . . ."

5. Opinion. The clue words are "I don't think . . ."

6. Fact. The speaker's statement is a fact—eight of the Web sites do recommend Acme tools. However, the Web sites' endorsements are opinions.

7. Fact. The speaker's statement is a fact—two of the Web sites do recommend Rutgers tools. However, the Web sites' endorsements are opinions.

8. Answers will vary, but the speaker seems to have made a good, solid, fair case for his recommendation. He has spoken openly and truthfully, and hasn't hidden any facts.

Activity 3.8: Understanding Group Dynamics

1. Call him Mr. Mason, because that is what the other apprentice calls him.

2. A simple question might be directed to Rich Benton. You already know him, and he has volunteered to help you.

3. A complex technical question might best be directed to Karen Aldridge. While she is new on the job, she is the friendliest, and she also has a good reputation for keeping up with the latest advances. You could ask Jim Mason or Zach Sullivan, but both prefer to be left alone.

4. Jim would probably divide the groups into more experienced people and less experienced people. In the first group would be Zach and Karen, and maybe Rich. In the second group would be you and Mike. If Jim is going to teach a new technique that Rich isn't familiar with, he might decide to include Rich in the second group.

5. Most likely, you'd become friendly with Mike, because you're both at the same point in your careers. And, of course, Rich is your friend already. Karen is a friendly person, so over time you could develop an excellent working relationship with her. Because Jim and Zach are so business-like, it would probably take a long time for you to become close with them.

Activity 3.9: Examining Differences in Speaking Styles Between Men and Women

Answers will vary.

Activity 3.10: Self-Assessment: Do You Speak Effectively?

Answers will vary.

Activity 3.11: Identifying Gossip and Lies

1. e, 2. g, 3. g, 4. e, 5. e, 6. l, 7. g, 8. e, 9. l, 10. g

MODULE 4

Activity 4.1: Making a Presentation

Presentations will vary.

Activity 4.2: Planning Meetings

Suggested answers:

SCENARIO #1:   This situation would call for a meeting. All employees will be affected, and workers are sure to have questions. This meeting also provides the owners with a chance to present the good news to everyone at the same time and in a personal way. A meeting is a better choice than, say, an e-mail or memo.

SCENARIO #2:   There is no need for a meeting of all 25 people, because only two of them are breaking the rules. Instead of a large-scale meeting, Michelle should meet with Roger and Mark separately, one to one, and explain the rules.

SCENARIO #3:   While workers' paychecks are of major concern to them, this is truly a small error, so a meeting is probably not needed. One way to get the information to workers effectively might be to send out an e-mail. Another way would be to attach a memo to each paycheck explaining what has happened.

SCENARIO #4:   This situation calls for a meeting of the company's top people to make a plan for moving forward. Large projects always require many meetings to coordinate the efforts of all the teams involved.

Activity 4.3: Reading an Agenda

1. The Newton Townhouses
2. August 3, 2002
3. 11:30
4. Two
5. Electrical
6. Phyllis Minichetti
7. 4:15
8. Permit planning

Activity 4.4: Practicing Assertiveness, Avoiding Aggressiveness

Suggested responses follow.

Aggressive	Assertive
Hey! Either show up on time, or I'm reporting you to the foreman. I'm sick of waiting around for you to start my job.	I'd appreciate it if we could get to work at the same time. This is a two-man job, and it doesn't make sense for me to stand around waiting to begin the day's work.
What were you thinking? I asked you to deliver those parts here by Tuesday, not Friday! It's already Thursday and you're two days late. I want to talk to your manager about this.	There must have been a miscommunication. I needed the parts here by Tuesday, not Friday. What can we do to get the parts here as soon as possible?

Aggressive	Assertive
The only car you should ever buy is one made in America. If you buy any foreign car, you're not a good American, and I want nothing to do with you.	I feel pretty strongly that Americans should buy only American-made cars, but I know there are other opinions.
Why are you always interrupting me when I speak? For God's sake, just shut up for a minute.	I would really like to be able to finish a complete thought. Could I ask you to let me finish before you begin answering?
Waiter, take this hamburger back right now. I asked for it well done, and it's only medium. Are you deaf, or is the cook just stupid? And don't think I'm paying for it unless I get it cooked *exactly* the way I want it cooked.	Waiter, I asked for this hamburger to be cooked well done, but it's only medium. Could you take care of this for me?

Activity 4.5: Practicing Etiquette

1. F, 2. F, 3. F, 4. T, 5. F, 6. T, 7. T, 8. F, 9. F, 10. T

Activity 4.6: Conveying Bad News with Sensitivity

Suggested answers:

1. Brad, I'm very sorry to have to tell you this, but your grandmother passed away last night.

2. Everyone, we're running behind on this job. We need to ask everyone to pitch in by working 15 hours of overtime per week for the next few weeks. This job is important to the company, and we would really appreciate your help.

3. While you are very qualified for this job, at this time the management believes that Jack is the stronger candidate. But we want to encourage you to apply the next time a promotion becomes available, because we think you've got what it takes.

4. Your father just called. Your mother has been involved in a car accident. Let me drive you to the hospital.

5. Dave, I am sorry to tell you this, but I can't see you anymore. You're a great guy, but things just aren't working out. I hope we can stay friends.

Activity 4.7: Increasing Your Awareness of Diversity

Answers provided in text.

Activity 4.8: Understanding Diversity in Yourself and Others

Answers will vary.

Activity 4.9: Recognizing the Potential for Conflict

POSSIBLE SOURCES OF CONFLICT:

1. Martin may resent Kate because he expected the promotion and didn't receive it. She got the job he was expecting. She is also younger and less experienced than he is.

2. Sam may have a negative reaction to Raul because Raul is Mexican, and Sam's mother had been mugged in Mexico.

3. Raul may have a hard time working for Kate. He owned his own company and may be used to being the boss, so it may be hard for him to take orders from someone else.

4. Trevor may not like Kate because he has a bossy older sister, and he may not want to work for a woman.

5. Mary may not fit in on the team well because of her background, and she's not as experienced as several of the other team members.

Activity 4.10: Resolving Conflict

Answers will vary.

Activity 4.11: Self-Assessment: How Well Do You Handle Conflict?

Self-assessment: Answers will vary.

Activity 4.12: Resolving Conflicts: A Quick Quiz

1. c, 2. c, 3. c, 4. a, 5. a, 6. b, 7. d, 8. b

MODULE 5

Activity 5.1: Setting Reading Priorities

SUGGESTED ANSWERS:

7 The new issue of *Sports Illustrated*

*2 A memo from your company's fire safety inspector, outlining new safety procedures

6 A piece of mail from the National Arbor Day Society, asking you to contribute money

4 A letter from your company's benefits department, outlining changes in the tax law and how these changes will affect your pension

5 An e-mail from your brother in another state, attaching electronic pictures of his new motorcycle

*1 A revised blueprint of the project you're working on

8 An advertisement from a company offering stock in a start-up Internet company

*3 An e-mail from your boss outlining the hours you're expected to work next week

Other answers are possible. Some guidelines: The revised blueprint should have top priority, because it could affect the very next step you take. The fire safety memo should also have top priority, because most likely the company will want you to begin using the new safety procedures *immediately*. The e-mail from your boss is important, but it doesn't need to be read first, because your hours are already set for this week. Still, it will be helpful to know your schedule for the following week. The letter from the benefits department includes important information you should know, but it most likely doesn't affect your life right now.

Items 5–8 are all personal items that you can read as you have the time and desire. You can read the e-mail from your brother and the solicitation letter from the National Arbor Day Society quickly. It will take more time to get through the new *Sports Illustrated*. The stock offering is mostly likely junk mail that can be thrown away.

Activity 5.2: Highlighting for Improved Comprehension

Passage A
The Nature of Soil

To make use of the samples taken during subsurface exploration, it is necessary to understand something of the nature of soil, types of soil, and how they react under various circumstances. This topic, in all its facets, is a complete study in itself, and we deal here with the subject only as it pertains to construction.

For engineers and architects, *soil* denotes all the fragmented material found in the earth's crust. Included is material ranging from individual rocks of various sizes, through sand and gravel, to fine-grained clays. Whereas particles of sand and gravel are visible to the naked eye, particles of some fine-grained clays cannot be distinguished even when viewed through low-powered microscopes.

All soils are made up of large or small particles derived from one or more of the minerals that make up solid rock. These particles have been transported from their original location by various means. For example, there are notable deposits of *eolian soil* in western North America, which were deposited by wind. There are also numerous deposits of *glacial till*, a mixture of sand, gravel, silt, and clay, moved and deposited by glaciers. Other soils have been deposited by the action of water, whereas others, known as *residual soils*, consist of rock particles that have not been moved from their original location, but are products of the deterioration of solid rock.

Soil types, as determined by particle size, are as follows:

- *Cobbles and boulders*: Larger than 3 in. (75 mm) in diameter
- *Gravel*: Smaller than 3 in. (75mm) and larger than #4 (5mm) sieve (approximately 1/4 in.)
- *Sand*: Particles smaller than #4 (5 mm) sieve and larger than #200 sieve (40,000 openings per square inch)
- *Silts*: Particles smaller than 0.02 mm and larger than 0.002 mm in diameter
- *Clays*: Particles smaller than 0.002 mm in diameter.

For purposes of establishing the abilities of these soils to safely carry a load, they are classified as *cohesionless soils, cohesive soils, miscellaneous soils,* and *rock*.

Cohesionless soils include sand and gravel—soils in which particles have little or no tendency to stick together under pressure. Cohesive soils include dense silt, medium dense silt, hard clay, stiff clay, firm clay, and soft clay. The particles of these soils tend to stick together, particularly with the addition of water. Miscellaneous soils include glacial till and conglomerate. The latter is a mixture of sand, gravel, and clay, with the clay acting as a cement to hold the particles together.

Rock is subdivided into *massive, foliated, sedimentary,* and *soft or shattered*. Massive rocks are very hard, have no visible bedding planes or laminations, and have widely spaced, nearly vertical or horizontal joints. They are comparable to the best concrete. Foliated rocks are also hard, but have sloping joints, which preclude equal compressive strength in all directions. They are comparable to sound structured concrete. Sedimentary rocks include hard shales, sandstones, limestones, and silt-stones, with softer components. Rocks in this category may be likened to good brick masonry. Soft or shattered rocks include those that are soft or broken but not displaced from their natural beds. They do not become plastic when wet and are comparable to poor brick masonry.

Passage B
The History of Paint

Craftspersons in the painting trade have a long history. Paint has been used as a form of decoration since prehistoric times. Early cave dwellers used plants, clay, and water to make paint. They used this paint to decorate their bodies and the walls of caves. Most of what these early people painted were lines that formed pictures. The people of ancient Egypt used paint in tombs, palaces, and on temple walls using colors which they prepared from the soil. By 1500 B.C., they imported dyes such as indigo and madder. From these they made blue and red **pigments.** Pigments impart color and other properties to paint. The Egyptians were the first to use protective coatings. They applied forms of pitch and balsam to seal their ships. They also developed and used water-based paints produced from freshly-burned lime (whitewash) with milk curds as a **binder.** A binder serves to bind or cement the pigment particles together upon drying of paint.

The Greeks, Romans, and others copied Egyptian painting practices. The early Greeks developed painting into an art form. They not only decorated flat surfaces, but painted human beings, wood panels, and vases. Paint was widely used by the Romans, who are credited with the introduction of white lead as a pigment in 430 B.C. The ancient Romans used stencils to paint borders on wall surfaces. They also painted stone and plaster to look like granite and marble. The Roman Empire collapsed in the 400s A.D. After that, the art of paint-making became lost to the western world until the middle ages (500 to 1450 A.D.), when the English and other Europeans began making and using paints to paint churches, public buildings, and the homes of the wealthy.

In Asia, the first pigments was developed before 6000 B.C. Coloring components included natural ores and organic pigments. Binders included color crayons sometimes made from boiled rice. **Vehicles,** the liquid part of paint in which pigments are dissolved or dispersed, were made from gum arabic, egg white (albumin), gelatin, and beeswax. The Chinese are credited with the use of lacquer as early as the Chou dynasty (1122 to 221 B.C.). During the Ching dynasty, the Chinese developed iron oxide to produce the color red.

Paint manufacturing began in Europe around the 1700s. Then, manufacturers ground pigments and oils on a stone table with a round stone. Their paints were made for limited private use. The Industrial Revolution in England changed this. In the late 17th century and early 18th century, power-driven machinery was brought into the paint-making process. At this time, **white lead,** a white pigment obtained from lead sulphate, become more widely available. These new machines and white lead allowed for the development and production of protective, anti-corrosion paints used for protecting metal structures such as bridges. The first varnish factories were started in Europe beginning with England in 1790

In the 18th century, there was a general increase in the availability of vehicles and pigments. White lead was put to more uses. Also, there was an extensive extraction of linseed oil from the flax plant. Paint grade zinc oxide was also developed. By the 19th century, paint manufacturing changed. For the first time, the two basic ingredients, vehicle and pigment, were mixed together before distribution.

The evolution of materials technology throughout the 20th century has produced a proliferation of paint and related products. Today, linseed oil is found in only a few paints and in some putty and caulking compounds. After World War II, the dye and plastics industries also began extensive research and development of new painting-related products. The dye industry created new pigments, while the plastic industry developed new **polymers.** Polymers are substances in which the molecules, consisting of one or more structural units, are repeated any number of times. Synthetic **resins** were produced as new binders for paint that provided significant improvement in weathering, water resistance, toughness, elasticity, and resistance to chemical exposure. These binders included alkyds, phenolics, chlorinated rubbers, vinyls, latexes, and acrylics. Resins are natural or synthetic substances which, when heated, are soluble in drying oils and solvents.

Shortly after World War II, new paints containing epoxy and urethane resins and zinc-rich coatings began to be produced in the United States. Over time, these coatings were enhanced by the development of high-quality **solvents** and **additives** that improved their application and performance properties. Solvents are liquids used in paints to dissolve pigments and other materials. Solvents evaporate during drying. These high-performance materials became the main coatings for protecting steel in industrial environments. Waterborne (water-based) coatings using acrylic latex binders were first introduced in the early 1950s. Their use gained in popularity during the 1950s and 1960s because they were easy to use and nontoxic.

During the latter half of the 20th century and up to the present, advances in painting materials and methods of application have been driven by increased concerns about health, safety, and the environment. In the United States, the passage of the Clean Air Act in 1970, and its amendments in 1990, mandated the containment of all sources of air pollution including carbon-based solvents generally classified as **volatile organic compounds (VOCs).** Oil-based paints use VOC solvents such as mineral spirits to keep them liquid until they are applied. Upon evaporation into the atmosphere, VOCs react with nitrous oxides (combustion compounds from automotive emissions and the burning of fuels) and sunlight to form ozone and air pollutants. Ozone is an unstable form of oxygen that is highly reactive. Ozone in the Earth's upper atmosphere (stratosphere) protects the Earth and its inhabitants from harmful ultraviolet radiation. However, ozone trapped within the Earth's lower atmosphere (troposphere) contributes to smog that can be hazardous to humans, animals, and plant life. Emissions of VOCs from painting and various other sources can also contribute to poor indoor air quality.

Today, because the Environmental Protection Agency (EPA) is requiring the elimination of air pollution, the environmental laws and regulations that limit the amount of VOCs in paint are increasingly restrictive. This means that fewer VOC-type solvents can be used, causing the focus of most new materials technology to be toward the development of better waterborne paints. Today's waterborne paints and coatings are made in a variety of resin types, such as epoxy, alkyd, vinyl, latex, acrylic, and others. They are as effective on outdoor surfaces as they are on indoor surfaces. Special coatings are made to protect metal, concrete, and other industrial **substrates** (surfaces being painted) in mildly harsh environments. Other types developed to comply with the air pollution laws include high solids and 100% solid materials. These are often difficult to apply, resulting in a number of paint manufacturers training and licensing painters to be exclusive applicators of their product(s).

Activity 5.3: Skimming for Main Ideas

1. soil
2. (a) cobbles and boulders, (b) gravel, (c) sand, (d) silts, (e) clays
3.

   (a) soil = all the fragmented material found in the earth's crust

   (b) largest = cobbles and boulders; smallest = clays

   (c) cohesionless soils, cohesive soils, miscellaneous soils, rock

Activity 5.4: Scanning for Information

1. Pigments are substances that give color to paint.
2. 1122 to 221 B.C.
3. volatile organic compound
4. Vehicles are the liquid part of paint in which pigments are dissolved or dispersed. White lead is a type of white pigment obtained from lead sulphate.
5. red

Activity 5.5: Finding Information: Using a Table of Contents I

1. b
2. d
3. a
4. d
5. d

Activity 5.6: Finding Information: Using a Table of Contents II

1. c
2. b
3. c
4. d
5. a

Activity 5.7: Finding Information: Using an Index

1. shy people, stress, time management, tobacco use, working with women
2. 116
3. False
4. 191–202
5. building a relationship with your supervisor; learning more about your supervisor; managing conflict with your supervisor; getting along with your supervisor

Activity 5.8: Finding Information: Using a Glossary

SET 1
1. c, 2. d, 3. a, 4. e, 5. b

SET 2
1. e, 2. a, 3. b, 4. d, 5. c

SET 3
1. T, 2. F, 3. F, 4. T, 5. T

SET 4
1. d, 2. b, 3. a, 4. a, 5. b

Activity 5.9: Looking for Keys to Comprehension I

1. b, 2. d, 3. c, 4. a, 5. b

Activity 5.10: Checking Your Comprehension I

1. c—note that whitewash by itself is not a binder; it must be mixed with milk curds to become a binder
2. d
3. d
4. b
5. a
6. a
7. b
8. d
9. c
10. d

Activity 5.11: Checking Your Comprehension II

1. d, 2. b, 3.d, 4.b, 5. b

Activity 5.12: Summarizing Information

TABLE A   Soil Types by Particle Size

Soil Type	Size (in diameter)
cobble and boulders	Larger than 3 in. (75 mm)
gravel	Smaller than 3 in., larger than #4 (5mm) sieve
sand	Smaller than #4 sieve, larger than #200 sieve
silt	Smaller than .02 mm, larger than .002 mm
clay	Smaller than .002 mm

TABLE B   Types of Rock

Type	Description/Examples	Comparable to
Massive	very hard; no visible bedding planes or laminations; widely spaced, nearly vertical or horizontal joints	Excellent concrete
Foliated	Hard, with sloping joints, which prevent equal compressive strength in all directions	Sound structured concrete
Sedimentary	Hard shales, sandstones, limestones, silt-stones with softer components	Good brick masonry
Soft/shattered	Soft or broken rocks, not displaced from their natural beds	Poor brick masonry

TABLE C   Timeline: Key Developments in the History of Paint

Period	Developments
Prehistory	Cave dwellers used plants, clay, and water to make paint; decorated bodies and cave walls with paint
Asia/6000 BC	First pigments developed; coloring components included natural ores and organic pigments
Egyptians/1500 BC	Used paint in tombs, palaces, temple walls; imported dyes; first to use protective coatings; developed whitewash and binder
Chinese/1122-221 BC	Used lacquer; used iron oxide to produce red
Greeks and Romans/430 BC	Developed painting into an art form; decorated wood panels and vases; introduced white lead
1700s/Europe	Paint manufacturing begins; white lead becomes more available; development of anti-corrosion paints; development of varnish; grater availability of vehicles and pigments
19th century	Vehicles and pigments mixed together before distribution
20th century through 1960s	New polymers and resins developed for better protection; solvents and additives developed to improve application and performance of paint; waterborne coatings introduced in 1950s
1960s through today	Paint developments driven by increased environmental concerns and Clean Air Act

TABLE D   Key Terms in Paint Production

Term	Definition
Vehicle	Liquid part of the paint in which pigments are dissolved or dispersed
Polymers	Substances in which molecules, consisting of one or more structural units, are repeated any number of times
Solvents	Liquids used in paints to dissolve pigments and other materials; evaporate during drying
Volatile organic compounds (VOCs)	Toxic substances used to keep paints liquid until they are applied
Pigments	Substances that give color to paint
Resins	Substances used as binders to provide improvement in weathering, water resistance, toughness, elasticity, and resistance to chemical exposure
White lead	White pigment made from lead sulphate
Substrates	Surfaces being painted
Binders	Substance that helps bind or cement pigment particles together upon drying of paint

Activity 5.13: Reading Memos

1. Carmen Cuneo
2. February 10
3. Frank Hightower
4. In the dumpsters provided
5. Danny Mahan, Nabco E&M, Nabco Service Company

Activity 5.14: Reading E-Mail

1. 8:53 P.M.
2. False
3. Mark Seitler
4. The trim around the table
5. An additional shelf for each cabinet
6. False
7. Dodge reports
8. True

Activity 5.15: Following Directions

7

201

4

0   [time]

12C

[name]

Activity 5.16: Following General Guidelines

1. c, 2. d, 3. a, 4. c, 5. a

Activity 5.17: Following Step-by-Step Instructions

1. F, 2. F, 3. T, 4. T, 5. T, 6. F, 7. F, 8. T, 9. F, 10. F

Activity 5.18: Using a Dictionary

1. d, 2. a, 3. c, 4. c, 5. a, 6. b, 7. d, 8. b, 9. a, 10 d

Activity 5.19: Using a Glossary II

1. T, 2. T, 3. F, 4. F, 5. T, 6. F, 7. F, 8. T, 9. T, 10. T

MODULE 6

Activity 6.1: Reading Illustrations

SET A:
1. plastering or parging, 2. tuck-pointer, 3. pointing trowel, 4. brick trowel, 5. It looks like a duck's bill.

SET B:
1. oxygen and acetylene, 2. red, 3. green, 4. four, 5. tip.

SET C:
1. end to end, 2. face to face, center to center, face to crotch, 3. end to center, end to face, 4. the center of the elbow joint, 5. the near edge of the elbow joint.

Activity 6.2: Reading Diagrams

SET A:
1. b, 2. b, 3. a, 4. a, 5. b

SET B:
1. c, 2. c, 3. d, 4. a, 5. b

SET C:
1. a, 2. b, 3. c, 4. d, 5. a

SET D:
1. b, 2. d, 3. d, 4. a, 5. c

Activity 6.3: Reading Tables

SET A:
1. T, 2. F, 3. T, 4. F, 5. F

SET B:
1. F, 2. F, 3. F, 4. T, 5. T, 6. T, 7. F, 8. F, 9. T, 10. T

Activity 6.4: Reading Maps

1. a, 2. c, 3. b, 4. d, 5.c

Activity 6.5: Reading a Web Page

1. T, 2. T, 3. F, 4. T, 5. T

Activity 6.6: Surfing the Net

Answers will vary.

Activity 6.7: Reading Measuring Tapes and Rulers

1. d, 2. d, 3. c, 4. d, 5. a, 6. b, 7. d, 8. a, 9. a, 10. c

Activity 6.8: Understanding Blueprint Terminology I

1. f, 2. c, 3. i, 4. a, 5. g, 6. d, 7. h, 8. b, 9. e

Activity 6.9: Understanding Blueprint Terminology II

Civil Plans	Architectural Plans	Structural Plans	Mechanical Plans
Also known as site plans	Also known as architectural drawings	Foundation plans	Piping and instrumentation drawings
Also known as survey plans	Floor plans	Roof framing plans	HVAC plans
	Roof plans		

Activity 6.10: Working with Blueprints: The Basics

SET A:
1. b, 2. d, 3. c, 4. c, 5. c

SET B:
1. T, 2. T, 3. T, 4. F, 5. F

SET C:
1. F, 2. T, 3. F, 4. T, 5. F

Activity 6.11: Reading Blueprints

SET A:

1. MJH

2. April 28, 1996

3. mechanical plan

4. 1234 First Street, Caliente, Nevada

5. zero

6. eleven

7. foundation plan

8. April 25th and May 4th

9. Dareya Cohen

10. residence

Set B:

1. plumbing

2. mechanical

3. architectural

4. architectural

5. electrical

6. civil/structural

7. electrical

8. architectural

9. mechanical

10. plumbing

Set C:

1.	e
2.	j
3.	b
4.	d
5.	f
6.	h
7.	a
8.	i
9.	c
10.	g

Set D:
1. T, 2. T, 3. T, 4. F, 5. F, 6. F, 7. T, 8. F, 9. F, 10. F

Set E:
1. b, 2. a, 3. c, 4.c, 5. d, 6. d

Set F:
1. c, 2. e, 3. a, 4. d, 5. b

Set G:
1. G, 2. F2, 3. G6, 4. 2 × 8, 5. 1/2″ × 4′ × 8′, 6. fireplace framing

Activity 6.12: Reading Isometric Drawings, Orthographics, and Schematics

SET A:

1. 30   3. no
2. 6   4. 1

SET B:

1. orthographic; it shows three sides of the object

2. schematic; it relies on a single line

Activity 6.13: Reading Specifications

1. c, 2. b, 3. a, 4. a, 5. b, 6. d, 7. c, 8. c, 9. a, 10. d

Activity 6.14: Reading Materials Lists

1. b, 2. a, 3. b, 4. c, 5. c, 6. a, 7. d, 8. d, 9. c, 10. a

Activity 6.15: Managing Your Information Load

1. b, 2. d, 3. d, 4. a, 5. a

Activity 6.16: Distinguishing Fact from Opinion

1. F, 2. O, 3. O, 4. F, 5. F, 6. O, 7. O, 8. F, 9. F, 10. O

Activity 6.17: Critical Reading I

What is the source of this information?	This information comes from a paid advertisement in a newspaper. The purpose of most ads is to sell something.
How much expertise or experience does the source of this information have? (Who is Peter Price-Jones? Does he even exist? What exactly is the "Independent Wealth Association"?)	What kind of newspaper would run an ad like this? Is the paper a respectable one, such as *The New York Times*, or is it an unreliable tabloid, such as *The National Enquirer?* Most likely, the latter.
	Does Peter Price-Jones really exist, or is he a made-up "spokesman" for a phony company? Who are the quasi-anonymous people who give testimonials at the end of the ad?
How do I feel about this information? Why do I feel this way?	It's hard to believe that someone can become wealthy simply by quitting his job and working a few hours from his home each day. This ad offers NO specific information on what the "money-making system" is.
Does this information match my previous knowledge or experience? (Based on what I know, how much of this advertisement can I believe?)	Anything that sounds too good to be true probably is. The ad really loses a lot of credibility by repeating several times that the booklet is "free," and then asking you to send $9.95 to cover postage and handling.
What do my friends, co-workers, and supervisors think? (What would other people say if I showed them this ad?)	Most people would advise you not to waste your money by sending for this booklet.

Sending $9.95 would be extremely inadvisable. It seems that the only person getting rich off this scheme is Peter Price-Jones.

Activity 6.18: Critical Reading II

1. a. In the introductory paragraph, only two of the three elements needed to start a fire are listed (fuel and heat). The missing element is oxygen.
   b. Point #2 should say "*Never* smoke or light matches. . . ."
   c. Point #3 should refer to "self-closing" metal containers, not "non-closing" metal containers.
   d. Point #6 should say "*Never* remove the tag from the extinguisher. . . ."

2. These mistakes are dangerous. You should report them to your boss immediately. Doing so could save someone's life!

MODULE 7

Activity 7.1: Writing for Laypeople

Suggested responses (other answers are possible):

1. Ensuring that workers comply with Occupational Health and Safety (OSHA) regulations is an important part of every foreman's job. OSHA is an agency of the U.S. Department of Labor that oversees many aspects of workplace safety.

2. When moving heavy equipment in crowded areas, be sure to use a signaler. A signaler is someone outside the vehicle who helps the driver move the vehicle safely and avoid accidents.

3. When working with gas-powered machinery, open windows or vents to avoid carbon monoxide poisoning. Carbon monoxide (CO) is an odorless, deadly gas caused by exhaust. Also make sure that you're careful when working with ammonia.

4. The plans for this building don't show a window on the north wall.

5. Mrs. Cowen, please be careful in this area. Excess bits of solder are going to be flying around, and they're dangerous. Plus, there's going to be a lot of waste material from the soldering, and it's dangerous too.

Activity 7.2: Considering Your Audience

1. a, 2. a, 3. b, 4. b, 5. c

Activity 7.3: Writing Self-Assessment

Answers will vary.

Activity 7.4: Writing Objectively, Economically, Clearly, Simply, and Legibly

Suggested answers follow. Other correct answers are possible.

EXERCISE A: WRITING OBJECTIVELY

Pros:
1. Will foster clear, nonstatic communication

2. More reliable than old walkie-talkies

3. Can be used on other job sites and other projects—good investment for the future

Cons:
1. Requires the outlay of cash, plus monthly bills

2. Other teams may feel we are getting "special treatment"

3. Cell phones are easily lost because they're so small, and can be broken easily because they're delicate

Possible note:

I would like to request the purchase of cell phones for all five members of Team B. There are several good reasons to justify this purchase. First, given the size of our job site, effective communication among the team members is essential. Second, the walkie-talkies we have been using are unreliable and full of static. We have almost made some large errors due to problems with them. Third, these cell phones can be used by different teams on different job sites when we have completed this project, making them a worthy investment for the future.

I understand that cell phones are more expensive than the technology we're using, and that other teams may feel that we are receiving special treatment if Team B gets cell phones and they do not. However, I feel that cell phones are a worthy investment. To address the equity issue, perhaps the cell phones can be used by each of the teams on a rotating basis, to ensure that no one feels left out. Also, even though cell phones are small and delicate—and therefore easily lost or broken—I feel that we can be trusted to take good care of these phones and ensure that they remain in good working order.

EXERCISE B: WRITING ECONOMICALLY

Suggested rewrite:

Trench and excavation safety are critical on any construction site. An *excavation* is any man-made cut in the earth, formed by removing soil. A *trench* is usually a narrow excavation that is deeper than it is wide, with a maximum width of 15 feet.

When working around excavations, use the following precautions:

1. Don't place tools or other objects within two feet of the trench. They could fall into the trench and hurt people working down there.

2. Don't attempt to jump over or straddle the trench. You could easily slip and fall in. Always walk around the trench.

3. Don't jump into a trench. You could twist an ankle or hurt yourself in some other way. Always use a ladder to get down into the trench.

4. Erect barricades around the trench so that others are not exposed to danger.

5. Inspect trenches daily to be sure that they are properly shored up.

6. Don't work in trenches filled with water. You could get electrocuted.

EXERCISE C: WRITING CLEARLY AND SIMPLY
Suggested answers (other correct answers are possible):

1. All workers must put on a hard hat before entering the construction site.

2. A *confined space* is a space large enough for a person to work in, but with limited means of entry or exit. Some examples of confined spaces are silos, tanks, hoppers, pits, and vaults.

3. For your safety and health, use your personal protective equipment (PPE) properly. Inspect it regularly. Care for it well. Wear it in all situations that call for protection. Never alter it in any way.

4. Anyone who shows up for work drunk will be fired. Liars and thieves will also be fired.

Activity 7.5: Answering the Five W's

SCENARIO A: (POSSIBLE RESPONSE)

Who?	The memo will be distributed only to those workers who actually work in the field. Therefore, secretaries and other in-house staff will not need a copy. The audience is therefore only a subset of the company's full staff.
What?	The specific subject will be good housekeeping rules—and rules of professionalism for working in people's homes. Note that you should be careful in how you phrase the memo, for it is very likely that some workers are more guilty of good housekeeping offenses than others. You don't want to offend those workers who are already behaving in a professional manner.
Where?	The memo concerns expected behavior while working in a private residence.
When?	You have only one week to prepare this memo, so you should get started right away. Your boss will surely want to read it over before he attaches it to the paychecks, so you'll want to get it to him early so that he has the chance to suggest changes.
Why?	JP Construction has been receiving complaints about sloppy housekeeping. The purpose of the memo is to remind workers to be respectful of their clients and to prevent further complaints.

SCENARIO B: (POSSIBLE RESPONSE):

Who?	This e-mail is aimed at supervisors only. Supervisors are then expected to communicate this information to the people who work for them.
What?	The specific subject of your e-mail is clear: the new procedure for ordering tools. It will be important to indicate exactly when the new procedure will be instituted. Also, because there may be questions, your e-mail should encourage supervisors to call you, talk to you, or e-mail you if they have questions about the new procedure.
Where?	The new procedure will be instituted throughout the company, so it is relevant everywhere.
When?	The new procedure will become effective six weeks from now. However, it is best to give workers as much notice of such changes as possible. So, the sooner you send out the e-mail, the better.
Why?	The purpose of this e-mail is clear: To make the new tool-ordering procedure perfectly clear to supervisors.

Activity 7.6: Eliminating Irrelevant Details

PASSAGE A: ALCOHOL AND DRUG ABUSE ON THE JOB

Alcohol and drug abuse costs the construction industry millions of dollars a year in accidents, lost time, and lost productivity. The true cost of alcohol and drug abuse is much more than just money, of course. Abuse can cost lives. ~~Abusing alcohol and drugs really is not a good thing.~~

Using alcohol creates a risk of injury for everyone on the job site. ~~And when I say everyone, I do mean everyone.~~ Many states now have laws that prevent workers from collecting insurance benefits if they are injured while under the influence of alcohol or illegal drugs. ~~Some think that this is not a fair system, while others find it very just and reasonable.~~

You don't have to be abusing illegal drugs like marijuana, cocaine, or heroin to create a job hazard. Many prescribed and over-the-counter drugs, prescribed for legitimate reasons, can affect your ability to work safely. Amphetamines, barbiturates, and antihistamines are only a few of the legal drugs that can affect your ability to work safely or to operate machinery. ~~Horseplay can also cause job hazards.~~

PASSAGE B: THE IMPORTANCE OF TEAMWORK IN THE CONSTRUCTION BUSINESS

More than any other industry, the construction industry relies on *teamwork*. There are very few, if any, construction projects that can be completed by one person. ~~Teamwork is also important in other businesses as well, such as car manufacturing and assembly line work. Ford Motor Company is very proud of the teamwork displayed by its employees.~~

Suppose you're putting up a skyscraper. How could you get the plumbing done without the plumbers? How could you get the electric lines installed without the electricians? How could the building be built without engineers, architects, and design professionals? How could you know how best to spend your time if you didn't have a foreman to direct you? Of course, you *couldn't* complete the project without the contributions of many people with different training and talents. This is why teamwork is so important. ~~Cost management and savvy management skills are also important.~~

Teamwork entails more than simply working alongside other people. ~~Much more, actually. Teamwork requires many things.~~ For a team to be successful, *all* the workers must actively contribute. Teams don't benefit from loners or people who think they're above it all. Think about sports like hockey and basketball, where players help each other score goals or make baskets. Those individual players aren't playing for themselves. They know that winning the point for the team is more important than getting glory for themselves. ~~Maybe someone should tell that to some of those hotshot NBA players who think that they're more important than their teammates.~~

Note that the sports analogy is acceptable in this passage, because it helps to make a point.

Activity 7.7: Writing Persuasively

Answers will vary.

Activity 7.8: Writing Step-by-Step Directions

Answers will vary.

Activity 7.9: Writing General Guidelines

Answers will vary.

Activity 7.10: Writing Summaries

(Highlighted Text)

The Foreman's Job

On a construction site, the foreman is not "one of the guys." In fact, the foreman's job differs from the average worker's job in several ways.

Most importantly, foremen are responsible for monitoring all aspects of a project, and making sure *all* the pieces come together. They must ensure that everyone on their team does his or her job well. They must deliver a quality job on time and on budget. They must coordinate various tasks, making sure that people are working together in the way that makes the most sense.

In contrast, the average worker's job is much more focused. For example, if you are a carpenter, you work on specific tasks, and you do what the boss asks you to do. What you do contributes to the final product. Your boss is the person responsible for that final product.

In general, supervisors have five main responsibilities. First, foremen are responsible for quality and productivity. They make sure that quality work gets done on time. They ensure that workers are using the most efficient tools, equipment, and procedures. They're always watching to make sure that workers aren't wasting time or supplies, and they're always looking for ways to do the job better or more efficiently. Second, foremen coordinate the team's efforts. Foremen make sure that a project runs smoothly. They assign different tasks to different workers, then make sure that all those tasks come together. Most of the time, foremen are both overseeing their own group of workers *and* working with people who are even higher up in the company. Third, foremen are responsible for cost control. Construction is a very profit-oriented industry. To be profitable, a job must come in at or under the budgeted costs. To this end, foremen make sure that no money is wasted, that contractors don't overbill and suppliers don't overcharge. Because time is money, foremen also watch to make sure that workers are reporting to work on time, taking reasonable lunch and coffee breaks, and putting in a full day's work. Fourth, foremen are responsible for their workers' safety. While safety is everyone's responsibility, the foreman is in charge of ensuring the safety of every worksite. Because of strict laws and legal responsibilities, foremen tend to be very, very strict about safety rules. Finally, foremen provide leadership. Foremen act as team leaders. Their job is to motivate workers and to make them feel like an essential part of the team. Foremen also serve as teachers, and sometimes as counselors if their workers are facing problems on the job (or at home).

SUMMARY:

While the typical worker focuses on just one aspect of a project, a foreman is responsible for the entire project. Foremen have five main responsibilities:

1. Quality and productivity management
2. Coordination of team efforts
3. Cost control
4. Safety
5. Leadership and motivation

Activity 7.11: Working with Cause/Effect, Classification, and Comparison/Contrast

Answers will vary.

Activity 7.12: Synthesizing, Analyzing, and Evaluating Information

Answers will vary, but given the need to do this project on a very tight budget, Bradford seems like the best choice. If Bradford had a reputation for being difficult to work with or for doing poor-quality work, it would not be the best choice. But Bradford's work is acceptable and reasonably priced, so it is a good choice.

Activity 7.13: Exploring the Writing Process

Answers will vary.

Activity 7.14: Writing Clearly and Directly

1. We will need more workers in July.
2. We aren't hiring now.
3. John is an excellent worker who can do many things at once.
4. We think we should use aluminum instead of copper.
5. Marie's boss knew that she'd been late for three days.
6. Construction professionals tend to work fewer hours in January, February, and March, when the days are shorter.
7. Until we hire more workers, our current employees will need to work overtime.
8. The hammer costs about $16.

Activity 7.15: Choosing Words Carefully

SET A: CONNOTATIONS
1. a, 2. c, 3. b, 4. a, 5. c, 6. d, 7. b, 8. b

SET B: SPECIFIC LANGUAGE

1. Do not subject this material to heat for more than three seconds.
2. We should ask the contractor to submit the bid by next Friday.
3. We're meeting in the conference room at 2:30 P.M. on Wednesday.
4. Employees can't take vacation time between September 21 and December 21.
5. Brickmakers make their bricks in a very hot kiln that is heated to at least 500 degrees.
6. Please ask Joe, Frank, and Rich to meet me at 8:30 tomorrow morning.
7. Mary is allergic to seafood. Eating it could be very dangerous to her health.
8. The coffee was old, cold, and full of grinds.
9. Please divide these 100 nails into four batches of 25 nails each.
10. For emergencies, dial 911.

Suggested Answers to Activities

Activity 7.16: Filling Out Forms

Employment application—answers will vary.

TIME CARD

Employee Name: [NAME]								
Employee #: 15358		Project Name: Orchard Beach Condominiums						
Week Ending Date (Saturday): 9-15-01		Project#: 988-C						

DESCRIPTION:	CODE	M	T	W	T	F	S	TOTAL
Supervision								
Demolition Clean Up								
Construction Clean Up								
Final Clean Up								
Demolition	840		5					5
Floor Prep & Patch	390					4		4
Hand Excavation/Backfill								
Concrete Patch	960		3	2				5
Concrete (Walls) (Slabs)								
Concrete (Sidewalks) (Stoops)								
Masonry	420	8				4		12
Structural Steel								
Miscellaneous Metal								
Wood Stud Walls								
Wood Blocking (Walls) (Roof)								
Wood Trusses & Bracing								
Field Frame (Roof) (Soffit) (Fascia)								
Sheathing (Walls) (Roof)								
Other Carpentry (Please list):								
Finish Soffit and Fascia								
Inter. Trim (Jambs, Trim, Casing, Base, Handrails)								
Custom Woodwork & Millwork								
Prefab (Cabinets) (Tops)								
Damp-Proofing	555			1	8			9
Drain Tile								
Insulation (Rigid) (Fiber)								
Roofing & Felt								
Caulking								
Metal (Doors) (Frames) (Hardware)								
Wood (Doors) (Hardware)								
Windows (Wood) (Aluminum) (Interior)								
Drywall (Hanging) (Finishing)	680			5				5
Toilet (Partitions) (Accessories)								
Misc. Specialties (Please list):								
Meeting								
Travel (Job to Job only):								
Punch List Items: (Please list if other than above)								
TOTAL HOURS:		8	8	8	8	8		40

	Mon.	Tues.	Wed.	Thurs.	Fri.	Sat.
Daily - Job Time In:	7⁰⁰	7⁰⁰	7⁰⁰	7⁰⁰	7⁰⁰	
Daily - Job Time Out:	4⁰⁰	4⁰⁰	4⁰⁰	4⁰⁰	4⁰⁰	
DAILY - Job Superintendent's Initials:	MR	MR	dm	MR	dm	

NOTES/COMMENTS:
I would like to request a
vacation day on 12/8/01.

LETTER OF TRANSMITTAL

Roberts Construction Associates, Inc.

849 East Washington Avenue
Madison, Wisconsin 53703
Office: (608) 257-0500   Fax: (608) 257-4374

RE: Newark Shopping Plaza   **DATE:** [today's date]
                                                         JOB NO.: 8950

ATTN: Roger MacAlester

TO: Meyerson Development Corp.
550 State Blvd.
Trenton, N.J. 08609

WE ARE SENDING YOU: [X] Attached   [X] Hand Delivered   [X] Specifications

[X] Shop drawings   [ ] Prints   [ ] Plans   [ ] Samples

[ ] Copy of letter   [ ] Change order   [ ] Cut Sheets   [ ] _____

COPIES	DATE	NO.	DESCRIPTION
4	2-16-01		Complete set of specifications
6	2-18-01		Complete set of shop drawings

THESE ARE TRANSMITTED as checked below:

[X] For approval   [ ] Approved as submitted   [ ] Resubmit _____ copies for approval

[ ] For your use   [ ] Approved as noted   [ ] Submit _____ copies for distribution

[ ] As requested   [ ] Returned for corrections   [ ] Return _____ corrected prints

[ ] For Technical Review [ ] Reviewed   [ ] For Bids Due _____ 20 _____
    and Comment

[ ] RETURN ORIGINAL TO:

REMARKS:

cc: ___ Monica Sluzak _____
    ___ Ethel Johnson _____

                                          SIGNED: ___ (Your Name) _____

MODULE 8

Activity 8.1: Writing Memos

MEMO

To: Christopher Daniels
cc: Mike Elias, Barbara Kennedy

Fr: [Your Name]

Date: October 7, 2000   3:30 p.m.

Subject: Late Employees

The following employees have been late more than once in the last thirty (30) days:
• Peter Fallow—late 3 times
• Jake Larrone—late 2 times
• Laurie Rowen—late 5 times

Activity 8.2: Writing E-Mail

From: [Your Name]
Date and Time: November 15, 2001   9:15 a.m.

To: hal.franklin@jjconstruction.com
cc: ben.mahwah@jjconstruction.com
                  maxine.wyckoff@jjconstruction.com

Subject: Incorrect Delivery

☐ Normal Priority   ☑ Urgent Priority

Hal,

Allendale Supply delivered the wrong parts yesterday. We ordered 5000 units of Part No. 6755. Instead, they delivered 6755 units of Part No. 5000. Mark Green signed for the order, not realizing there was a mistake.

    We need the correct shipment by next week to keep the project on schedule. Can you give Jeff Sommers a call and ask him to take care of this?

Thanks,
[Your name]

Activity 8.3: Writing a Business Letter

SouthWest Construction

4751 Gallegos Blvd., Albuquerque, NM 87114
Phone: 505-555-5487   Fax: 505-555-9087
E-mail: southwestconst@aol.com

September 15, 2001

Mr. Jason Dell
Survey Director
New England Surveying
3937 Commonwealth Avenue
Boston, Massachusetts 02118

Re: Visit

Dear Mr. Dell,

Allow me to introduce myself. My name is [Your name], and I am the Director of Surveying at SouthWest Construction in Albuquerque, New Mexico.

I read your interview in *Surveying Quarterly* with great interest. I am very impressed with your work and the new techniques you have pioneered. In fact, I find that your work and mine is very similar.

I will be in Boston next month on October 22, and would very much like to meet with you to discuss how combining our research and work efforts might benefit us both. Would you be available at all that day to meet with me? I would be happy to come by your office, or meet you at any other convenient location.

My phone number is 505-555-5487, or you can reach me via e-mail at southwestconst@aol.com. I will follow up with you next week, but if you'd like to call me, I will be happy to speak with you at any time.

Sincerely,

[Your Name]
Director of Surveying

[Your initials]/hs

cc: Jack Zilsky, President, SouthWest Construction

Activity 8.4: Using Visual Aids in Your Writing

Answers will vary.

Activity 8.5: Writing a Progress Report

Progress Report
Prepared by: [Your Name]
Date: August 17, 2001

Project: Cedarwood Townhomes, Statesboro, GA
Progress for the Period: July 15—August 15, 2001

Prior Progress against Deadlines

- Ten model units were due to be completed by February 15, 2001— Successfully completed on February 13
- Buildings A, B, and C were due to be complete by June 15, 2001— Successfully completed, but one week late: June 22.

Progress this Month

Deadline this month: Landscaping for Buildings A, B, and C was due to be complete by August 15. This work is not yet complete, because the garden center was unable to deliver all the necessary landscape shrubberies on time. We expect to receive those shrubberies on August 20th, and to complete the landscaping by August 23.

Work Remaining

- Next main deadline is completion of Buildings D, E, and F by October 15, 2001. All buildings have been framed out and filled in, and all plumbing systems are in place. Work on finishing interiors is expected to be complete by October 1, and all roofing will be complete by October 15. We're right on target.
- Final deadline is November 30 for completion of Buildings G, H, and I. Buildings G and H have been framed out, but we have run into problems with the soil for Building I. Soil analysis is being conducted. Results are expected August 30th. Depending on results, engineers, architects, and designers may have to be consulted. Buildings G and H are on schedule for being completed by the November 30 deadline, but Building I could lag behind by as much as a month.

Summary

While we have encountered some delays in meeting deadlines, the delays up until this point have been fairly minor. Cedarwood Townhomes is very much on target for completion by the end of this year. The most serious issue is the soil surrounding Building I. By the time of the next progress report, the soil analysis will have been performed and we will have a better sense of the effects on Building I. It makes sense, though, to plan for at least a one-month delay on finishing that building.

Activity 8.6: Writing Field Reports

SCENARIO A:

Mid-State Plumbing, Inc.

Company and Location: Marine Bank, Ft. Lauderdale, FL

Description of Problem: Clogged toilet.

Action Taken to Correct Problem: Plunged toilet. Cleared blockage.

Date: May 23, 2001   **Plumber:** [Your Name]   **Fee:** $175

SCENARIO B:

Smith Brothers Heating and Air Conditioning
Belleville, NJ

Location of Call: Newark, NJ

Description of Problem: Central A/C unit not working. Motor burnt out.

Action Taken to Fix Problem: Motor replaced from stock.

Hours spent on call: 2 hrs.   **Technician:** [Your Name]   **Date:** 3/3/02

Activity 8.7: Practicing Proofreading Skills

DOCUMENT B:
The inaccuracies are underlined and in boldface.

Section 16741 [should be 16471]
Telephone Service Entrance

PART 1 GENERAL

1.00 [should be 1.01] SUMMARY

   A.   This section covers the work necessary to provide and install a complete **pathway [should be raceway]** system for the building telephone system. The system shall include telephone service entrance raceway, equipment and terminal backboards and empty **3/8 [should be 3/4]** inch conduits to telephone outlets.

1.02 RELATED SECTIONS OF THE PROJECT MANUAL

A. <u>Section No.</u>   <u>Item</u>

09900   Painting and Staining

16111   **Conduct [should be Conduit]**

16130   Boxes

16159 [should be 16195]   Electrical Identification

1.03 QUALITY ASSURANCE

A. Telephone Utility Company: **Northeastern [should be Southwestern]** Bell Telephone Company

B. Install work in accordance with Telephone Utility Company's rules and regulations.

PART 2 PRODUCTS

2.01 TELEPHONE TERMINATION BACKBOARD

A. Material: Plywood.

B. Size: 4 × **6 [should be 8]** feet, 3/4 inch thick.

PART 3 EXECUTION

3.01 EXAMINATION

A. Verify that surfaces are **read [should be ready]** to receive work.

B. Verify that field measurements are as shown on the Drawings.

C. Beginning of installation means installer **excepts [should be accepts]** existing conditions.

3.02 INSTALLATION

A. Finish paint termination backboard with durable enamel under the provisions of Section **09090 [should be 09900]** prior to installation of telephone equipment. Color to match wall.

B. Install termination **blackboards [should be backboards]** plumb, and attach securely at each corner. Install cabinet trim plumb.

C. Install **pull wire [should be galvanized pull wire]** in each empty telephone conduit containing a bend of over 10 feet in length.

D. Mark all backboards and cabinets with the legend "TELEPHONE" under the provisions of Section 16195, **ELECTRICAL [IDENTIFICATION].**

END OF SECTION **6741 [should be 16471]** - TELEPHONE SERVICE ENTRANCE

Activity 8.8: Writing with a Computer

1. T, 2. T, 3. F, 4. F, 5. F, 6. F, 7. T, 8. F, 9. T, 10. T

Activity 8.9: Correcting Commonly Misspelled Words

1. accommodate
2. Wednesday
3. parallel
4. omission
5. recommend
6. license
7. succeed
8. separate
9. disappointed
10. neither
11. mileage
12. occurred
13. practically
14. permissible
15. Therefore
16. February
17. schedule
18. equipment
19. desperate
20. independently

Activity 8.10: Distinguishing Between Commonly Confused Words

1. site
2. imminent
3. principle
4. It's
5. loose
6. passed
7. except
8. There
9. you're
10. their

11. advice
12. among
13. effect
14. than
15. inferred
16. dessert
17. accepted
18. Whose
19. through
20. they're

Activity 8.11: Practicing Proper Usage

1. a lot
2. would have
3. supposedly
4. all right
5. anyway
6. regardless
7. thus
8. supposed to
9. himself
10. off

Activity 8.12: Practicing Grammar Skills: Capital Letters

1. My favorite co-workers are Sally, Bill, and Terry.
2. I just read a book about the Civil War in America. That was the war that ended slavery in the United States.
3. [correct as is]
4. This year, the company is giving everyone a week's vacation between Christmas and New Year's Day.
5. I go to a Catholic church, but my neighbors attend the Baptist church in the next town.
6. [correct as is]
7. The foreman asked, "Has anyone seen the blueprints?"
8. My favorite subject was always math, because I was never any good at English.
9. In all jobs, it pays to be bilingual. If you work in Texas, it helps to speak Spanish.
10. After I hurt my back on the job, I went to see a doctor.

Activity 8.13: Practicing Grammar Skills: Colons and Commas

SET A: COLONS

1. My favorite months are May, October, and November.
2. I would recommend the following course of action: Send in a letter of inquiry, then call to ask for an interview.
3. [correct as is]
4. What I can't decide is whether or not to ask for a promotion.
5. These are the best workers on my team: Mary Washington, Karl Jeffries, and Tony Gold.

SET B: COMMAS

1. It seems to me that everyone deserves a second chance.
2. The deadline is May 15, 2002.
3. I would rather work in Florida than in Georgia.
4. [correct as is]
5. [correct as is]
6. As noted in my letter of June 17, your bill is three months overdue.
7. I really enjoy working as a carpenter, but I also enjoy the masonry aspect of construction.
8. Would you ask Oliver, Beth, and Lily to meet with us at four o'clock?
9. [correct as is]
10. [correct as is]

Activity 8.14: Practicing Grammar Skills: Exclamation Points, Question Marks, and Semicolons

1. [correct]
2. Frank asked for volunteers to attend the convention; Zeke and Josh raised their hands.
3. I didn't expect him to do something like that!
4. [correct]
5. Do you think we have enough money in the budget to purchase new tool belts for the staff?
6. The tower came crashing down; I ran as fast as my legs could carry me.
7. There are 14 million people in New York City. Isn't that amazing?
8. Tom is a rapid talker and a slow worker; Jim is a slow talker and a rapid worker.
9. [correct]
10. Are you free to work overtime on Friday night?

Activity 8.15: Correcting Sentence Fragments

1. S

2. F. On the way to work, seeing the fire engine racing through the streets, I knew something was very wrong.

3. F. Please come to my office on Friday.

4. F. I finally bought a new pipe wrench, which I desperately needed.

5. S

6. F. Falling to the ground is a terrible way to start the day.

7. S

8. F. I saw the foreman, whose name is Jack.

9. F. Ted called in sick three times last month: on the 8th, 12th, and 17th.

10. S

Index